Living Lines

Living Lines

Form Drawing Inspiration for Steiner-Waldorf Teachers

Henrik Thaulow

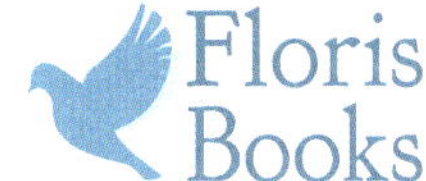
Floris Books

Translated by Vivienne Moss Kravik

First published in Norwegian as *Levende linjer Levende tanker: Formtegningsøvelser i grunnskolen* by Antropos Forlag in 2016
First published in English by Floris Books in 2019
First published in North America in 2020
Text and illustrations © Henrik Thaulow unless stated otherwise
English version © Floris Books 2019

British Library CIP Data available
ISBN 978-178250-610-2
Printed and bound in Great Britain
by Bell & Bain, Ltd

 Floris Books supports sustainable forest management by printing this book on materials made from wood that comes from responsible sources and reclaimed material

Contents

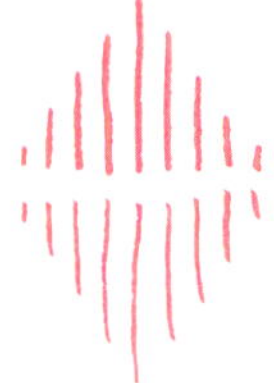
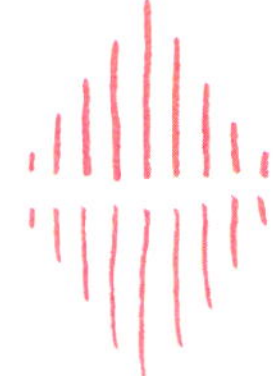
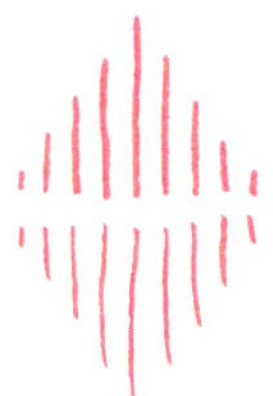
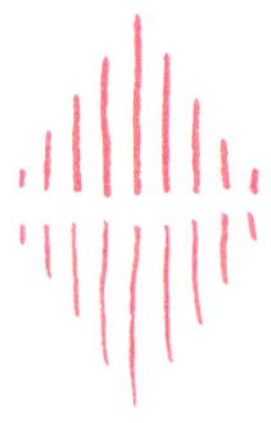

Introduction

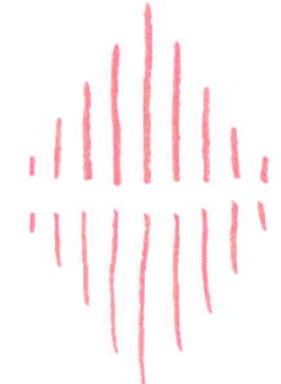
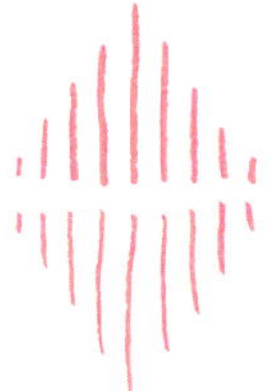

Have you ever doodled patterns and then enjoyed colouring in the gaps? Scribbled on a piece of paper while talking on the phone? Or built structures or figures without thinking about what they're going to be? If the answer is yes, then you have played with form. You have practised form drawing.

You've probably also drawn a freehand circle: that is, one based on your own idea of what a circle is, not one copied from an image. Human beings have a fantastic ability to pick up on the ideas and principles of shape, and form drawing is a way of exploring them.

When you play with form, you're free to do what you want. You use your understanding of how forms relate to one another and your aesthetic instinct. Form drawing can be as enjoyable and expressive as dancing or playing music, for both adults and children.

This book draws on my many years of experience with pupils in Waldorf education, and I have been inspired by many Waldorf teachers who, collectively, have researched this subject for almost 100 years. I have gathered images from nature and cultural life that have inspired new form-drawing exercises.

Form drawing is key to the artistic, playful mind. I hope that this book can assist you as a teacher to find new ways of encouraging this playfulness and creativity in your pupils.

How to use this book

Living Lines is divided into three main parts:

1. Part 1, 'Getting Started', describes form drawing and its purpose, as well as providing an overview of which type of forms are suitable for particular situations and age groups. It also provides practical suggestions on type of paper, drawing tools, use of colour and the size of your drawings.
2. Parts 2–7 provide practical, step-by-step exercises tailored to each class. To get the most out of the exercises, I recommend reading Part 1 first. However, please don't regard the exercises as templates to adhere

to exactly. My hope is that they provide creative inspiration for you to explore and develop the power of form with your pupils. In other words, it is up to you as a teacher to decide how much you want to demonstrate or explain and how much you wish to leave to the pupils to work out themselves.

You can complete the exercises in full or carry them out in part, and spend as much or as little time on them as you like. The exercises are grouped thematically and take pupils' abilities into consideration. I have presented the exercises alongside examples of pupils' work and other images, so that you can see form drawing in the context of the natural world and our cultural and social heritage. I hope the examples will inspire you to find your own *new* form drawings.

I have purposefully presented the exercises in a neutral grey, leaving it up to you to decide how to present them and in which colour. Pupils should use their coloured pencils, chalk, wax crayons, wax blocks and other materials.

You may come across unfamiliar terms while reading this book, for example plant names or mathematical terms like Fibonacci, fractals and so on. In these cases, it is up to you to decide whether to research further. The purpose of *Living Lines* is not to focus on a form's relationship to particular plants, geometry or the relationship between numbers, but to train the eye to focus on the form itself.

3. Part 8, 'Further Thinking', places form drawing in a wider context, and I explain my own approaches and theories. I am particularly interested in form drawing in relation to movement and life processes, and here I describe this in the context of living lines and living thoughts. I have also gathered together some of Rudolf Steiner's thoughts on form drawing.

Part 1: Getting Started

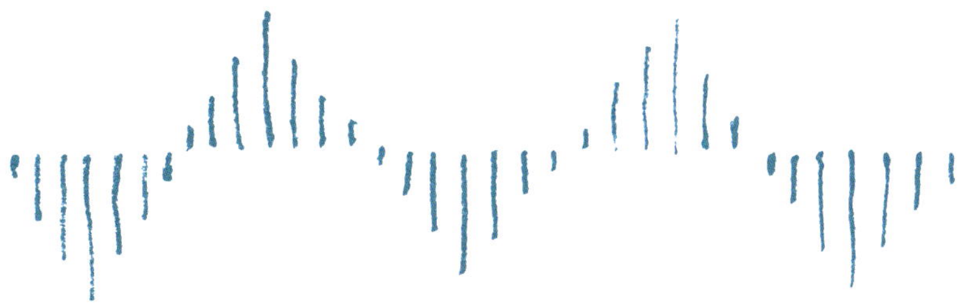

What Is Form Drawing?

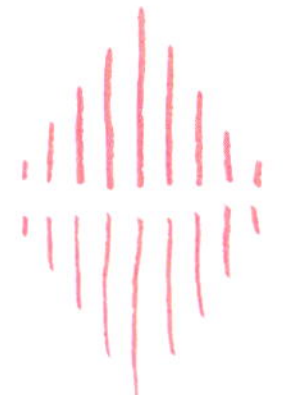
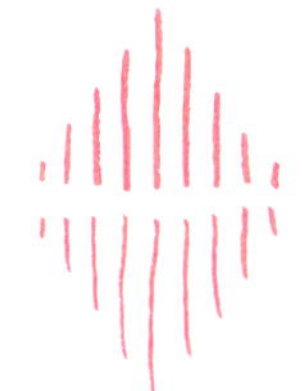

All children love to play with lines. Even two and three year olds can scribble, and before long they move on to making more orderly circle- or cross-like figures. Children instinctively explore form, and indeed it is an intrinsic part of human nature to look for shapes and patterns, both in what we hear and in what we see. Just as our ears detect patterns in what is audible, our eyes notice form in what is visible. Think of how we appreciate music and art.

Patterns speak for themselves; there is no need for them to resemble anything or be explained. A line can be more than a mere symbol or drawing: it can possess its own inherent aesthetic orderliness, give form to geometrical shapes such as circles and squares, or express movements and processes.

Form drawing is an exercise in exploring the line on its own terms. By this I mean that the non-figurative or abstract figures are based on the form's own construction, structure and what it instantaneously expresses. If this sounds difficult to comprehend, don't worry – working through the exercises will help.

Aesthetic problem-solving

In the classroom, teachers often give pupils examples, either by writing on the blackboard or by explaining, yet when it comes to form drawing pupils are not expected to copy their teacher. Instead, the intention is to enable pupils to understand the *idea* of the form and then recreate and develop it on their own. No one should try to exactly copy a freehand circle from the blackboard, with all of its errors. It is the *idea* of the circle that we draw.

Rules define the window of activity for pupils. Take the drawing of a border, for example. Pupils intuitively understand the elements that make a border: lines are the same height and progress according to a regular rhythm and so on. This means that teachers can trust pupils to express the idea of a border themselves without intervention, although of course details of construction can be discussed and explored during the process.

Geometrical shapes like circles, triangles and squares are easy to comprehend, but complex forms in nature and culture can be more difficult. They may be visually pleasing or interesting, but the way they are composed or structured might be unclear. Through form drawing you will be able to explore and master these more difficult shapes, whether they take in principles of form in geometry, culture or nature. Pupils will learn by simultaneously exploring and creating.

As the example of drawing a freehand circle shows, when you comprehend the idea of a form you might feel more directly connected to the form and your creative process than when you draw something from observation. In the latter case, you have more distance from the object you are drawing because it is outside you; you are copying it after having studied the way it appears at a certain place and time. In form drawing, these stages are merged together: you are intrinsically connected with the inner picture of an idea that you are recreating.

Form drawing is about exploring form, finding out which different forms can be connected, and how they can be mastered. When drawing a form, your aim is to complete it, make it whole.

I call this process *aesthetic problem-solving*, and it strengthens the ability to think flexibly and holistically. In this way, form drawing is a type of reasoning that in turn develops the ability to reason in other contexts, whether in school subjects or in life.

Why draw freehand?

A circle can be completed by using a compass: starting at a central point and setting a radius. However, this is a purely technical exercise, as your hand is doing nothing but activating the instrument. The final product is perfect, but it is an expression of the compass's work, not your own.

We can easily provide pupils with rulers and compasses so that they can draw shapes such as circles, squares and triangles with precision. Yet in doing so we deprive them of their own activity, development and learning. If shapes are drawn freehand, pupils must be actively creative and competent, and thus the forms remain living notions.

Form drawing provides simultaneous learning and practice. There is a reciprocal developmental relationship between the movement of the hand and the movement of thought. While drawing, the drawer is dynamically engaged with their own imagination as well as the activity of the hand. In this way, form drawing is a way of thinking, a way of finding solutions based upon creative and holistic pictorial thinking.

When pupils are ready for the challenge of

geometry lessons, they can leave aesthetics as the starting point for problem-solving and switch to logical thought to solve tasks and problems. Pupils will be able to think logically to solve problems, because they will have developed problem-solving skills as a result of form drawing.

Our ability to create form

We find forms and patterns everywhere we look in nature as a consequence of the principles of form in living organisms. Patterns can sometimes be difficult to spot, but even in apparent chaos a principle of form is present in one way or another. We can easily recognise, for example, wave patterns in water, star shapes in a snowflake and trees constantly dividing into branches. The principles of form are everywhere, even in the most amorphic substances.

In plants, the principles of form are dependent on conditions of light, type of soil, water and so on. Chance and the complexities of these exterior conditions mean that the 'perfect' version of a form is not always realised in reality. Yet we have the ability to comprehend this. We can still draw the form in its idealised, if more simplistic version.

Pupils can practise identifying shapes and patterns in the complex world of nature. They can search for hexagonal patterns in a snowflake, meandering paths of water or structures in clouds. Nature offers an endless variety of geometrical tendencies, rhythmical patterns, movements and other principles of form, and the exercises in Part 2 draw many examples from the natural world.

Thus form drawing can train our perception of natural processes, and help us understand the dynamics of nature. Exploration and the testing out of ideas is more important than results and the finished product. If you have grasped the idea of a form, you are free to develop it further, following the form's inherent sense of order. On the whole, nature is only capable of reproducing its own good ideas. The individual, on the other hand, is free to make choices. In this way, humans have always created their own cultural expressions.

Form drawing in relation to other subjects

Form drawing introduces pupils to forms inherent in nature and objects, and allows them to apply their human abilities of abstraction and creativity. It can enrich all subject areas, whether helping to understand the form of the landscape in geography, a culture's diverse modes of expression in history, beauty in mathematics, the structure of lettering, elegance in gymnastics, or the rich diversity of aesthetic qualities in the sciences.

What form drawing is *not*

Form drawing provides endless opportunities, but if you wish to develop new exercises you need to know what is *not* considered form drawing. It is important to keep form drawing separate from traditional drawing, which belongs with other subjects on the curriculum. In the diagram below, activities and skills encompassed by form drawing are inside the circle, and those outside the circle belong to traditional drawing.

The four headings in the figure show what form drawing is and is not: this, I hope, will help you to easily recognise when you have gone beyond form drawing. However, these definitions are not intended as limitations but rather as sources of inspiration and possibility. They provide space for activity.

Order

Geometry
Mathematics
Logic
Calculation

Figuration

Naturalism
Imitation
Tracing
Copying
Photography

Symbol

Pictogram
Emblem
Indirect

Chaos

Chance
Intuition
Spontaneity

Here is some further explanation of the terms in the diagram:

- *Figuration* means observational drawing, directly copying our surroundings.
- *Symbols* are forms that often have definite meanings, which means that pupils cannot develop them further.
- *Order* means forms that can be measured against something that is objectively correct (for example, circles, squares, rectangles, triangles, symmetries, repetitions). These are exercises where pupils can correct themselves with practice.
- *Chaos* as an opposing factor can encourage spontaneity, improvisation and toying with exploratory ideas to see what might happen.

When thinking about the aims of form drawing, it is wise to avoid figuration and symbols. However, the interchange between order and chaos can be helpful.

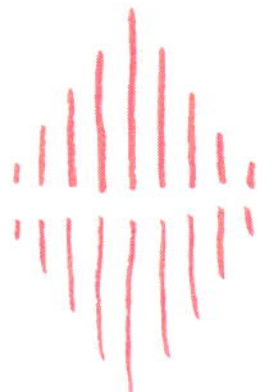

Basic Forms

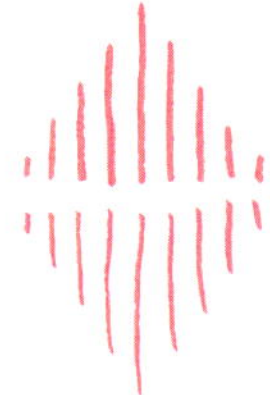

Just as when we listen to music we are able to recognise basic elements like tone and rhythm, we can recognise basic elements and principles in the many forms we encounter in the world.

The two basic elements: straight and curved lines

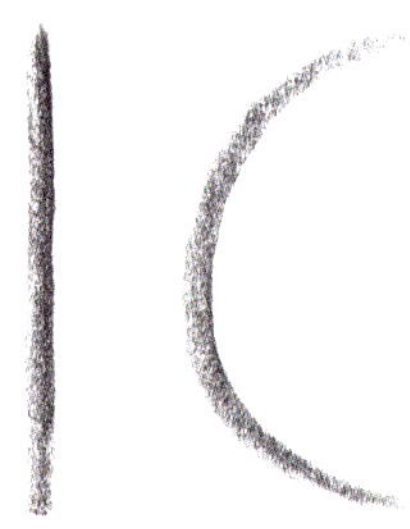

There are two basic elements in all forms: straight and curved lines.

Straight and curved lines do not symbolise qualities; they are two separate qualities in their own right and they exist because we use our abilities in two different ways when we draw them. They also exist as a result of observing them in different ways, by which I mean that we follow forms with our eyes in the same way as we follow them with a pencil when we draw them. Presenting the concepts of 'straight' and 'curved' to pupils is a good introduction to the subject of form drawing.

To help you to understand, draw curved lines on a sheet of paper. Draw quickly, then slowly, long ones and short ones, wide curves and narrow. Feel what this does to you. Do the same with straight lines, and feel the difference. You have just completed preparatory work for your first form drawing lesson: you can now describe the qualities of straight and curved in your own words.

It is best to find your own way of expressing yourself, but here are a few key concepts that may help.

The straight line

- Has direction and intent
- May have a decisive clarity and quality of 'light'

- Possesses regularity, structure and definition
- Can also express division, callousness and stagnation
- Lacks the curved line's life and movement

The curved line

- Brings movement, life and tension
- Can also bring unpredictability and even darkness
- Can interrupt a whole figure because it constantly introduces new elements
- Has a life of its own
- Can end in chaos if not helped by the qualities of the straight line

Basic forms: the circle and the cross

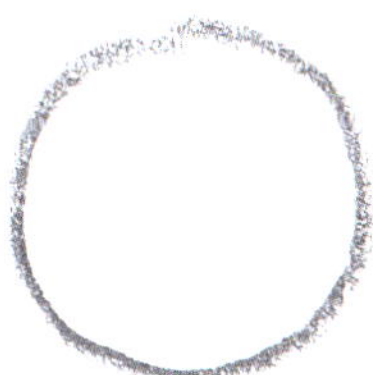 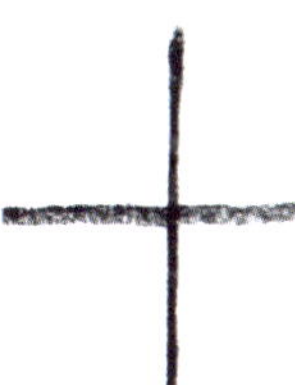

Straight lines and curves are found everywhere, but the mother and father of all forms are the circle and the cross. The circle is wholeness and gathering. The cross is division and separation. (See pp.201–3 for a more detailed discussuion of the relationship between imagination and the act of drawing.)

Basic forms of movement: the figure of eight and the spiral

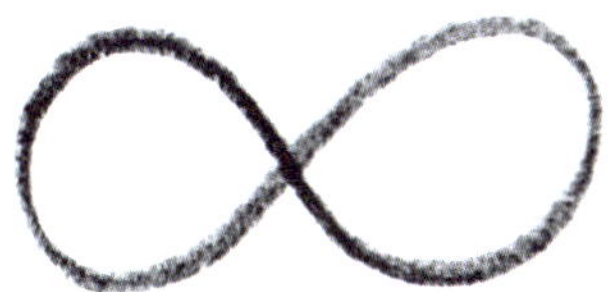 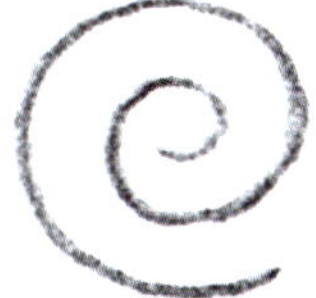

Both the figure of eight and the spiral are, in their own way, dominant in both process and movement, and they provide the basis of many different exercises for pupils. Unlike the cross and the circle, these forms are only partially defined. In other words, whether the figure of eight and the spiral have been 'mastered' is left to a pupil's own judgement.

The figure of eight is also known as a lemniscate. It is first and foremost rhythm, like the swing of the pendulum searching for balance between two points. It also alters the perspective of space; what turns inward on one side turns outward on the other. We experience such fluctuations in our daily and annual rhythms, externally and internally, in the beating of our heart and the expansion and contraction of our lungs. We can see this rhythm in an infinite number of phenomena. The rhythm of the figure of eight is balance and being. It is existence.

The spiral is development and movement, from centre to periphery, or from periphery to centre. It is growth and metamorphosis. It is connected to time: not to life as existence, but as a process.

All of these basic elements and forms can seem simple and even banal as drawing exercises, but they are demanding for younger children because they all involve a type of aesthetic problem-solving. Even the circle, with its strict and well-defined contours, needs to be 'solved' step by step by doing the activity itself. I recommend you respect these shapes by allowing your pupils sufficient time to explore them.

Types of Exercise

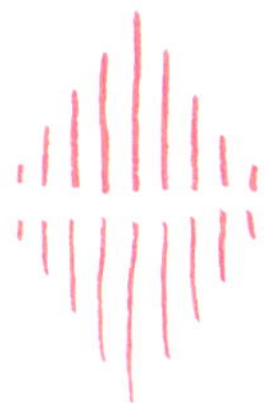
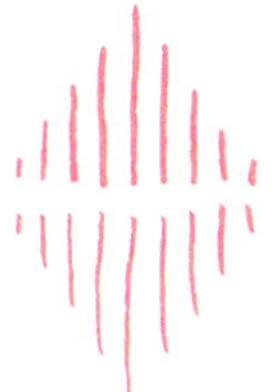

The exercises in this book can be broadly divided into four types. Often you will find that the categories overlap within the same exercise, but awareness of them will help you to navigate the world of form.

1. Line drawing

Line drawing is perhaps the richest and most enjoyable way of practising form. It makes it possible for pupils to experiment and begin to grasp the importance of movement. All of the figures described previously – circle, cross, figure of eight and spiral – can be included in line drawing in the form of borders, decorative elements or scribble-like figures. Borders are rewarding exercises because they can be simple or complicated, and so can be adapted to the individual pupil's abilities. Borders are playful and rhythmical, and can easily be built on by the pupil alone or with assistance.

2. The basic shapes

All forms relate to the cross and the circle and so elements of these are included in all the exercises. The square, rectangle, triangle, star and so on are related to the cross. Oval forms, egg forms and so on are related to the circle. There are many possible variants on and combinations of these.

3. Mirroring

Mirroring demands a particular type of problem-solving, and it can take many different directions and involve varying degrees of difficulty. For example, a form can be mirrored vertically on an axis so that the mirror image occurs on the opposite side. This is a challenging task, because the form must first be comprehended as a whole before it can be recreated on the opposite side. Gradually the level of difficulty can be increased, for example by mirroring on a horizontal axis. In these exercises you can practise and increase your understanding of symmetry, and you can observe this and its presence in nature and technology.

4. Development forms

The spiral and the figure of eight belong to the basic forms, but they also inherently include aspects of development and transformation – or lead to these. The spiral is repetitive yet transformational in the same way that a seed (intention) becomes a fruit (product). The figure of eight plays between the forms of the circle and the cross, between the outer and the inner.

All forms can be altered. They can change gradually, two or more shapes may belong together, or shapes may be related even though they differ. We recognise this in architecture and in the wonderful variety and richness of form that nature provides. This interconnectedness and the development of form are the most important elements in this book, and Part 2 comprises exercises that put this into practice. Many exercises offer a greater degree of freedom for pupils and will consequently be more challenging and demand sound guidance from you, the teacher. In all the exercises, it is essential to play and explore. The risk of getting lost must not hinder a journey into unknown territory.

Practical Considerations

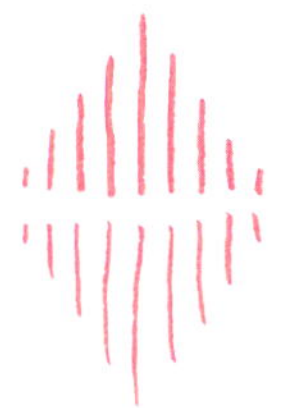
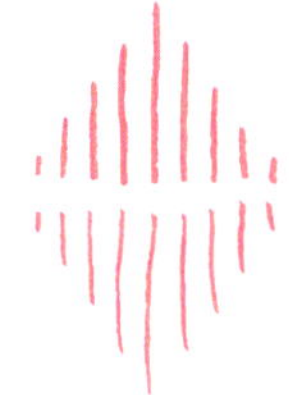

When beginning form drawing, you are bound to have lots of questions. How big should the paper be? What type of pencil should you use? What about colours? These are sensible questions to consider, and there is no correct answer. The only constant is that the form should take centre stage. Everything should support the form; nothing should disturb it. To facilitate this, here are some practical suggestions on how to get started with form drawing, based on my experience.

The hand

As described on pp.12–13, form drawing should be done freehand. The hand has remarkable sensory qualities, and with the correct tools it can work miracles. How to use your hand while form drawing will vary according to the purpose of the exercise and the complexity of the form. Some forms use long lines to be drawn in one movement; others demand supportive points and are to be drawn slowly and formed gradually, in increments. Sometimes it is more natural to use the whole arm when drawing; on other occasions the hand will rest on the paper and only the wrist and fingers will be moved.

Speed

You will probably find that pupils can become restless while drawing. At the beginning of a task, they may assume that it is something they need to finish quickly. They are influenced by our era's tendency to finish one job before going straight to the next, and then the next, and the next… However, the drawing process should take the time it needs, just as making music naturally does. Model this attitude by demonstrating your own ease when standing at the blackboard and draw forms at your desired tempo.

Drawing tools

The choice of drawing tools is important. They should give the correct amount of resistance: some crayons can be too waxy and stick to the paper, thus giving a stop-start motion, particularly when a pupil progresses to moving their wrist and fingers, which makes them unsuitable. Coloured pencils are excellent for smaller exploratory tasks, especially as pupils become older. Chalk on the blackboard is also excellent, as it stimulates experimentation. Which drawing tool to choose depends on the scale you are working to and how colours are being utilised: block wax crayons work on large sheets, coloured pencils are better for work on a smaller scale.

The size of the form

Children can naturally judge the placement of lines on paper themselves from an early age – this is easily observed in nursery children's drawings. So that they do not lose this ability as they grow older, it is important to gradually renew this awareness of scale so they can get used to covering the paper while simultaneously maintaining the 'breathing space' around the edge.

The thickness of the line

Each line should be reasonably thick, but not so much as to make the form unrecognisable. Nor should it be so thin that it is difficult to see. The line thickness can be defined or increased in certain places after the form has been drawn to provide strength and dynamism.

The starting point

Before you begin to draw a line, consider the sheet of paper and adapt the starting point to the space available. Take into account the line's finishing point, colour and thickness. By doing so, you can work creatively with even the simplest elements. It is helpful if you consider in advance where the starting point on the sheet should be before your pupils start drawing.

Direction

Pupils should get used to holding the sheet in the *same position* on the table. Teachers should decide the position for each exercise. Many exercises involve drawing lines in different directions, and there will always be someone who is tempted to rotate the sheet in line with the direction of drawing to make the work easier. This will limit what they gain from the exercise. Present this as an exciting challenge for pupils – it will soon become a habit they adopt.

The paper

A line always develops in relation to something, which in the case of form drawing is the format of the paper and its edges. In the same way, humans move in response to their environment, be it a room, a forest, a town square or a social setting. The bottom line is that we all grow and see ourselves in relation to the world around us. Even a single line can demonstrate the relationship between itself and the framework it inhabits. All the form-drawing exercises in this book explore this relationship.

Format

In most cases, format is not of vital importance. The sheet can be square or rectangular or something else if required.

Dimensions

The size of the sheet depends on the tools used to create the line. Generally, the more rudimentary the drawing tool and the pupil's motor skills, the larger the sheet should be. It is natural for younger pupils to move their entire arm; older pupils usually find it more natural to use their wrist and fingers. Of course, this varies according to the individual exercise, and the sheet should be appropriate to the task in hand.

Texture

The paper should not be too smooth, because it needs to provide a certain amount of resistance to the drawing tool employed.

Underlay

The type of underlay chosen is important. Bear in mind that table surfaces are often uneven, so give pupils a supportive base upon which they can place their drawings.

Colour

In form drawing, the colours are not as important as the figures themselves. However, consideration should still be given to choice of colour.

Black may be too harsh, and a grey pencil stroke somewhat boring for a child. Brown is soft and neutral and makes a viable alternative. Personally, I prefer drawing with colour.

If you choose to colour the form, remember that the form is the primary focus, and all colouring should support the form, not undermine it. It is important for you to have considered this prior to the lesson in order to provide sound guidance for your pupils, who tend to love colouring shapes after they have drawn them!

Colouring surfaces with complementary colours often works well. If lines are a warm yellow and red, an idea is to fill the open surfaces with lemon-yellow superimposed on blue so that green tones appear, carefully and sensitively, setting the powerful line in relief.

When considering colour combinations, the surface area to be coloured and the density of the colour are just as important as the actual colour combination. On a case-by-case basis, consider whether it is right to colour the form or if it is better to leave it as it is.

Drawings by real pupils throughout the book show examples of how colour may be used.

Mastering the process

A form must be practised before it can be mastered. Although I have not emphasised mastery in Part 2, where the exercises are located, I mention it here as a reminder to keep it in mind. To achieve successful practice sessions, the following tools are useful:

Individual blackboards

By using chalk on a board, pupils can feel that what they are doing is not too serious, as the drawing can be easily wiped away. This frees them to experiment and makes them less anxious about their results. The blackboards can be made from MDF board, A3 size, painted with blackboard paint.

Jotting sheets

Use cheap paper, for example scrap paper that can be recycled after use. This encourages pupils to practise and become involved in a process that is not focused on results. As with blackboards, jotting paper is a necessary component in form-drawing lessons that encourages the playful and exploratory aspects of the subject.

Individual workbooks

Pupils should also have their own workbook where they can draw what they have mastered. Remember that what is drawn in this book should still have the feeling of something fresh and new, to avoid the pupil becoming tired of the form they are working on.

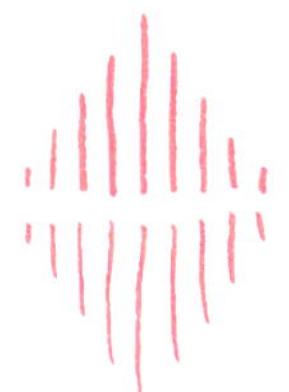 # Creating Your Own Form Drawings 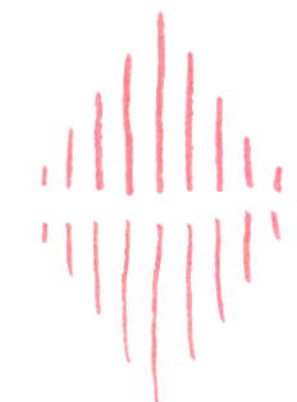

Part 2 presents a series of exercises for each class, but I encourage you to create your own exercises too. I also recommend that, whether using the exercises in this book or your own, you practise them before you present them in class. You have to own them so you can recreate them in front of the pupils. This will enthuse your pupils and encourage them to create and develop the form. There is an element of perpetual innovation in classroom dialogue, and this will allow you to gain direct experience of pupils' ability and on what level you should form future tasks.

Often, I use any paper I can find or the margin of my calendar for informal scribbling and jotting down drawings and forms in different ways. This is preparatory work. I create and recreate the shapes I'd like to use, and at the same time try to sense if they are something the pupils are capable of mastering. This concept becomes more concrete and understandable when you put it into practice. When you begin to draw, you will find that drawing is compelling and leads you to experiment further – and you will inspire the same in your pupils.

Interacting with your pupils

When you know what form drawing is *not*, you can allow yourself to be creative within the parameters of what it *is*. During the course of lessons, you will get a good idea of what your pupils can and cannot achieve. This is vital for both achieving a successful dialogue with your class and preparing your next lesson. You can increase the working pace or raise the difficulty level if the class is capable of this. Or you may, for example, spend more time on certain exercises if the class is enthusiastic and full of ideas. As a result, it is important that the exercises I have proposed for individual age groups are not viewed as rigid but rather as suggestions.

Personally, I never correct pupils' work unless a child asks for assistance. I provide positive feedback. I praise their work process and originality. I ensure that praise is individual and genuine. Form drawing is supposed to be playful and exploratory, and pupils naturally correct their own work within the aesthetic rules of the subject. I always make the rules clear – albeit with a twinkle in my eye – but only when I introduce the exercise to the class. I aim to create a trusting environment so that each pupil's creation can communicate something important: each person's individual mode of expression and style. Each pupil will leave their own indelible stamp on their drawings as they express their intentions and efforts. You will always find something praiseworthy.

Form drawing can produce extremely beautiful results, but this is not of primary importance during children's form-drawing lessons in school. Nor should we spend time worrying if the drawing is 'correct'. What is important is the process, and as a teacher you can easily recognise a pupil's endeavours on their way to form awareness. If results must be measured, do so by watching the pupils' joyous experiences surrounding the different forms, in exploring them and in the acquisition of knowledge that is achieved, step by step, from their own starting point. The most important results are far in the future, and most likely in totally different areas to drawing.

To copy or to create?

I hope now you will be inspired to undertake some practice work and that my words have even sparked a desire to create form on your own terms, employing your own aesthetic choices, where neither geometry nor nature are guiding influences. This might seem demanding or ambitious, but think of it as a path leading from binding geometry to free form. Try to separate the desire to create something perfect and universal, and instead commit yourself to something vulnerable and individual. This is a transition from moving along with something to initiating movement ourselves. In other words, instead of occupying the enclosed space of the circle, take control of the space in the spiral, transform space by mirroring, and create space when transforming form. Progress from copying to creativity.

Part 2: Class 2 Exercises

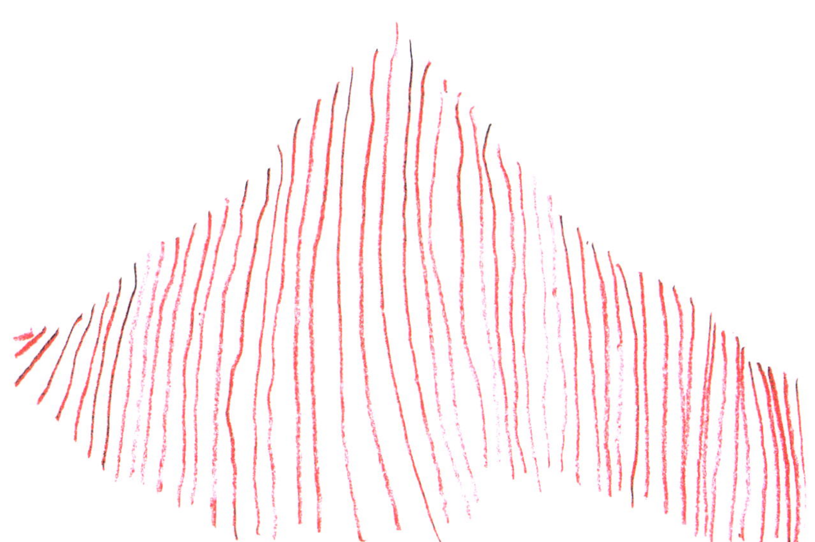

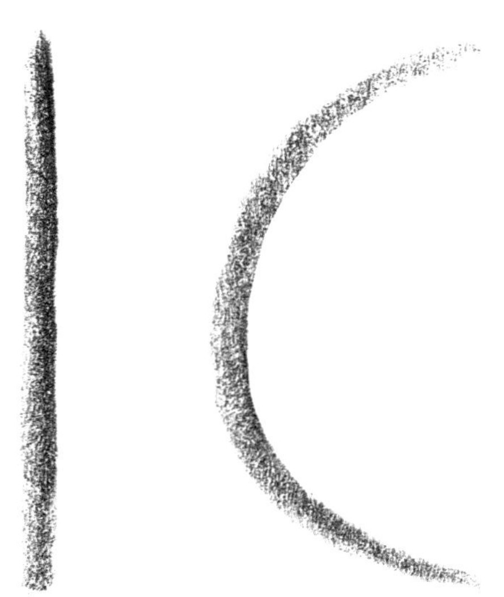

The straight line and the curve

The best place to start is with the simplest building blocks in all drawing: the straight line and the curved line. (See pp.16–17 for a reminder of these lines' qualities.) These are the basis of form drawing. You might think that these two lines are easy, but bear in mind that drawing a straight line and drawing a curved line are two diametrically opposed activities. For pupils in Class 2, these lines and the associated exercises will happily demand all their attention and effort.

To begin your lesson, draw a straight line and then a curved line slowly and carefully, while the class observes. Your pupils' interest will be awakened when they realise that you are not drawing the lines quickly and inattentively; they will note that there is a creative process behind these two different figures.

Your pupils can then attempt the same task, either on paper with good-quality wax blocks, or on small blackboards. They should use the same colour for both lines, so that the differences in the forms can be easily seen. Afterwards, pupils can draw both lines in their workbooks: their two very first form drawings. This is enough for the first lesson, and your pupils will feel a sense of accomplishment.

The cross

To explore the straight line further, ask your pupils about the difference between a vertical and a horizontal line. You will find that your pupils are full of ideas!

Draw a number of straight lines, putting them together in different ways. Start with simple combinations; more complex examples will be given later. Do this with care, taking your time. Something new always appears.

Eventually a unique form will appear that has even sides: the cross. Practise drawing crosses with your pupils. Begin with the vertical line and consider where this should start. There should be space above and below, so do not place it at the edge of the sheet. Instead, use the middle. The same approach should be taken with the horizontal line.

Ask your pupils to draw the cross in their workbook.

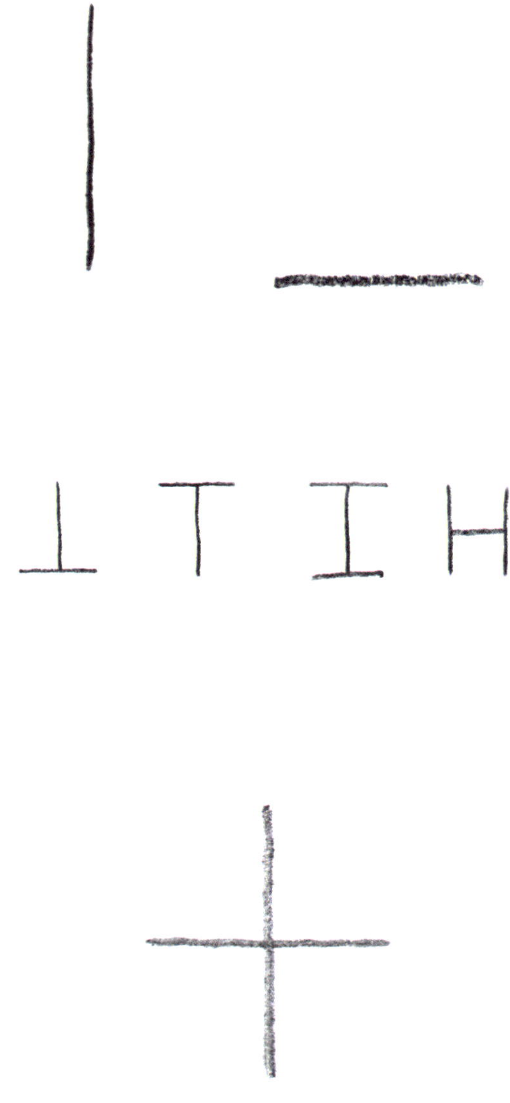

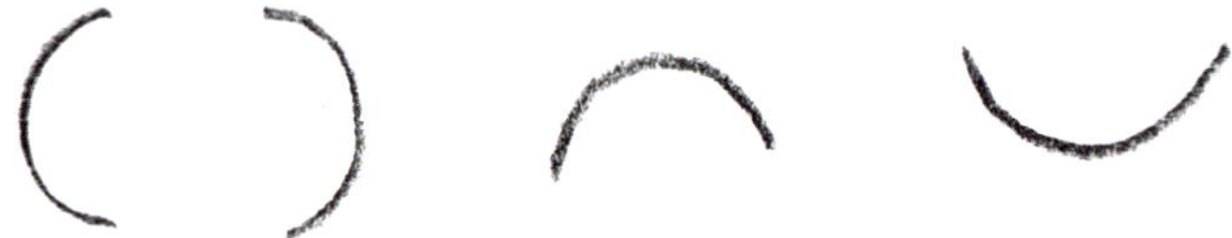

The circle

The curve can be explored in the same way as the straight line. Ask your pupils to draw lots of curved lines, long or short. How far can they take the curve? Finally, they will end up drawing a circle.

This is a basic form that pupils will return to regularly. It does not need to be drawn accurately; everyone understands the idea of the form, and your pupils will draw it as accurately as possible to the best of their ability.

Ask your pupils to draw the circle in their workbook.

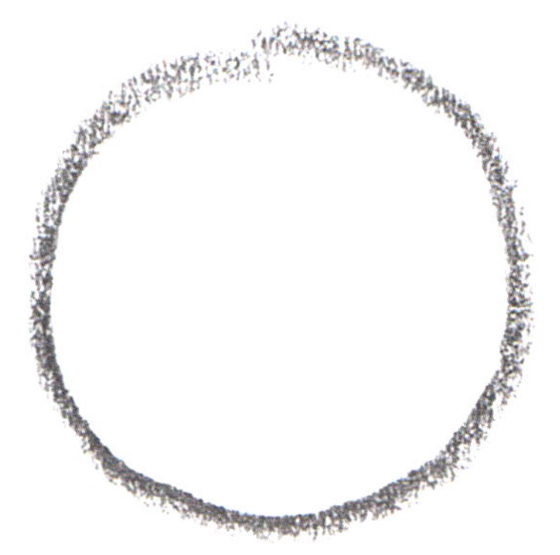

Developing straight lines and curves

Practise the straight line again, in all its simplicity. What happens if it is placed diagonally, or if two lines cross one another in different ways?

Demonstrate all of these exercises to your pupils with slow, relaxed and expansive movements. Encourage them to find new variations.

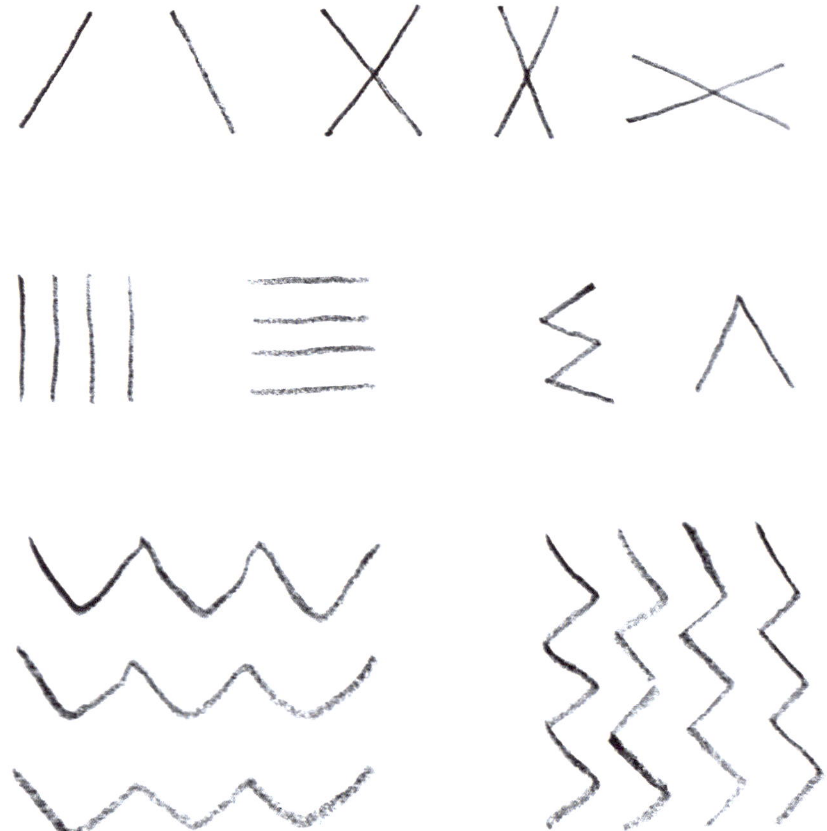

Now, combine curved lines in different ways. Repeat them so that patterns emerge. Use the whole sheet of paper.

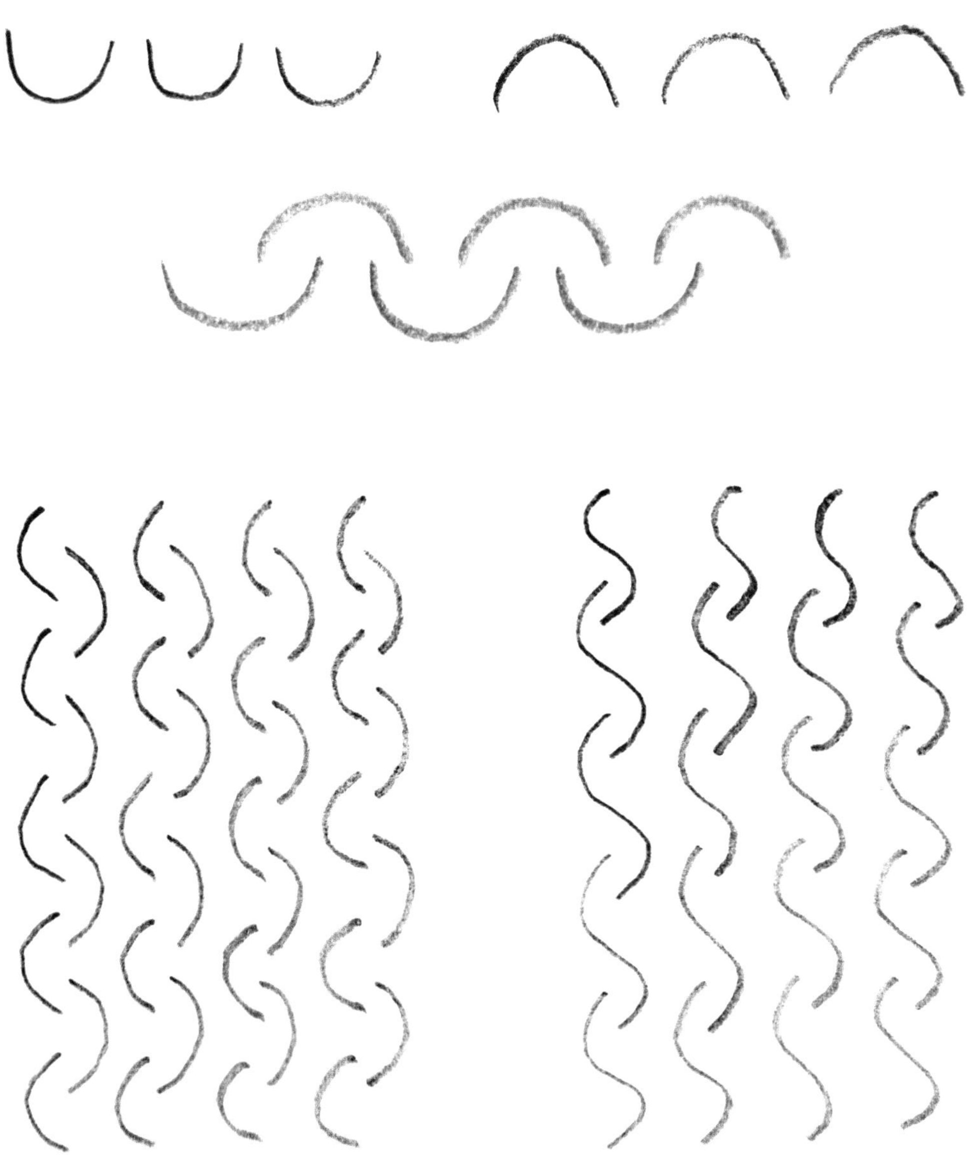

Here are examples of new exercises using straight and curved lines. Repeat this composition multiple times across the sheet of paper or blackboard.

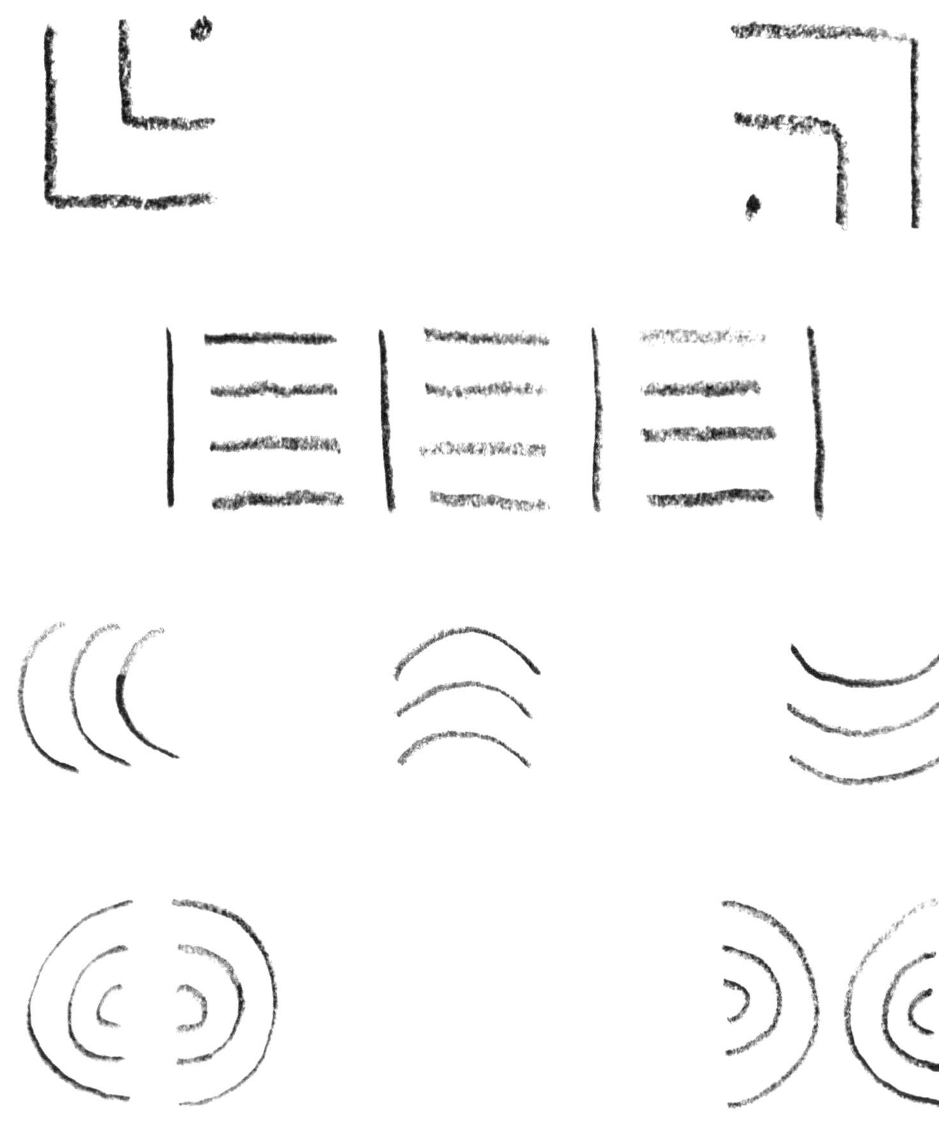

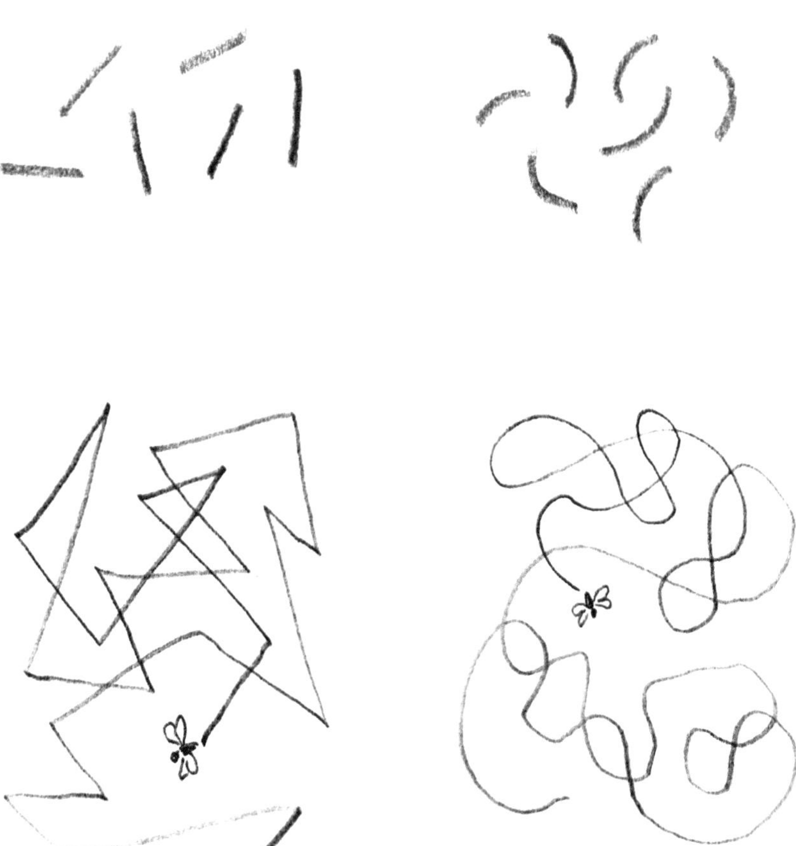

Try drawing straight and curved lines in different combinations. Allow pupils to draw only straight lines or only curved lines on a sheet of paper.

Make rules: for example, that all lines must be equally long, curved in the same way, that they move in different directions, that they not be allowed to meet and so on. Rules can give your pupils different areas to explore.

Another approach could be to look at a natural phenomenon, preferably something that moves, for example, a fly that buzzes round and round or a spider spinning its web across spaces. Ask your pupils to use straight or curved lines to draw their flight patterns.

Try different approaches to circles: draw
them inside or outside one another.

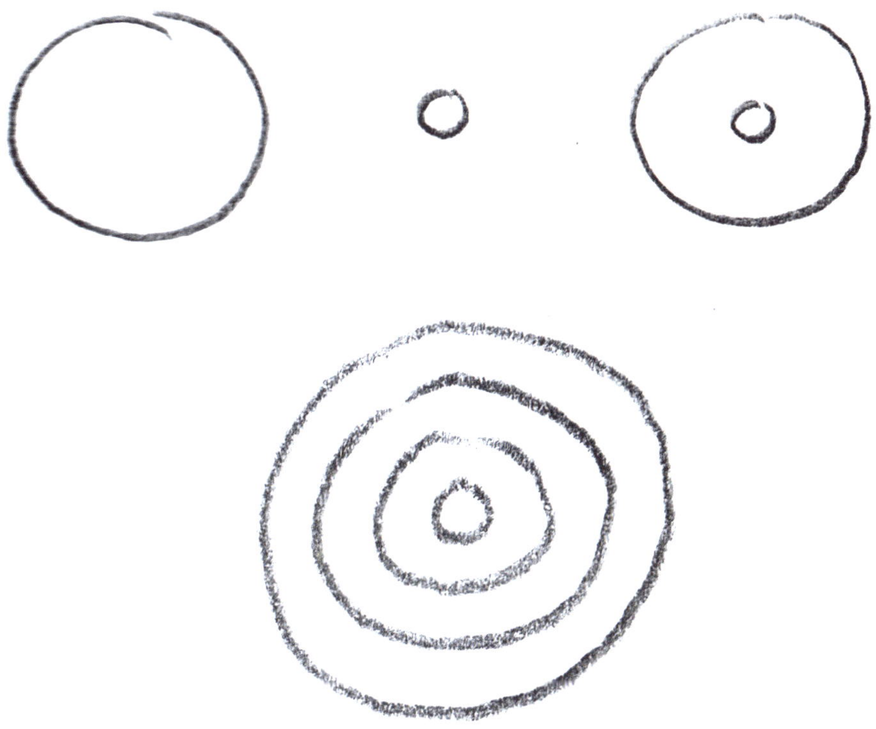

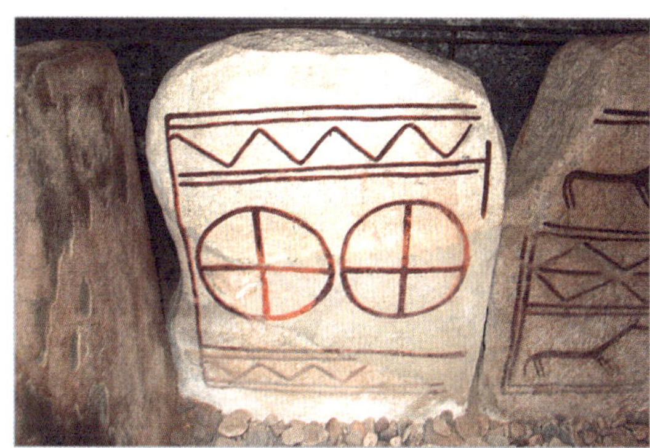

From a Bronze Age site, Kivik, Sweden

Draw a cross, then add more lines in the spaces between the original two. How many can you fit in? Ask your pupils.

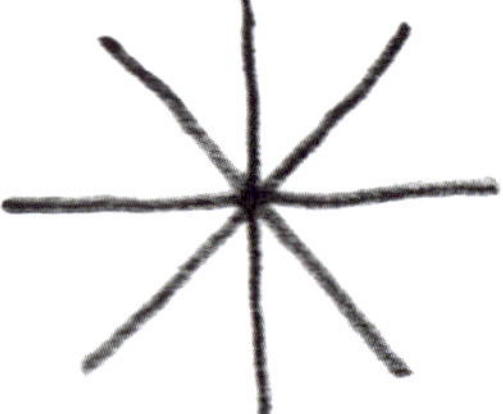

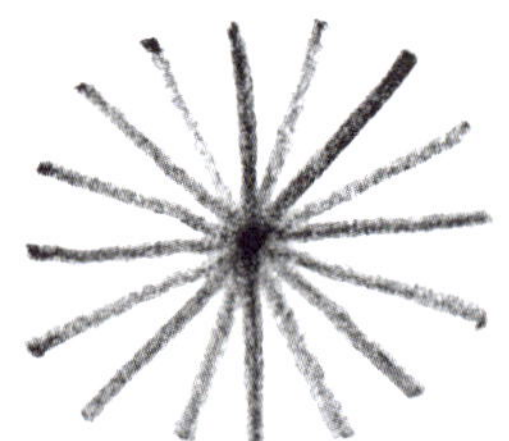

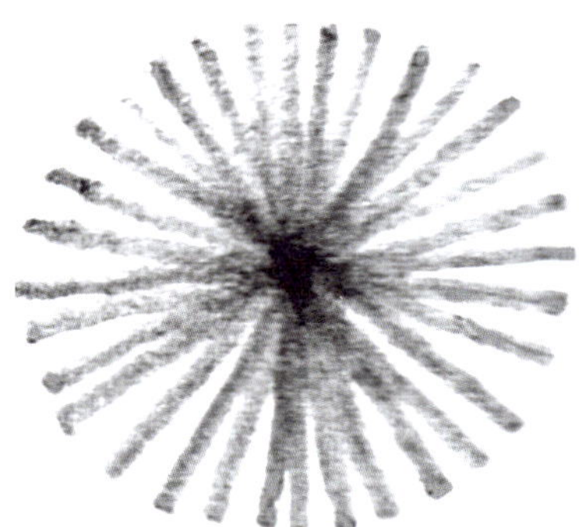

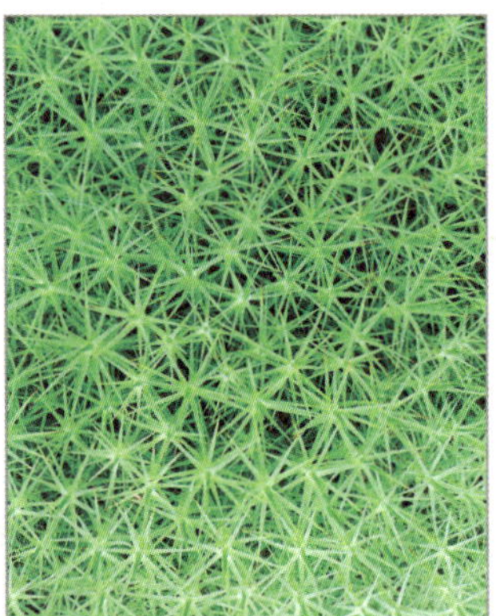

Moss

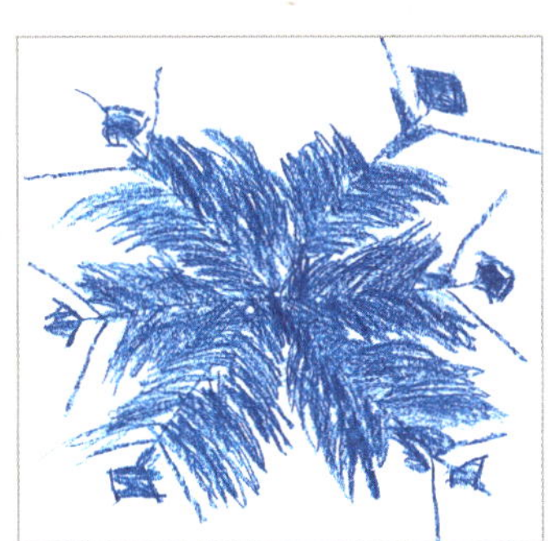

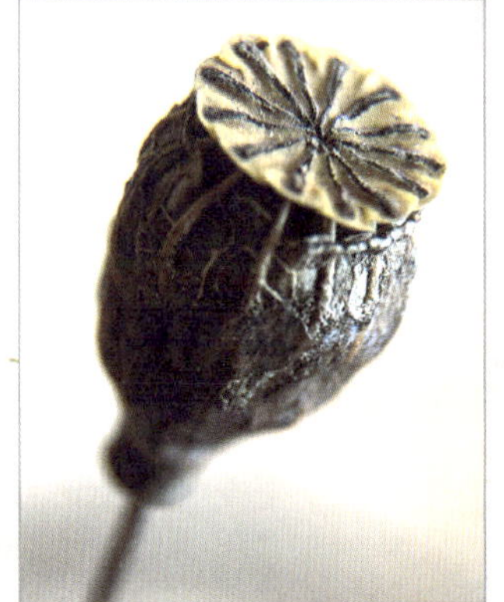

Poppyseed head

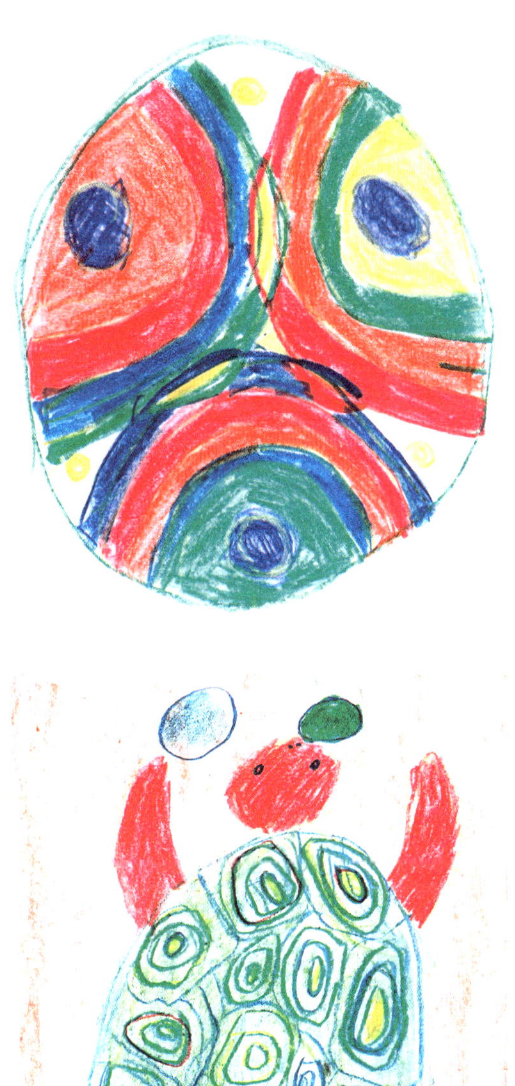

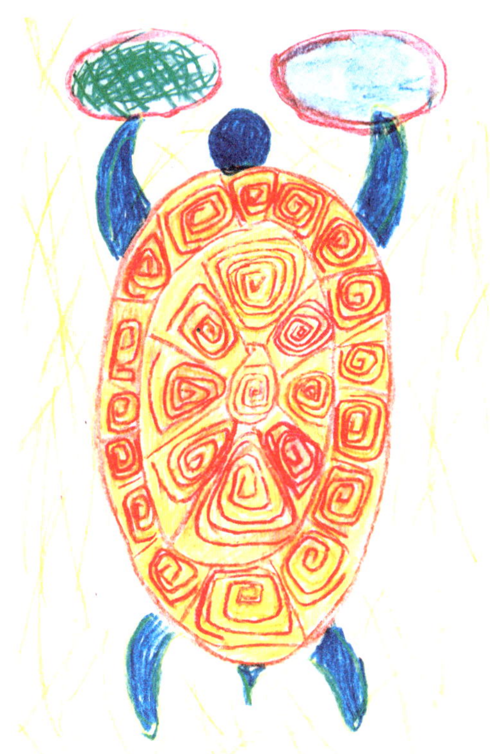

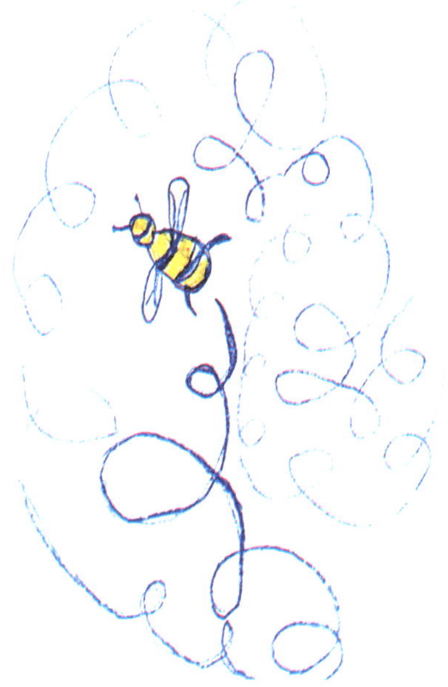

Here are some new challenges to try with straight lines. Draw a series of vertical lines that gradually increase and then decrease in height.

Note how new lines and shapes appear in addition to the ones that are drawn.

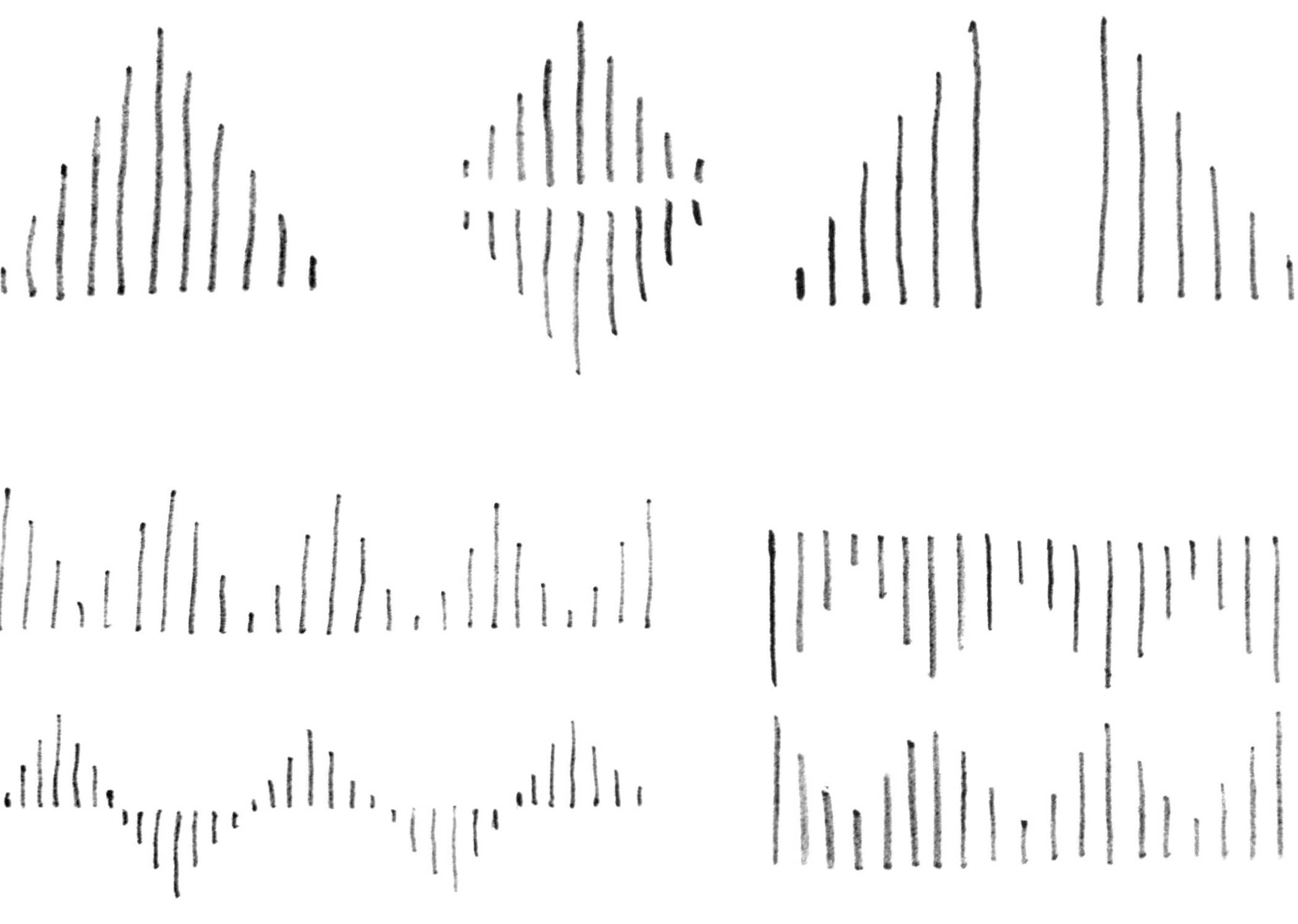

The pupil who drew this has understood the task well and produced a beautiful and dynamic drawing.

If you would prefer your pupils to achieve more regular results that look more like the examples on p.38, then reiterate the rules and ensure the class understands them fully before attempting the task again.

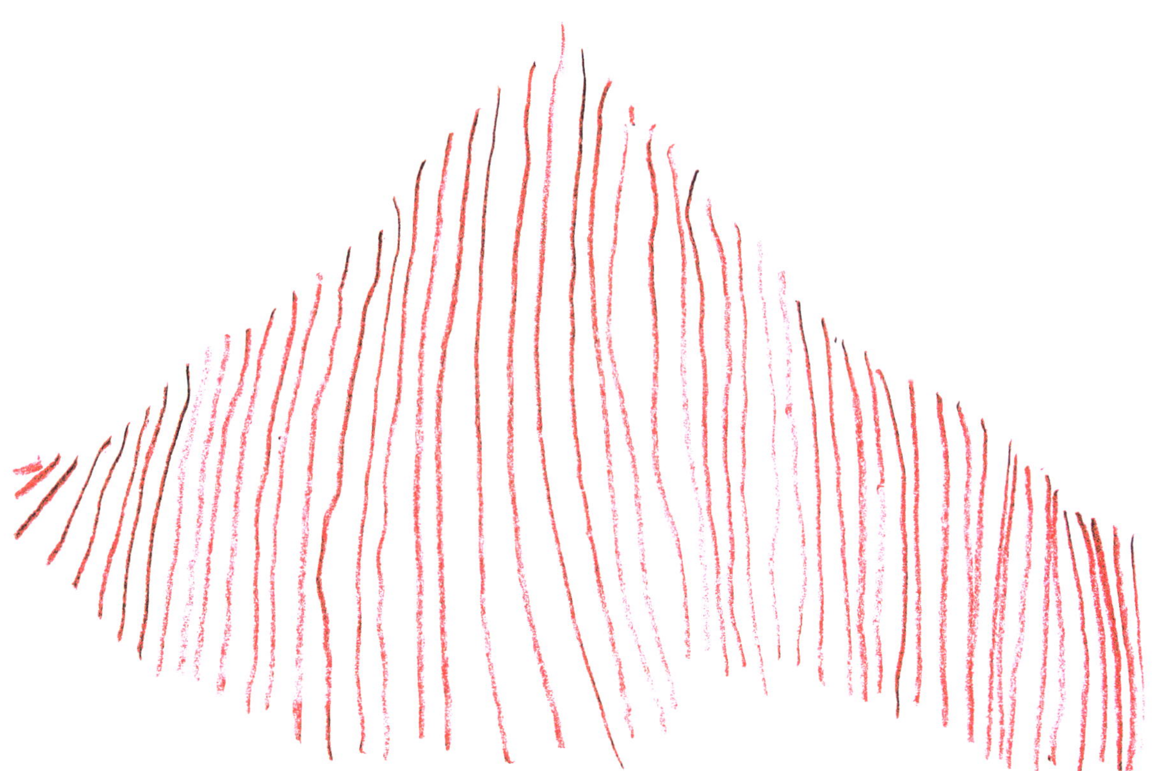

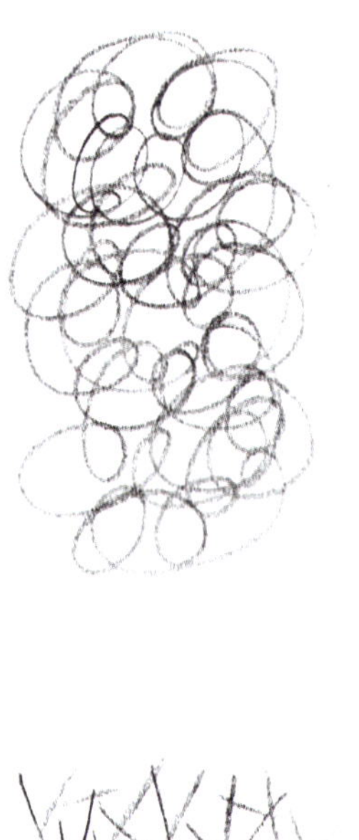

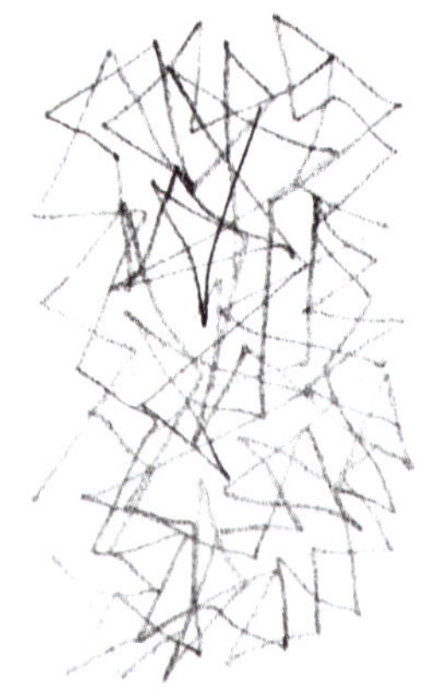

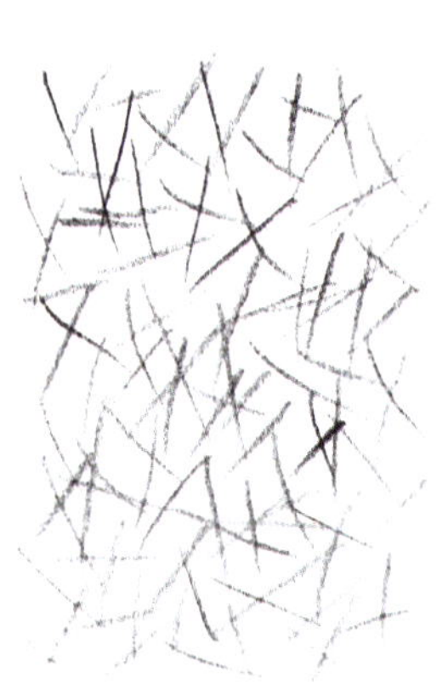

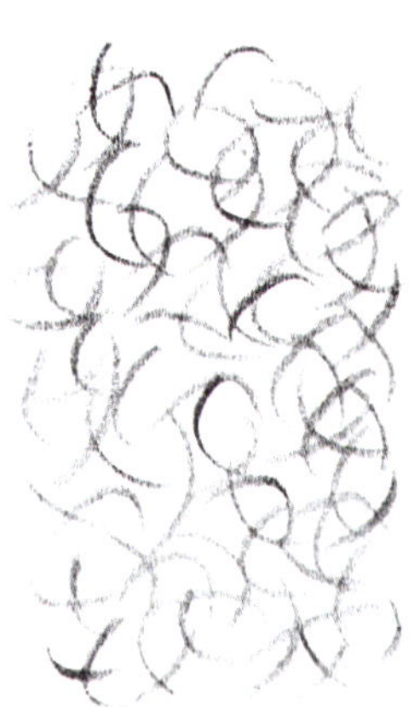

Build up momentum using lines and curves. Let pupils fill their entire sheet of paper with one complete unbroken line that travels in one direction. The loops can be the same size.

Next, try the same exercise with straight lines. The aim is to fill the paper in a pretty or pleasing way.

Now, create new challenges using different rules. The lower examples show the same exercise but this time with freestanding (that is, broken) lines.

It is important to decide in advance how regulated or free you will make the exercise for your pupils. Counterintuitively, it is often easier to learn with more restrictive exercises, and often more fun!

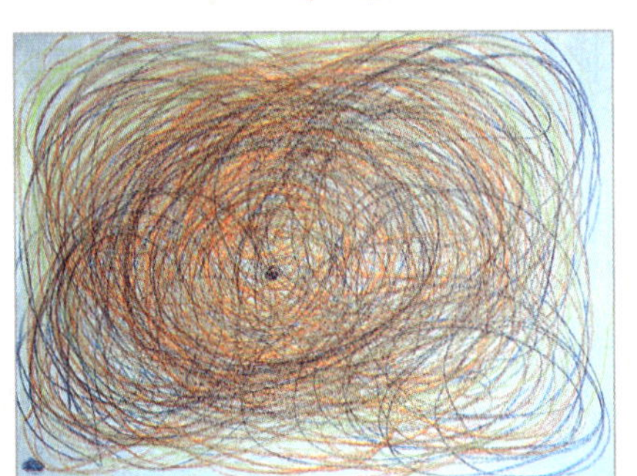

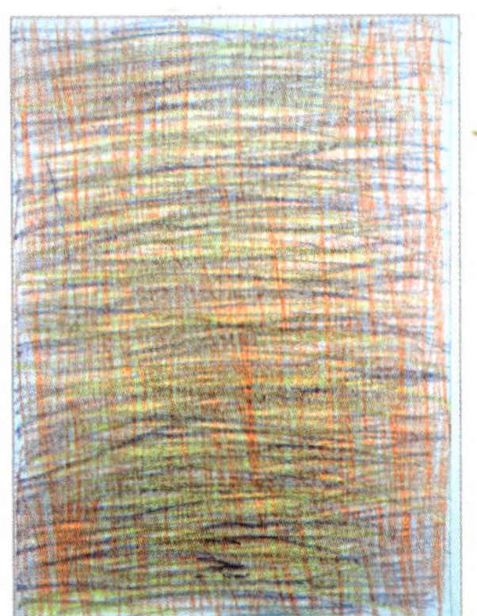

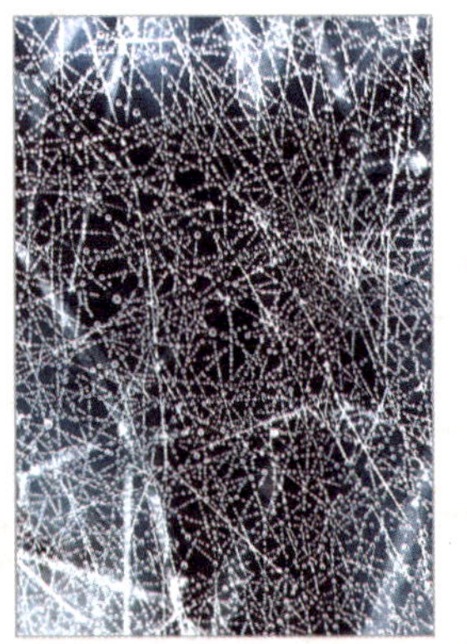

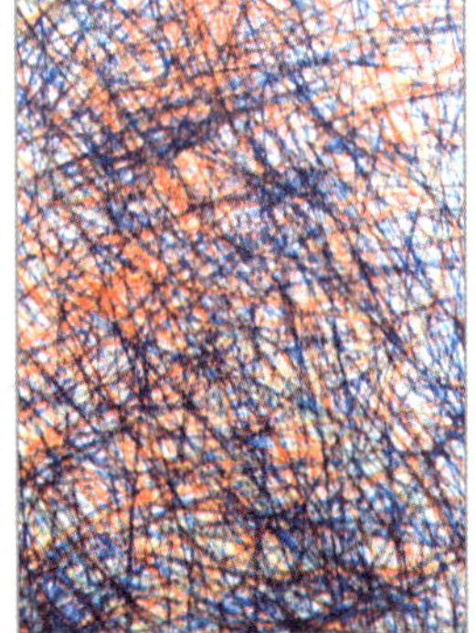

A spider's web with dewdrops

Borders

Borders are a recurring theme in form drawing, because they provide excellent challenges for the aesthetic senses. Making forms the same height and maintaining a regular rhythm require practice. Also, many borders have complicated twists that hone pupils' motor skills. When drawing borders, it will soon become clear to pupils that they are repetitive figures. Once they have understood this, they can make their own suggestions.

Meanwhile, here are a few borders to try out in class. The lower two examples are not horizontally symmetrical and can be turned upside down for variation.

You can also develop these examples by using curves instead of straight lines.

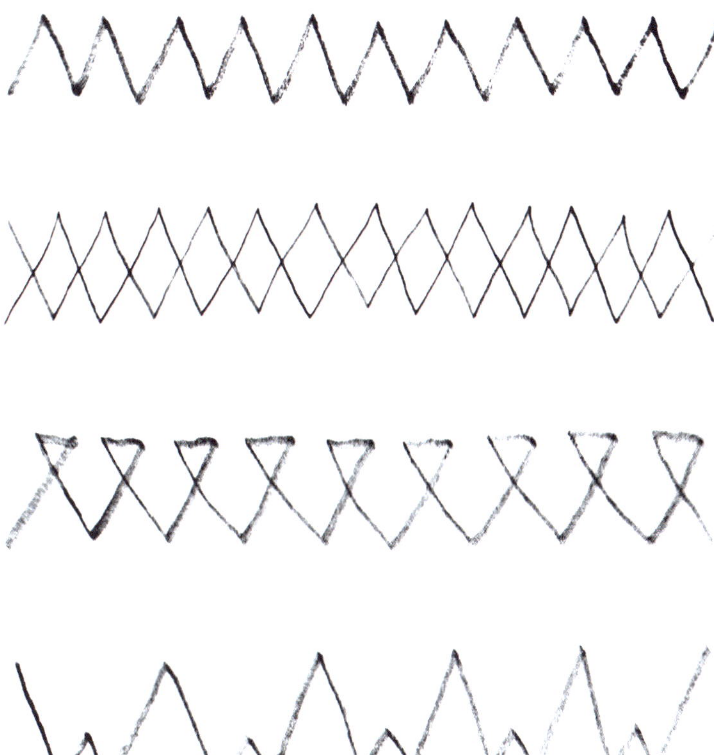

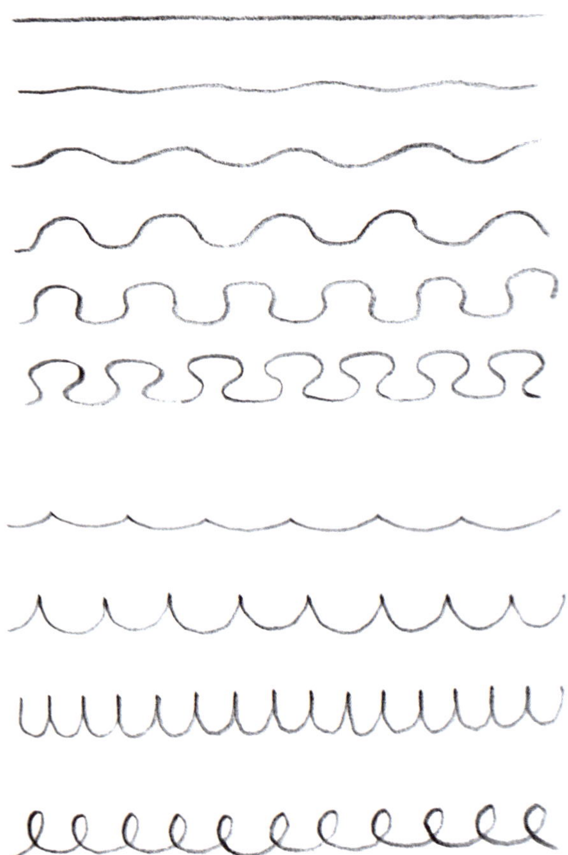

Developing borders

Soon after learning the basics, pupils will be able to start drawing different types of borders. For example, to develop a border from a straight line, ask the pupil to imagine that the straight line is something living in its journey across the page.

Using the whole sheet of paper, allow a straight line to develop as shown in the examples. Ask your pupils to develop what you have started on their blackboards.

The lower four illustrations show another way of developing the line. Allow your pupils to experiment and use their suggestions to develop new tasks.

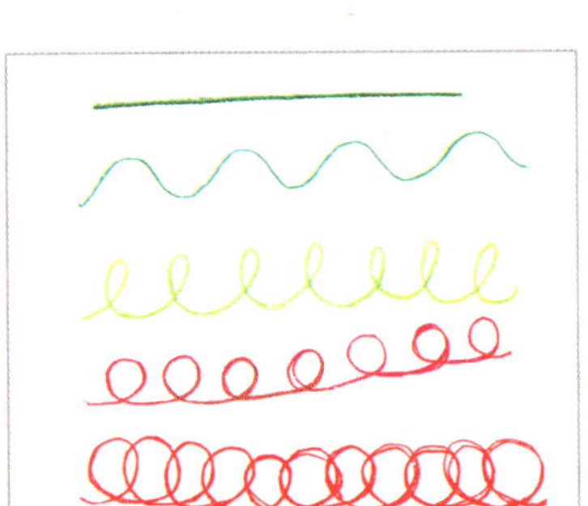

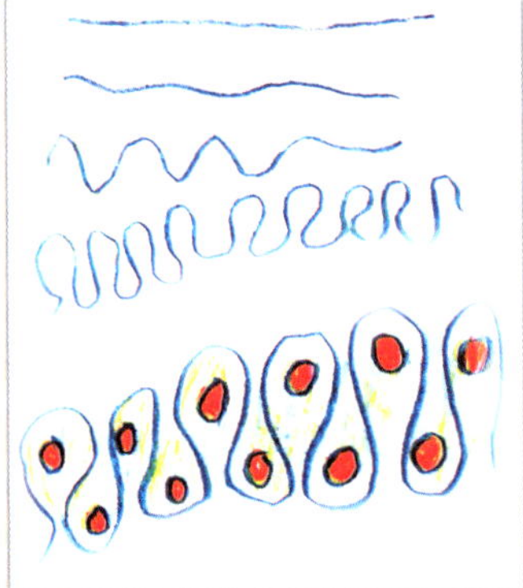

This border is a further development of the final example on the facing page. Pupils should practise drawing the border upside down (in other words, aim to mirror the image).

Next, they should draw the borders so that each loop is directly above another loop. This can be done initially with the 'backs' facing one another (see the example at the top of this page) and then with the loops facing one another (see the example in the middle of this page). This demands accuracy and is useful preparation for other related exercises.

Once they have grasped the concept, pupils can explore how such borders can be juxtaposed in many different ways: beautiful, exciting, elegant and fun. There are many solutions, but some may be too demanding for this level. I have suggested more advanced exercises for each class throughout the book.

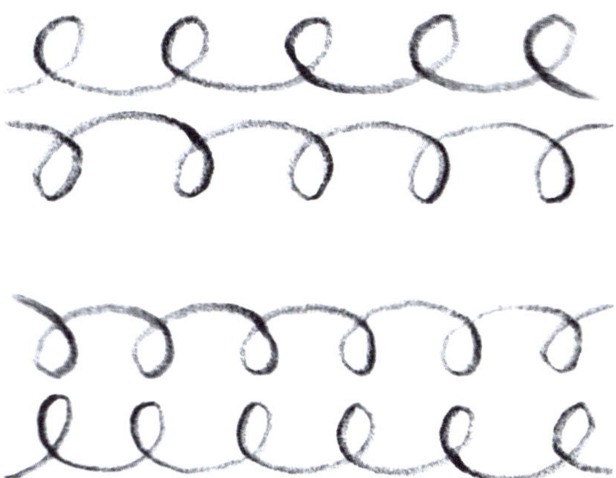

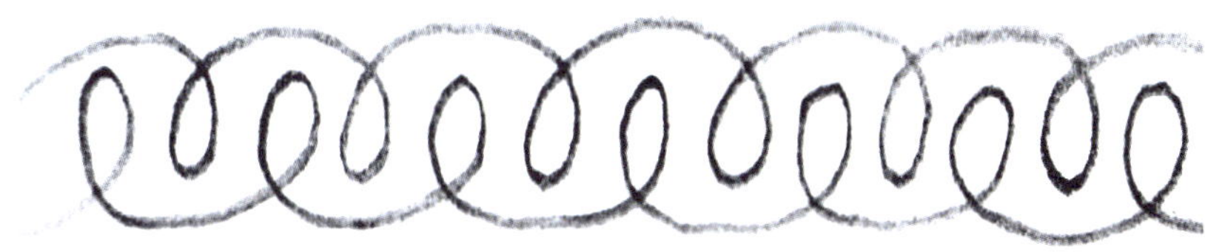

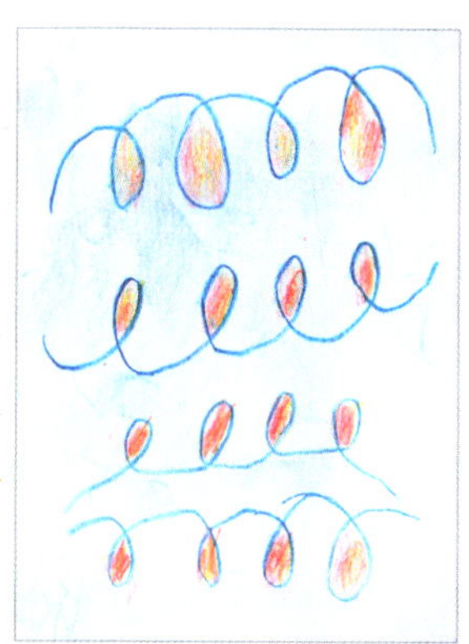

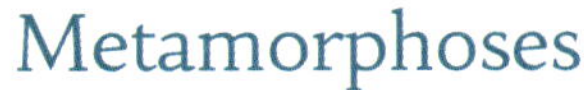

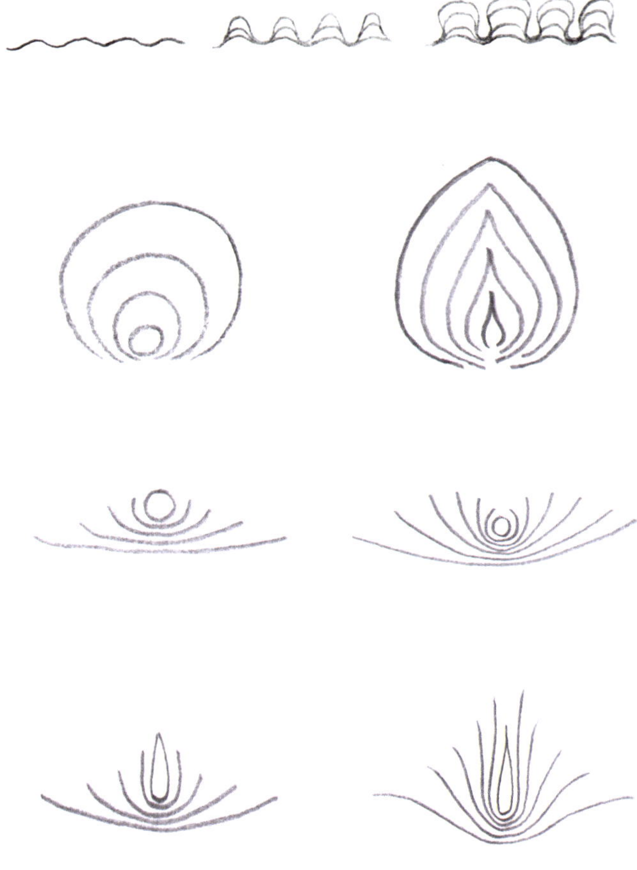

Metamorphoses

Forms can appear quite different and yet still be related, because of the gradual development of one figure. For example, the first border on this page is gradually developed by placing new, higher waves above the first line. This method allows pupils to experiment with different ideas to create new borders, and you should encourage them to take their concepts as far as they can. Try out different borders in which the elements stem from the same border or edge.

When working with single figures, start with the smallest element and develop outwards, as with the circles and teardrop shapes in the examples on the left. Try doing the opposite, beginning with a single large figure and working inwards.

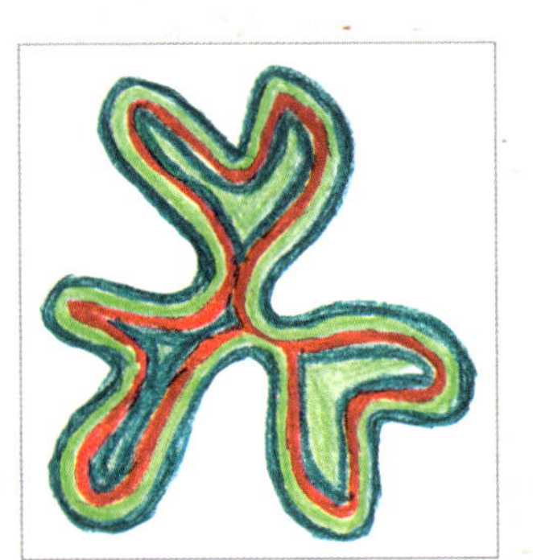

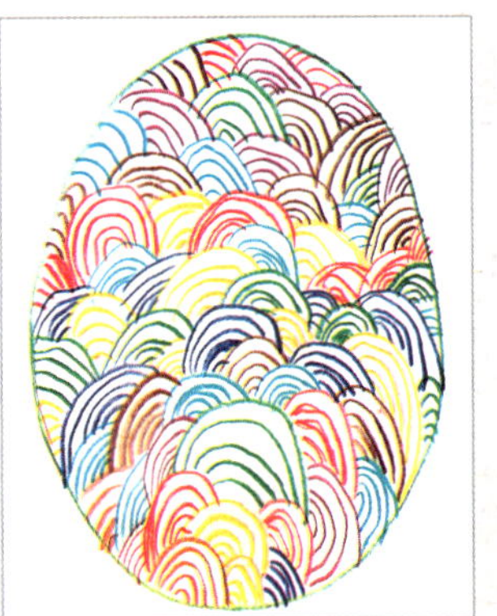

Find different solutions and approaches. Complete the exercises in large formats: use the entire sheet of paper or whole blackboard for each.

Draw a small figure on one part of the sheet, then add contours. Instruct pupils to make the gaps between the contours the same size (see the examples at the top of the page).

Another exercise involves distinguishing lines using colour or thickness. Draw one line, then use the same point of origin to add more, letting them diverge evenly (see the lower examples).

With the help of contours, any figure can be the starting point for interesting and often surprising transformations of form.

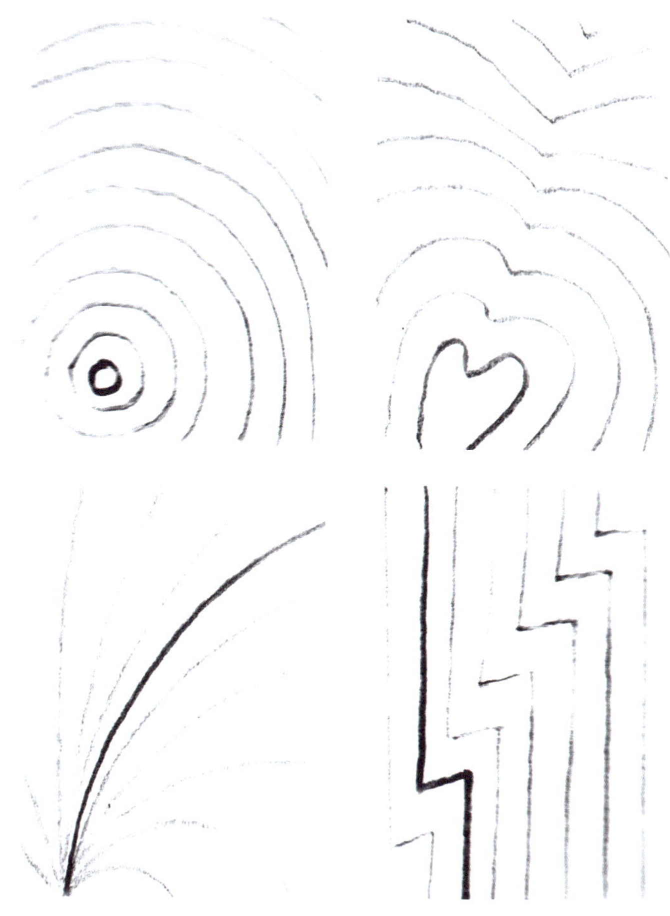

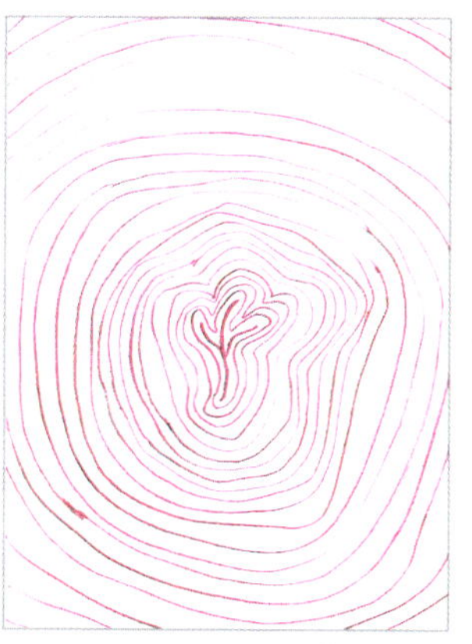

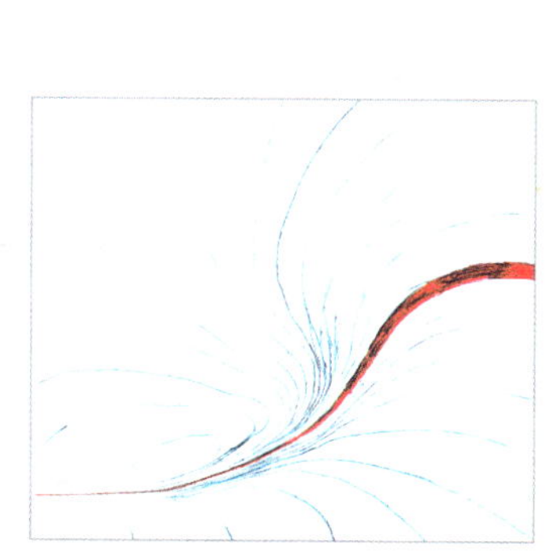

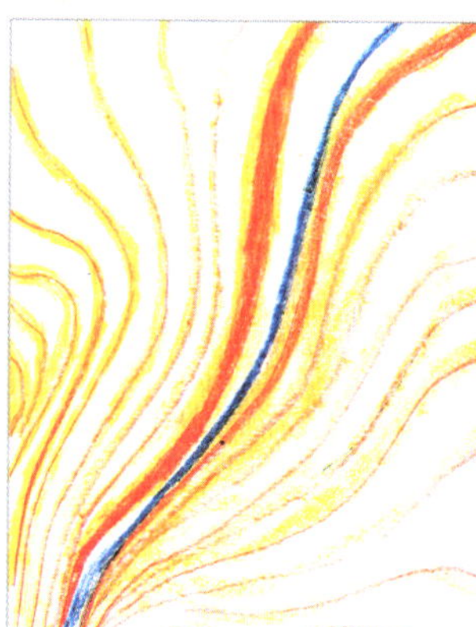

Draw a few points on a sheet of paper. Next, work systematically through the points, drawing around one, then the next, all the time maintaining the same distance between the lines. The illustrations below demonstrate different methods.

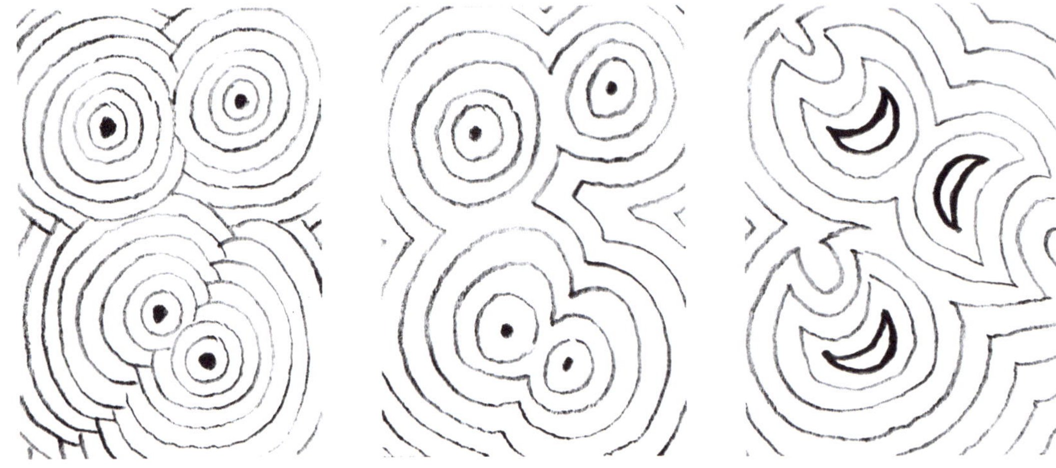

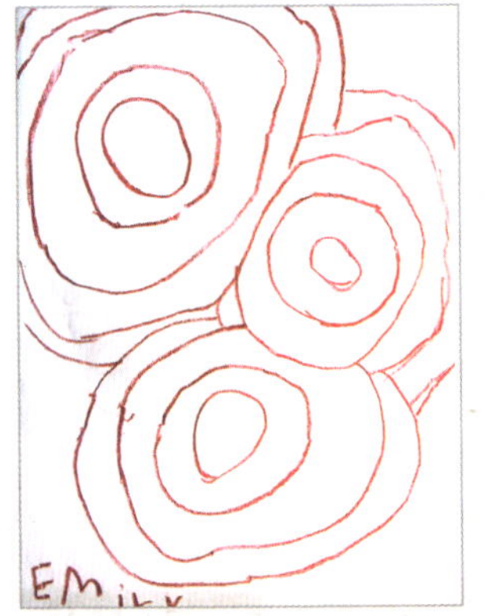

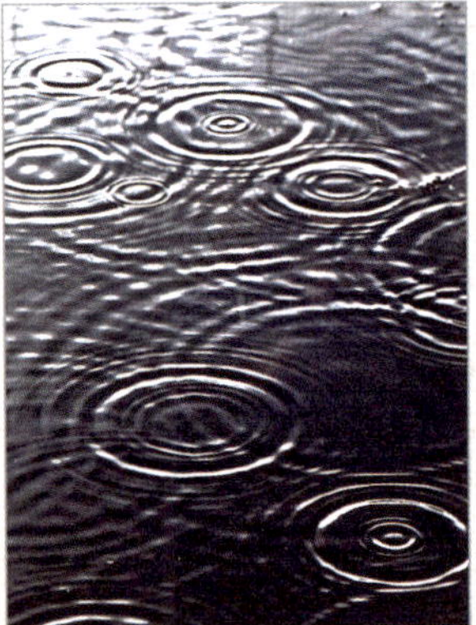

Raindrops on still water

Here is a plantlike transformation, progressing from one form to two to three and so on.

A line can develop while it is being drawn. I suggest that you attempt this exercise, then step back to consider the results. Is your line going where you first thought it would? When introducing this exercise to pupils, make suggestions on the blackboard and then ask the pupils to try their own versions.

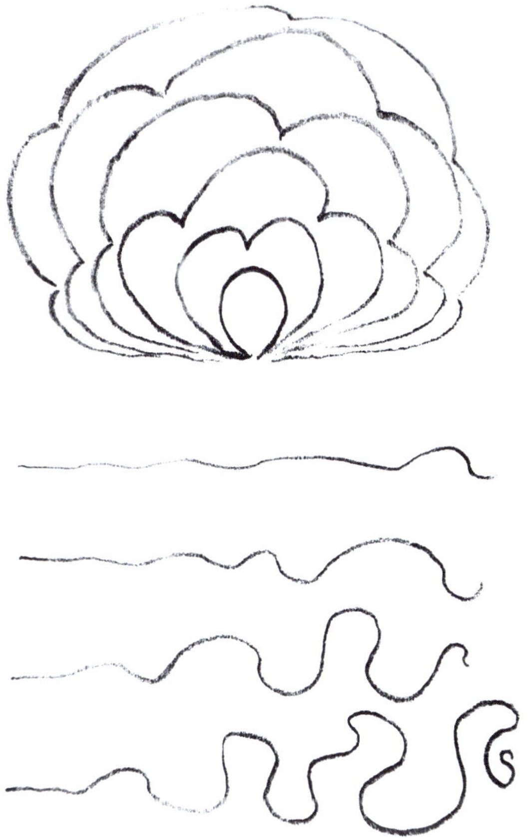

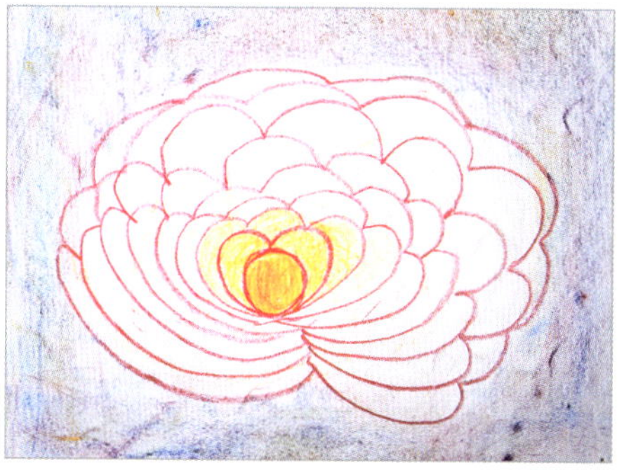

Spirals

It is important to introduce the basic form of the spiral carefully, as it will be explored in later classes. Consider the progress your pupils have already made and give thought to whether they are ready for this challenge yet. If not, you can delay starting work on spirals until Class 3.

If you deem your class ready, the spiral can be approached in many different ways:

- It can develop in a border pattern.
- It can have as many rotations as the pupils wish or can master.
- It can run inwards or outwards.
- It can have broader or narrower spacing between the lines. Alternatively, the space can increase or decrease as the spiral grows.

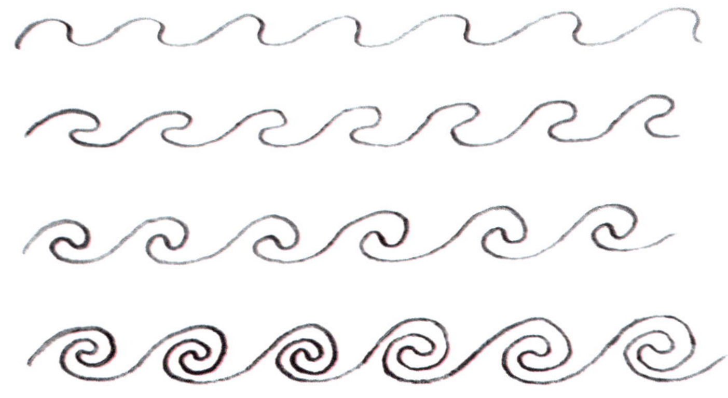

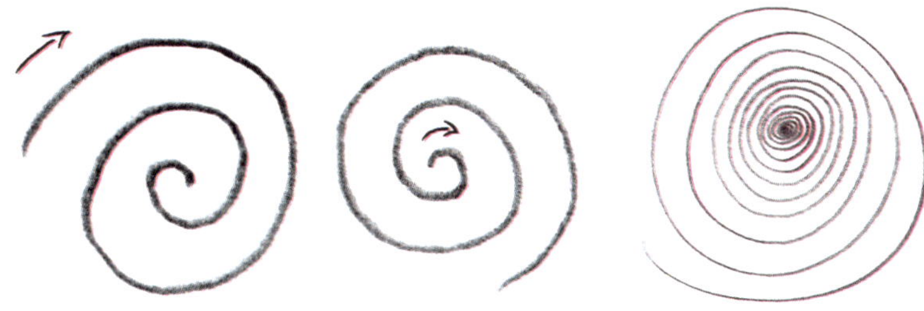

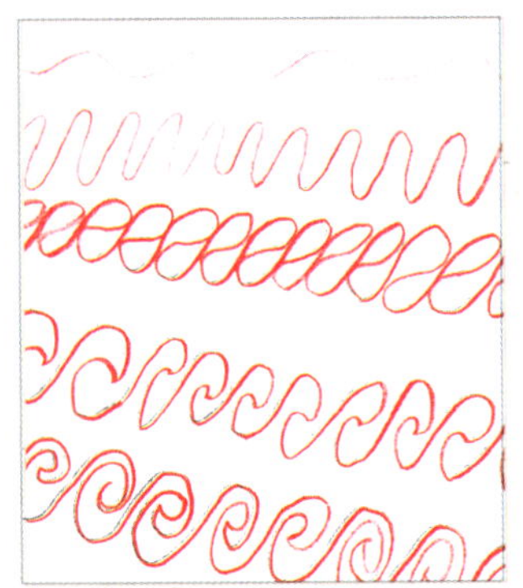

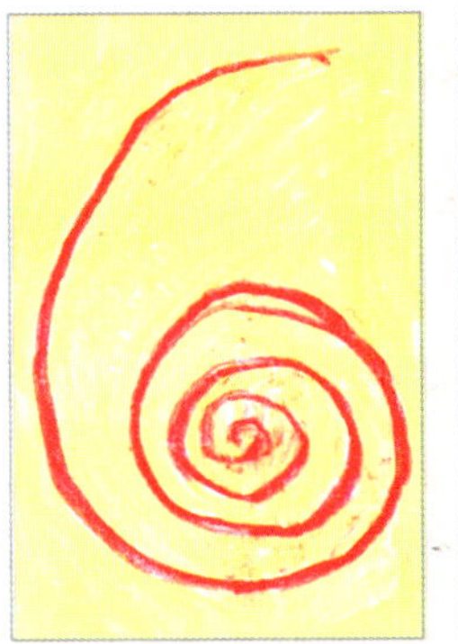

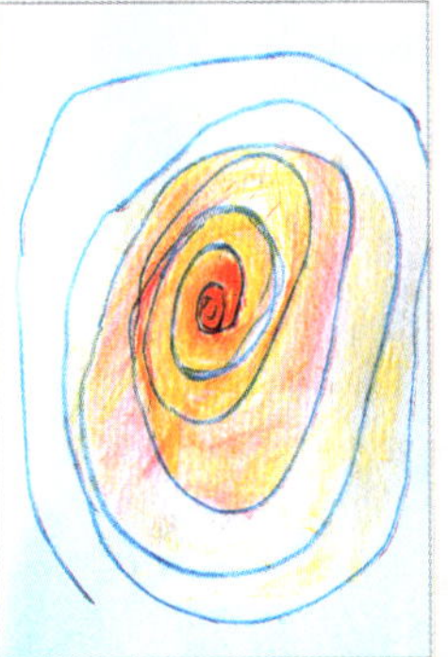

Some good exercises involve asking:

- For the spiral to look attractive, where should the line finish on its inward or outward journey?
- You may choose to draw lines that are equidistant on the inward path (for example, the width of two fingers). Where should the line finish to avoid breaking the rule?
- Or perhaps you'd prefer the distance between the lines to reduce as the spiral winds its way inwards. Where should it finish then?

Spirals can be drawn using straight lines as well as curved. To do so, start working on the upper edge of a straight line. You can develop straight-edge spirals in many different ways, as shown. One way of approaching the task is to use thick wax crayons or blocks.

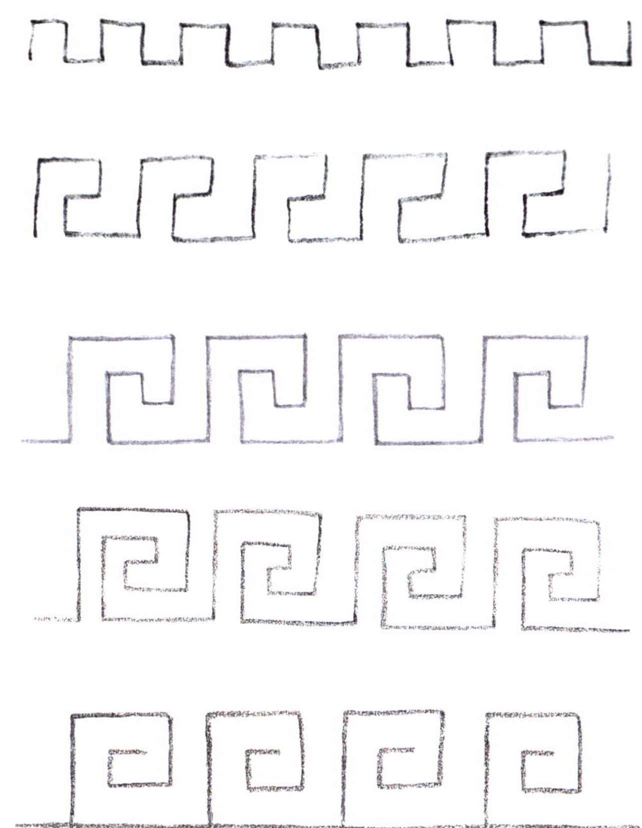

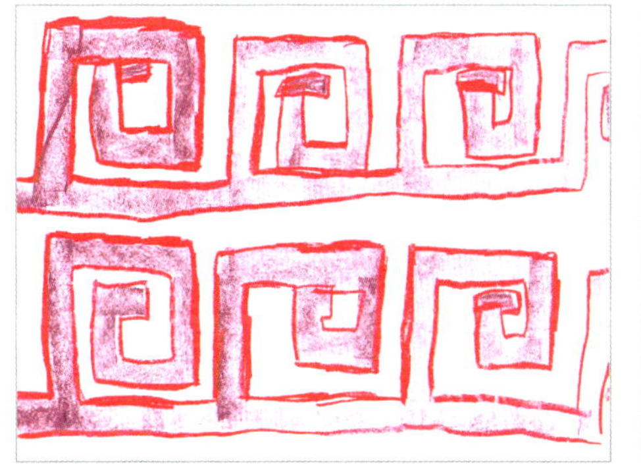

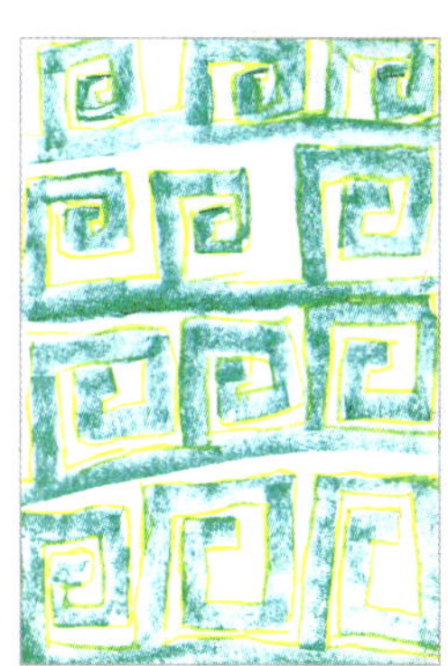

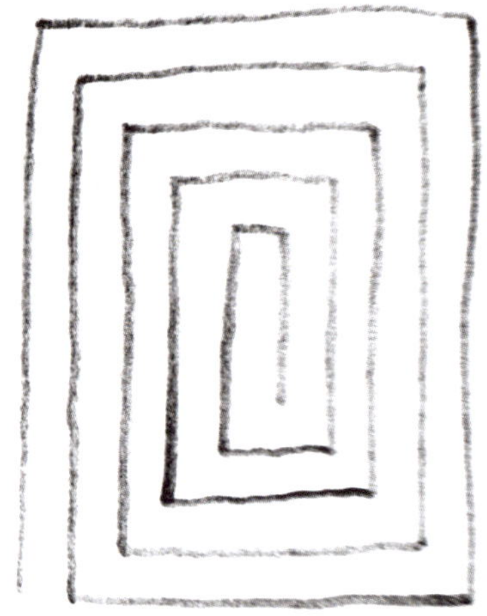

Challenge your pupils to draw a square or oblong spiral that runs inwards, and specify that the distance between lines should be equidistant, as shown. Where should the last and innermost line finish? This will always be up to the pupil, and as a result is a great exercise for learning to assess form.

One idea for colouring this form is to increase the depth of colour as you approach the centre of the spiral (see the examples of pupils' work).

In the figure below we see the spiral transitioning from one direction to another.

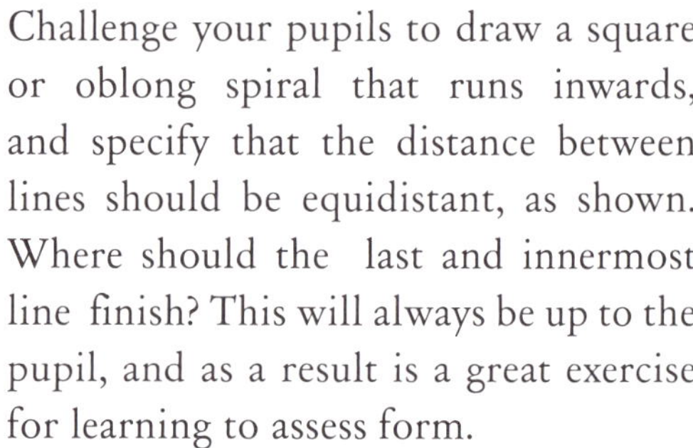

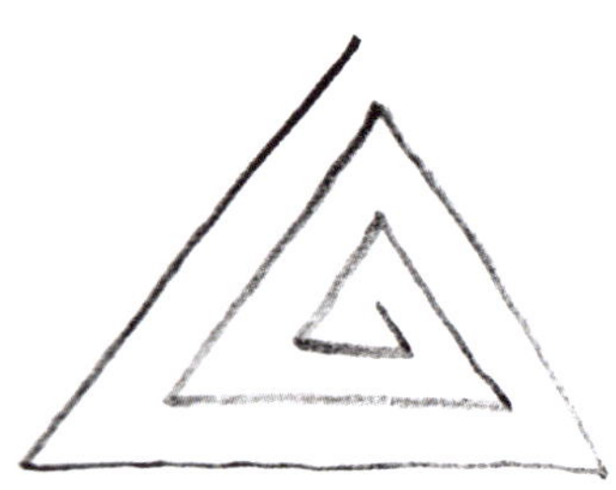

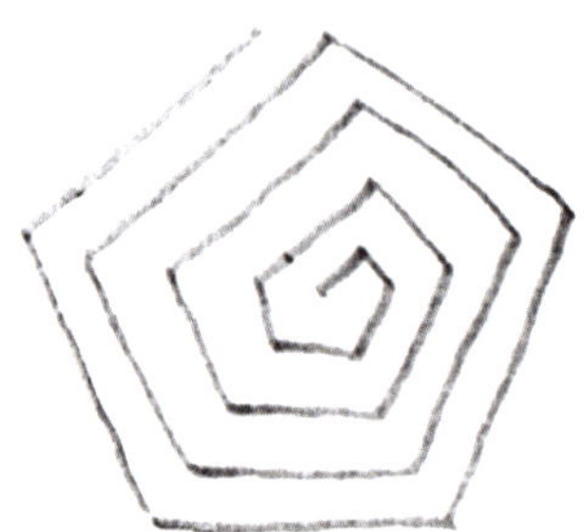

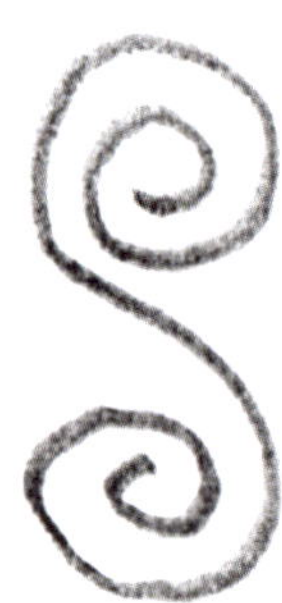

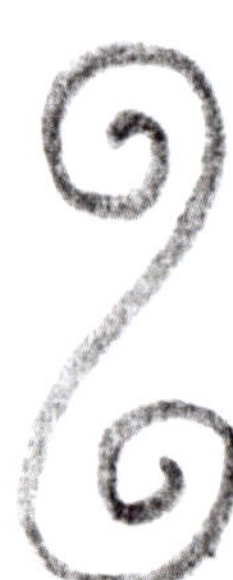

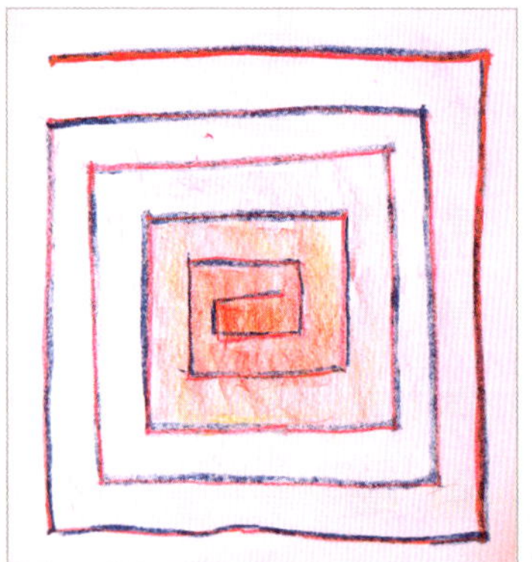

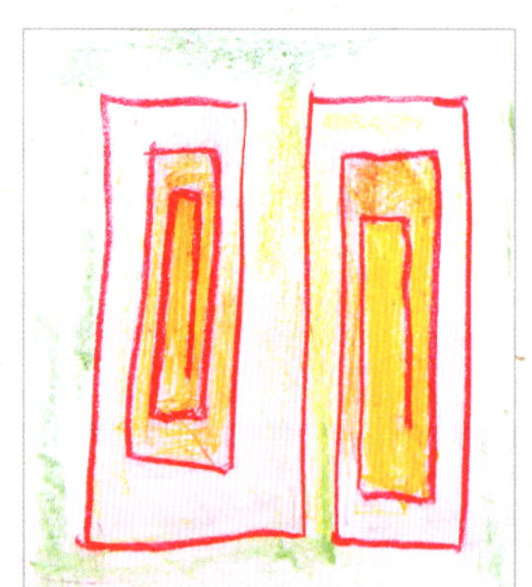

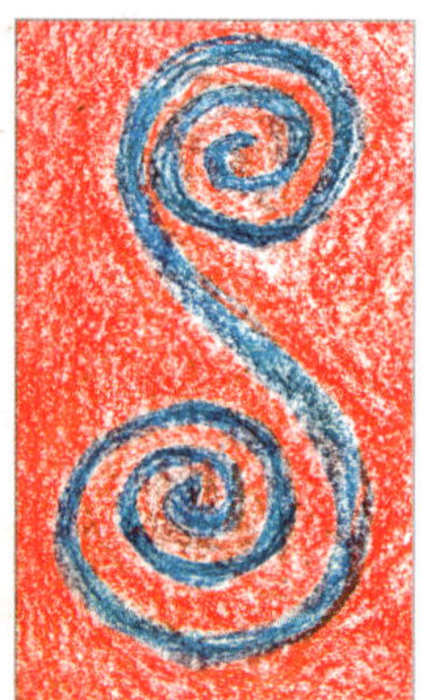

Take note of the challenging point where the direction shifts and try it with your pupils.

Ask pupils to alternate between practising spirals that twist in the same direction and those that change direction.

When pupils have drawn a spiral that changes direction, develop a new, additional spiral (see the central examples). The challenge here is to get all the spirals the same size and the same distance apart.

Next, draw several spirals from a central point (see the lower examples). Try to create even spacing as the lines curve.

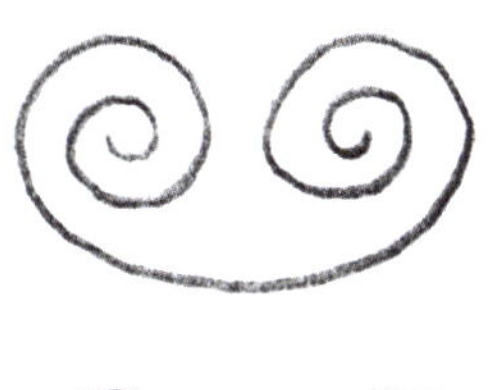

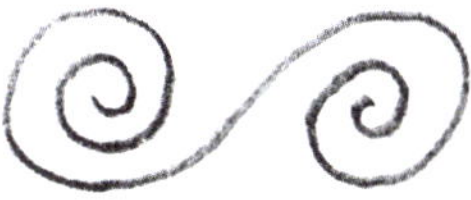

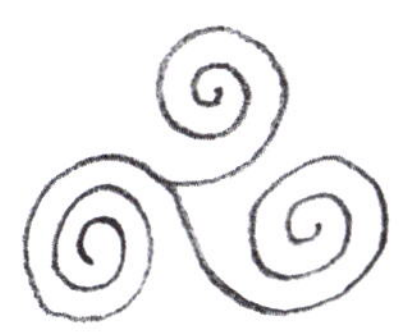

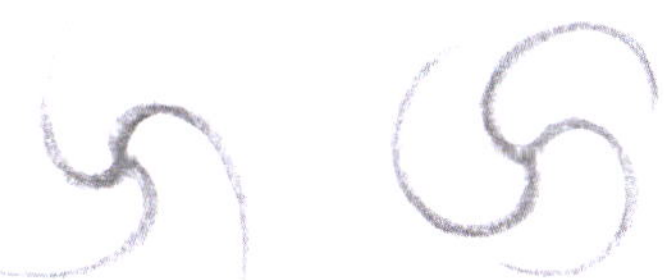
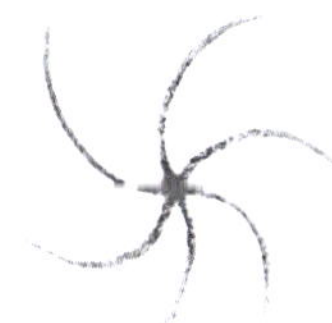

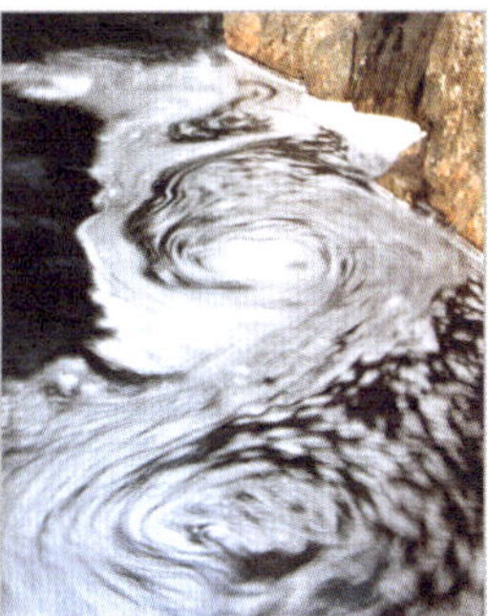

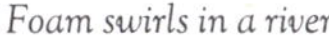

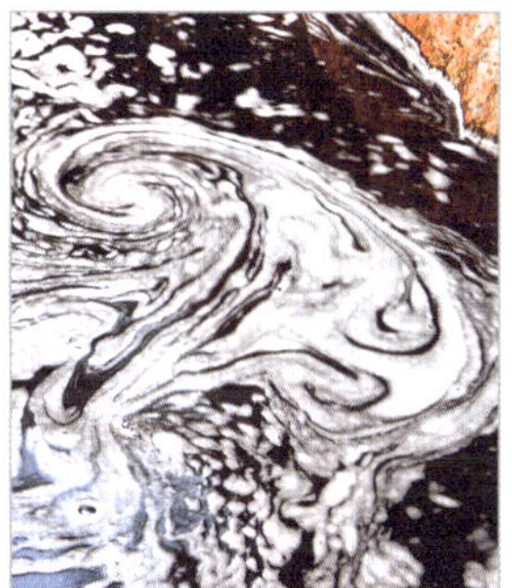

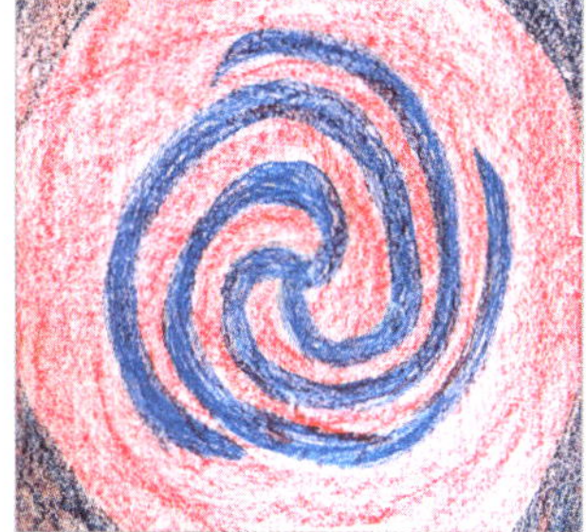

Foam swirls in a river

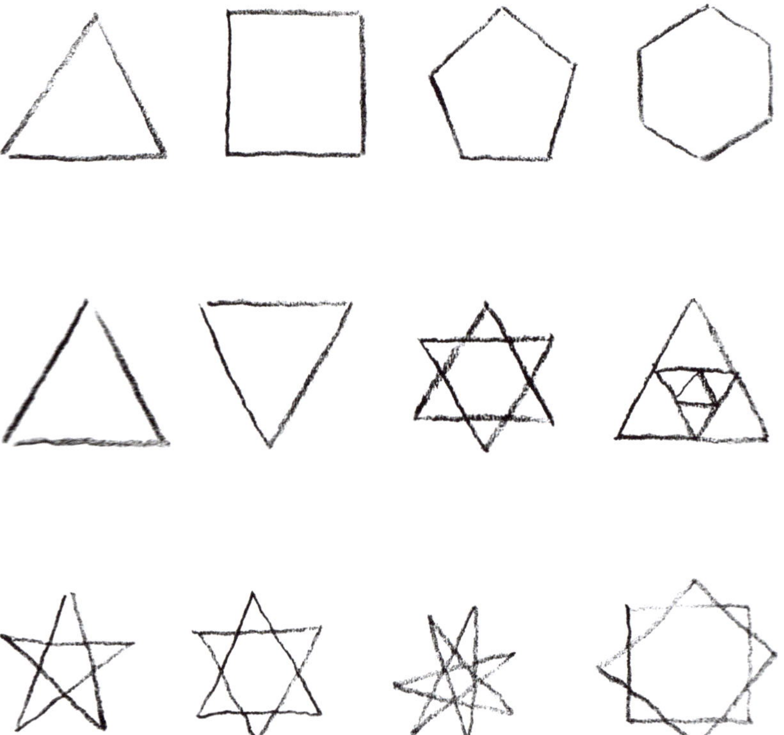

Mathematics

Drawing shapes helps us to gain a better understanding of numbers, as it allows us to visualise them as numeric forms with differing qualities. Form drawing can be used to illustrate the four forms of arithmetic; in the examples shown here, the concepts of plus, minus, multiplication and division are present.

All these exercises can be completed freehand, and pupils may also work together to construct these figures using thread or sticks.

What numeric secrets do star forms possess? Look at the examples of pupils' work here, then discuss these forms with your class.

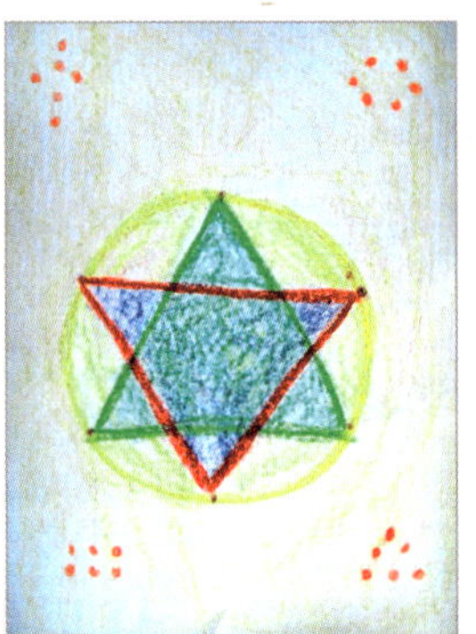
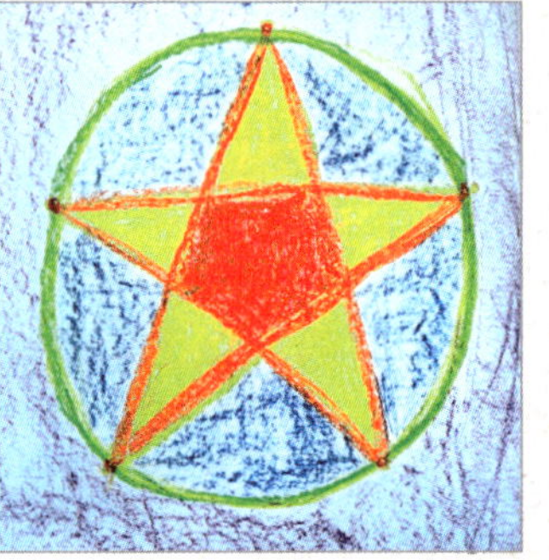

In the two examples above, we can see that it is possible to divide six by two and three, yet it is not possible to divide five by a number other than itself

By presenting numbers as shown in the illustrations on the right, we can grasp their qualities as well as the way they convey amounts.

In the centre are two examples of the number eight. Draw a circle and mark eight points at equal intervals around it. Now begin at the first point and draw lines to every second point. Next, draw another circle, mark eight points again, and draw lines to every third point. What happens in each example?

In the lower figure, twelve points are used. In this way, you can discover which numbers divide into twelve. Explore different possibilities.

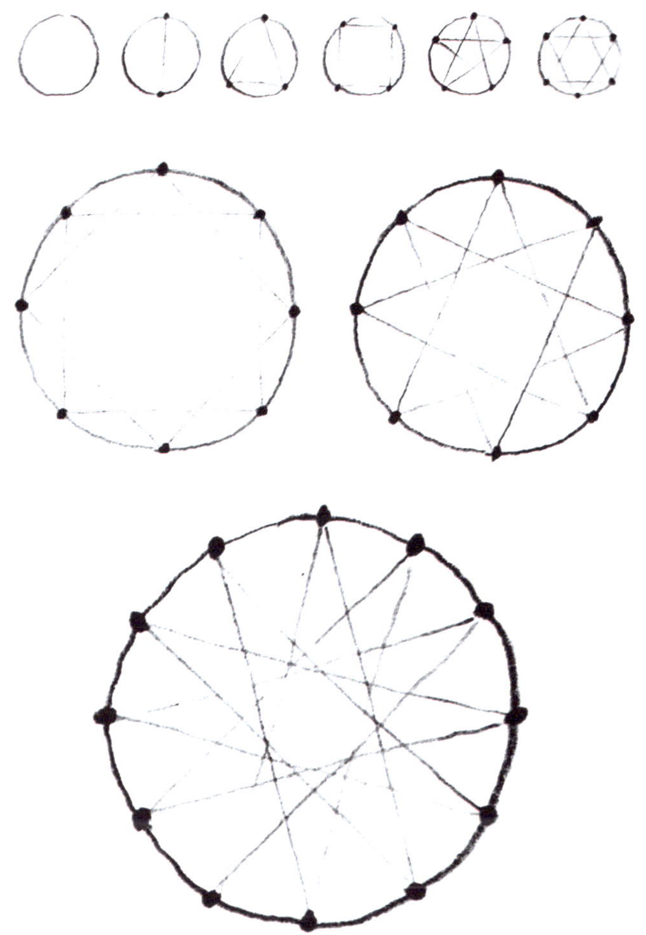

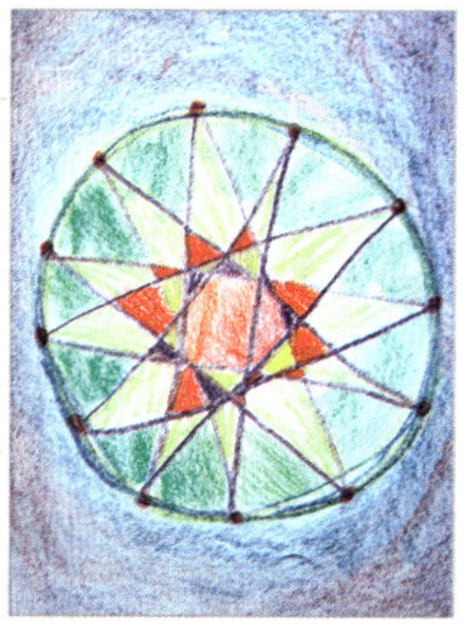

Part 3: Class 3 Exercises

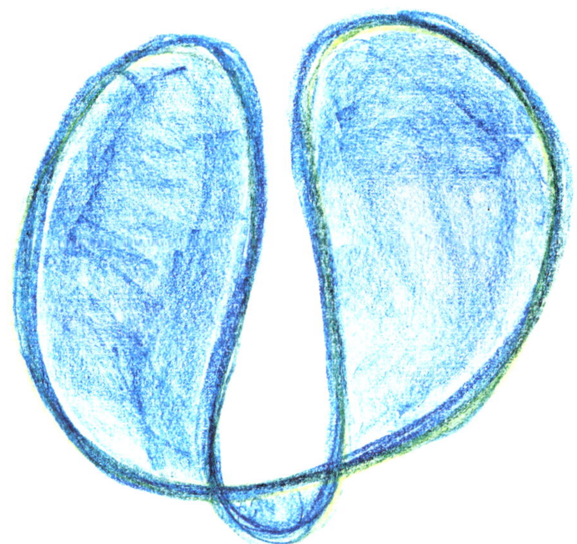

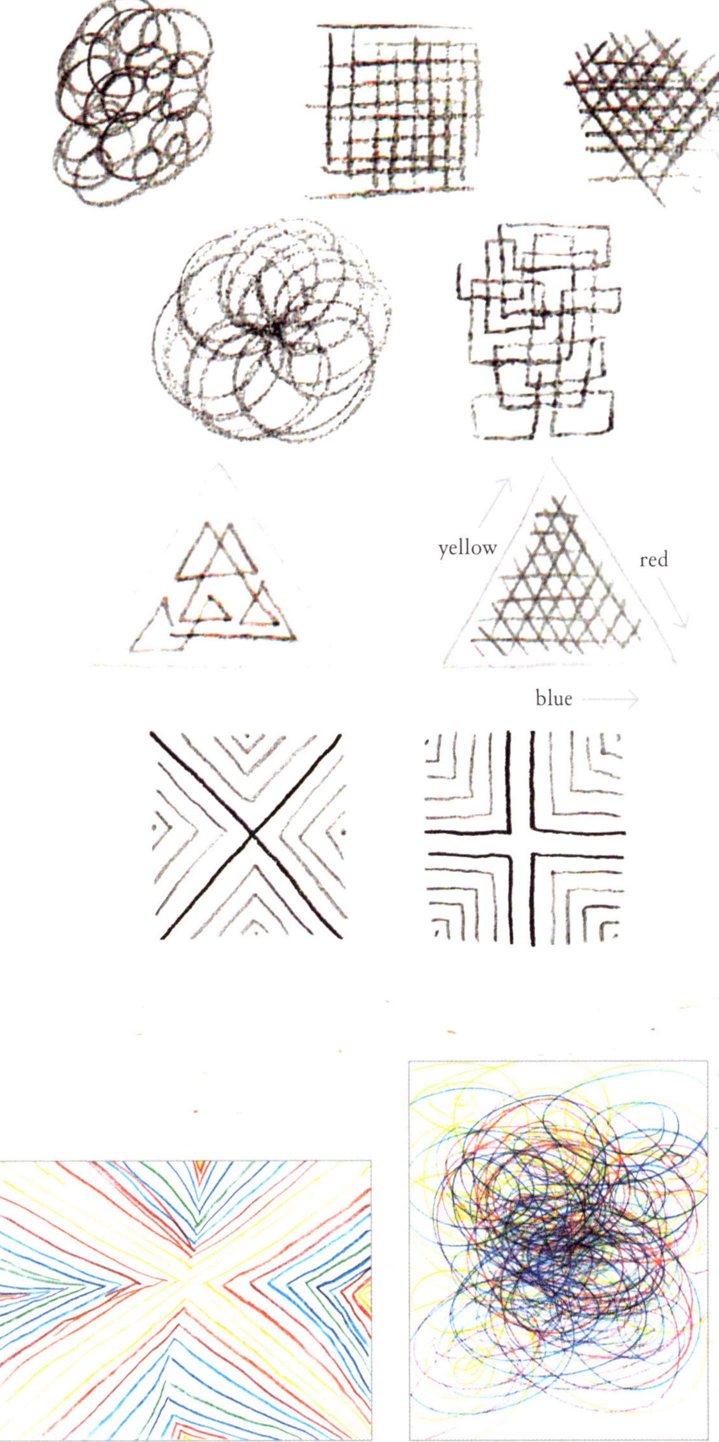

The straight line and the curve

You can reintroduce the straight line and the curve to your pupils in different ways. Here are two examples:

1. Use only curves of different sizes and which go in the same direction in an unbroken line.
2. Use only straight lines that go in two different directions, and decide if they should be short or long.

Ensure that your pupils understand. Remember, it is only when rules are clearly established that it becomes fun to play! Give pupils challenges using different rules or allow them to make up their own.

Within a framework of rules, pupils can practise their sense of aesthetic appraisal. They may choose to colour the differing directions of straight lines in different colours, or colour the areas between the lines.

Follow up with these relatively simple exercises using curved lines. See if your pupils are able to put them together as shown here.

Many form-drawing exercises have differing types of symmetry within them, for example up and down, left and right. They are part of the challenge of the exercises, and pupils will usually understand this intuitively without the need for explanation.

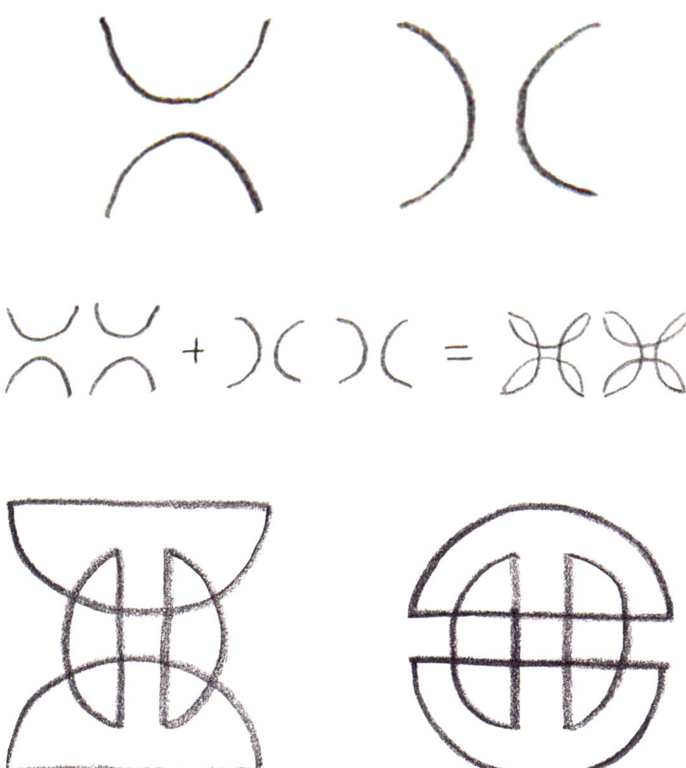

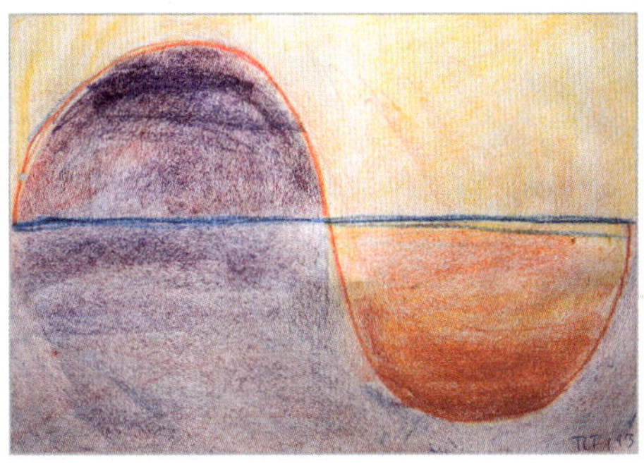

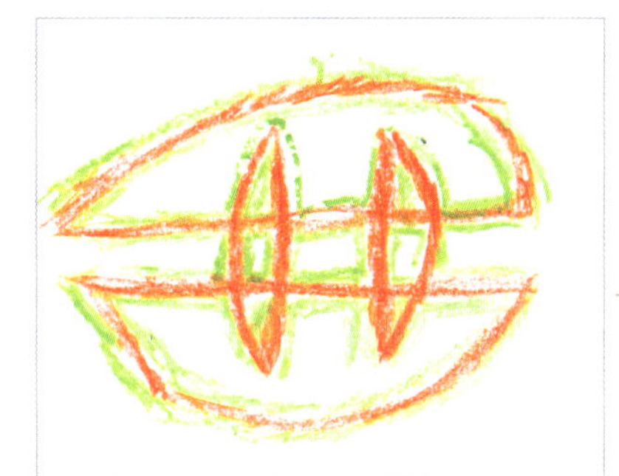

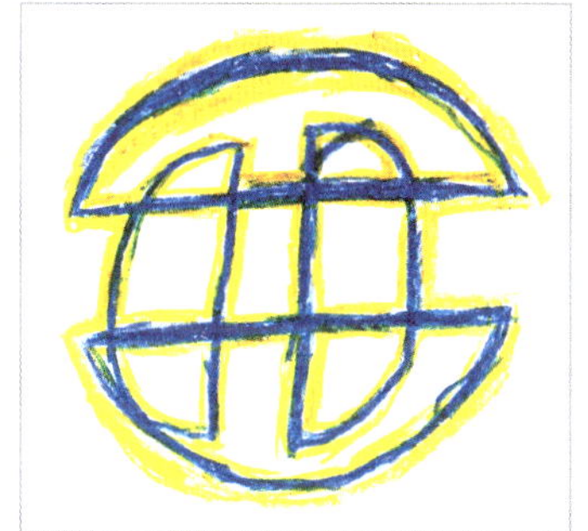

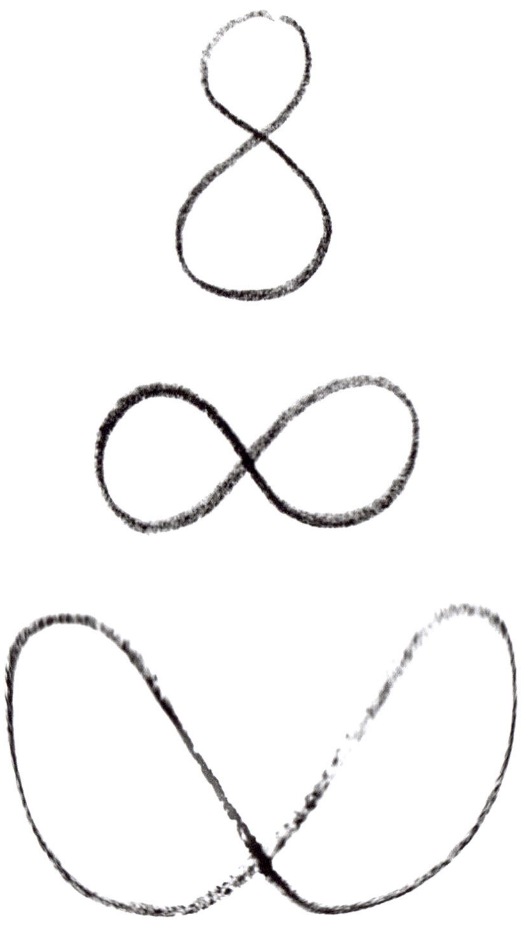

The figure of eight

The figure of eight is also referred to as a lemniscate (see p.17) or the sign of infinity. Take plenty of time with this basic form and pay attention to the challenging turning point in the centre. Changing the direction of a line might not seem difficult in a figure of eight, but pupils will have to tackle this particular problem later on in more complex forms, so it is important that they master the basics.

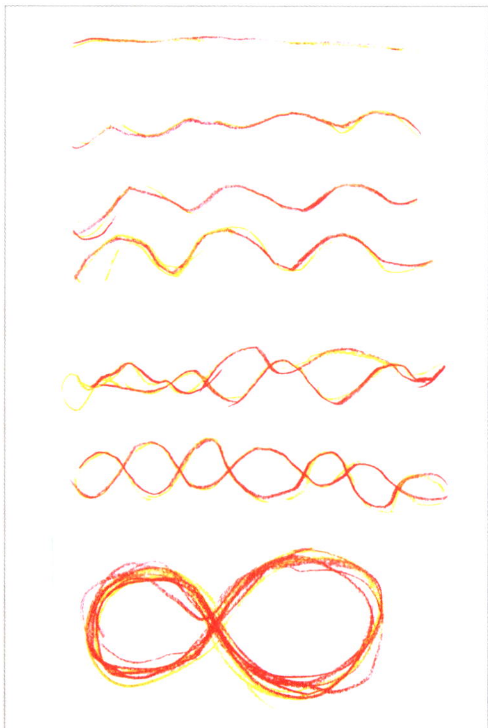

Now add a loop onto a figure of eight so that you end up with three loops. Let pupils experiment with this form in different ways by altering the size of the loops and the loops' positions in relation to one another.

Try putting two figures of eight together, using more loops if you wish. It looks easy, but for this age group it is a demanding task that requires preparation and practice.

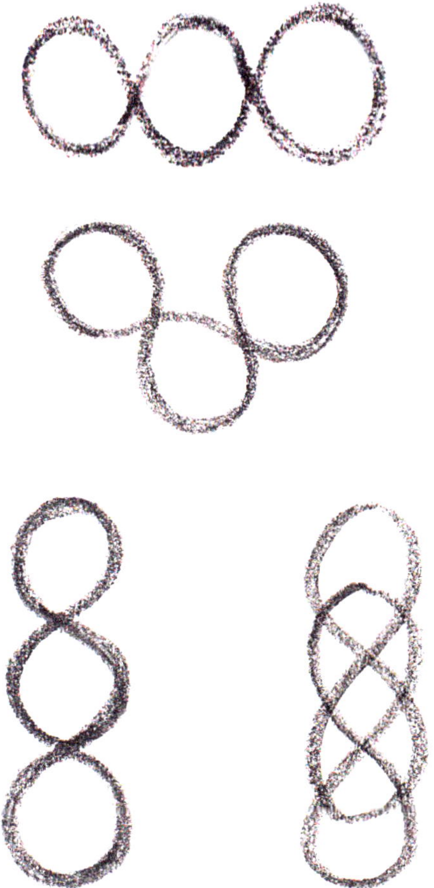

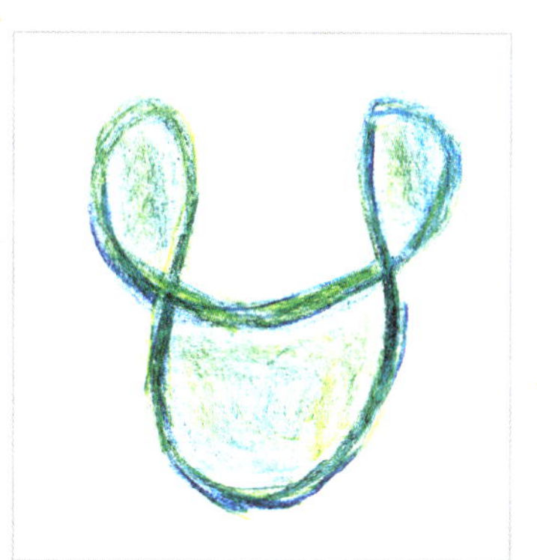

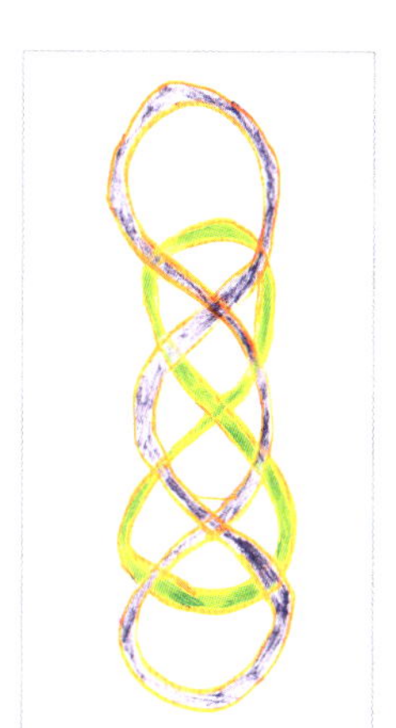

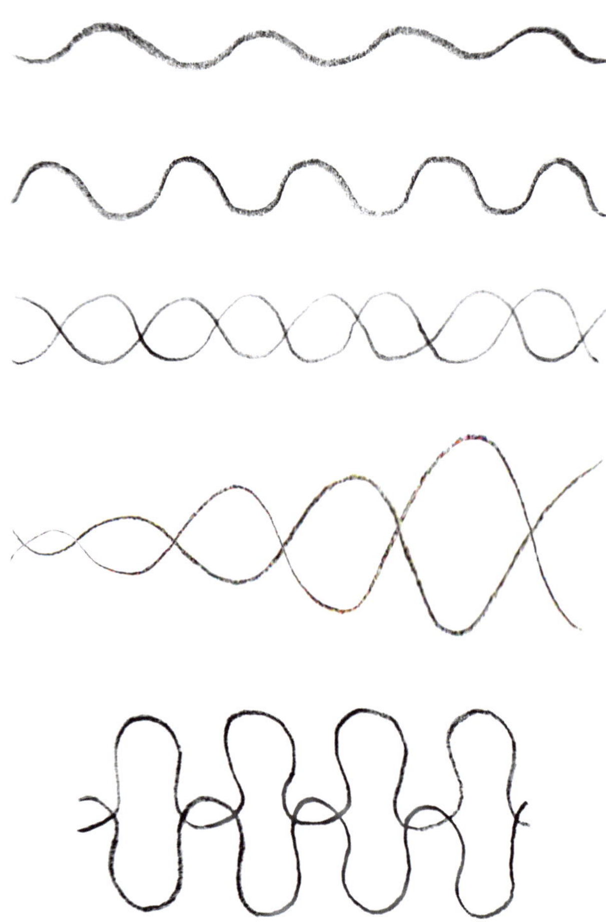

Borders

Borders provide many challenges and are always worth returning to. Pupils can experiment with juxtaposing or intertwining borders. What if the border is constantly expanded? What if borders partially intertwine?

You can provide your pupils with suggestions, but also encourage them to develop their own borders.

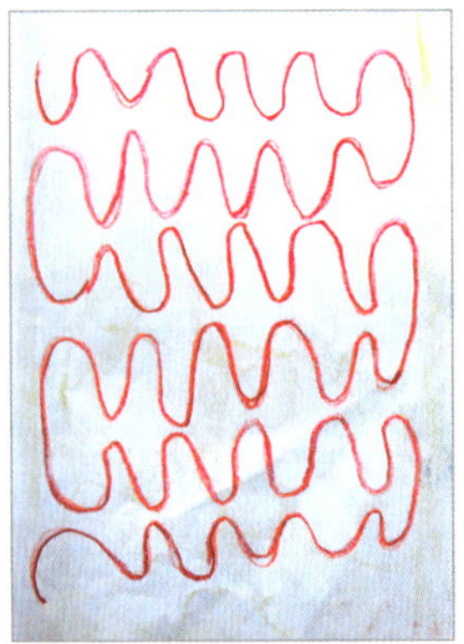

Start with simple borders again, then mirror these horizontally and put them together. Decorative elements such as dots can be added. Ask your pupils to consider which are most effective aesthetically and why.

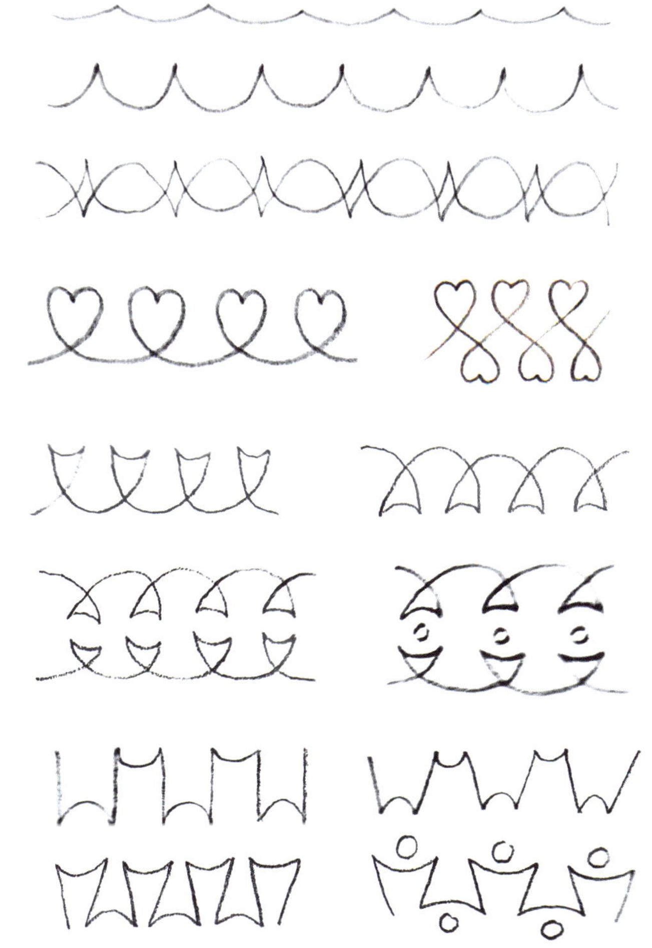

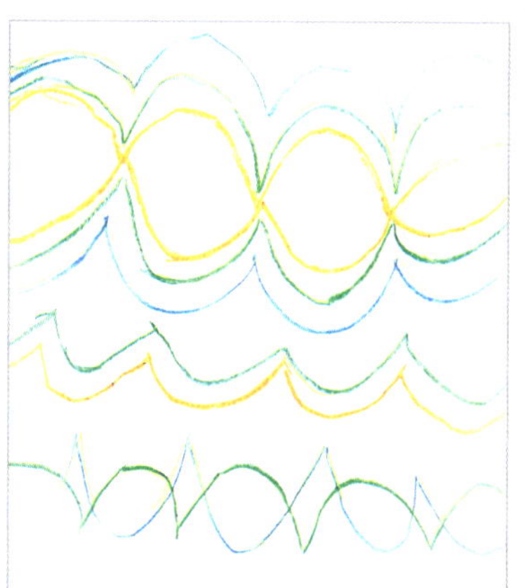

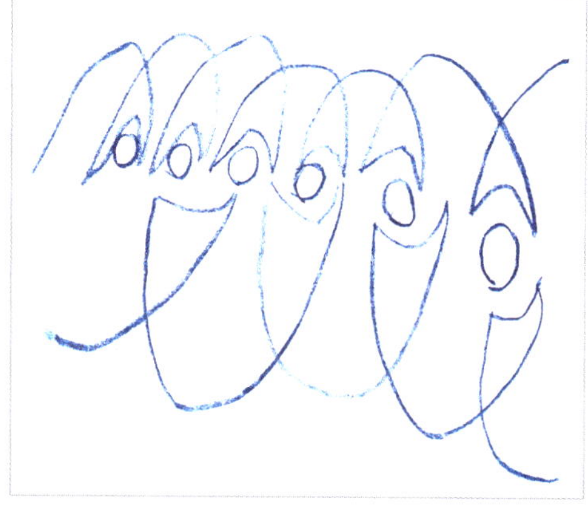

Angular forms can complement round forms. Here are different examples to discuss in class. Which ones do the pupils like best? Why?

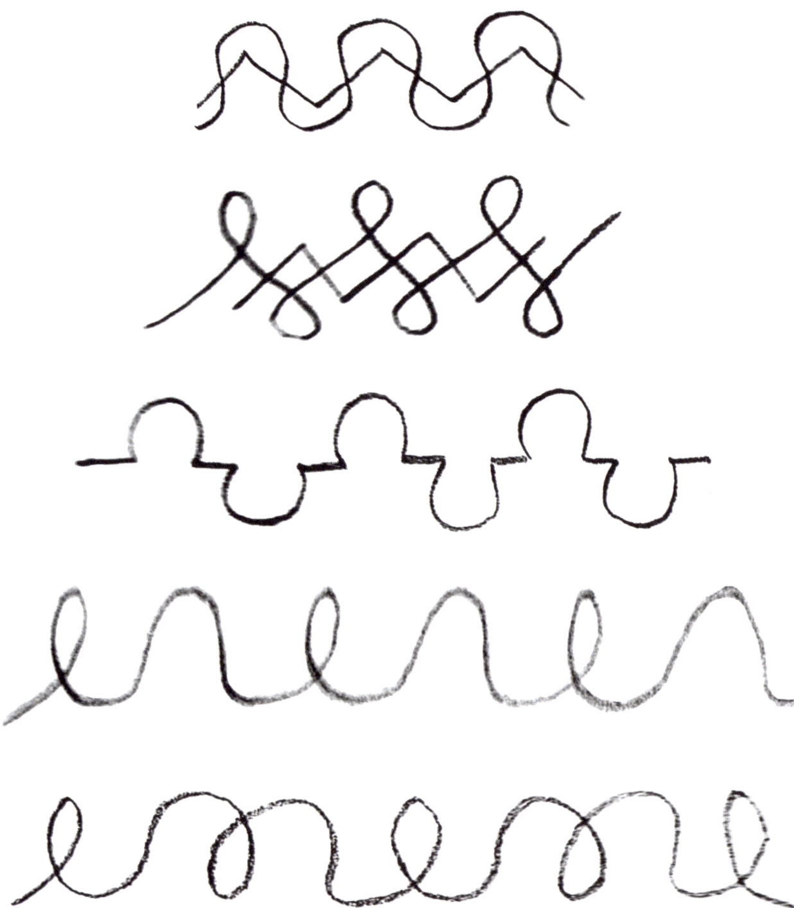

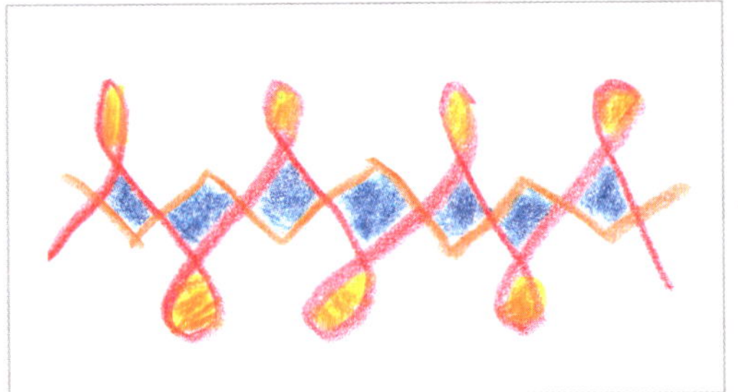

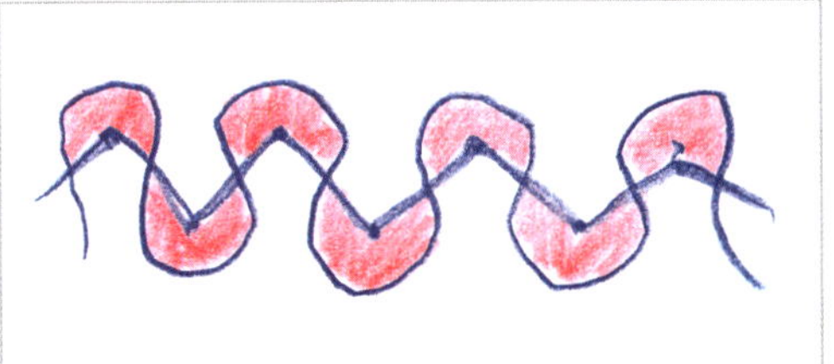

This simple border can be explored using small and large loops.

To develop this concept, draw the border along the edge of an imaginary circle and allow it to catch its own tail. A new complete form arises!

Now this new shape can be experimented with so that 'branches' appear. These can be thick or thin, many or few. How would the pupils like to colour them? Try it out with your class.

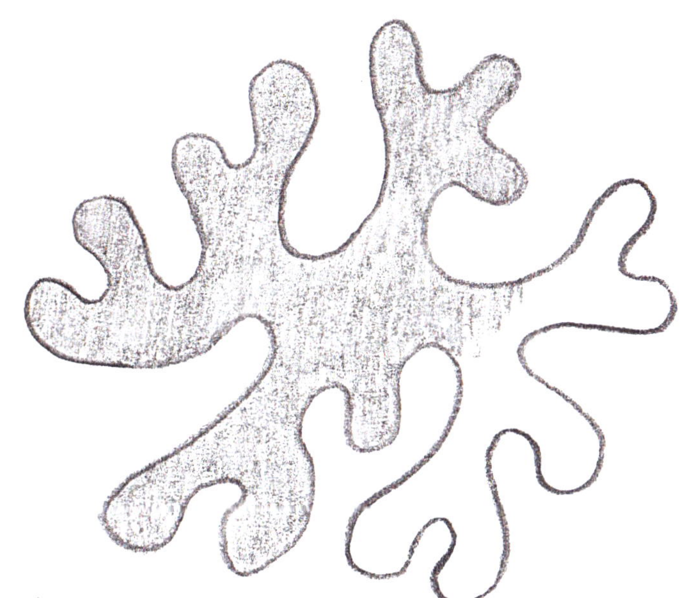

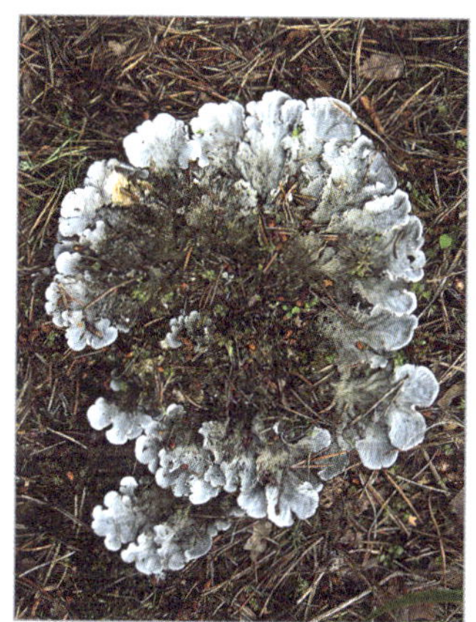

Moss in the forest

Mirroring

Draw a vertical line, which will act as a mirror. Next, draw a form on the left followed by its reflection on the right, or vice versa for left-handed pupils (see pp.19–20 and pp.209–14). You can introduce mirroring using the examples included here.

After a while, encourage pupils to make their own suggestions, either independently, in pairs or in groups of three, which will allow them to set tasks for each other to copy.

This can be done outside in sand, mud or snow. Soft rope is another useful way to discover and play with forms and mirroring.

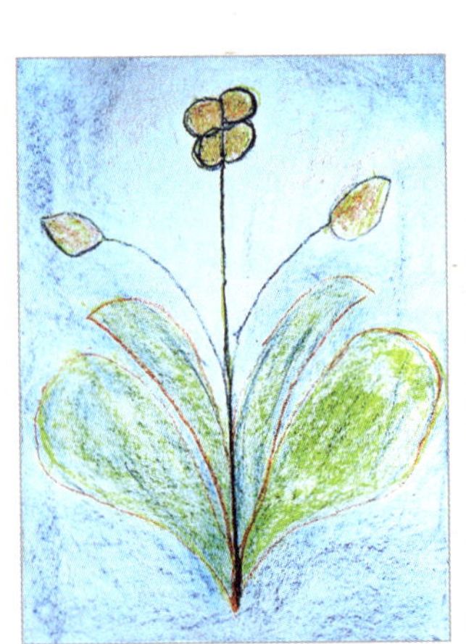

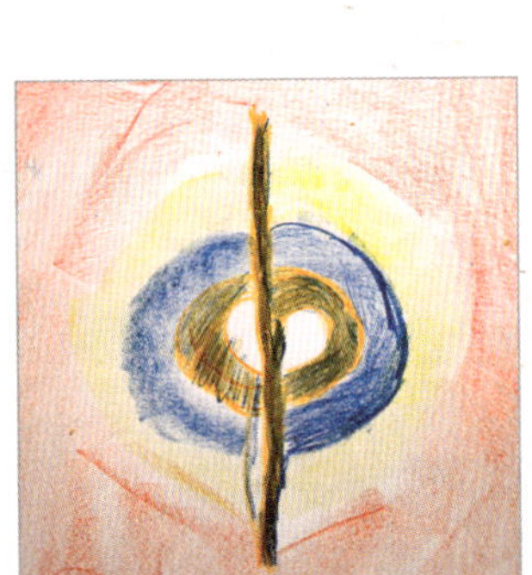

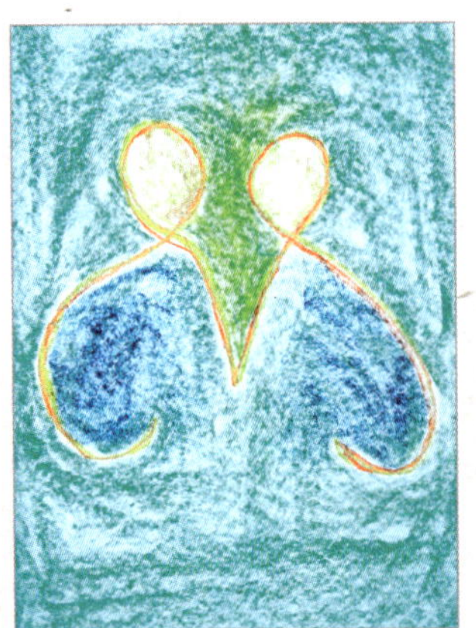

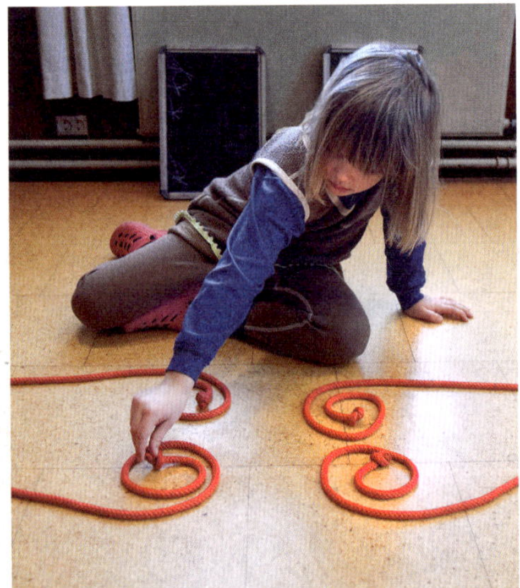

Mirroring can involve drawing numerous forms outside of one another. The forms may overlap one another if the central line is omitted.

Various patterns may emerge as a result of the symmetries used, which can grow to cover a whole sheet of paper.

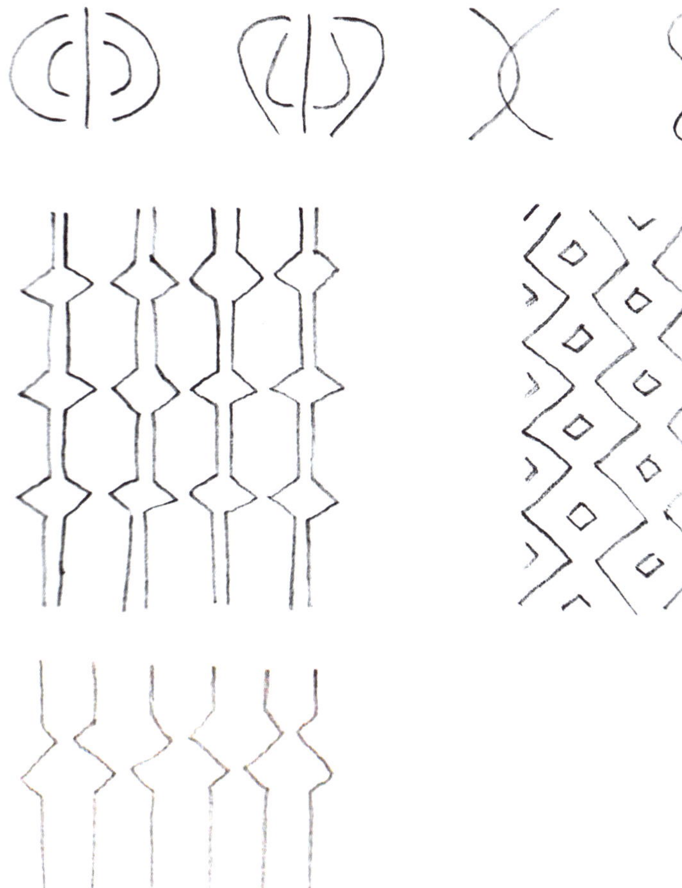

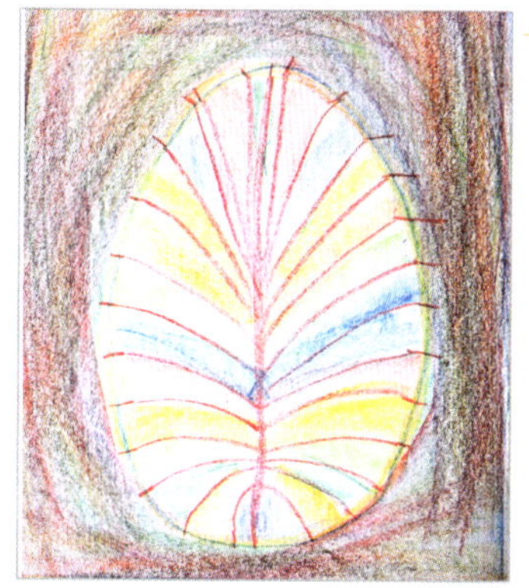

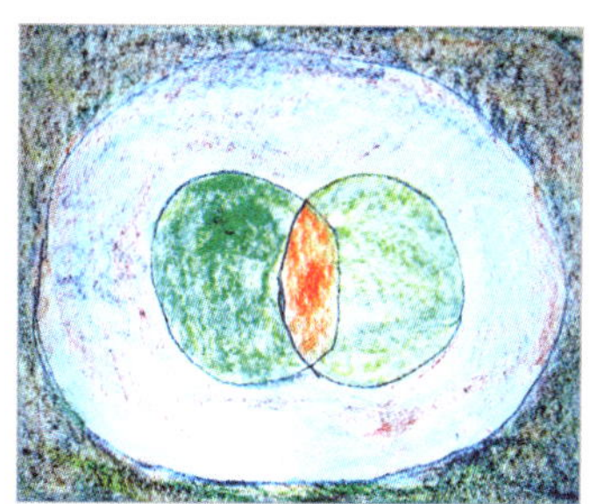

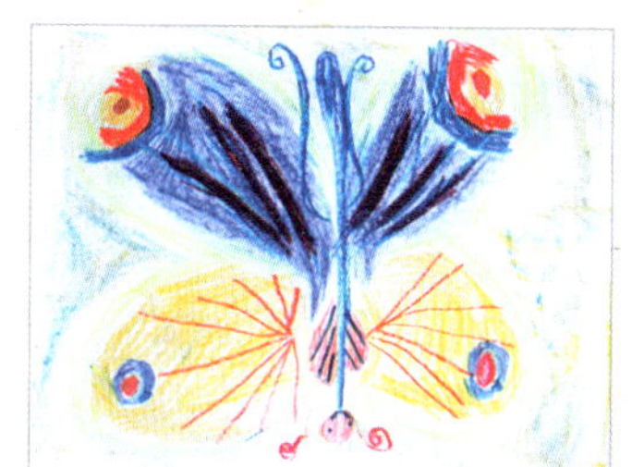

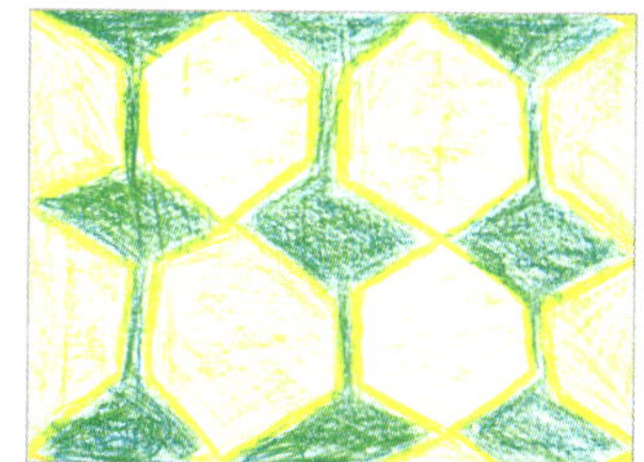

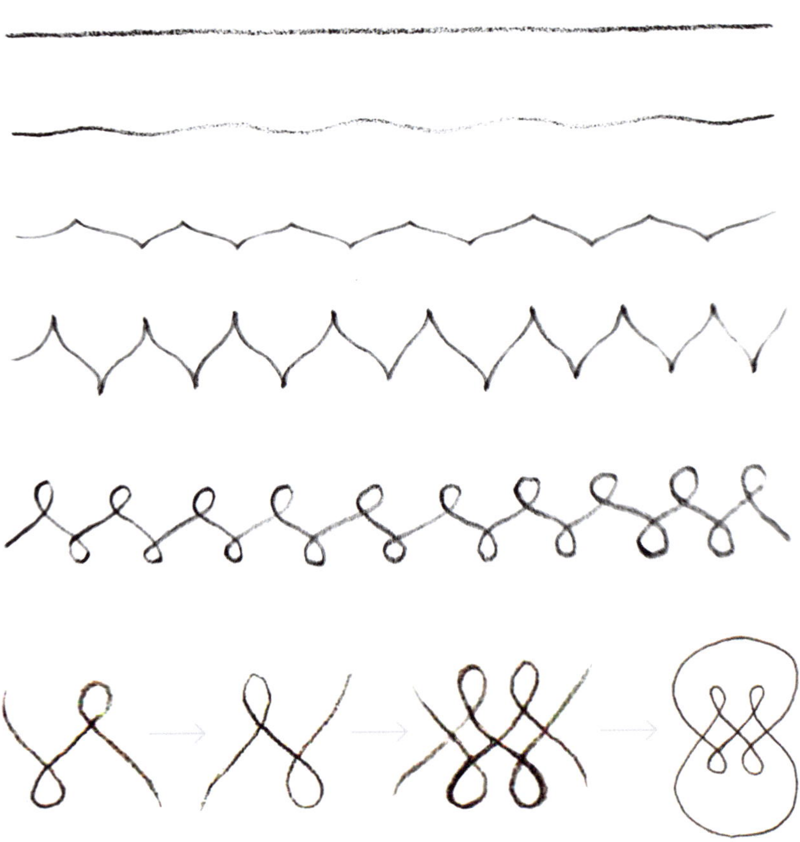

Developing borders

Allow a border to be built up from a single straight line. Make larger waves with each new line. As these gradually become more pointed, loops may appear. Test this out using small loops at the top and larger below, or vice versa.

From borders to ornamentation

In different borders we can find interesting ornaments or details by picking out fragments or sections. These can then be composed in different ways, and loose ends can be connected so that new forms emerge.

Here, two borders are combined. Note that the final figure consists of one continuous line.

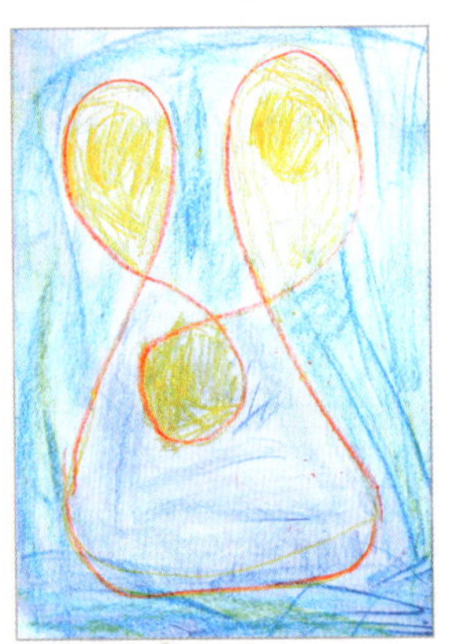

This border is put together in the same way as on the previous page, but the sections of ornament that have been extracted have three loops instead of two. Note that the final figure consists of two continual intersecting lines.

Why not explore alternatives in class?

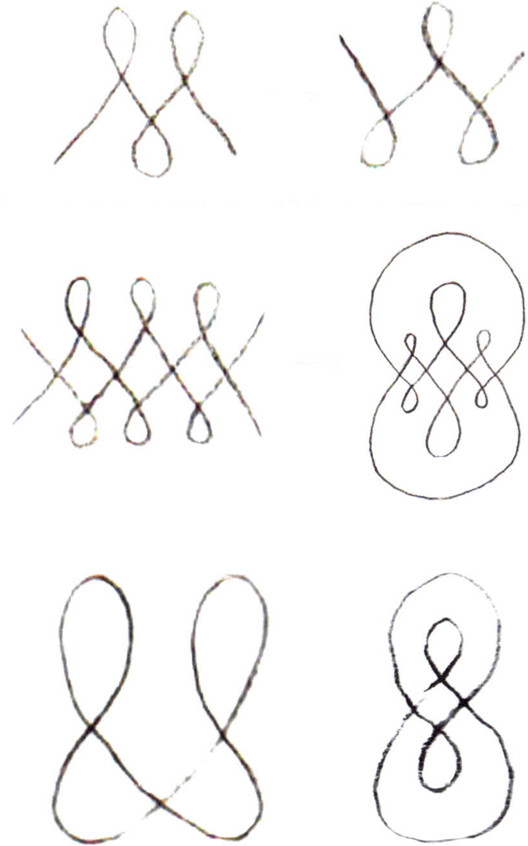

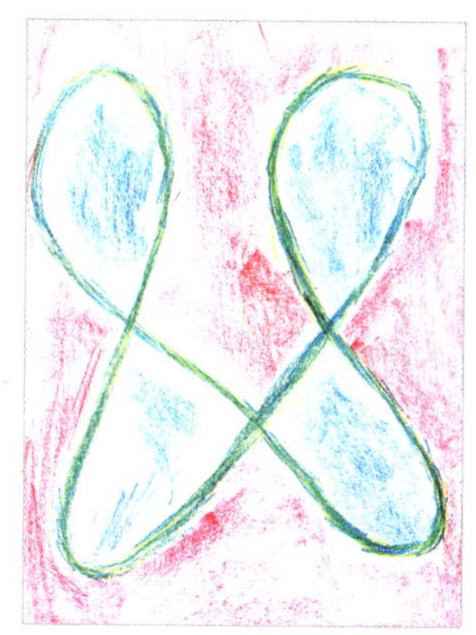

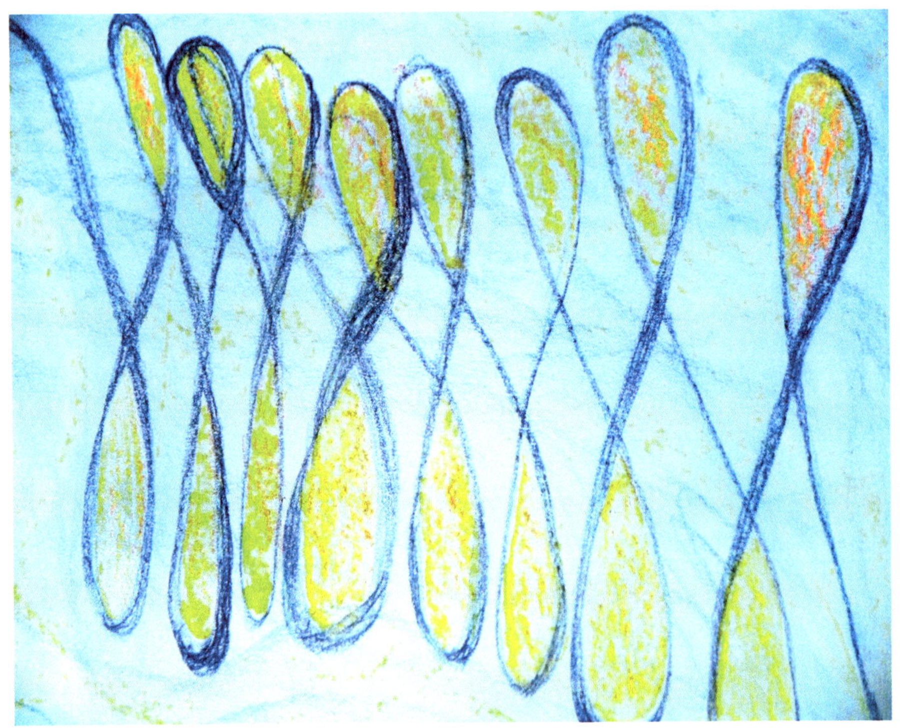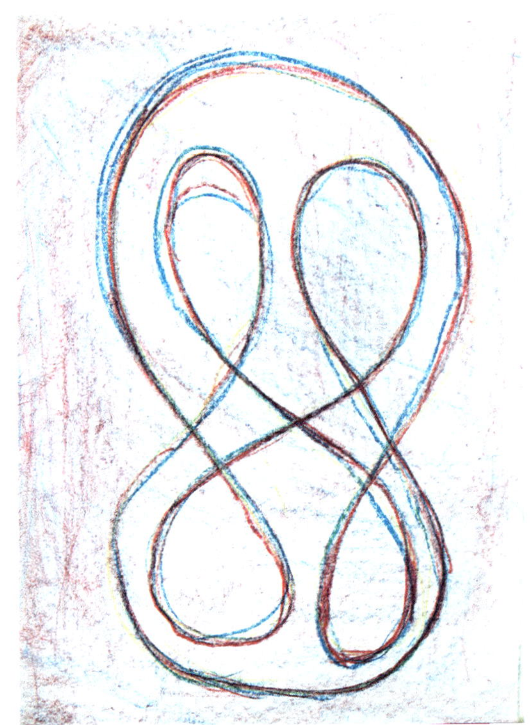

Pupils' work, Class 3

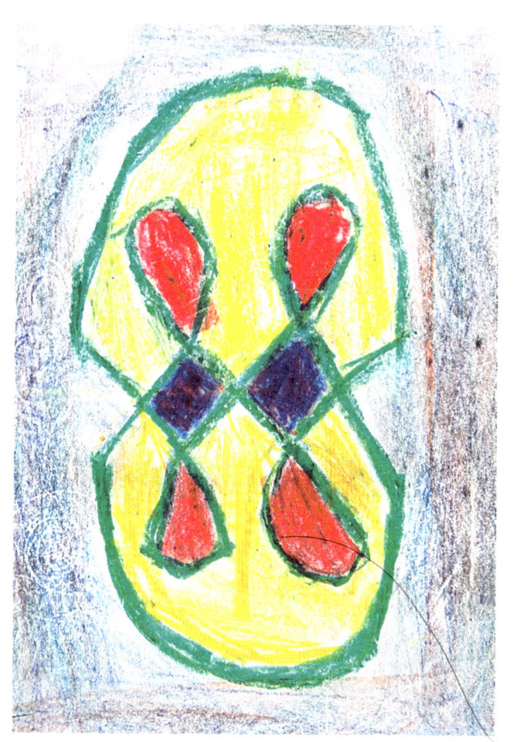

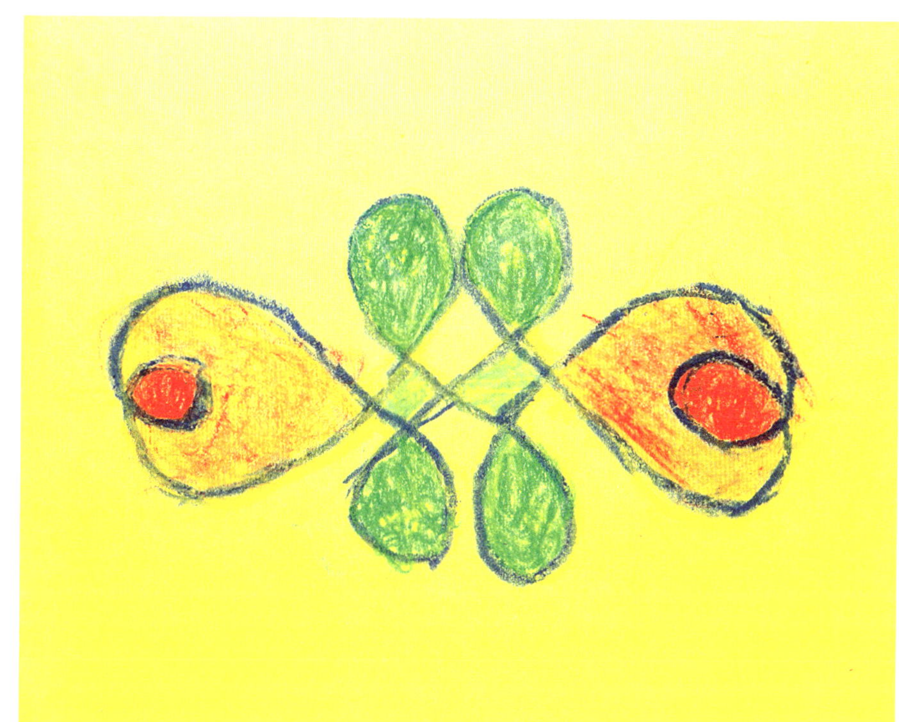

The spiral

The spiral is a recurring theme in form drawing. In this exercise, start on the outside and work inwards. When you reach the centre, continue the line and work your way back out again, as shown. The challenge in this exercise is to find out how many turns it is possible to make and to leave space for the spiral that works its way back outwards again.

The key, as in other exercises, is to work at a slow pace while making sure not to lose the flow and uniformity of the movement.

The spiral is drawn by beginning on the outside and working inwards, then changing direction at the centre and working outwards again. The space in-between is coloured in.

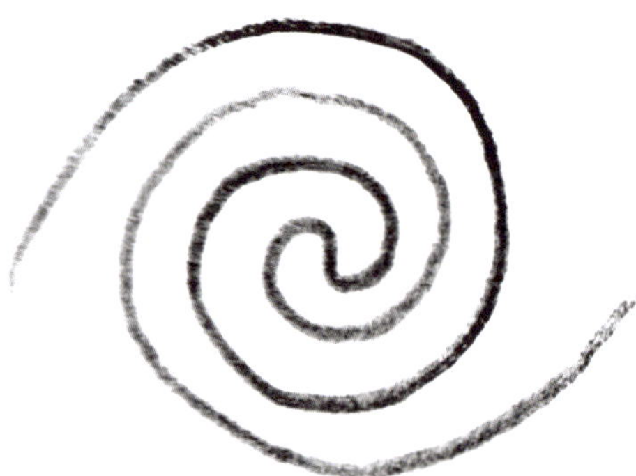

This exercise can be turned into a border, as shown below.

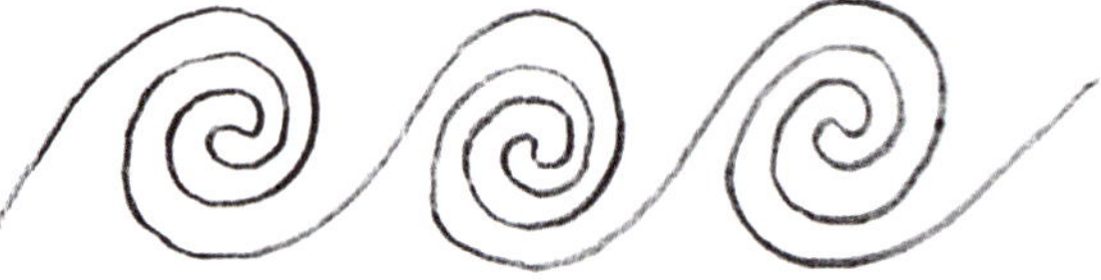

Start this exercise at the smallest, innermost curved lines. Next, draw the curve on the outside.

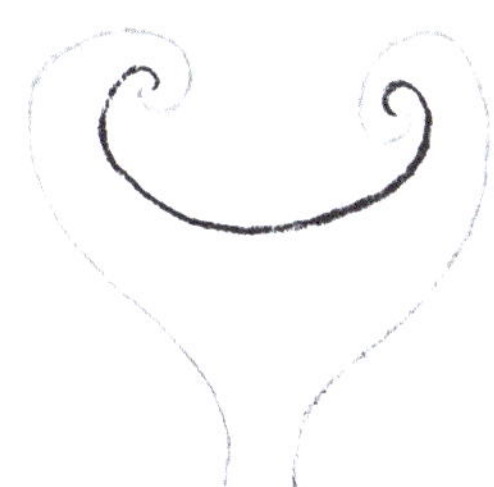

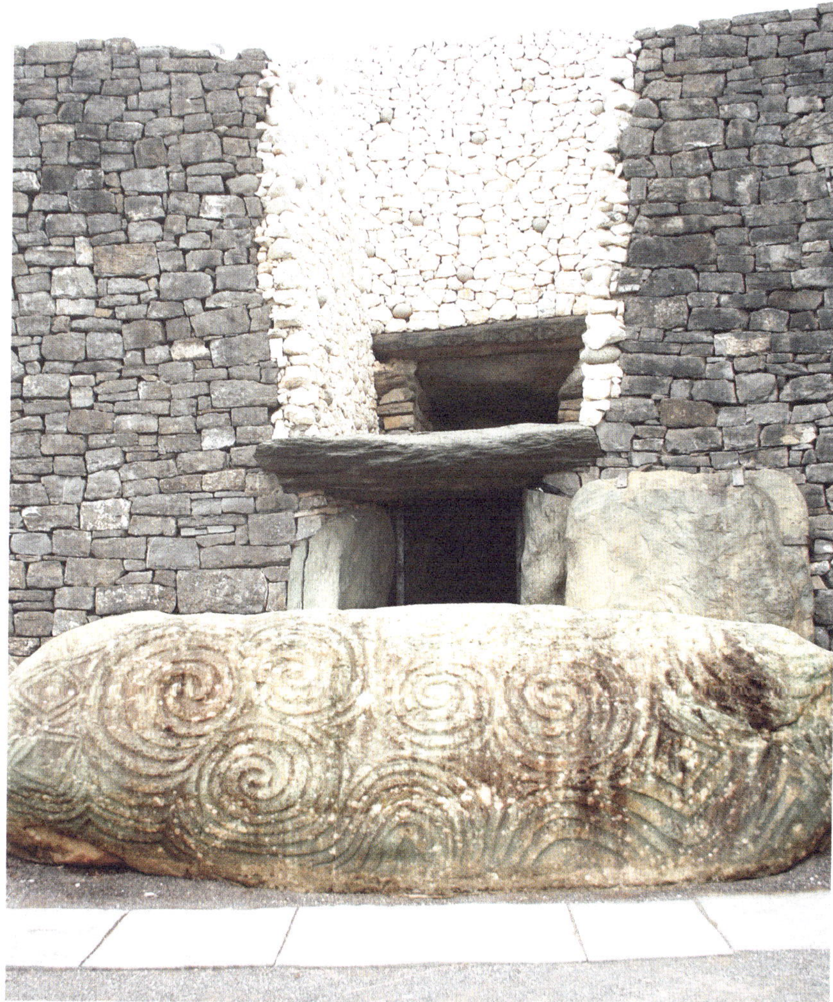

The entrance at Newgrange passage tomb, Ireland, built 3200 BC

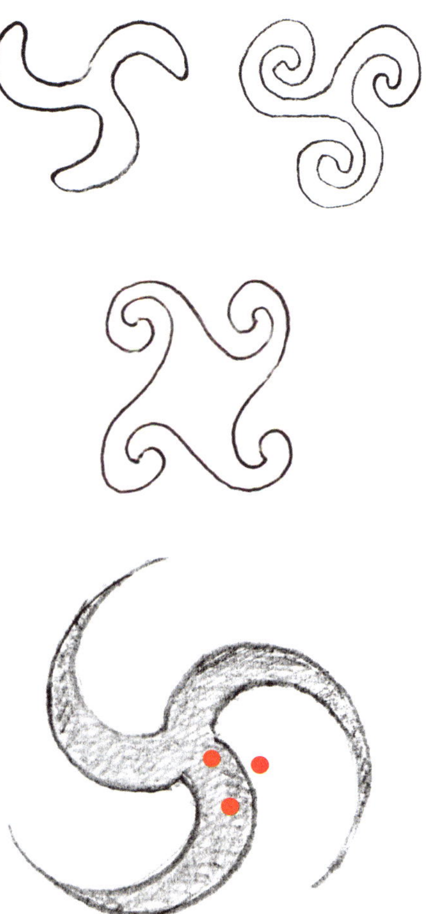

Drawing these spirals using a single line can be tricky. If your pupils find it too difficult, ask them to try the simpler exercise with the red dots.

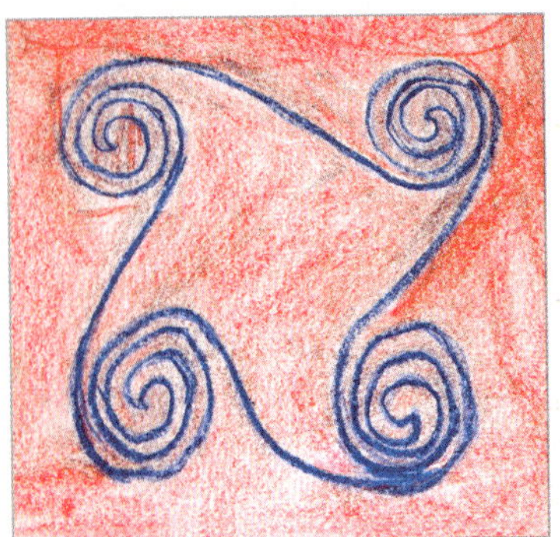

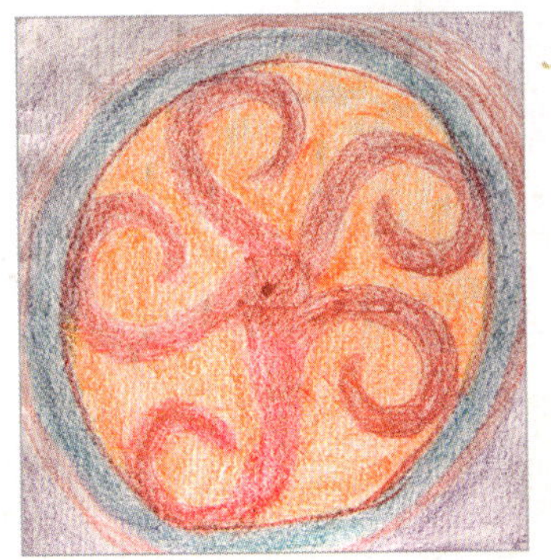

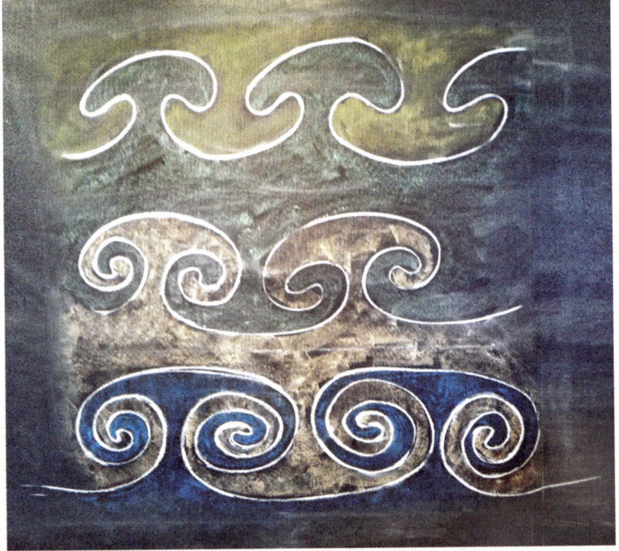

Blackboard drawing

Problem-solving

Explain to your pupils that this looped border is to be drawn around an imaginary circle and is supposed to catch its own tail. See if it is possible to make the ends meet so that the pattern is completed.

Next, pupils can try to create examples with fewer and fewer loops: try seven, then six, then five, and so on. How few loops can they use?

When they reach two loops, let the pupils solve the problem. They will have to choose between two possibilities: either they need to change the direction of the loop and make a figure of eight, which is the most logical solution aesthetically, or they can continue in the same direction and make a small loop inside of a larger loop. Discuss what works best in class. Are there other solutions?

Finally, what happens when there is only one loop?

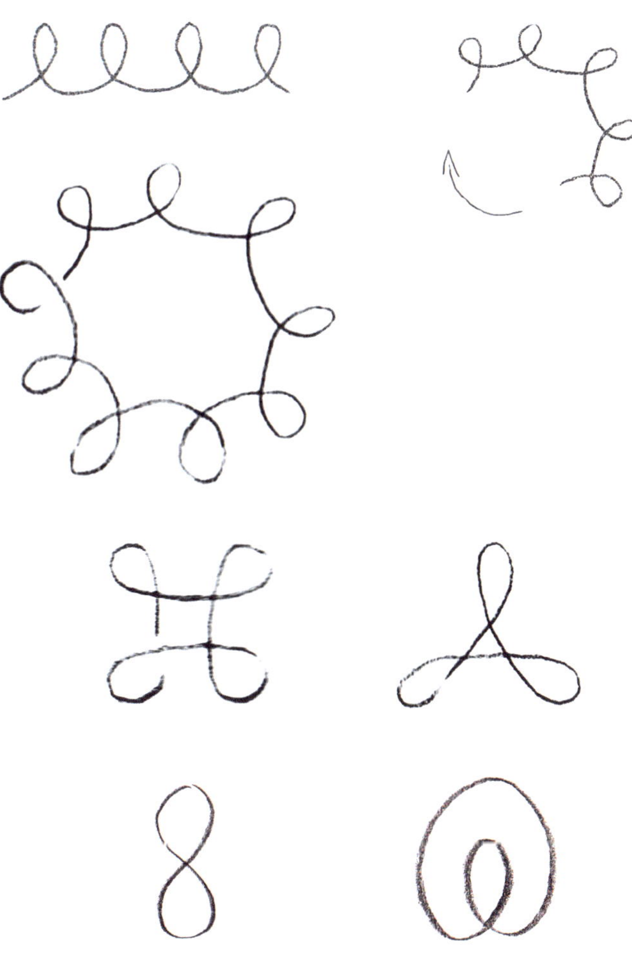

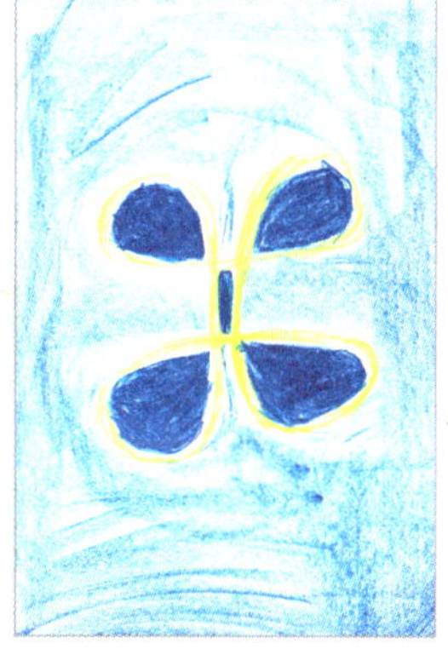

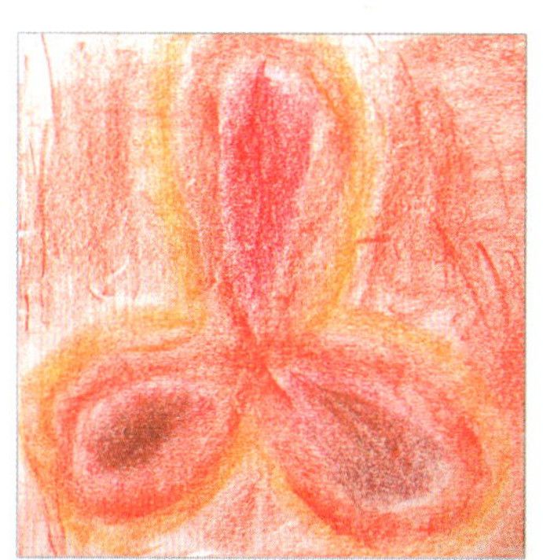

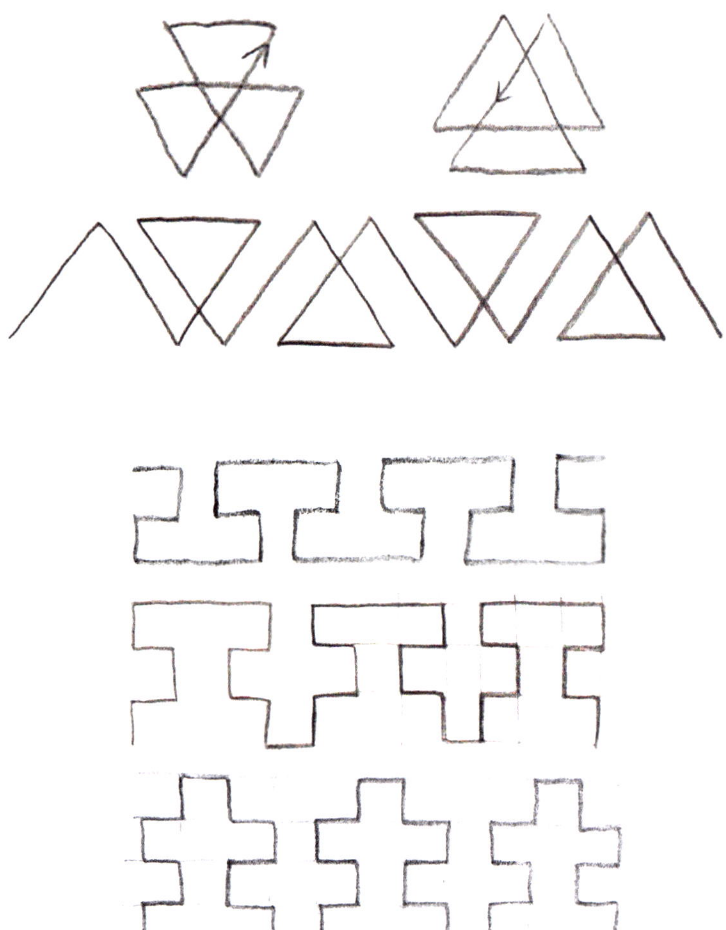

More complex exercises

Keep in mind that the exercises with triangle shapes shown here can be very demanding, so only set them for pupils who you believe are ready for them. These can be practised with rounded loops too (see p.90).

For these three border exercises based on squares, you can give guidelines to pupils or choose not to. It is an opportunity for pupils to find individual solutions and make them as complex as they are able.

The first of these three exercises looks the same if it is turned upside down. But what do you need to do to make the second one identical when it is turned upside down?

Repeat the task and add a square on top of each element: this is how the final figure is built up.

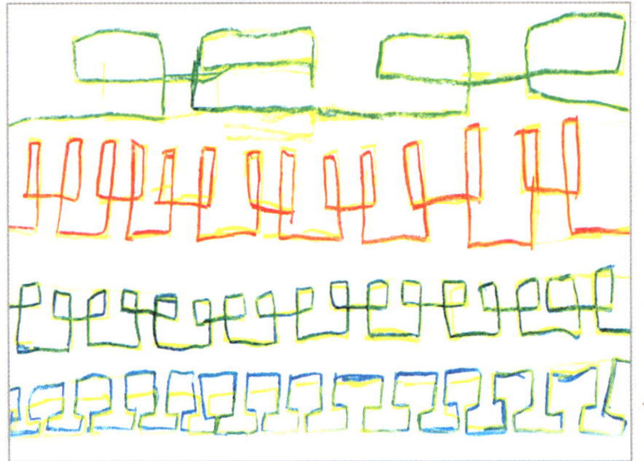

In this exercise, draw the thickest line first and loop the thin line around it. Use different colours for each line if you wish.

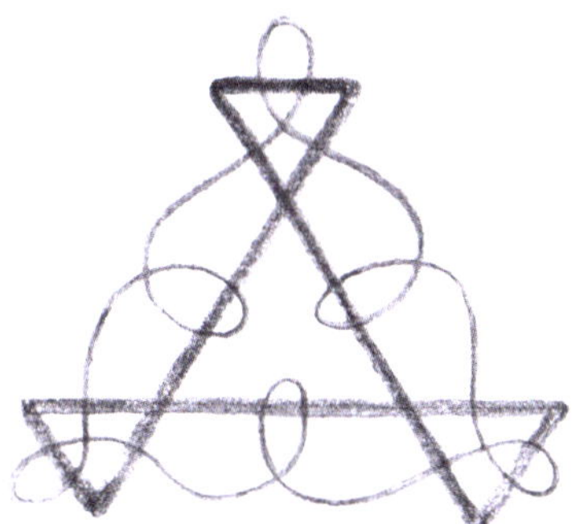

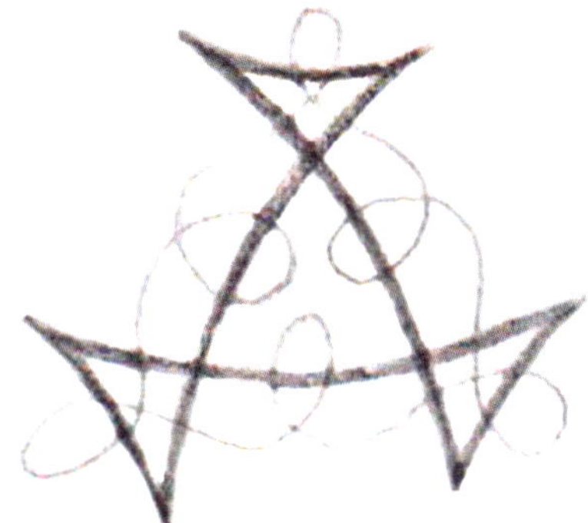

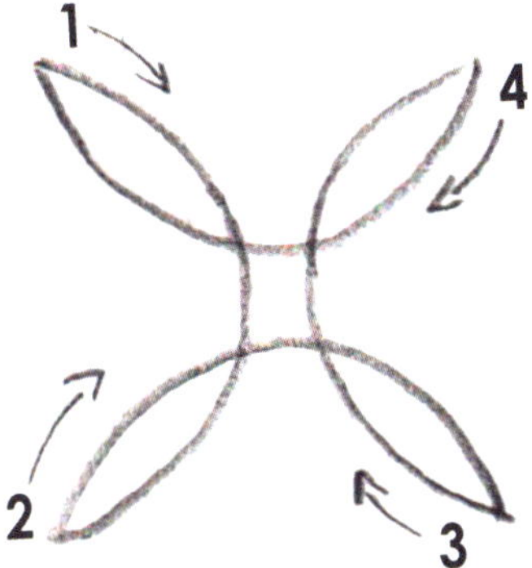

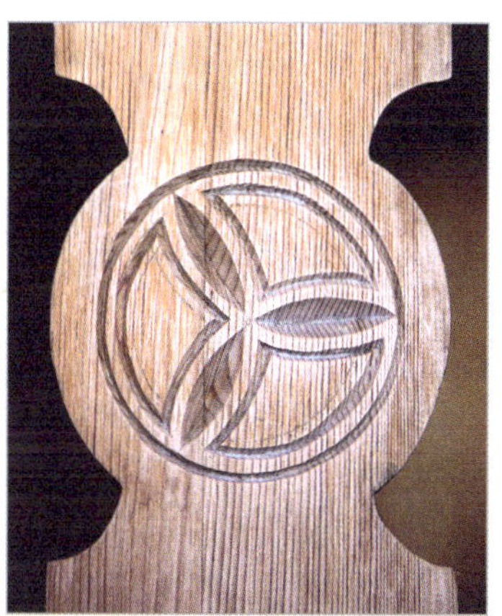

Interior detail from a Norwegian kitchen, 1901

Patterns

Patterns contain repetitive elements that can be developed as far as you like. The challenge lies in placing the forms pleasingly and filling the page. The expression 'pleasingly' is open to interpretation, but it allows the pupils to conduct their own aesthetic appraisals.

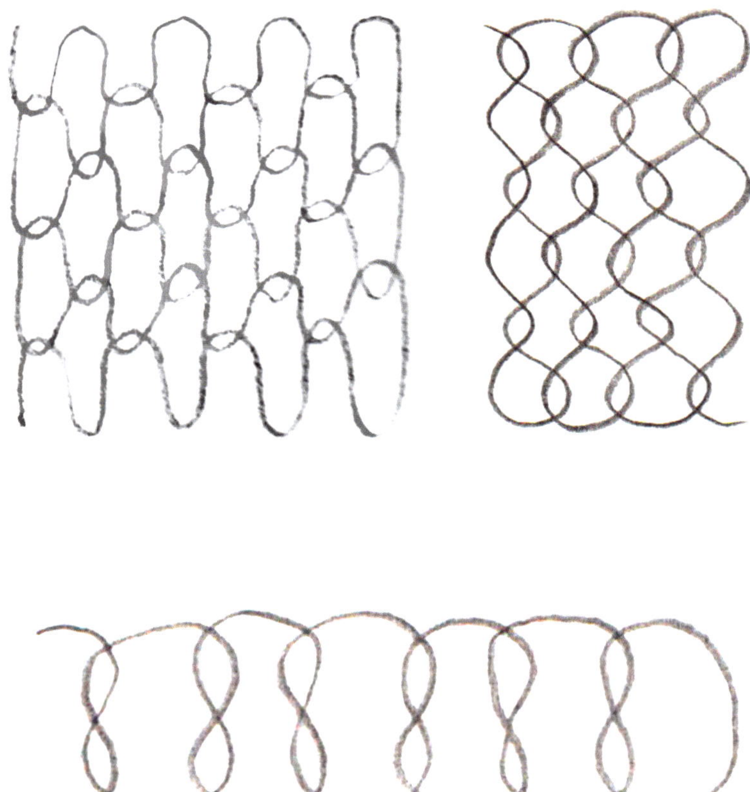

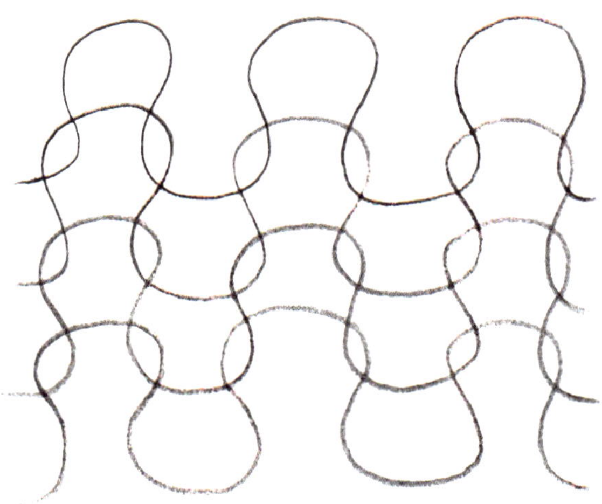

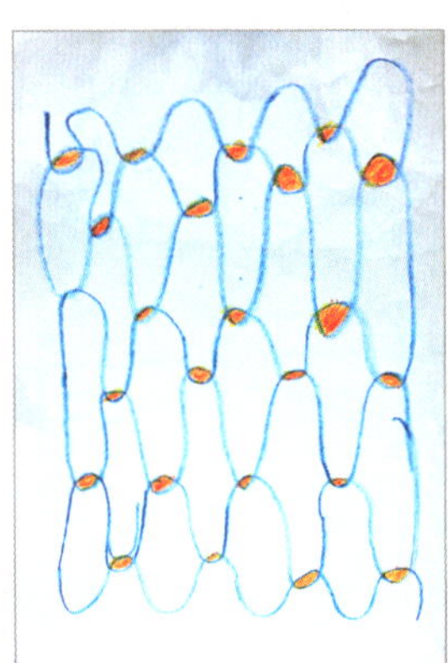

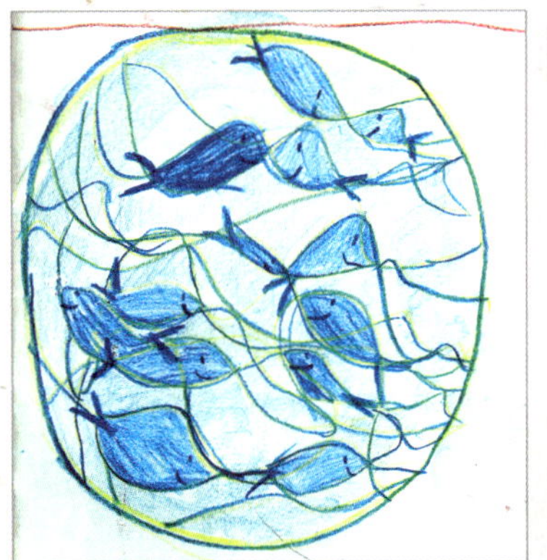

Asymmetry

A lot of form-drawing exercises are based on symmetry, as this is a natural aesthetic feature that children can recognise and work with. Many natural forms are also symmetrical, but in different ways: for example, a leaf with curved edges.

Draw a single line, mark points on it, then run a new line through these points, as shown. Next, draw another line that follows the outside of the contour you have just drawn, and continue doing this until the form is 'pleasing' or 'complete'.

There are many options here for individual variations. Exaggerate the forms as much as you like.

Starting with three loops (bottom) provides another option for asymmetry.

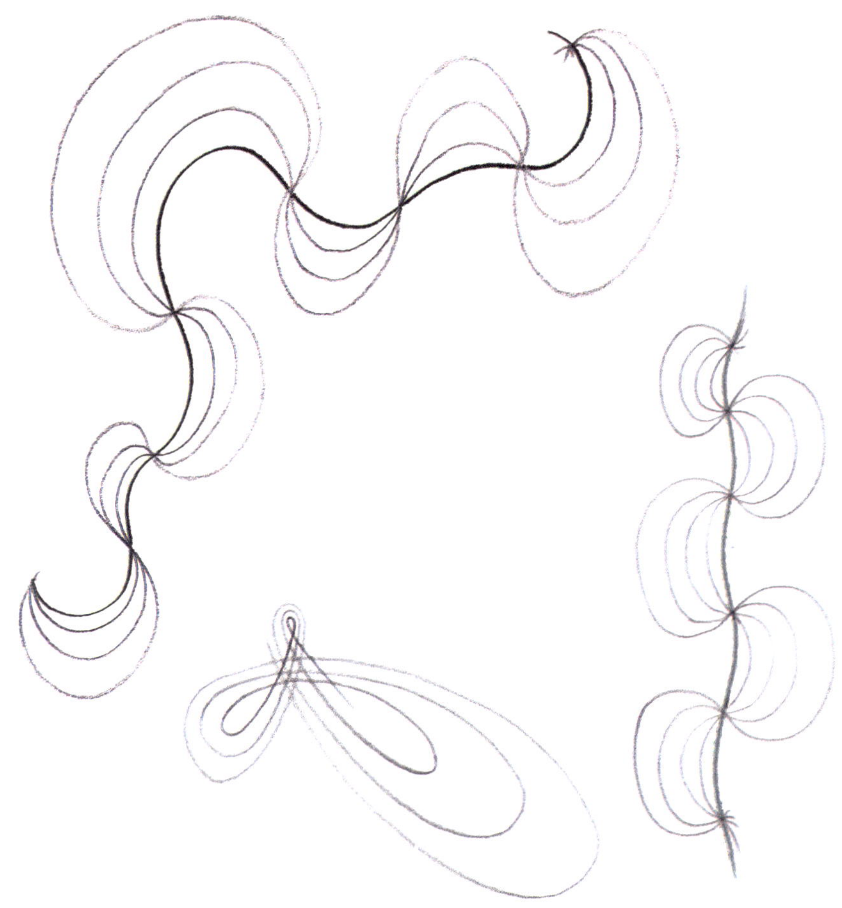

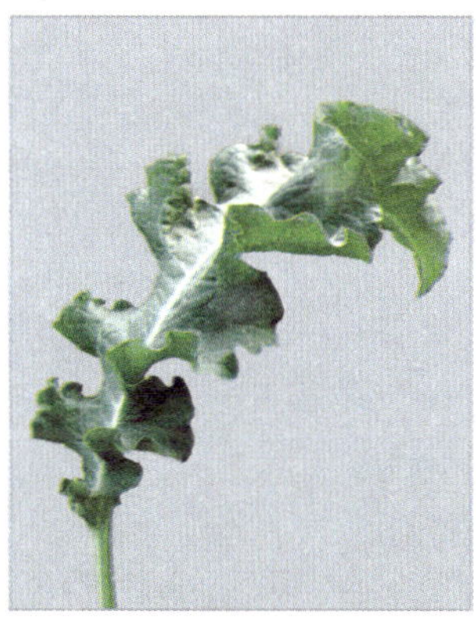

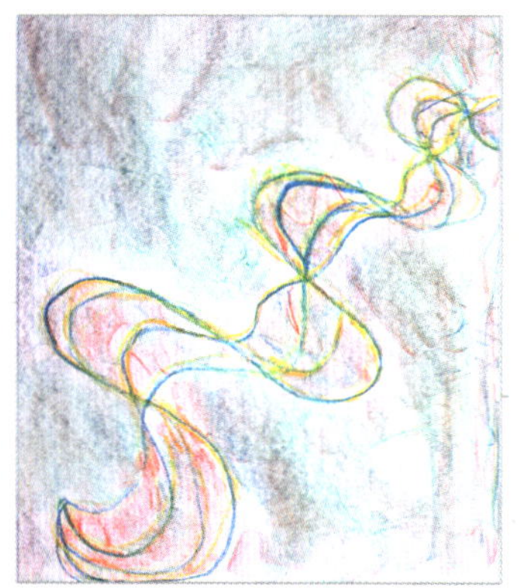

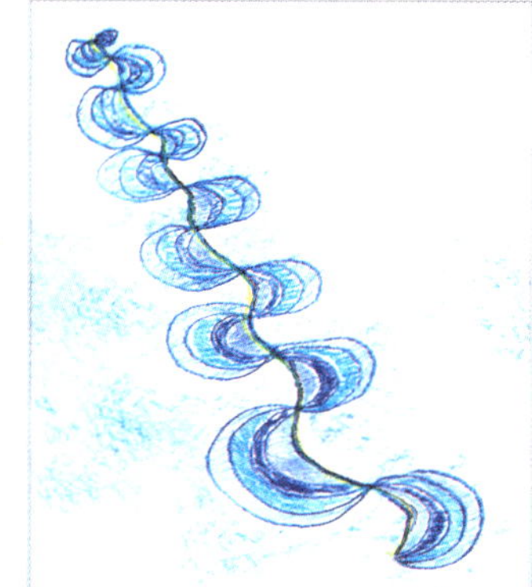

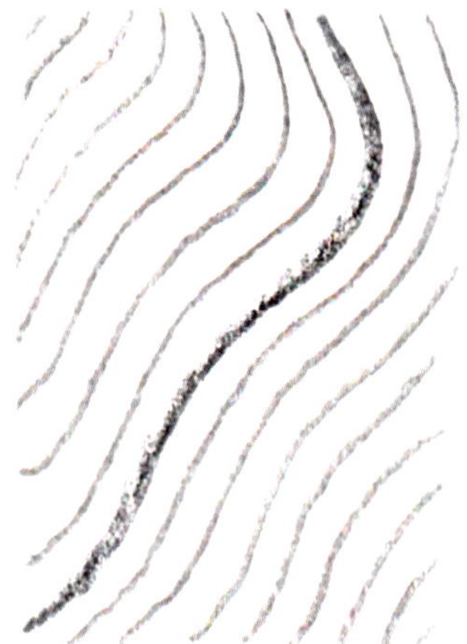

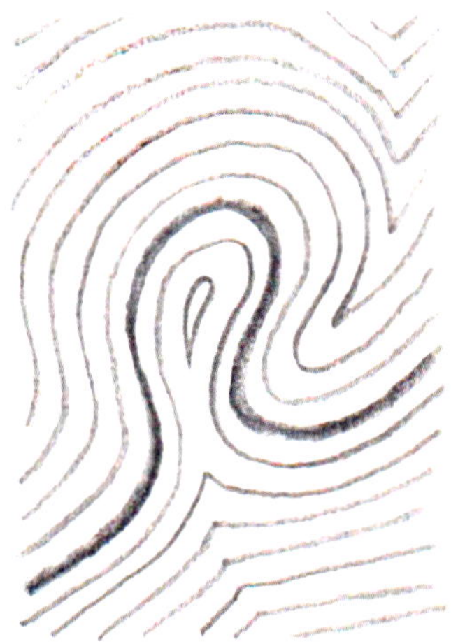

Metamorphoses

Draw a coloured line across the sheet (left). Then, in a different colour, draw more lines: the distance between them can be the width of a thumb, two fingers and so on, but ensure they are equidistant. Watch the pattern as it develops.

In the next exercise (right), draw a coloured line that bulges in such a way that a space appears within it, almost like a 'thumb' shape. Next, draw more lines, again ensuring they are equidistant from the original. Make a point of being strict with your pupils about this, for example instructing them that 'You must never get closer to the original line than the width of your thumb.' This means that they must make aesthetic choices. For example, when the small space closes, pupils will need to make a decision on whether there is room for the small droplet shape in the space.

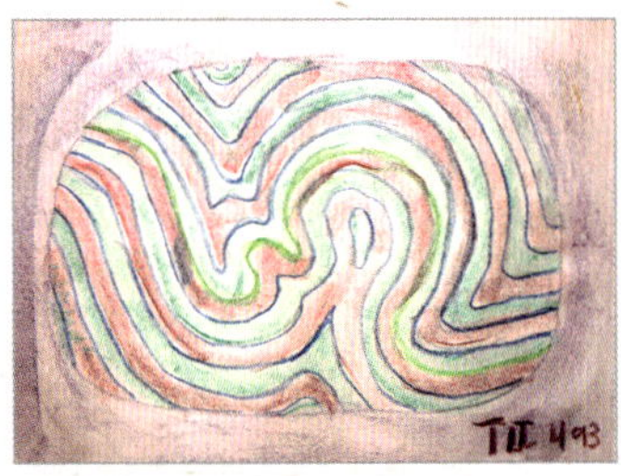

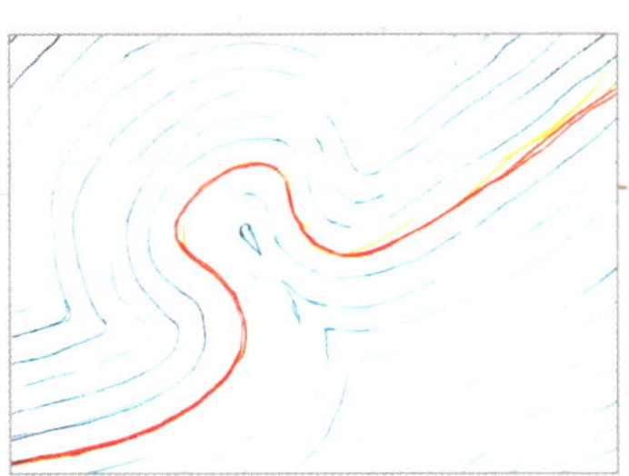

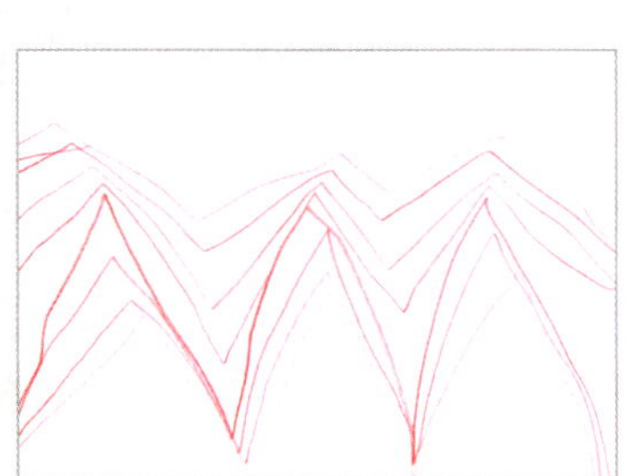

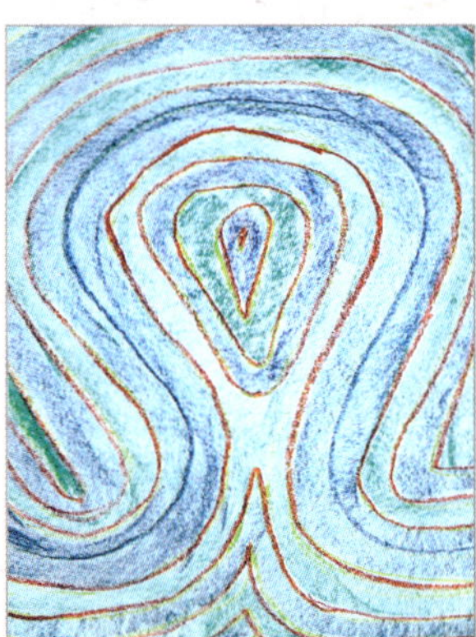

Try different lines, for example a branch shape or one with more curves, as shown. Pupils can start at different points on the first line and decide at what distance they wish to place the contour lines, always remembering to keep them equidistant.

Here we will also use a first line of one colour, but in this exercise new lines will converge at certain points and diverge at others.

Draw a coloured line across the sheet, then place points on it. In a different colour, draw more lines around the original one, approaching but not touching the points. These lines do not need to be equidistant from the original line. Pupils can find their own solutions in this exercise.

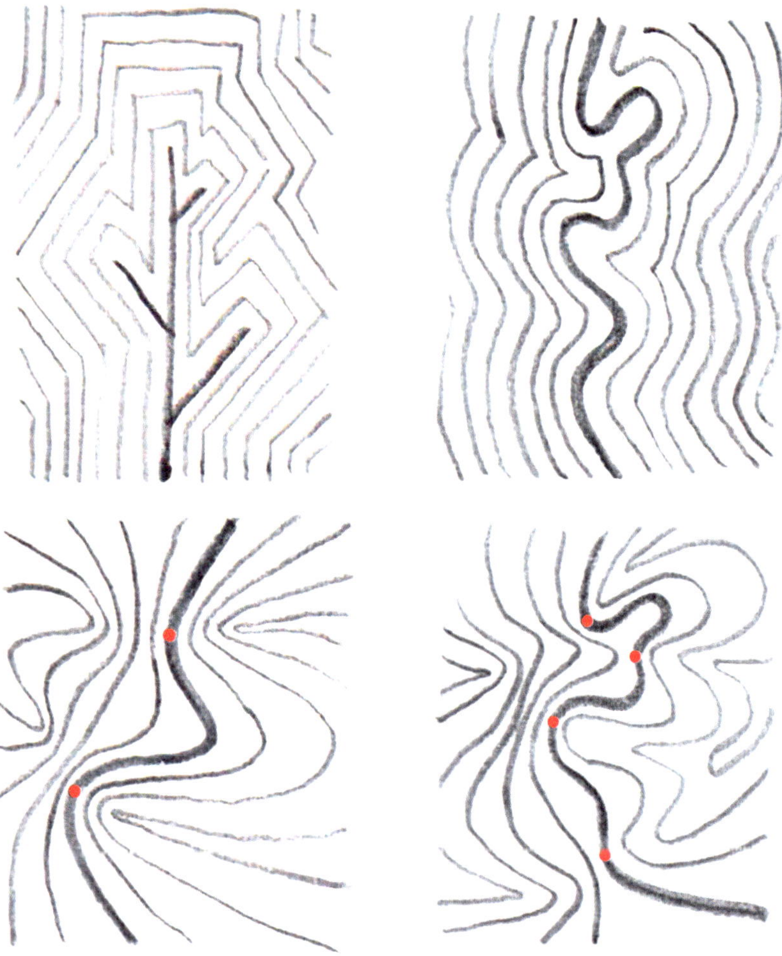

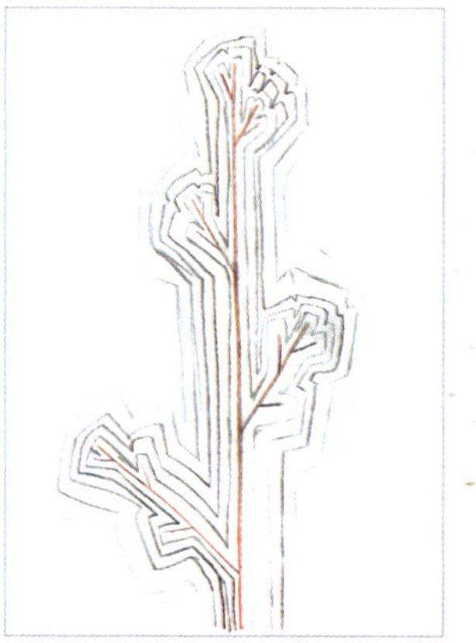

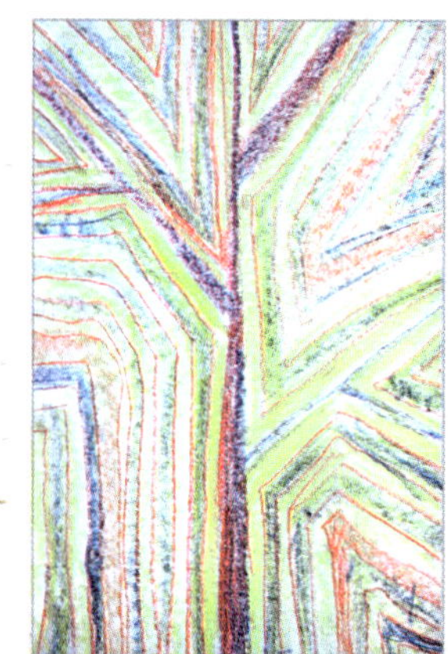

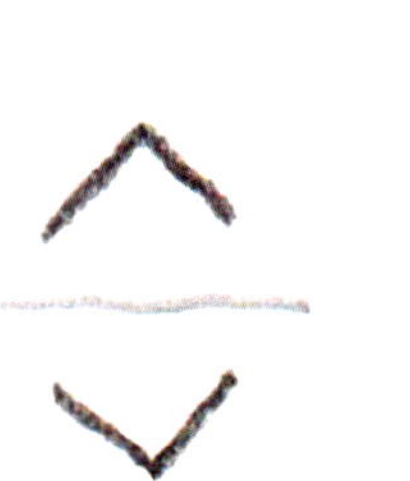

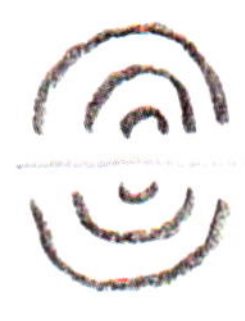

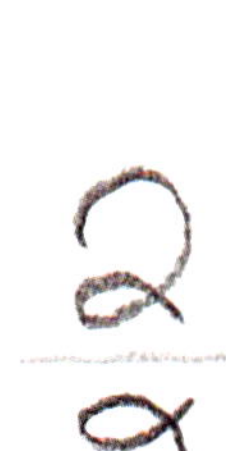

Horizontal mirroring

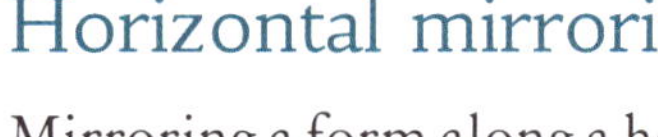

Mirroring a form along a horizontal axis is much more difficult than mirroring along a vertical axis. Look at the exercises shown, then begin carefully. Develop the exercises step by step.

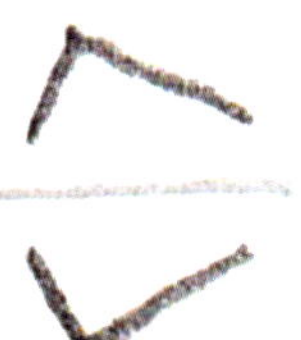

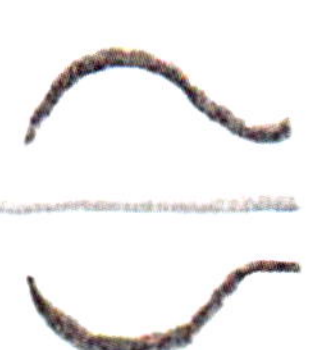

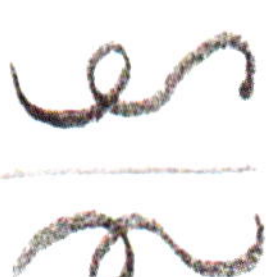

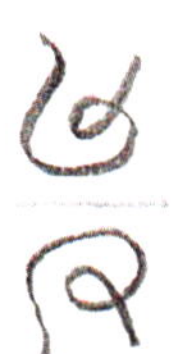

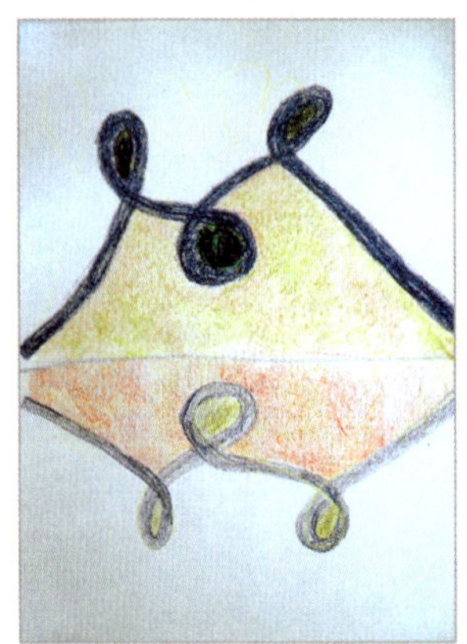

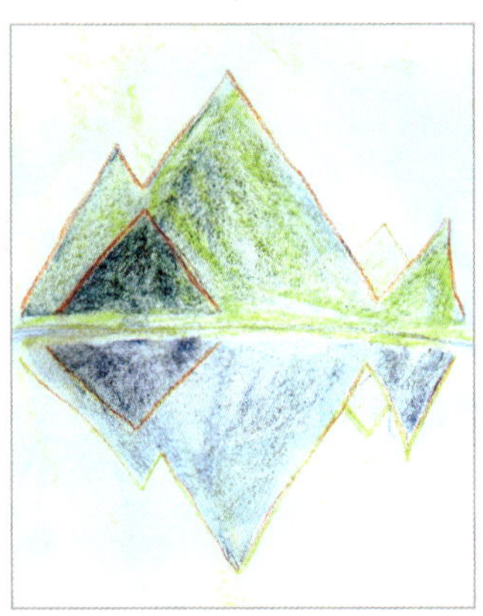

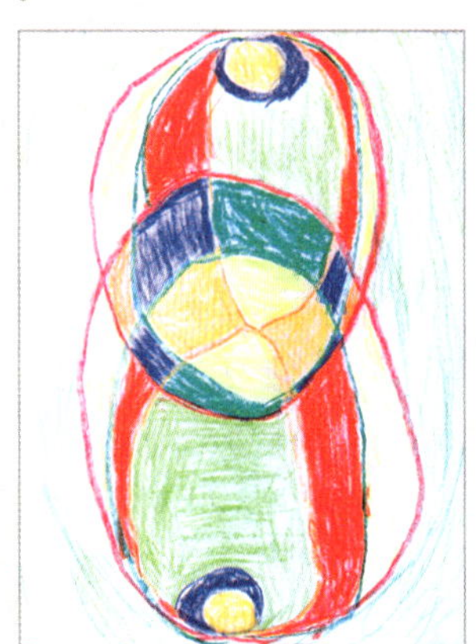

Honeycomb exercise

Draw a hexagon, then build the form outwards on all sides so it resembles a honeycomb.

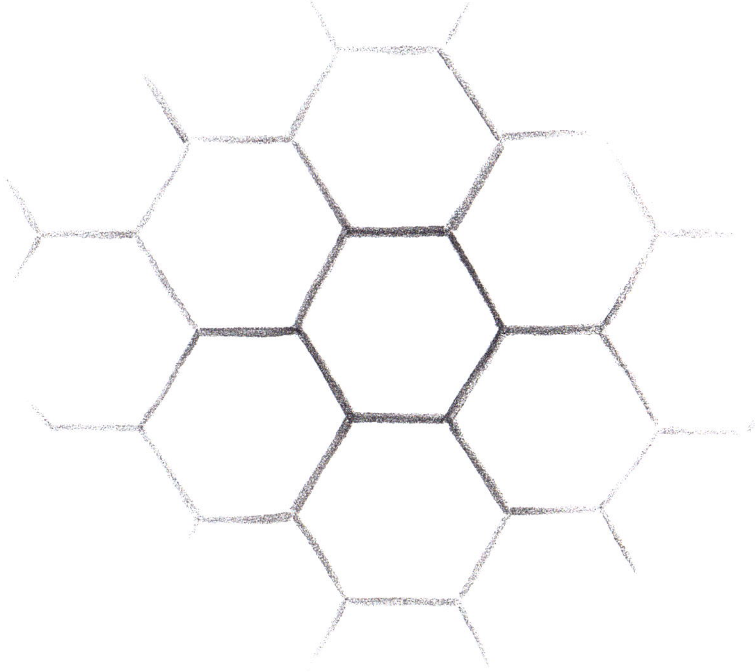

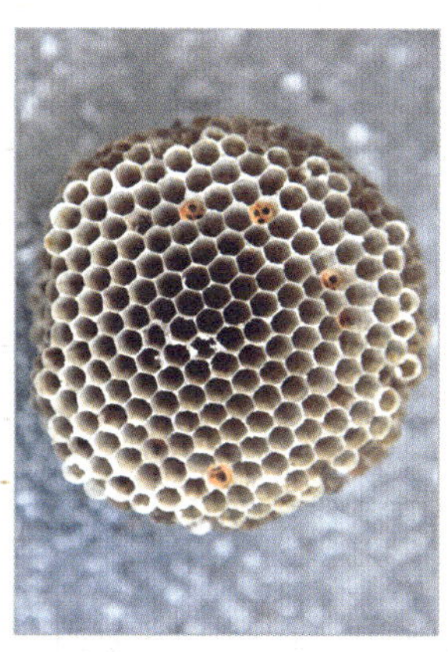

A wasps' nest

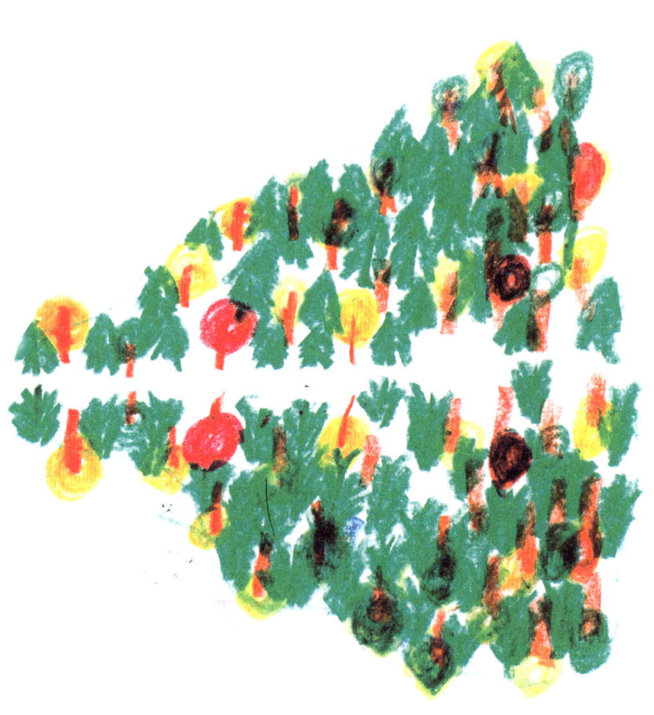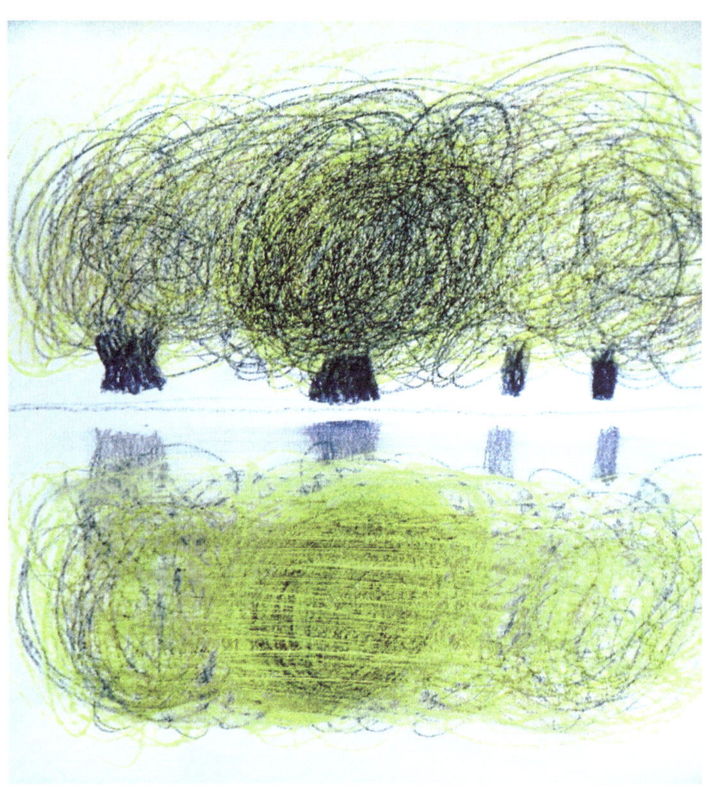

Pupils' work, Class 3

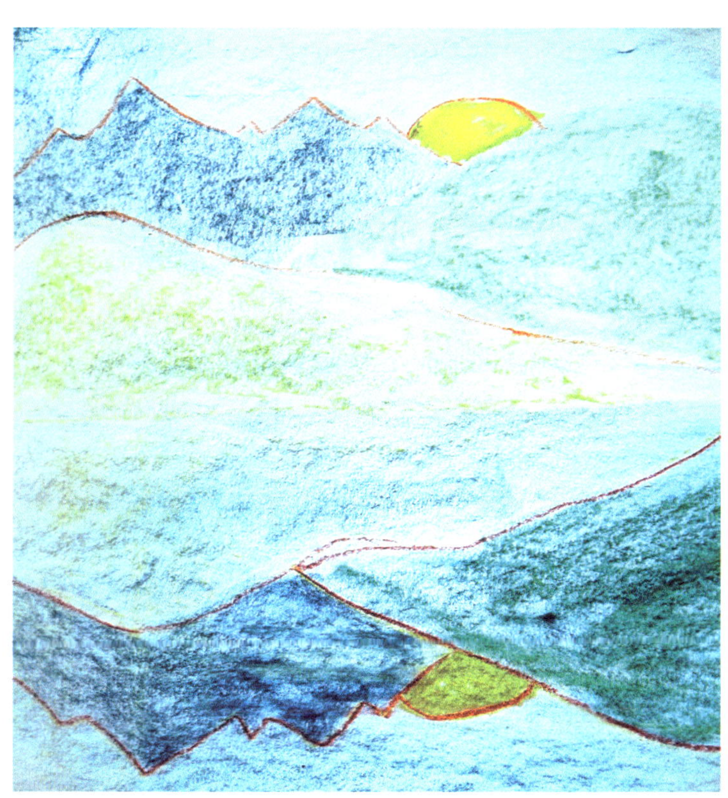

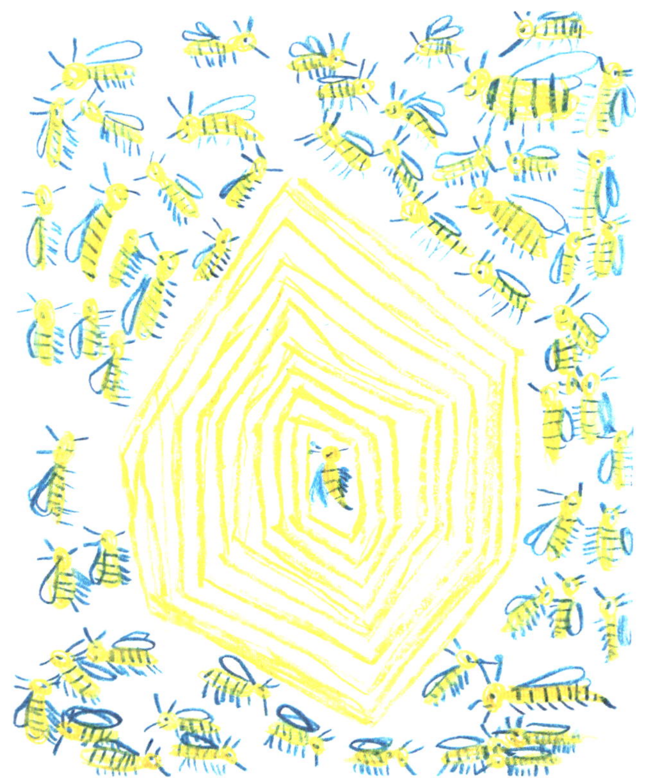

2 or 3

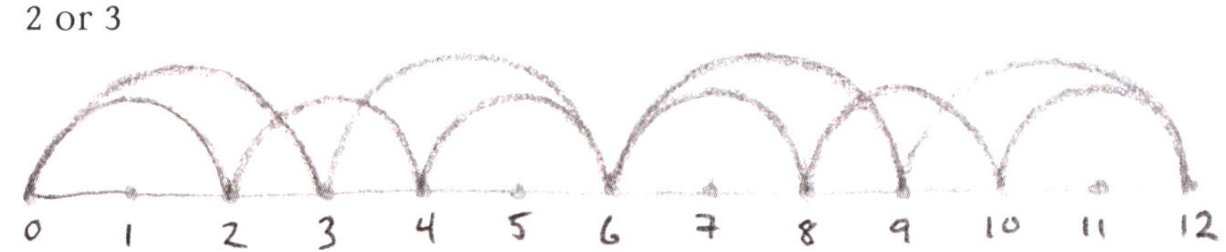

3 or 4

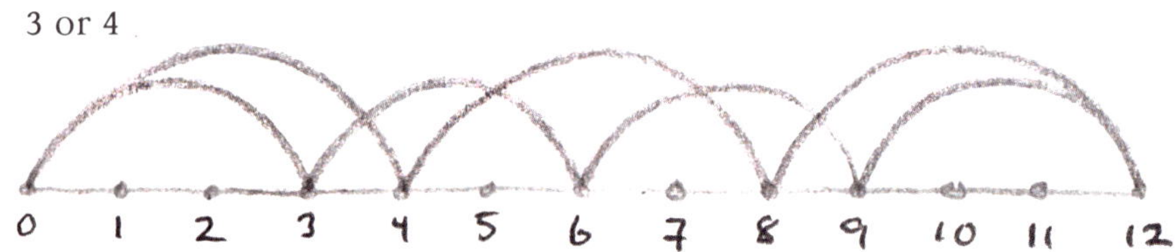

3 or 6

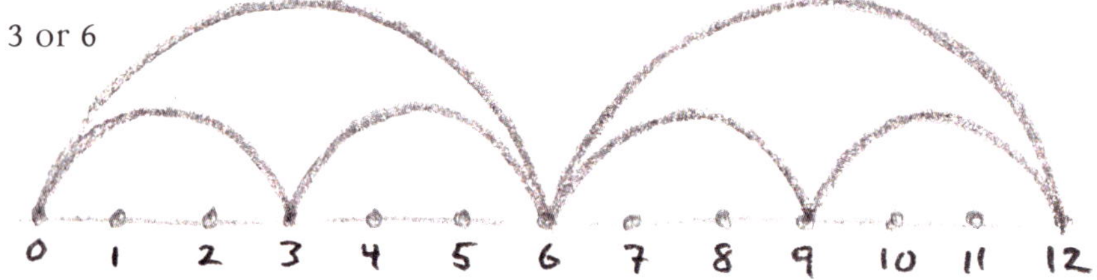

Multiplication

Visualisation, using forms and rows of numbers, makes mathematics more accessible to children. It is less abstract than pure numbers and mathematical terminology. Try drawing rows of numbers up to twelve, as shown.

Multiplication tables can be illustrated along these rows: the first example shows the two and three times tables, the second shows the three and four times tables, and the third shows the three and six times tables.

By presenting times tables in this way, rhythm and distances become visible. It is also possible to compare the different tables, see where they intersect and discover different numerical patterns. This is good preparation for a future understanding of the common denominator.

While drawing, colour each table carefully in its own individual shade.

Multiplication tables can also be visualised by using triangles and squares. This is a repetition of Class 2's first meeting with numbers and forms, where the number three was a triangle and four was a square. Here, the three times table is demonstrated using triangles and the four times table using squares.

Find different models to visualise more multiplication tables.

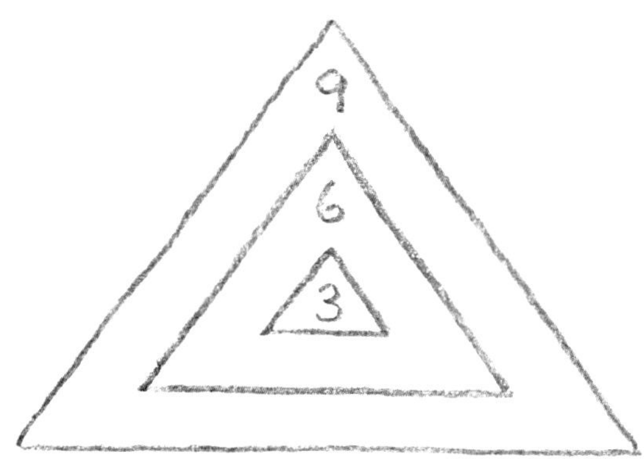

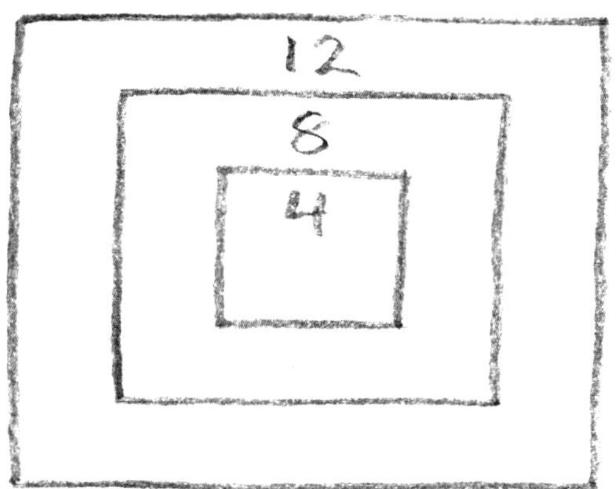

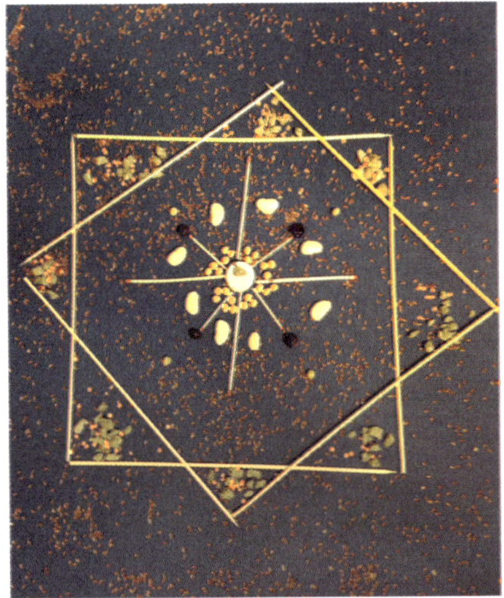 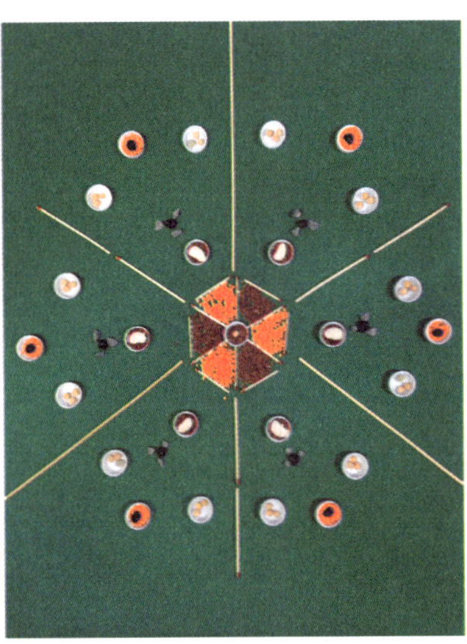

Using real objects

It is possible to make flowers, mandalas and other forms, and to mirror and build symmetries, using peas, beans, lentils, flaxseeds, matches, flower stalks and so on. It is a good idea to start in the middle and make four to six exits from the centre. Then build up the rest of the form.

This is a good exercise for group work. It is also a good way of practising aesthetics, geometry and how numbers relate to one another.

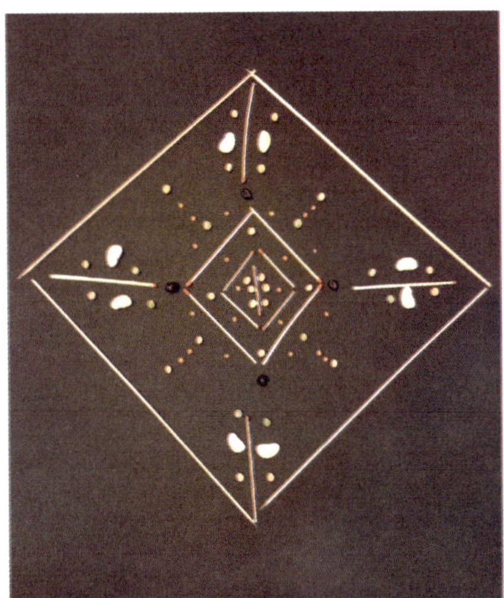 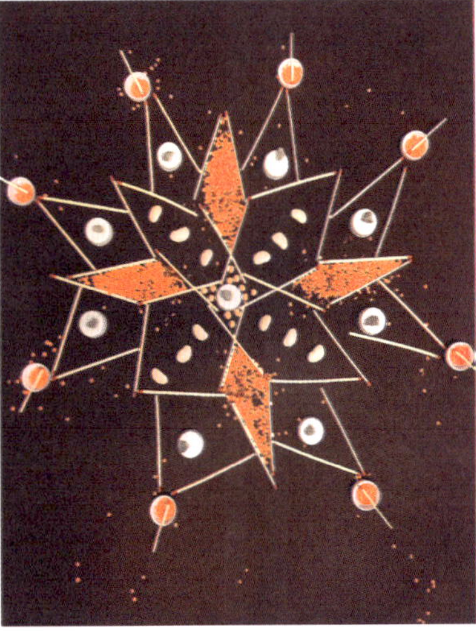

All pictures are from group work by pupils from Classes 2 to 10

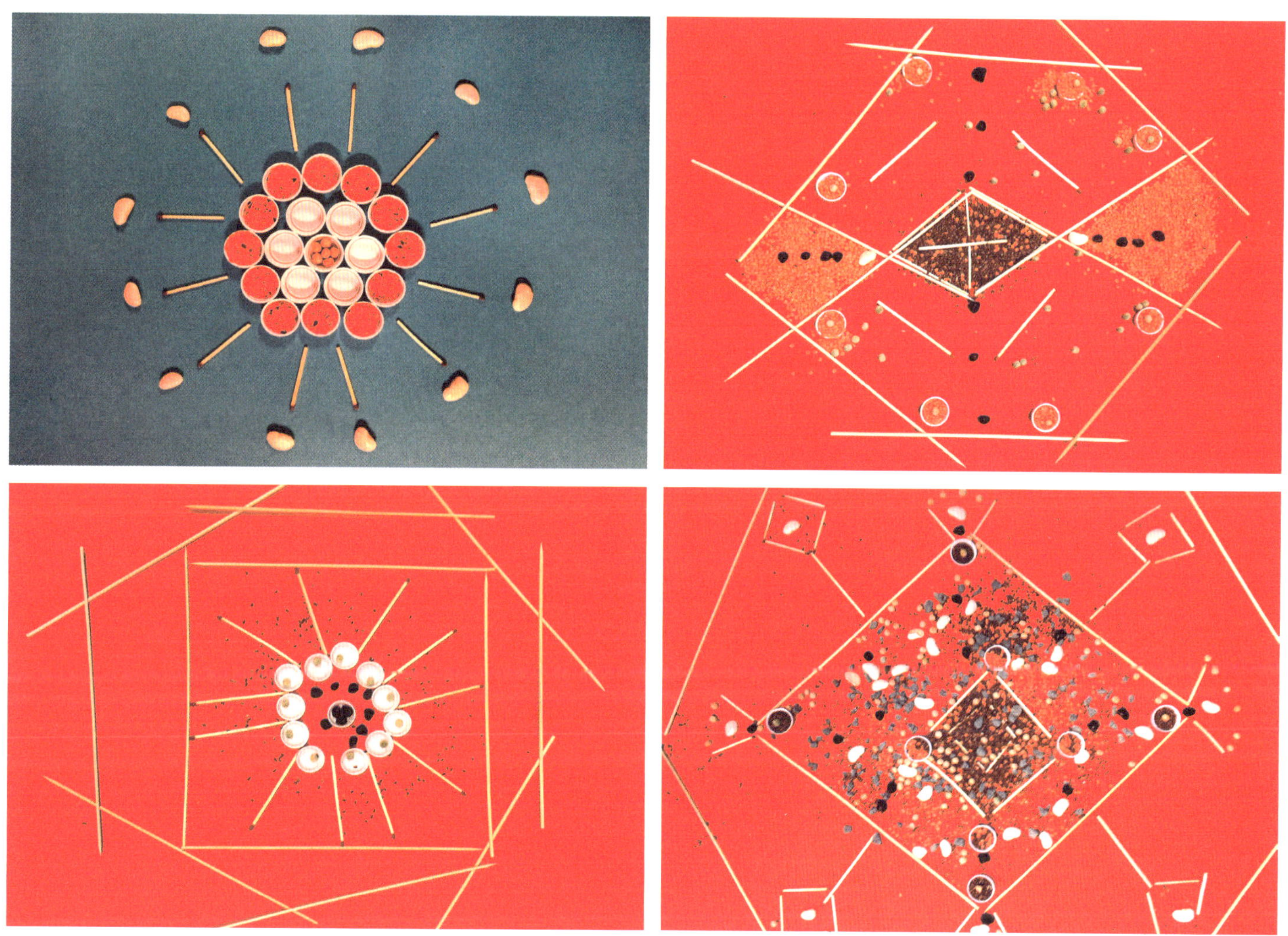

Part 4: Class 4 Exercises

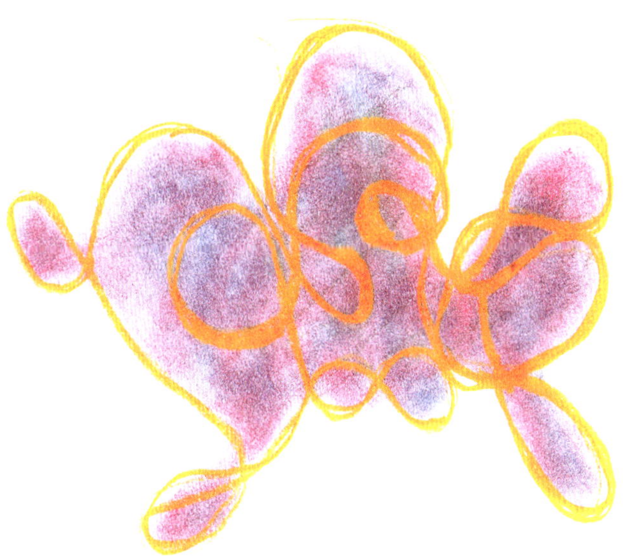

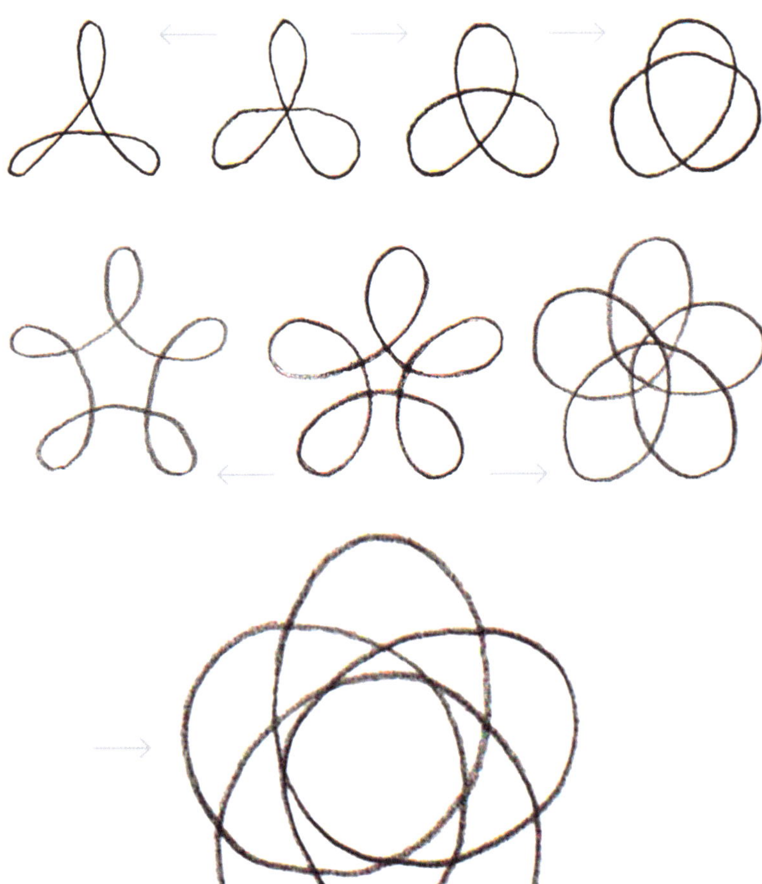

Movement and change

These exercises will develop pupils' understanding of how form can move and change. Encourage them to use their imagination and demonstrate flexibility in their ideas. Explain the challenges of the forms and wait until pupils have explored the figures themselves before you draw finished products in class.

This three-looped form (top) can be further developed in two directions, as shown. Try out the exercise yourself before giving it to the class. Allow your pupils to experiment individually and then discuss results with them.

Next, try using four or five loops (centre). The figure can be drawn in one line, or you can remain in rhythmic motion while adjusting the line, as shown in the pupil's example in bright yellow (below left).

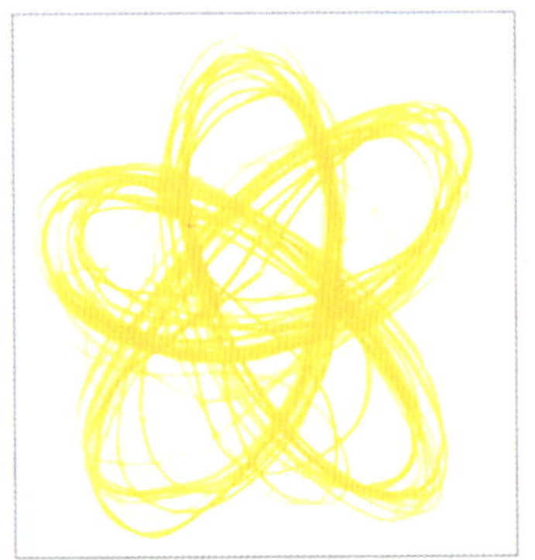

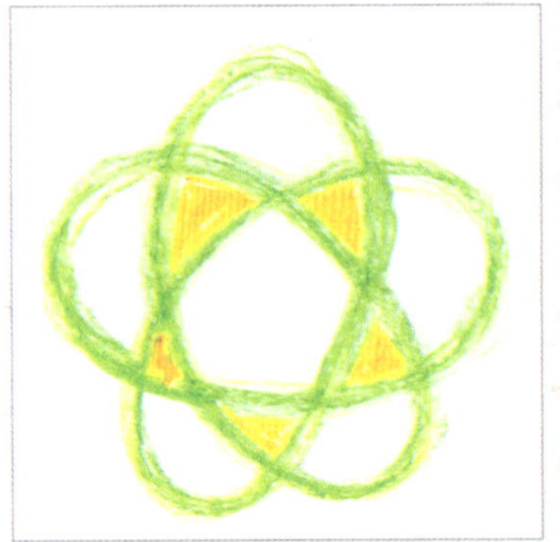

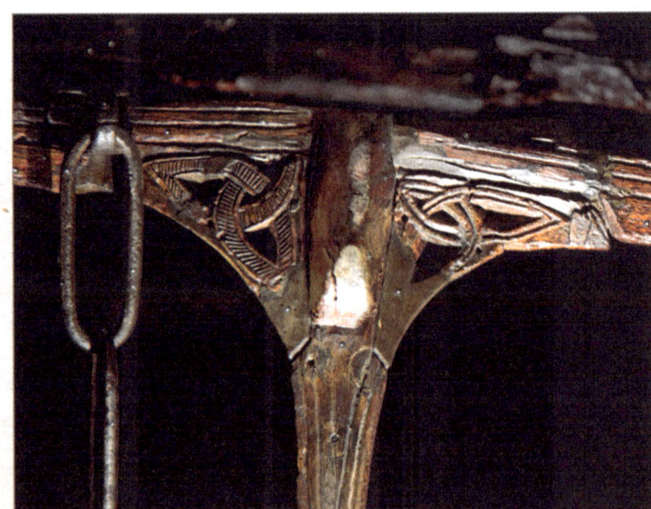

Detail from a Viking sleigh

Different forms may be superimposed upon one another to create beautiful ornaments. Using their experiences from the previous set of exercises, let pupils experiment to see which figures can be superimposed elegantly. The challenge is to place them so that they intertwine with clear, graceful lines. The forms should throw one another into relief, rather than overshadow one another.

Lines crossing one another more than once in the same place can lack clarity. To emphasise one of the forms, use a thicker line or another colour. It takes experimentation and practice to produce a proficient piece.

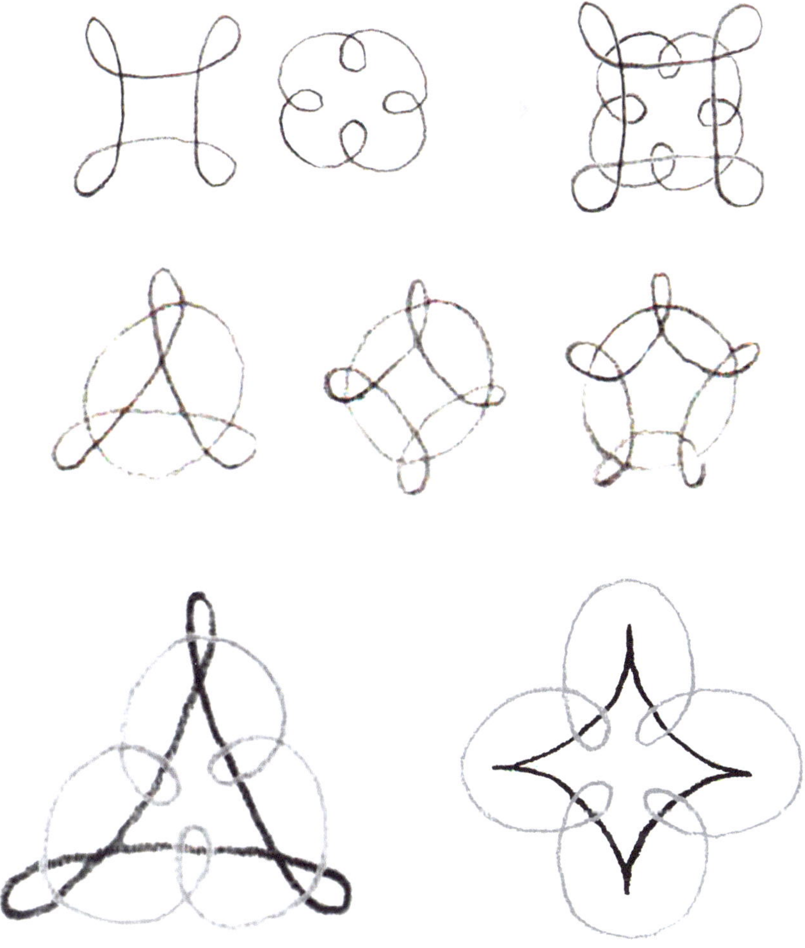

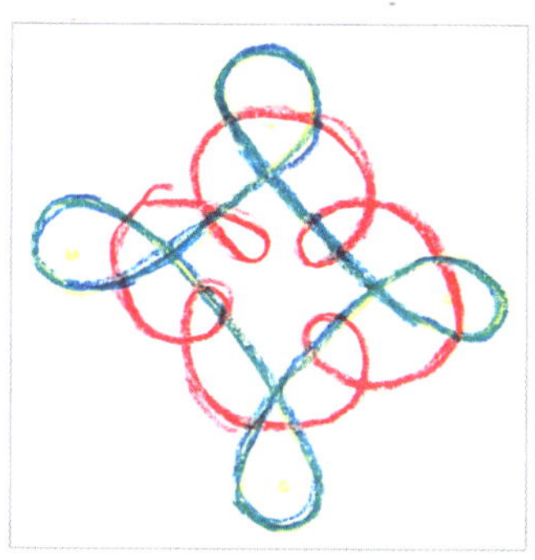

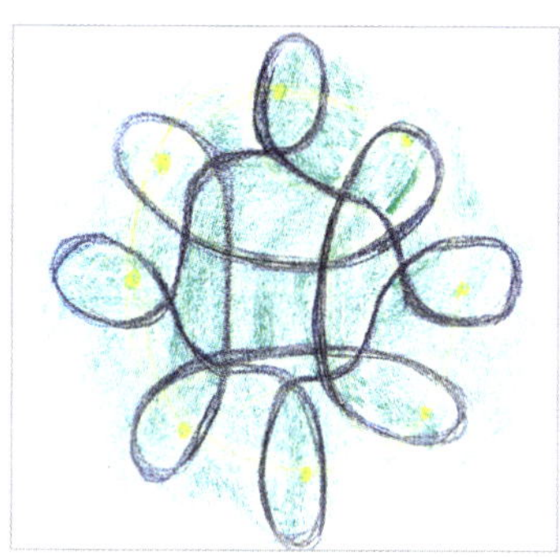

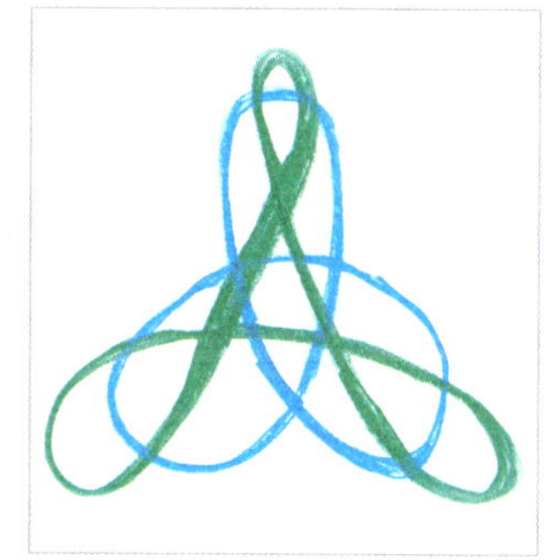

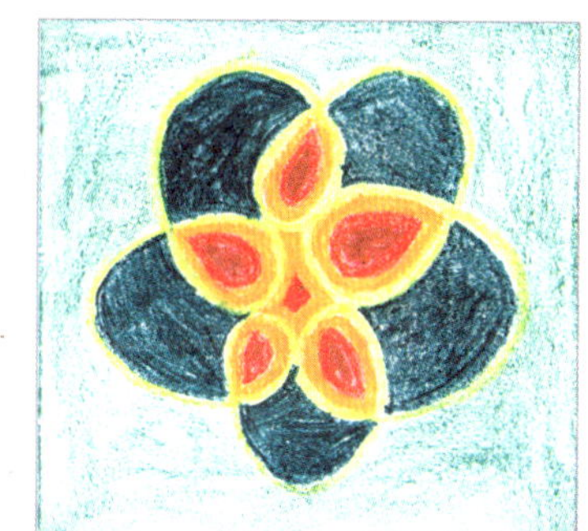

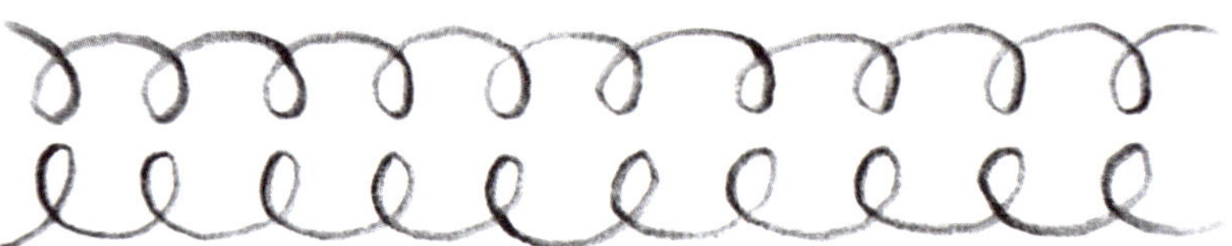

Let pupils experiment putting these two borders together in different ways and, if needed, assist them with suggestions after a while.

Once pupils have merged the borders as shown in the first example, pick out a motif from the border and tie the 'loose threads' together.

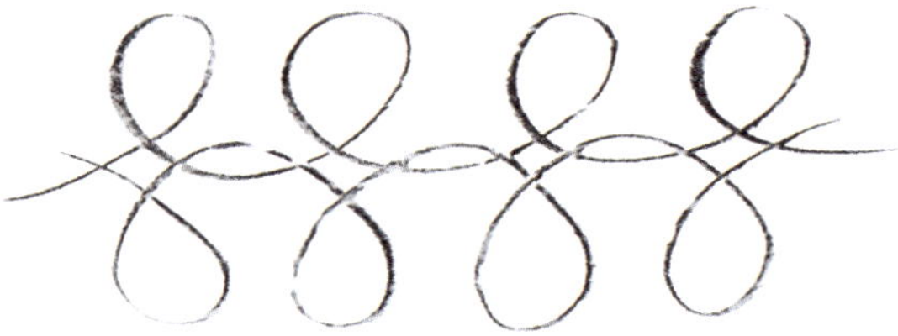

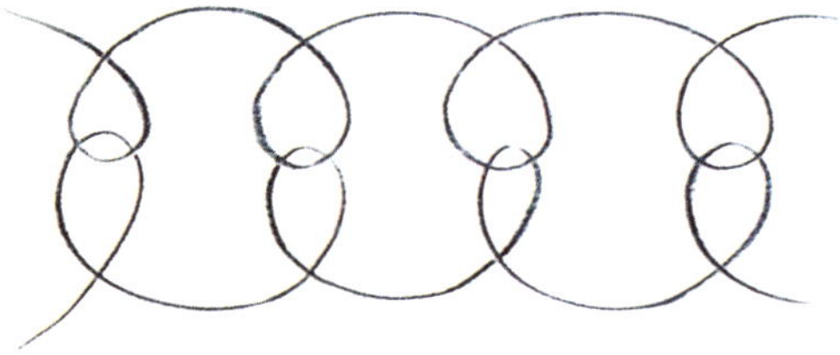

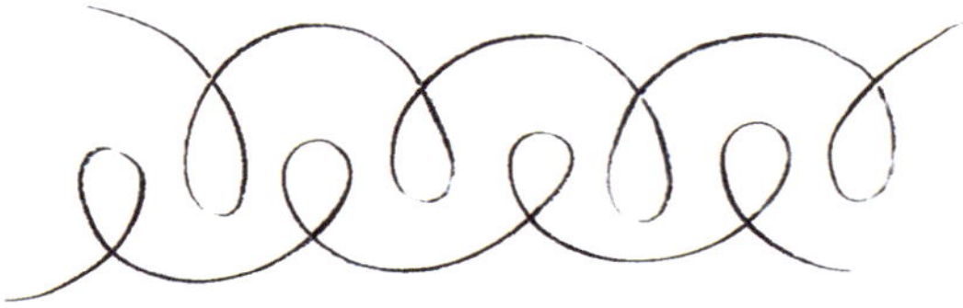

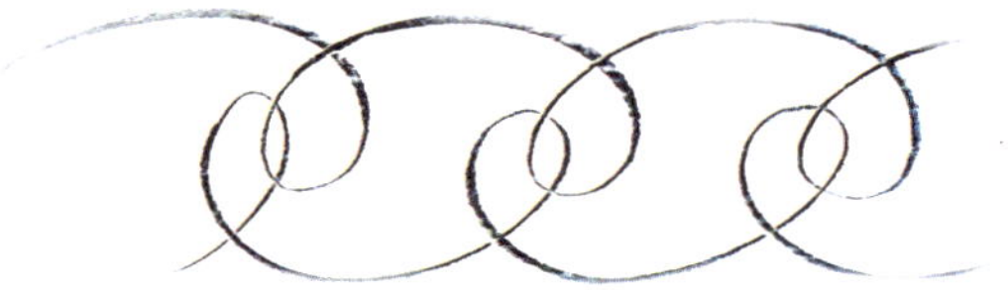

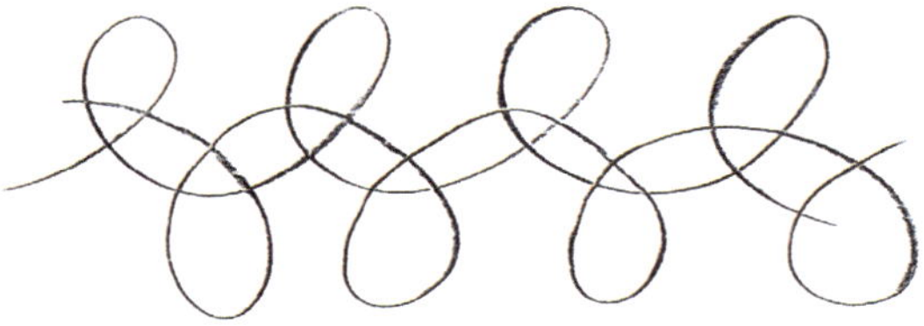

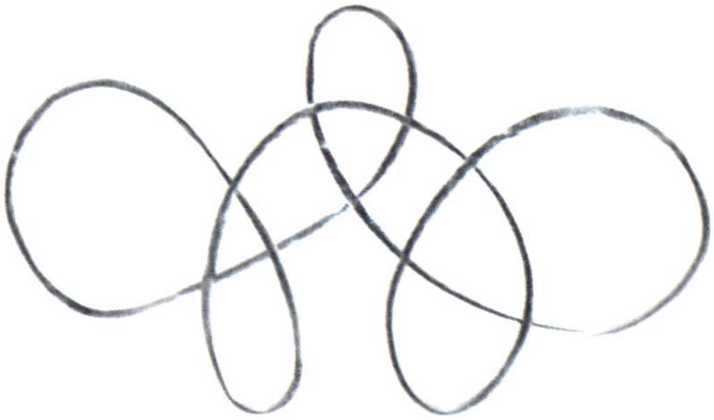

Here are other ways of merging the borders shown on the previous page. As before, pick out a motif. Next, let your pupils draw this as a large, attractive form. However, wait until Class 5 before attempting plaiting (see p.122).

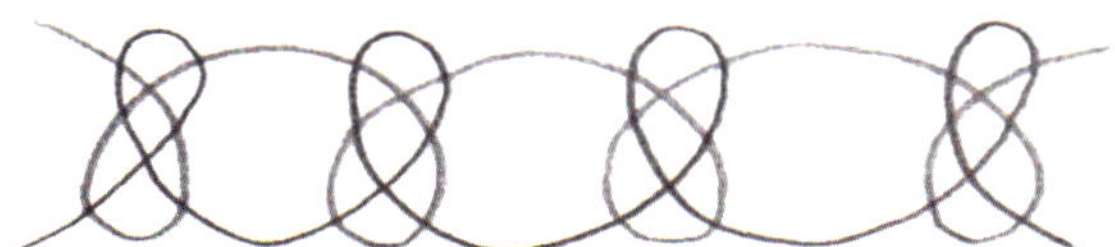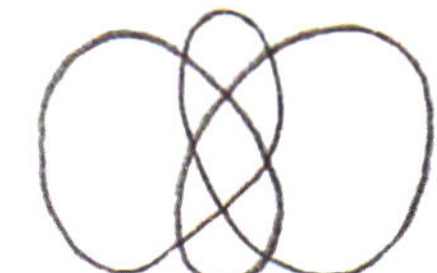

Consider whether your pupils are ready to attempt the lower figure. If so, start with the lighter line, then slowly and accurately superimpose the thicker line on top. This is an example of something pupils should be allowed lots of time to build up.

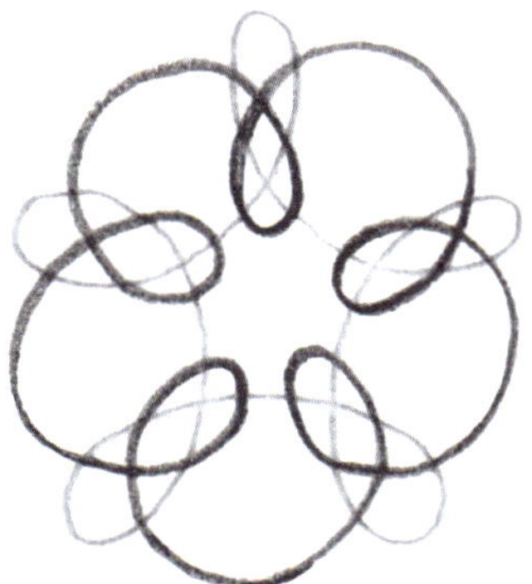

If colouring the form, ensure that the colour choice emphasises the harmony and beautiful symmetry in the pattern. You might even decide that the motif looks its best without colour.

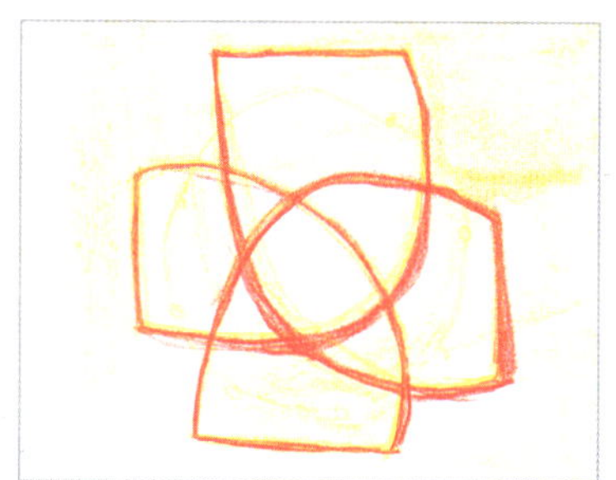

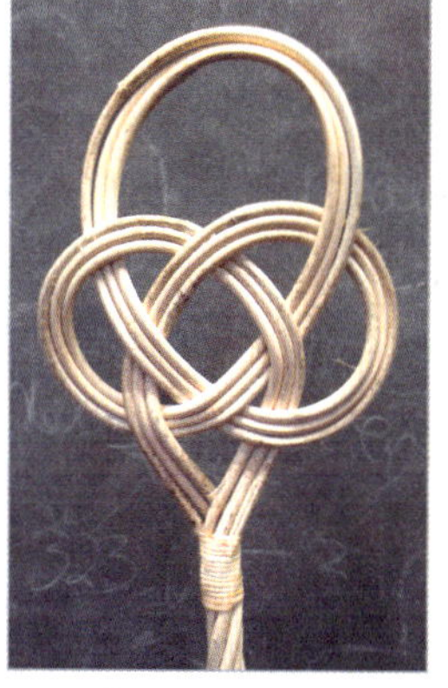

Carpet beater

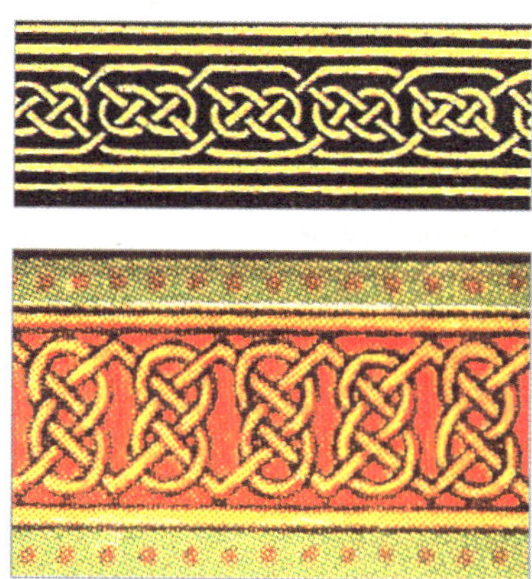

Celtic borders

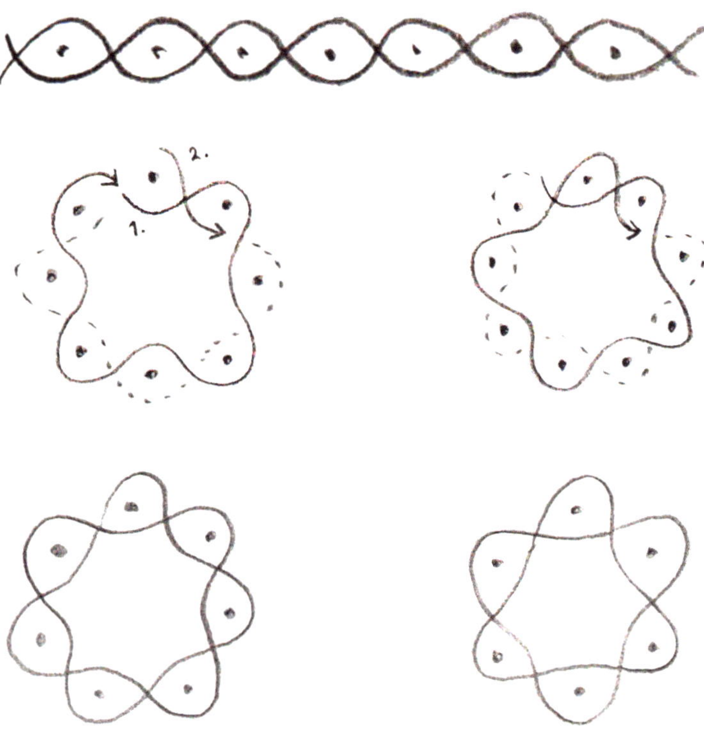

Aesthetic problem-solving

This exercise involves complex problems that will require pupils to think, and they do so best while using their hands and a crayon or chalk. When finished, ask them to draw the final product into their workbooks. However, what is more important is the joy of exploring the forms on paper. In this case, I advise generosity in setting the guidelines for rough work and jotting, allowing pupils to erase and fetch more paper as they need to.

To begin, make a row of points on a line and draw a border around them, as shown.

Next, draw the points again but this time in a ring, then draw a border around them in the same way, alternating between the inside and the outside. Do the lines meet themselves or not?

To develop the exercise, draw seven points in a circle and repeat the above. What happens now? What about when six points are drawn?

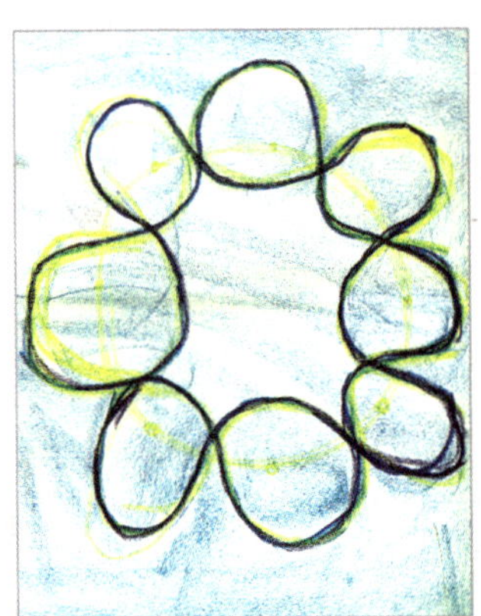

When the pupils have grasped the concept, they can experiment with fewer points.

How does the exercise work when following this rule: draw the line alternately on the inside and then the outside? It works every time, but let your pupils find out for themselves.

Finally, you can show them on the blackboard.

These exercises develop the previous ones, but also act as preparation for the Indian tradition of Rangoli (see p.96). Experiment with two or three rows of points. Is it possible to create a continuous line using only two rows or do you need three?

Note that drawing points is helpful when constructing complex figures, but they can detract from being able to see the form as a whole. After a while, pupils will become skilful enough to draw the figures freehand.

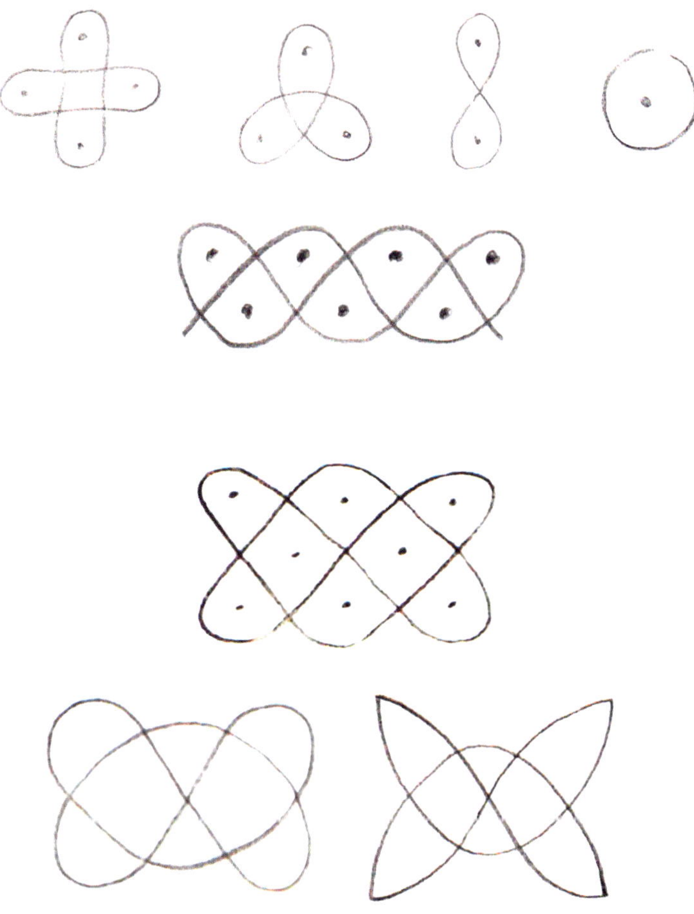

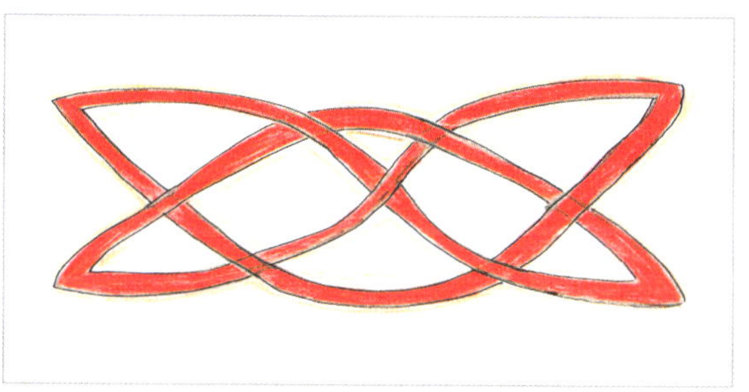

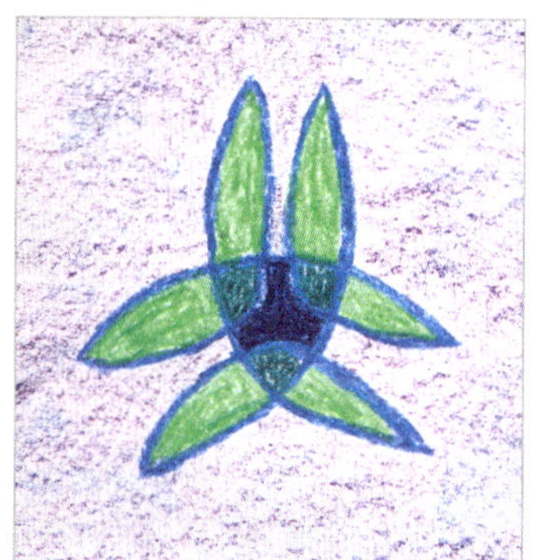

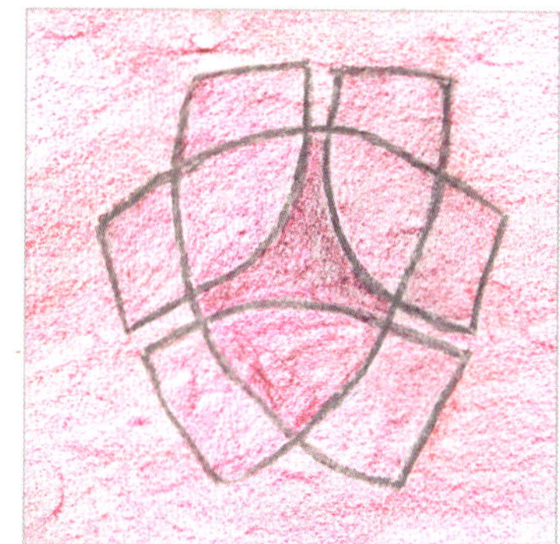

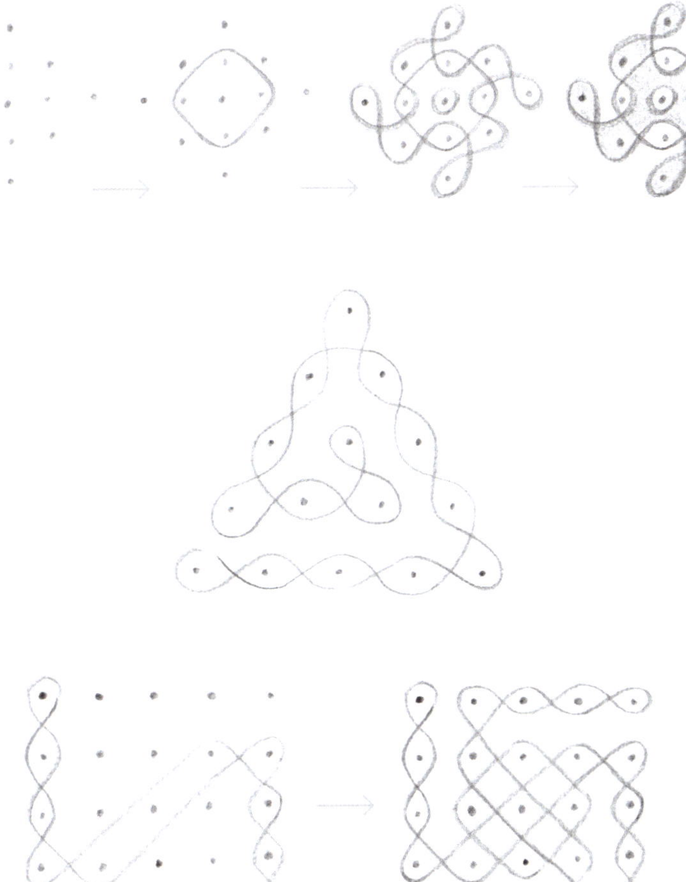

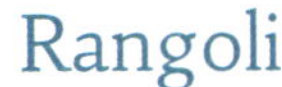

Rangoli

The inhabitants of the Indian state of Tamil Nadu have a morning ritual in which they draw different forms in front of the entrance to their houses. They take a small amount of rice flour between thumb and forefinger from a small bowl, and then rub their fingers together to gradually release the flour in a line approximately twenty centimetres in length. Their elegant and rhythmical movements make these beautiful forms appear each morning afresh, and in the same place. There are often coloured versions too. This is called Rangoli.

See the illustrations for examples of how to develop a Rangoli pattern. The triangle is fascinating; while drawing you have to use your intuition to place the line systematically on the outside or the inside of the points. Try using triangles with several points along the edge.

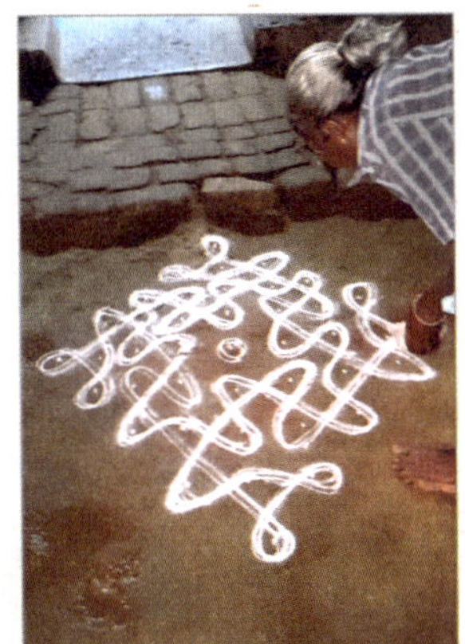

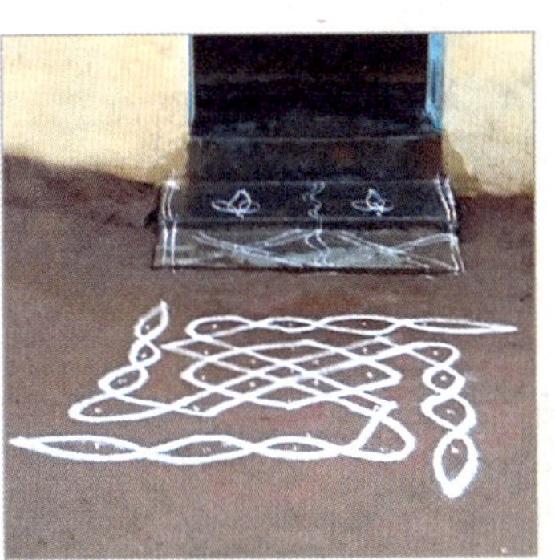

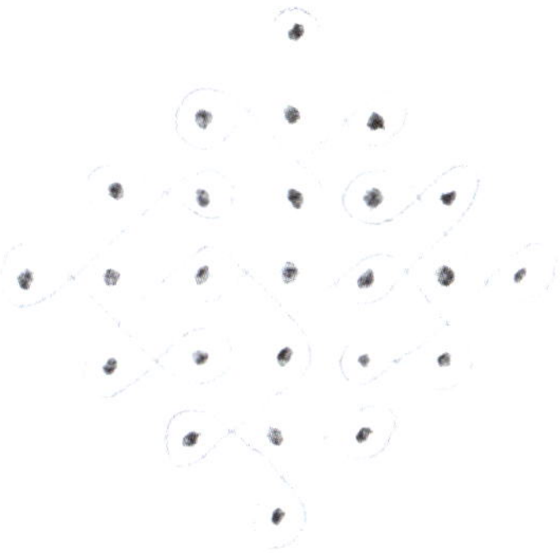

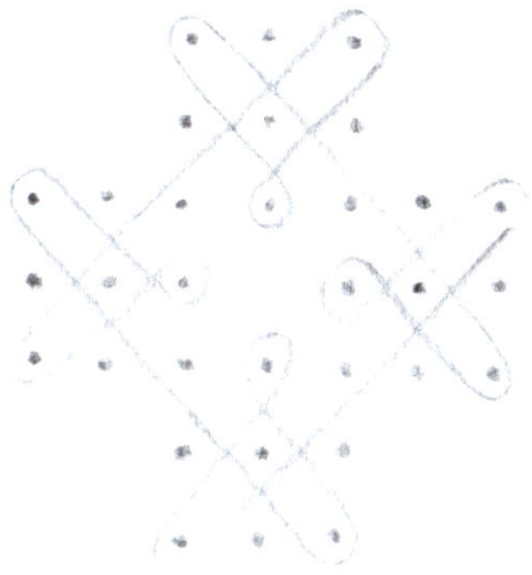

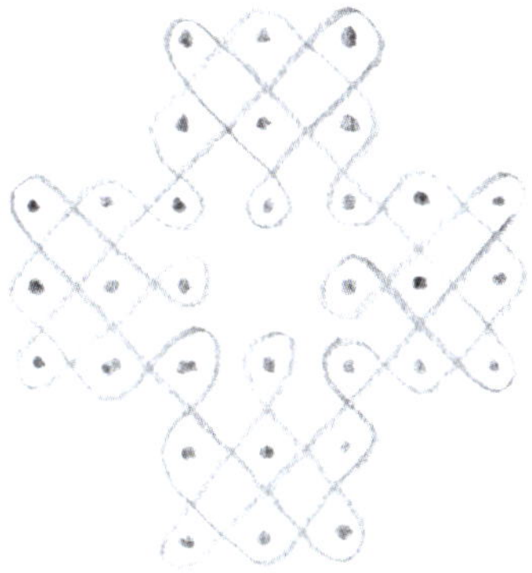

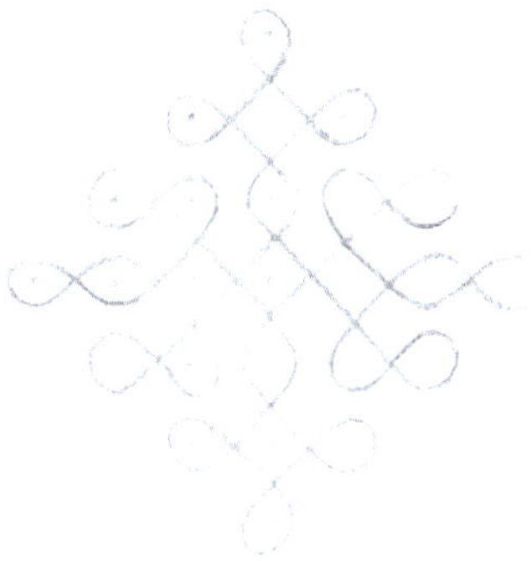

Although the two figures
directly above look similar,
they are slightly different.

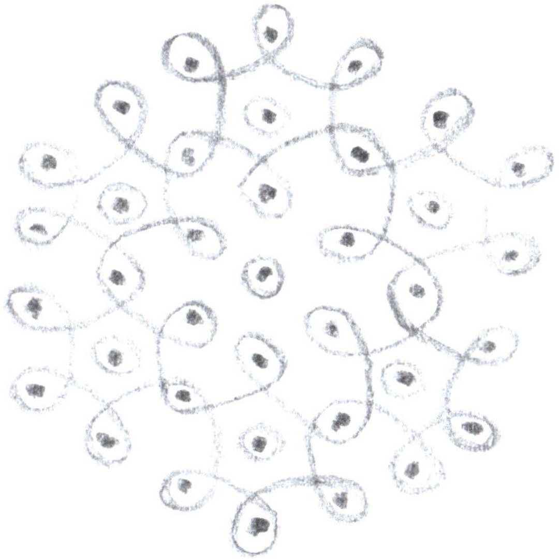

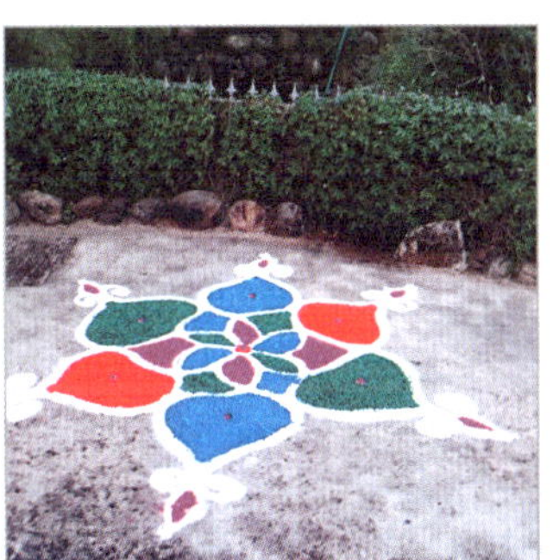

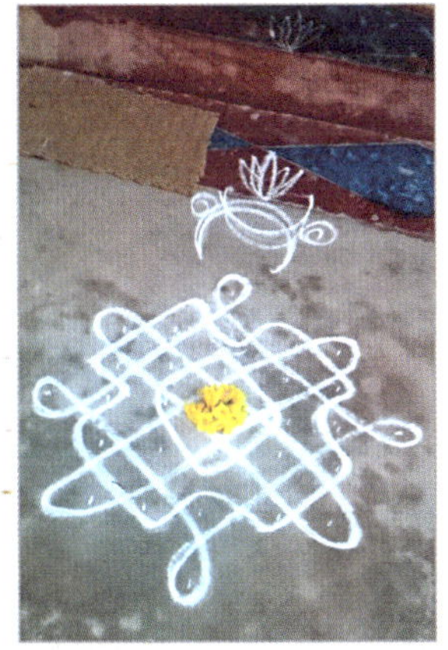

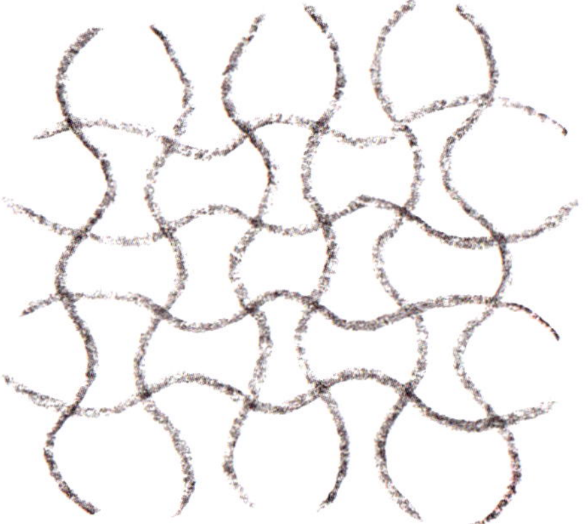

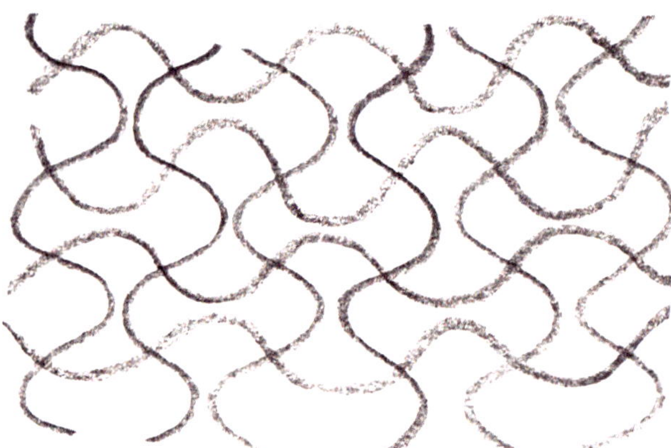

Wallpaper patterns

All of these 'wallpaper' patterns consist of vertical and horizontal lines that cross over. They differ in the distance between the lines, along with their arches and loops, which decide their form and degree of difficulty. These types of pattern can go on for as long as you like.

The examples given here will stretch your pupils' abilities. Allow them to explore new methods themselves, too, and to challenge one another.

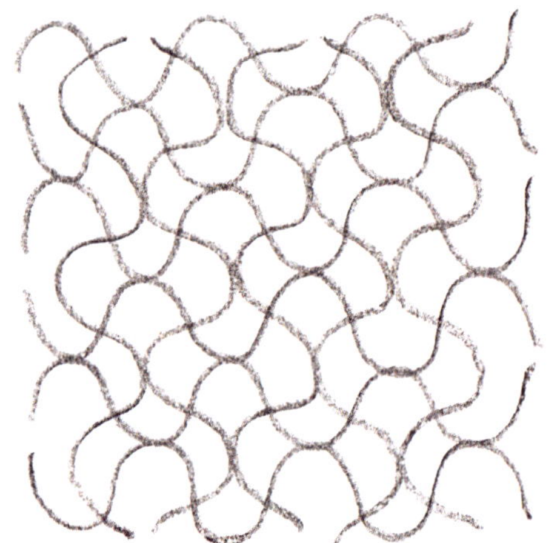

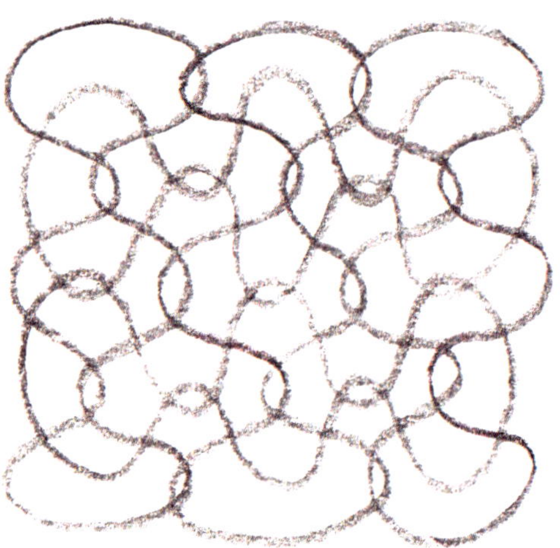

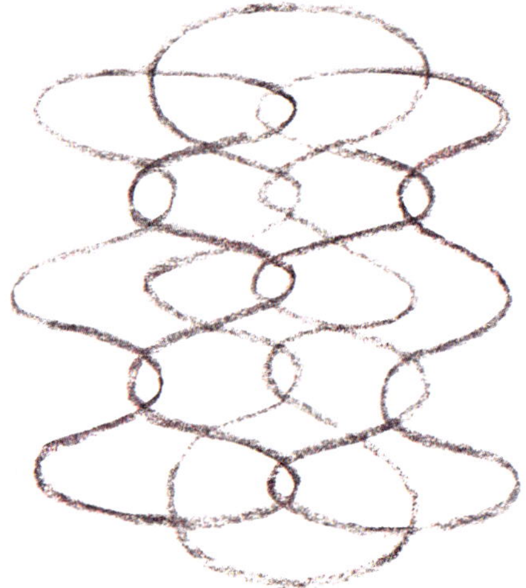

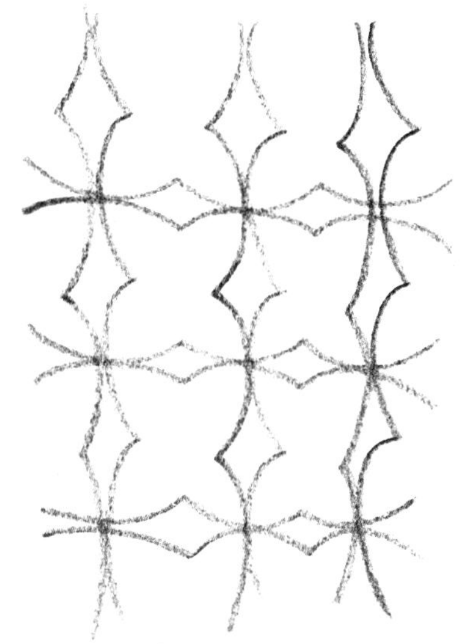

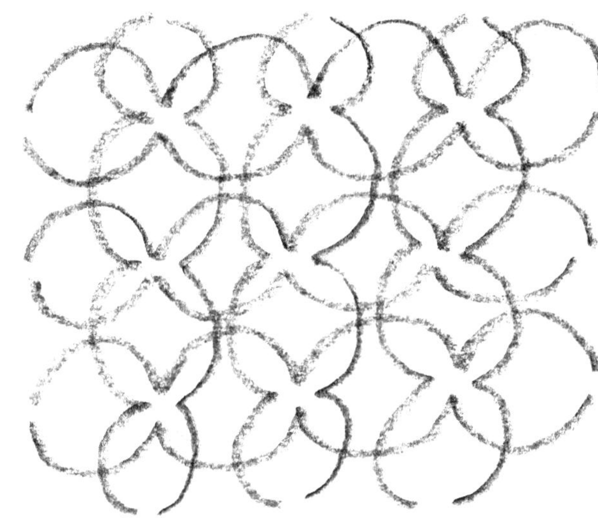

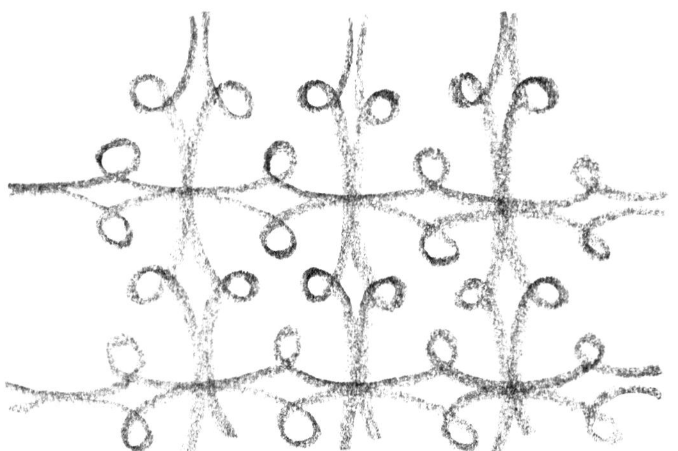

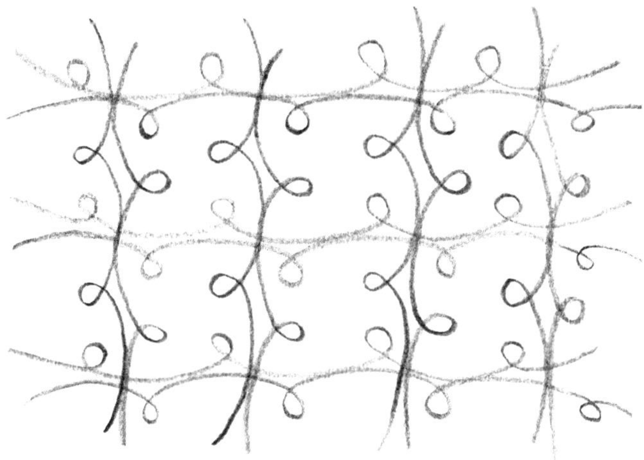

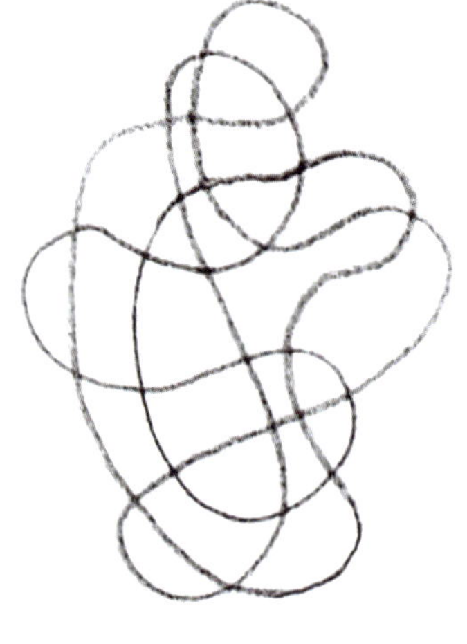
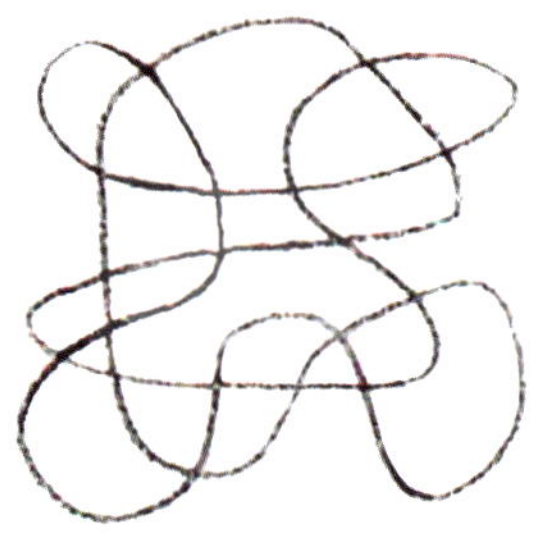
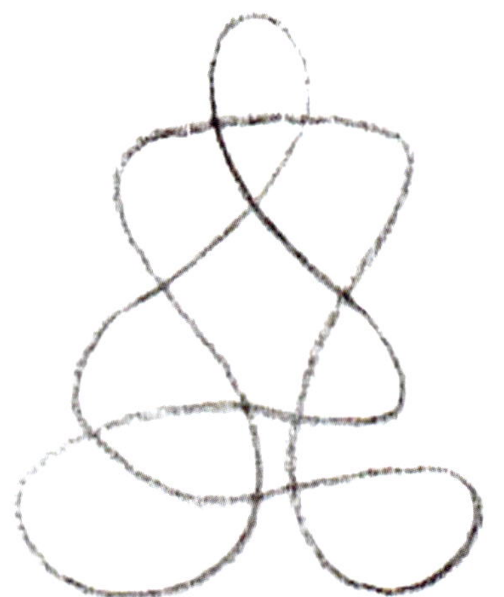
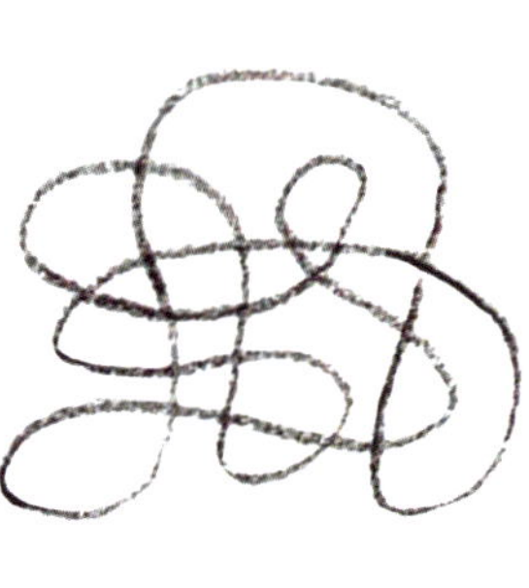

Living patterns

Ask your pupils to let a line wander over the paper while following these rules:

- End the line by linking it to its starting point.
- Don't allow the line to cross in the same place more than once.
- Leave plenty of space between the forms that arise.
- Don't make it too complicated.
- Use the entire surface of the paper.

Why not make up your own rules?

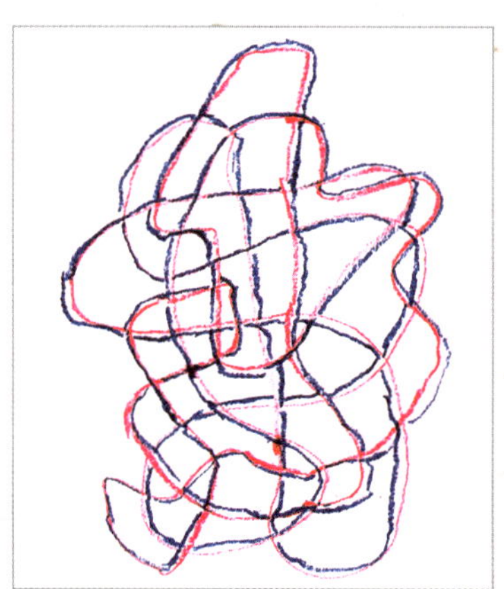
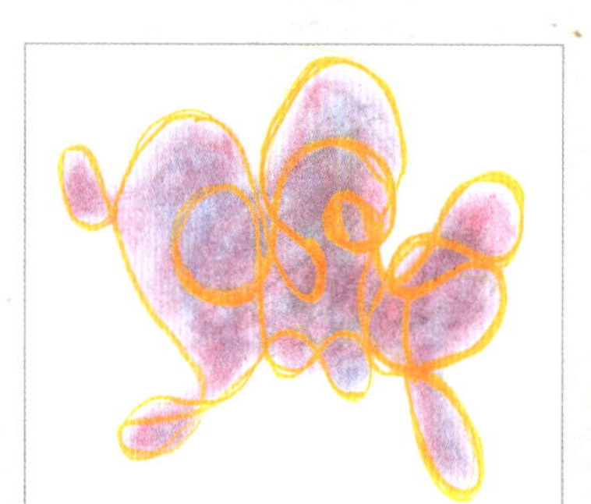
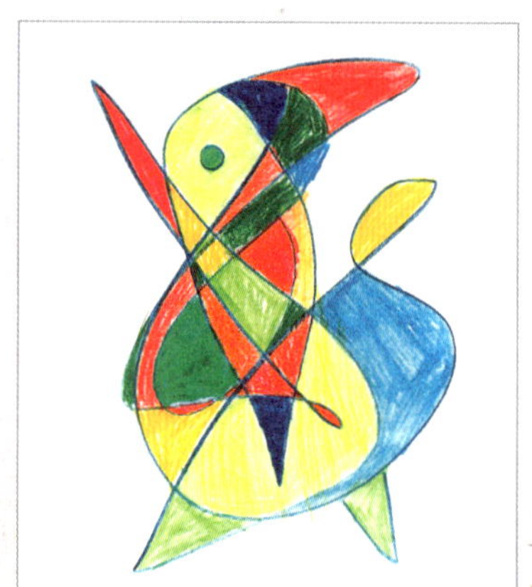

Movement

Drop a sheet of A4 (US letter) or A5 (Half letter) paper onto the floor and ask pupils to draw what they observe, without explaining anything else. Allow them to play with this beautiful, swaying form. Afterwards they can approach these zigzag patterns in different ways. Let pupils find their own versions.

This exercise is a good example of how movement helps us to recognise the principles of form. The oscillating form breathes in and out, representing momentary stillness between movements.

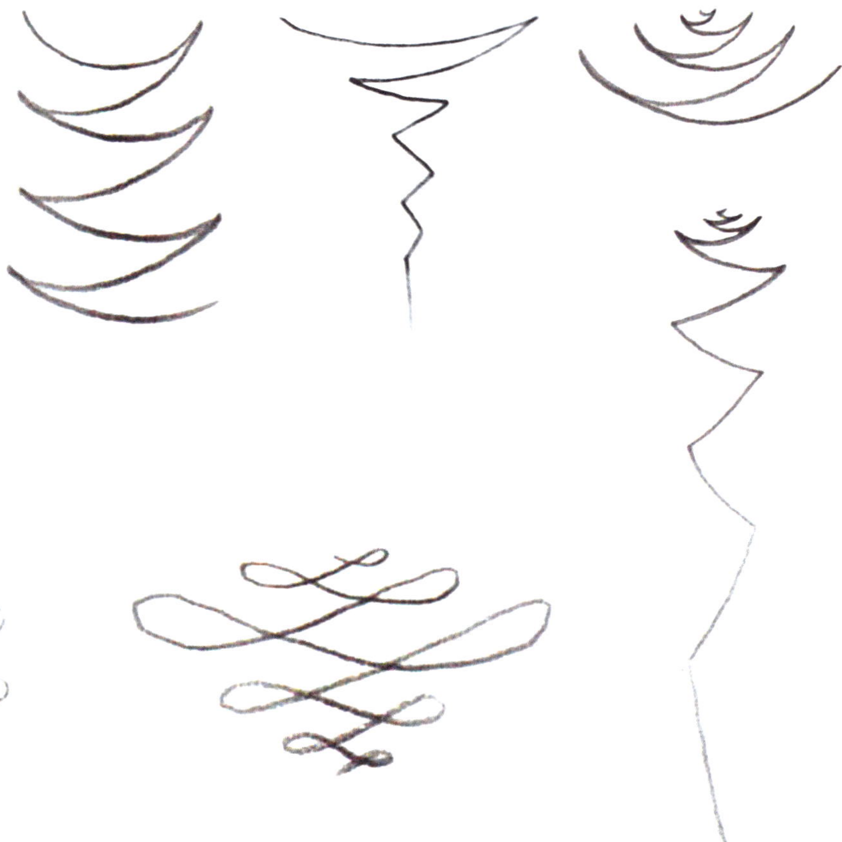

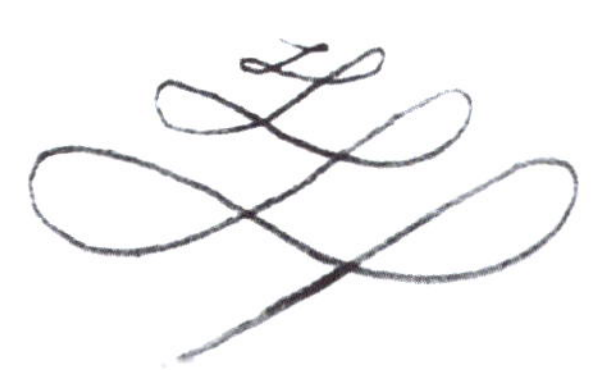

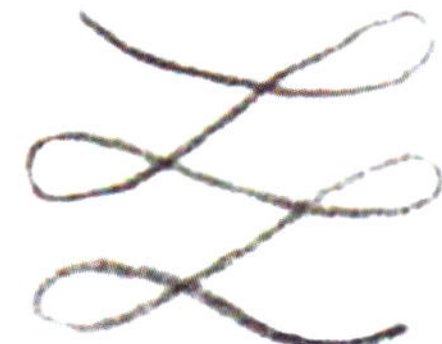

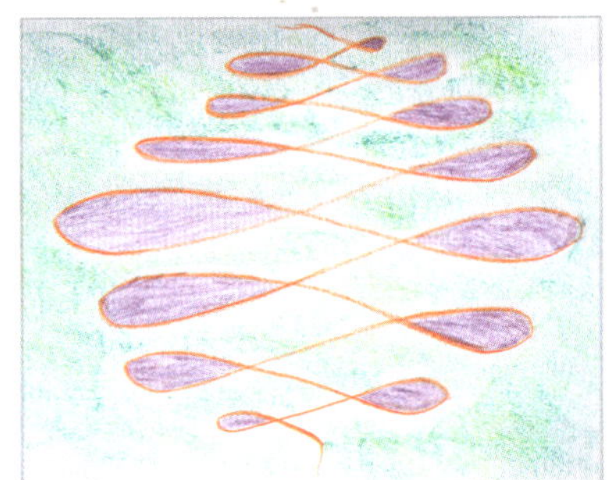

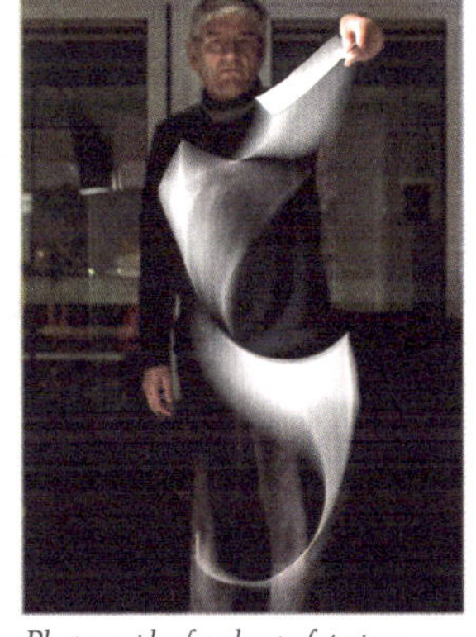

Photograph of a sheet of paper falling (two seconds' exposure time)

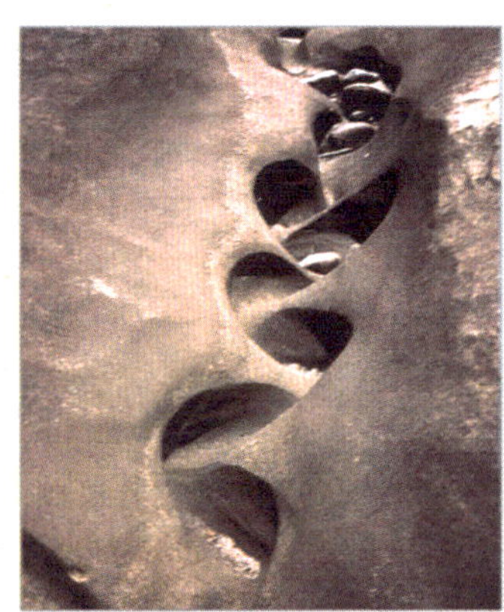

Thousands of years of moving water has left traces in the rock of Piccaninny Creek, Australia

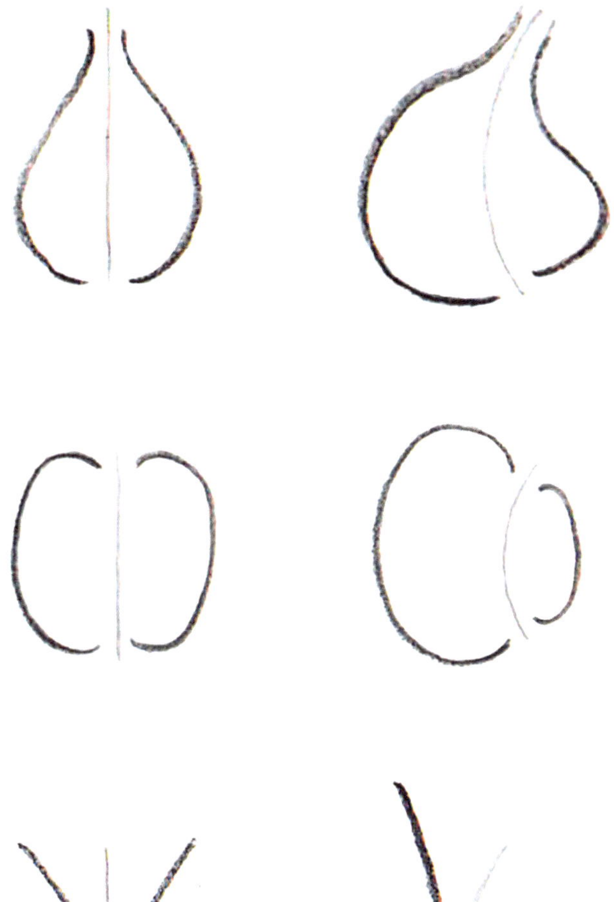

Curved mirrors

Mirroring using a vertical line will already be familiar to your pupils, but how will they cope if the mirroring line is curved? Demonstrate the examples on the blackboard and then let pupils experiment to understand the principles behind them. It may help to ask pupils to look into both convex and concave mirrors and observe their effects before completing the task. It is possible to arrive at different solutions from the same point of origin.

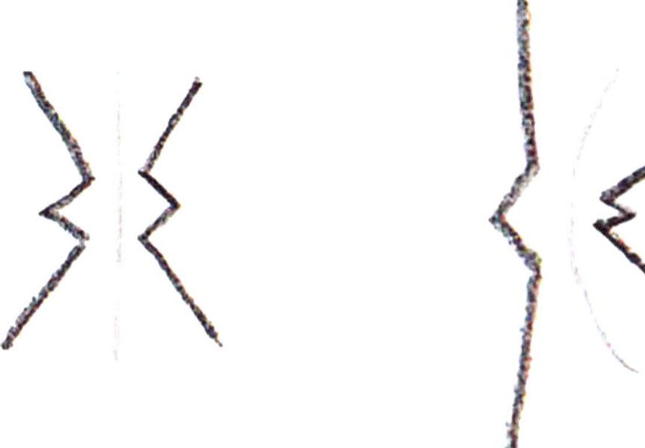

Through the mirror

The line to be mirrored can cross the vertical axis (or mirror) in different ways, as shown.

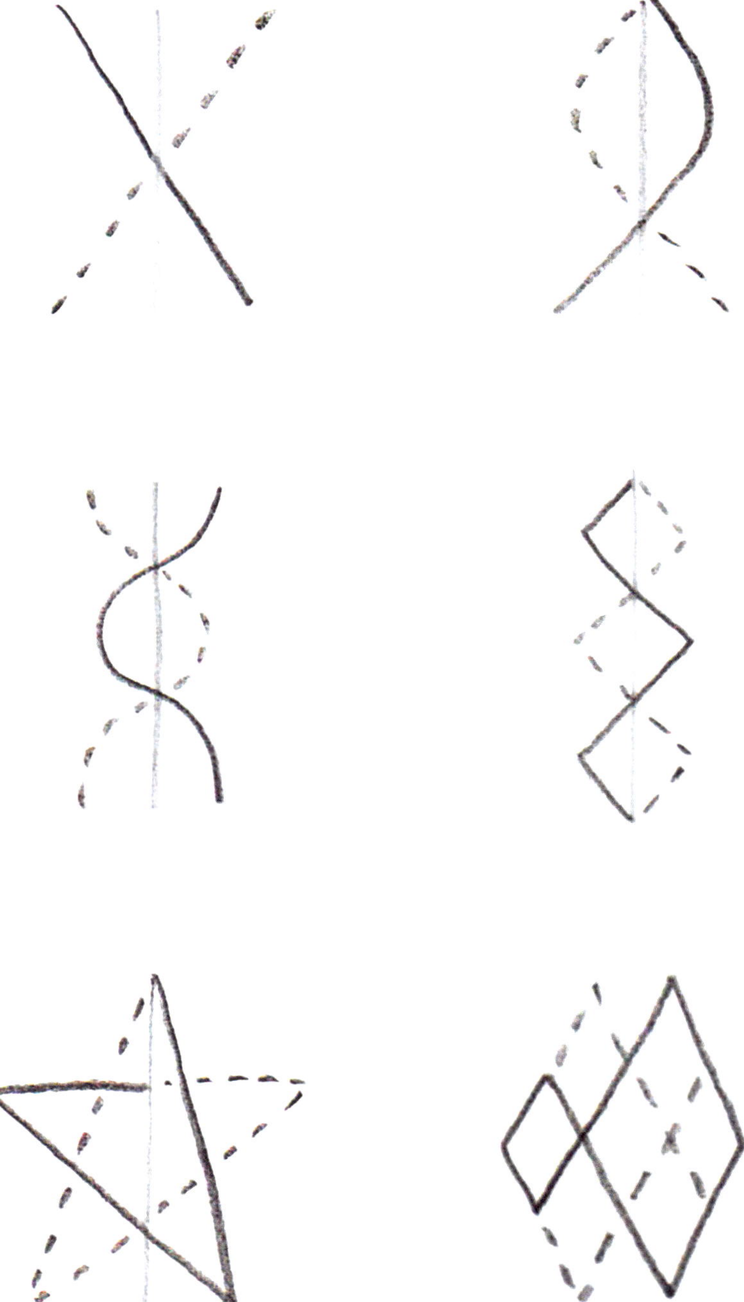

Horizontal and vertical mirror

Here, mirroring is shown on both horizontal and vertical planes.

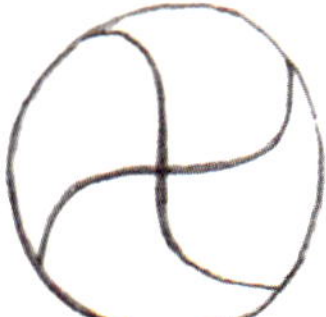
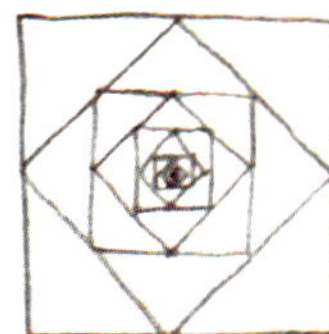
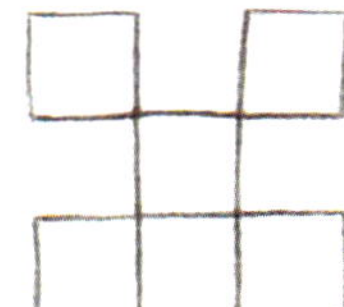

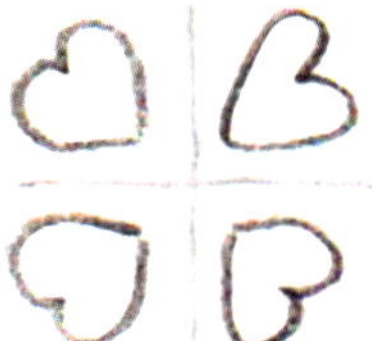
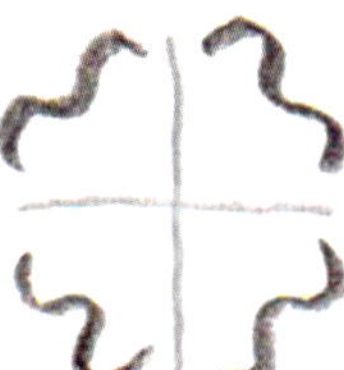

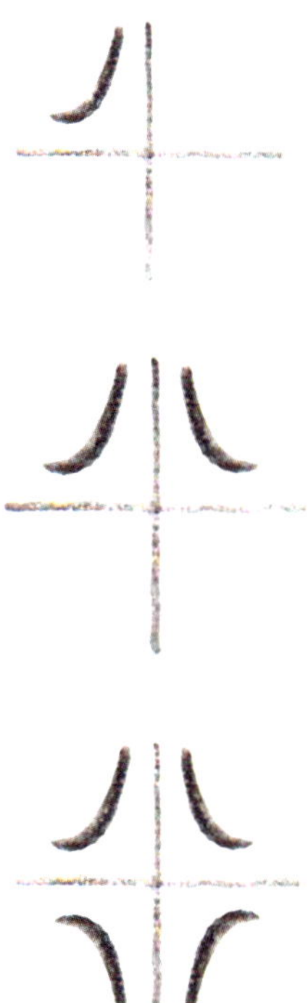

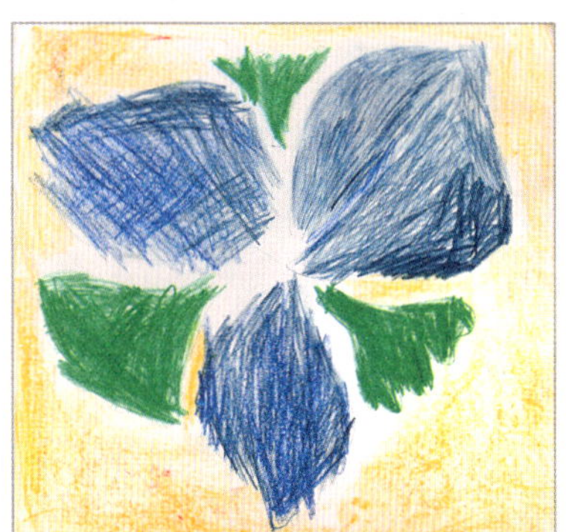
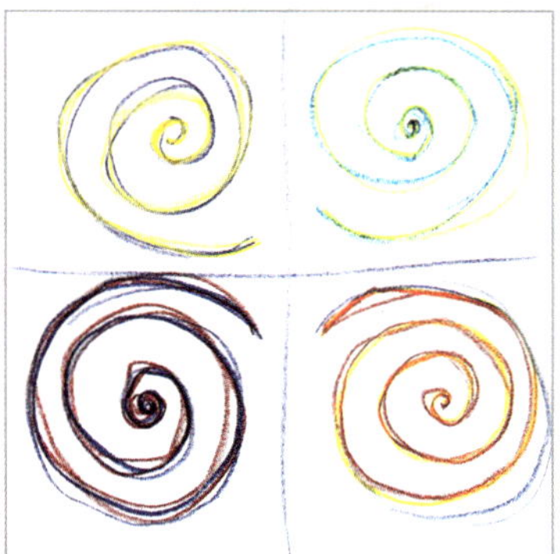

Central point symmetry

You can also practise symmetry around
a central point, as shown.

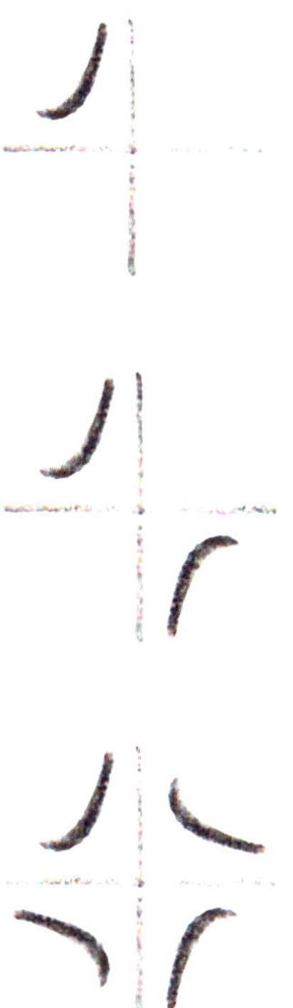

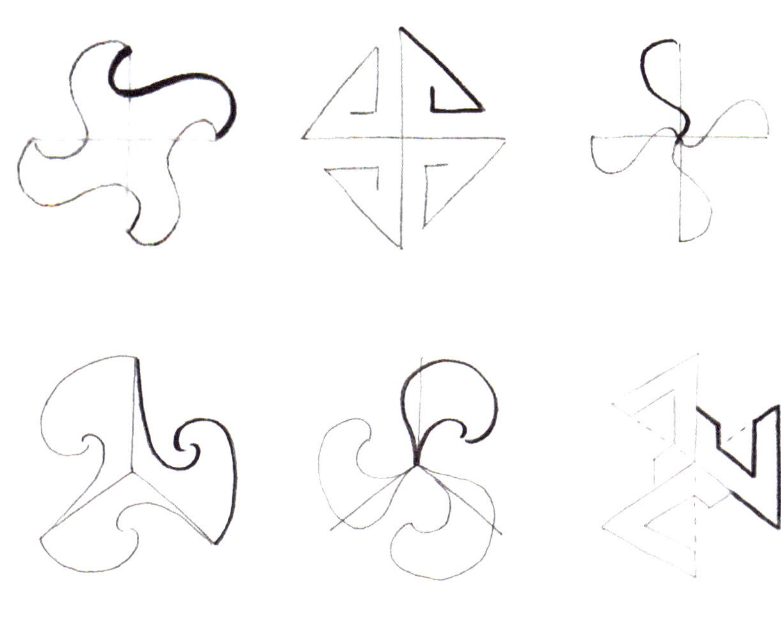

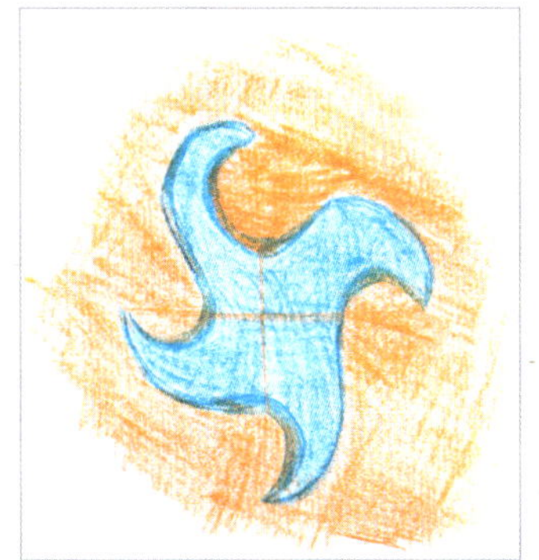

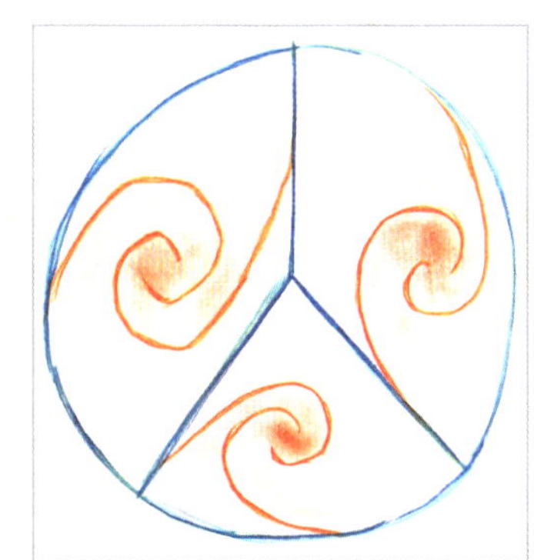

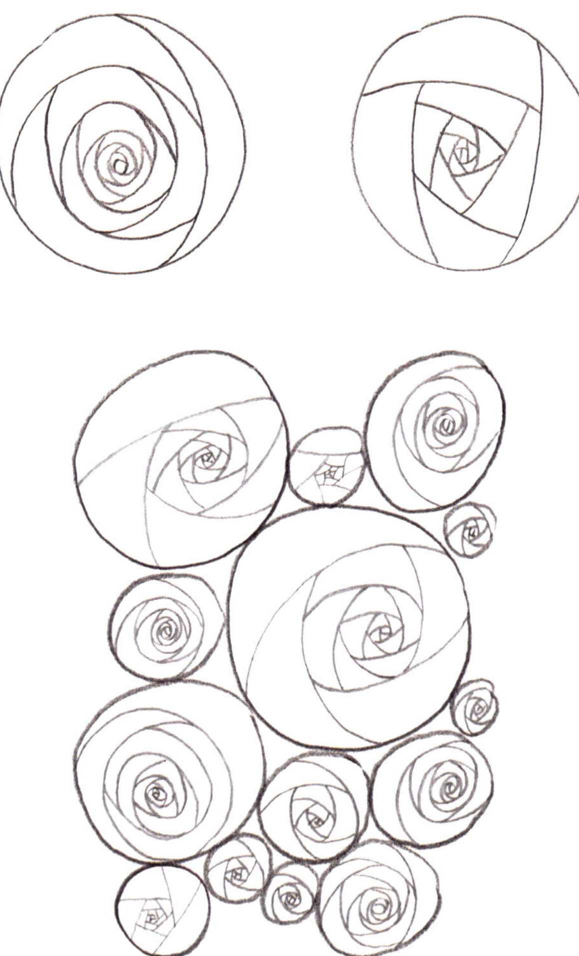

Flowers

Draw a circle, and then continue the line so that a 'crescent moon' shape appears. (The crescent can vary in width.) Begin your next line in the midpoint of the crescent moon to create another one, and continue inwards in this way until it is natural to stop.

Many pupils will understand the method of construction simply by looking at a demonstration on the blackboard, but some pupils might need verbal assistance from you during their first attempts.

Build up a whole bouquet of flowers.

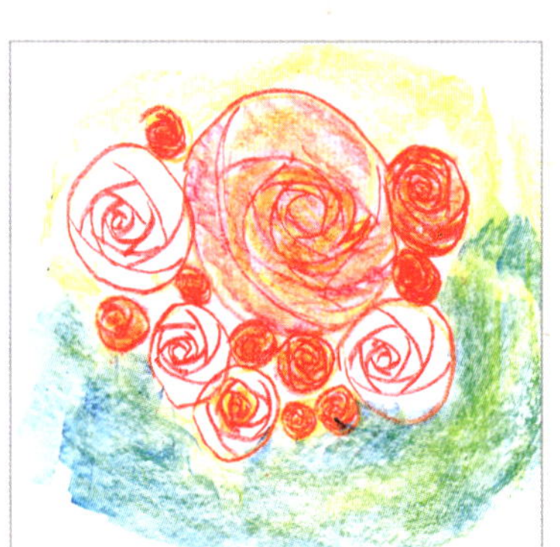

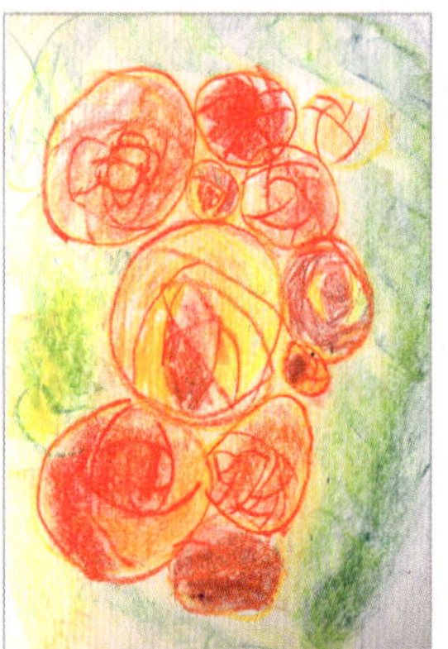

Draw loops that intersect at the same point to make 'petals', as shown top left. Continue doing this until a beautiful flower appears. Remember to tell your pupils to make all the petal loops the same size, for the sake of practice.

You can repeat the exercise using different-sized loops (top right). Or explore different possibilities, such as drawing loops that meet at the top at the same point (lower left).

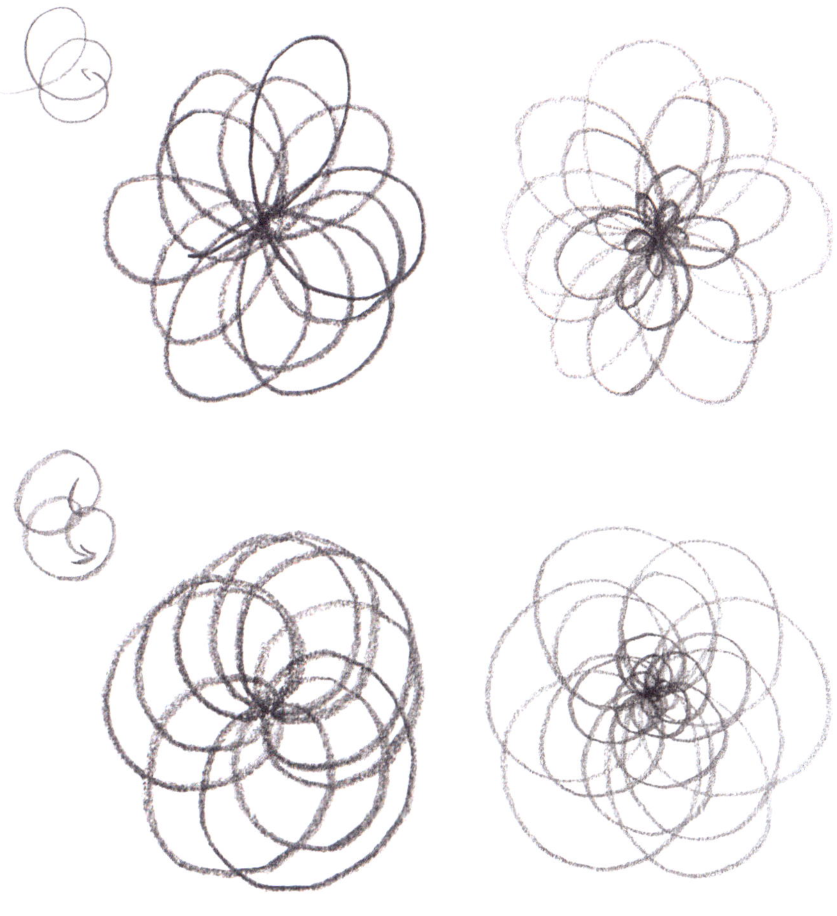

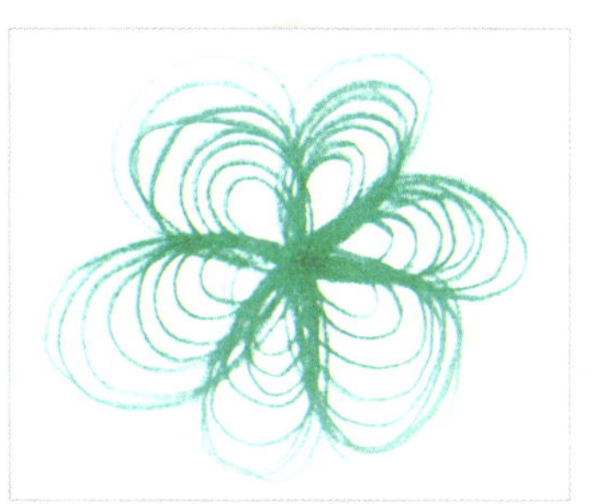

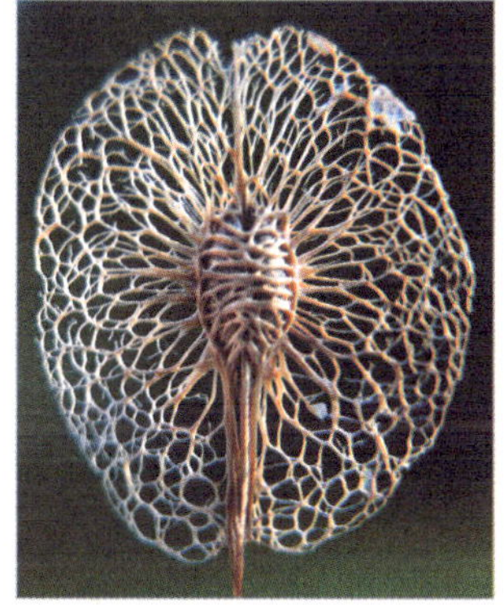

Seeds

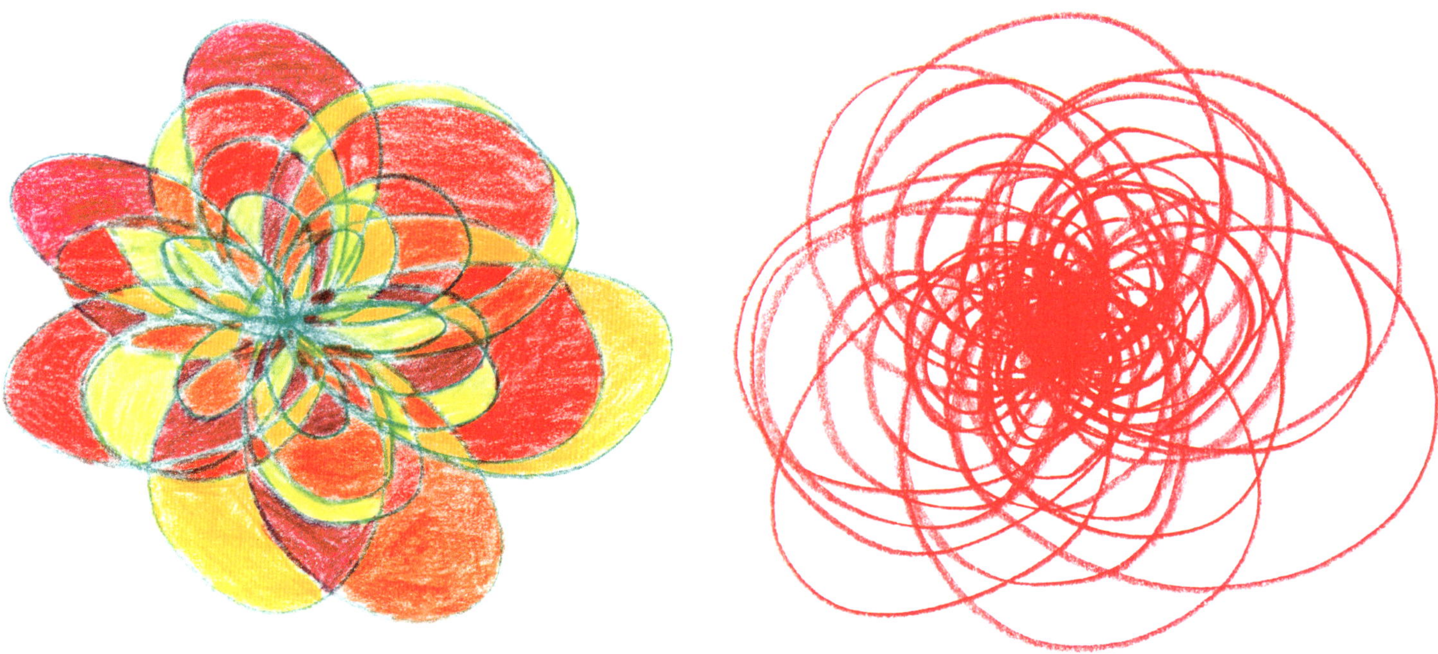

Pupils' work, Class 4

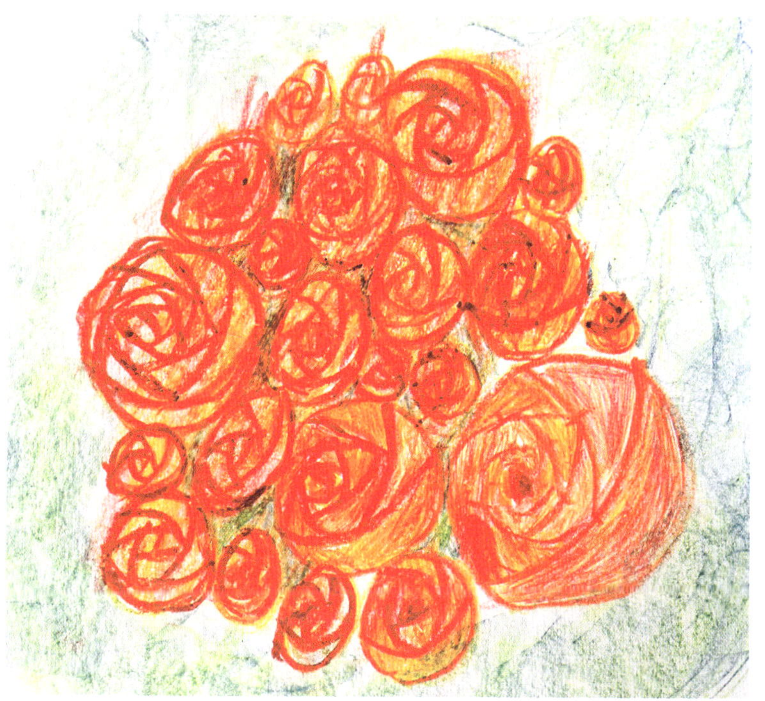

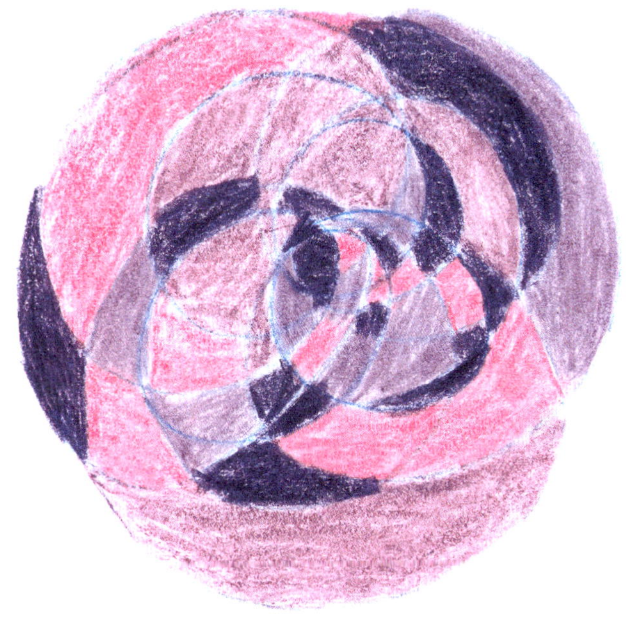

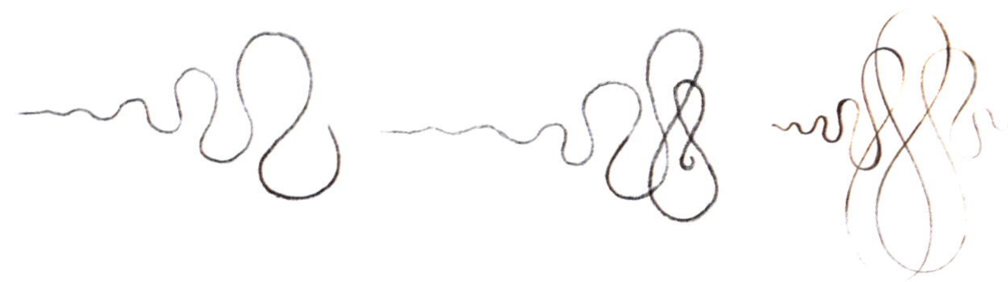

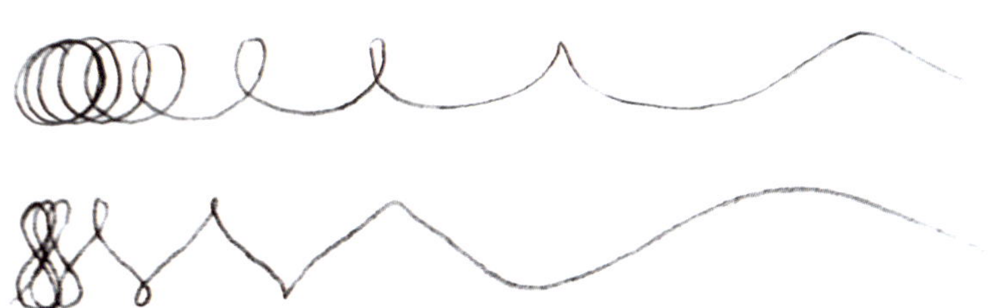

Metamorphoses

In these exercises we will metamorphose forms. First, let a line develop rhythmically, up and down or from side to side, varying your pace.

Next, draw a circle or a figure of eight a few times, without moving your hand. Then move your hand to one side, first slowly and then gradually speeding up.

Play with a U shape, or let a circle gradually curve in on itself and out the other side, as shown in the lower examples. Use colours to show how what was once on the outside gradually transfers to the inside – and vice versa. One way of approaching the circle exercise is to draw all stages of the process before the lesson on separate sheets, then ask your pupils to put them in the right order.

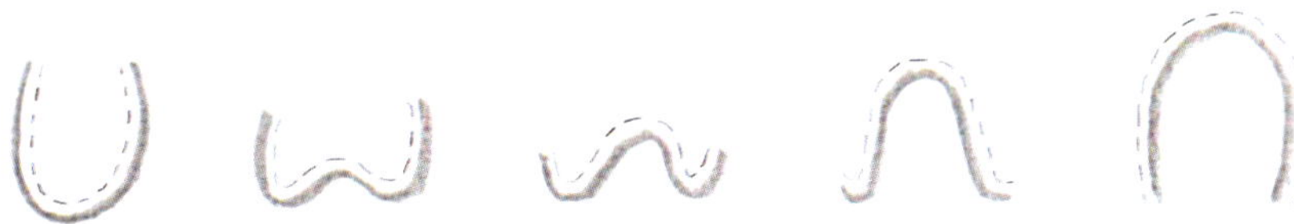

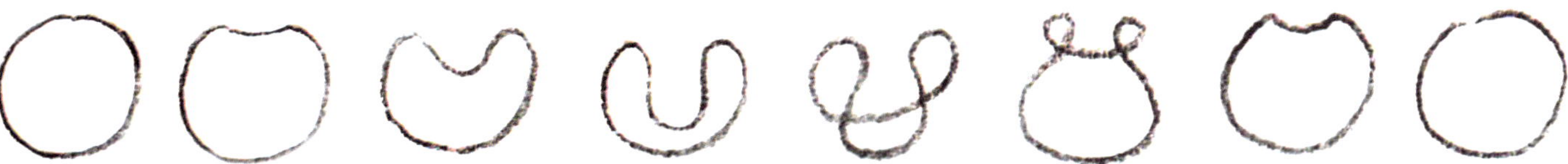

It is difficult to progress from the metamorphoses shown on the upper right to those below, so instruct your pupils to practise on small blackboards or paper before copying them into their workbooks.

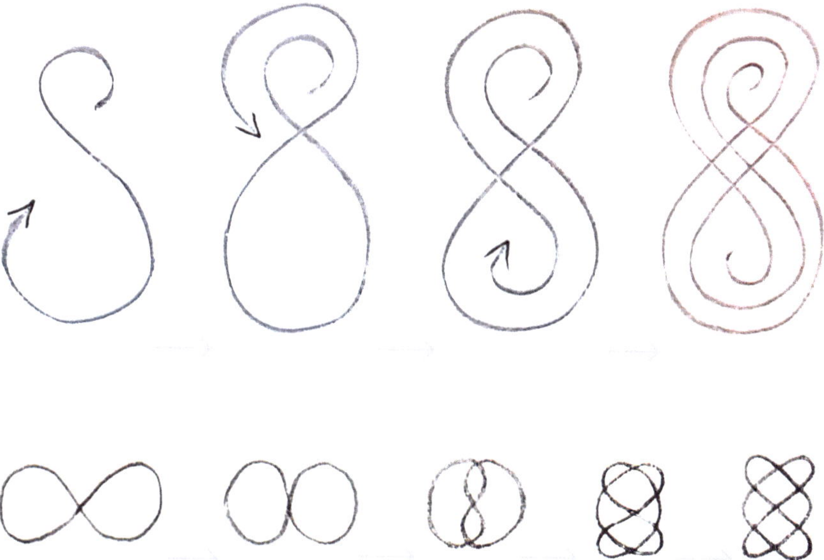

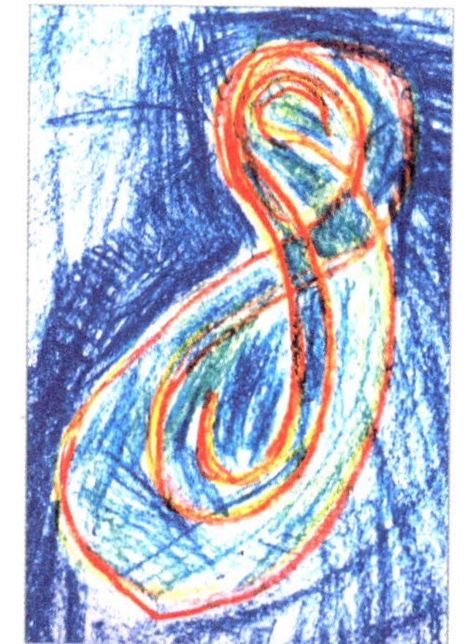

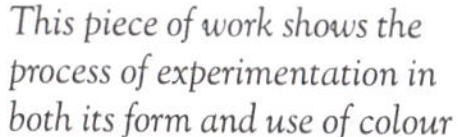

This piece of work shows the process of experimentation in both its form and use of colour

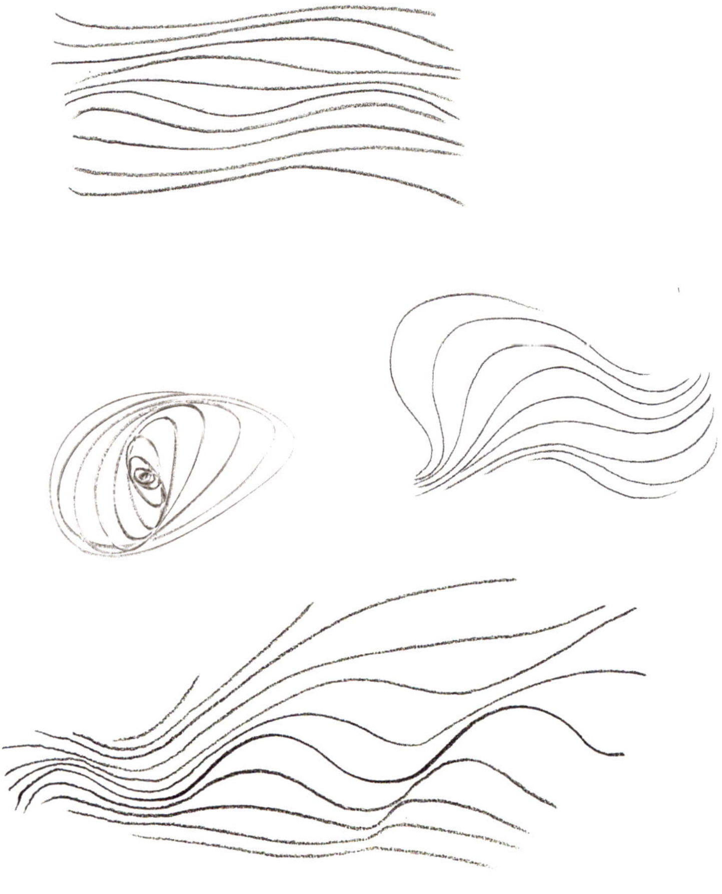

These exercises explore free-form transformations. Start anywhere on the page and allow a wave or irregularities to develop. Let pupils judge for themselves when their drawing is finished. Talk to them about why they decided to stop at that point.

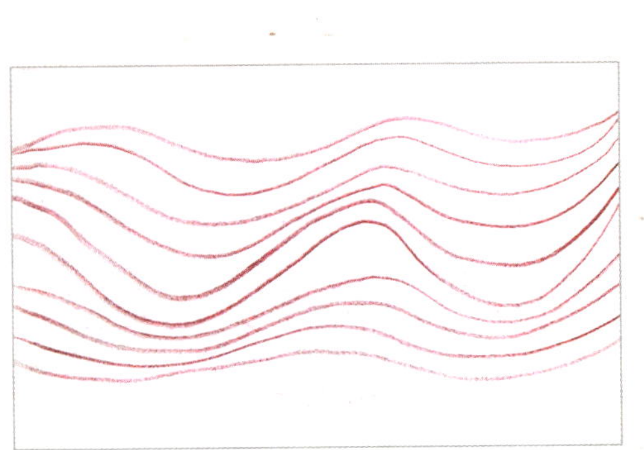

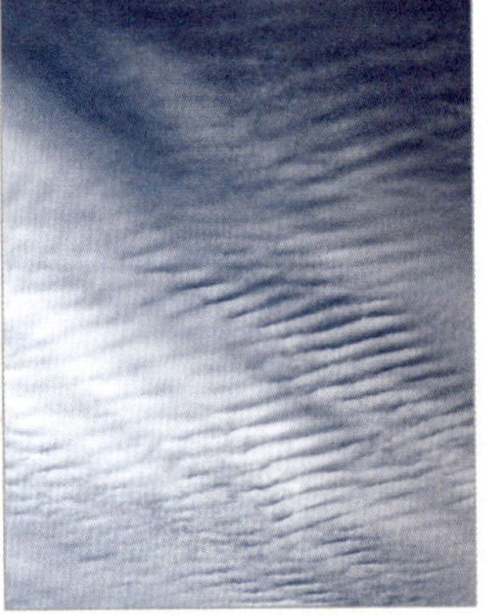

Cirrocumulus or herringbone clouds

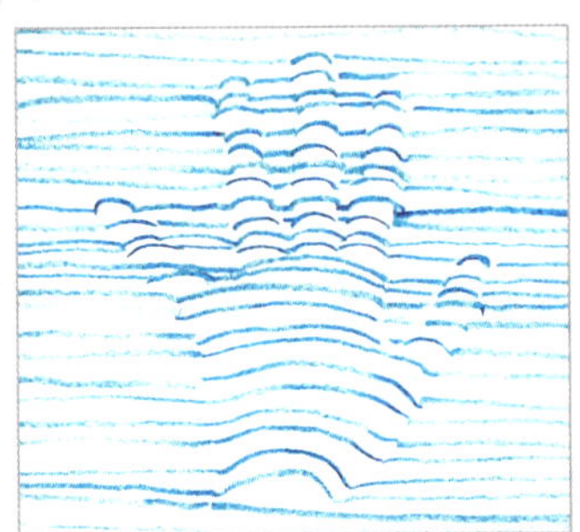

The illustration to the left is the result of a pupil's experiment. They placed their hand on a sheet of paper and drew around it with a faint line. The horizontal lines were drawn in afterwards and curved each time one entered the space where the fingers were originally

Now try these transformations. Start drawing a small ring. After several turns, create a small swelling to make a new form arise. Follow its course closely before adding more undulating elements.

In the exercise below, draw a square, and then inside draw another, smaller square at an angle so that each of the corners of the inner square touch the sides of the original square. Repeat this as far as possible. Finally, set four or more of your completed squares together, as shown.

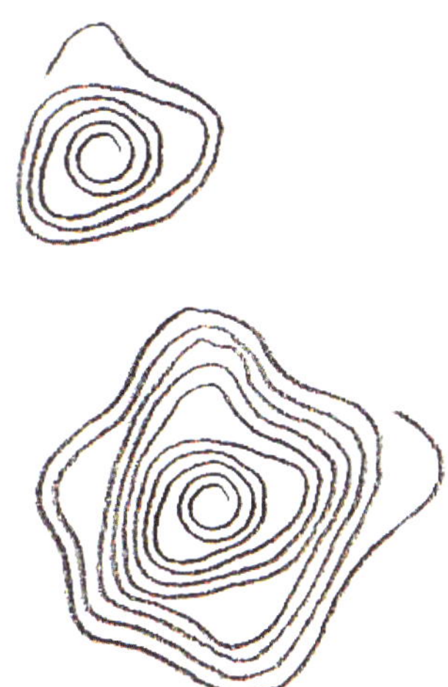

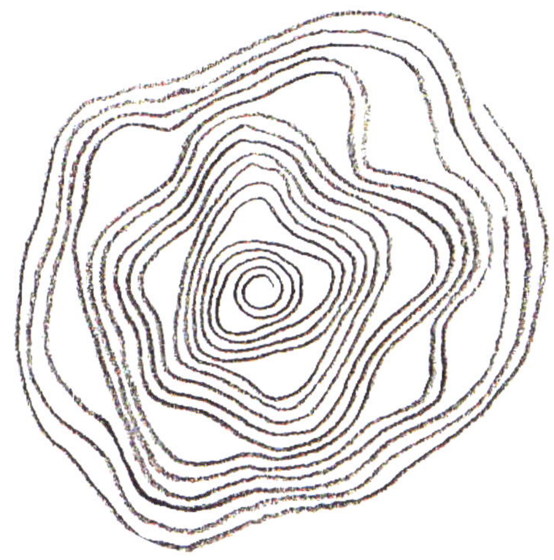

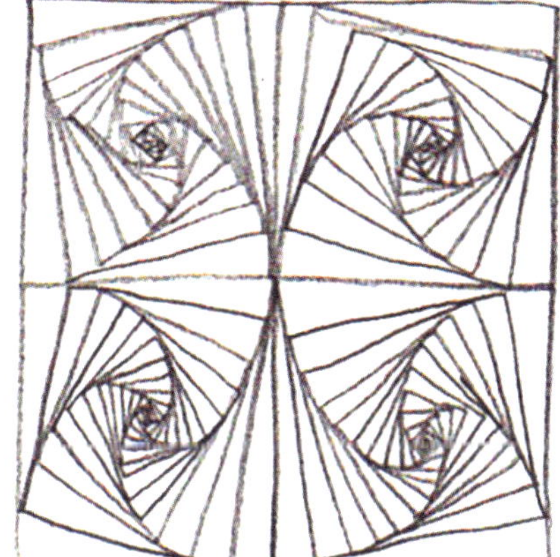

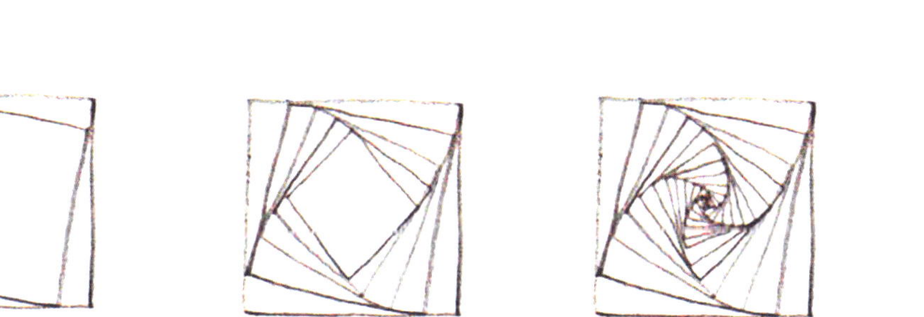

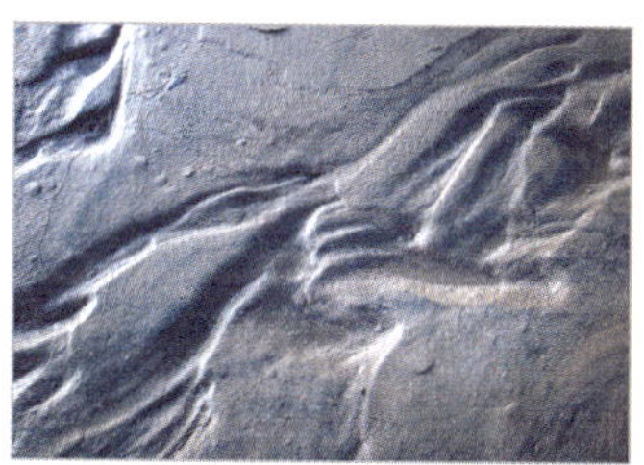

Tracks from running water in sand

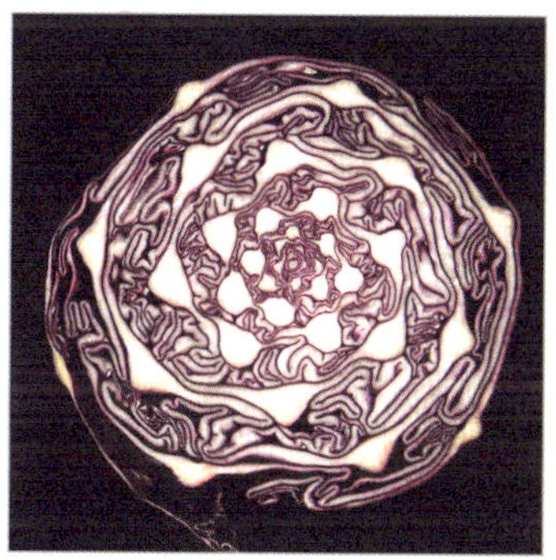

Sliced red cabbage

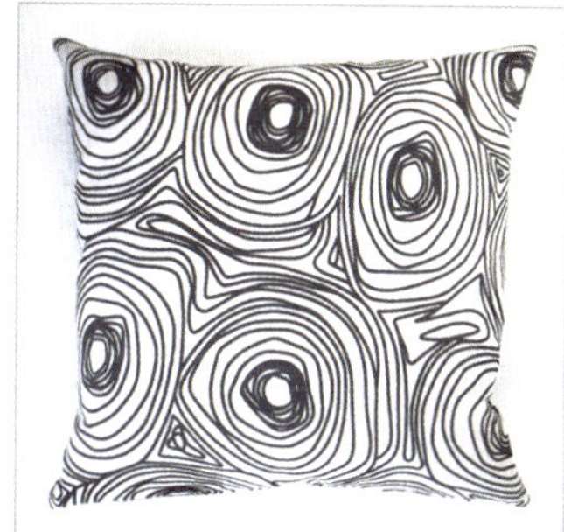

Decorations on a cushion, Museum of Contemporary Art, Oslo

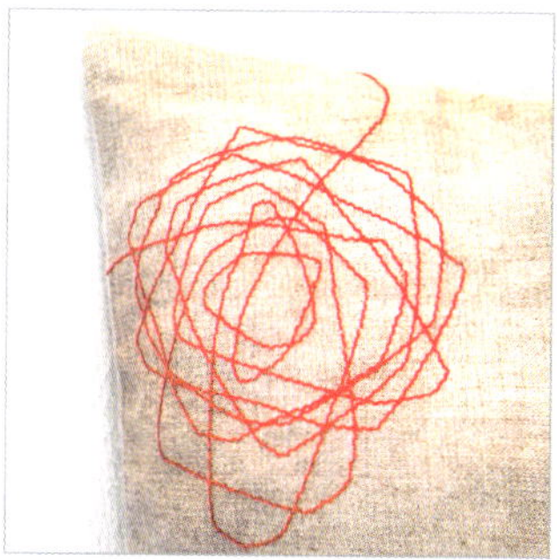

Embroidery on a cushion, Museum of Contemporary Art, Oslo

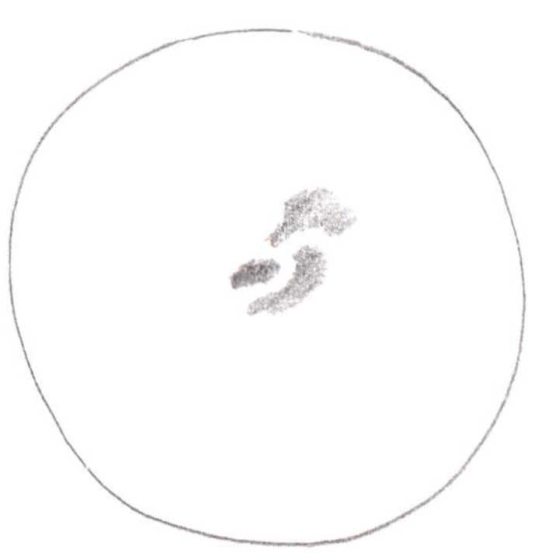

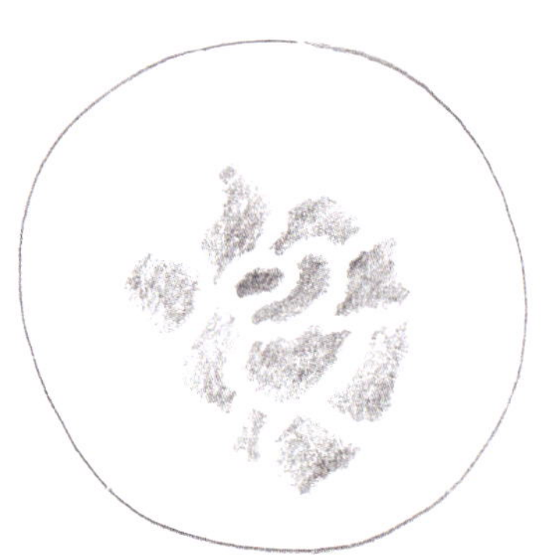

Self-organising patterns

These structures are built around one form. In the example, a circle acts as the boundary for a non-figurative form to be drawn in the middle. Draw more forms, keeping them equidistant from one another. Finally, define all the figures with a heavy outline.

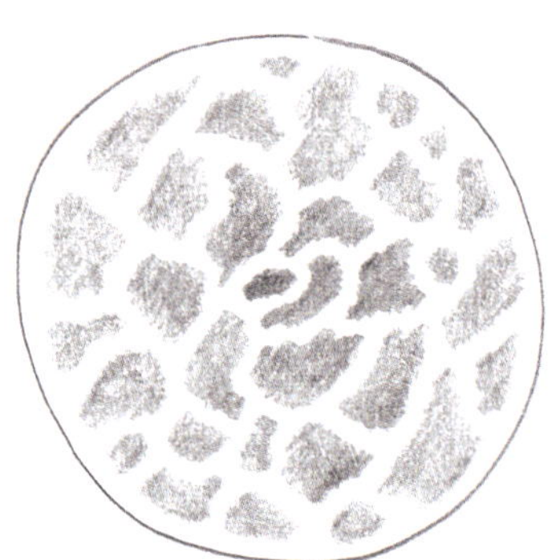

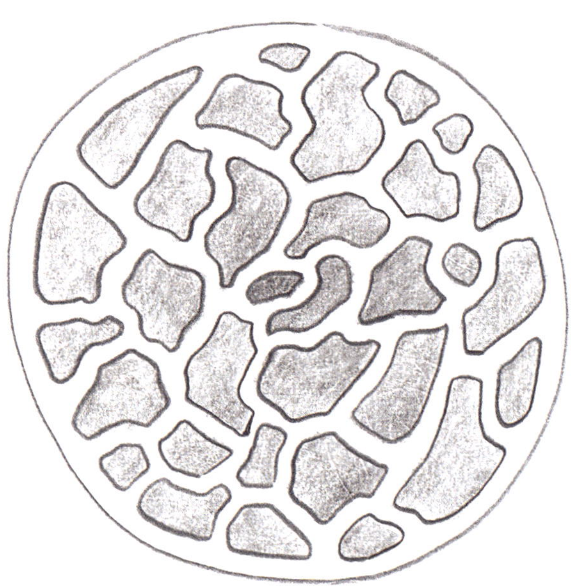

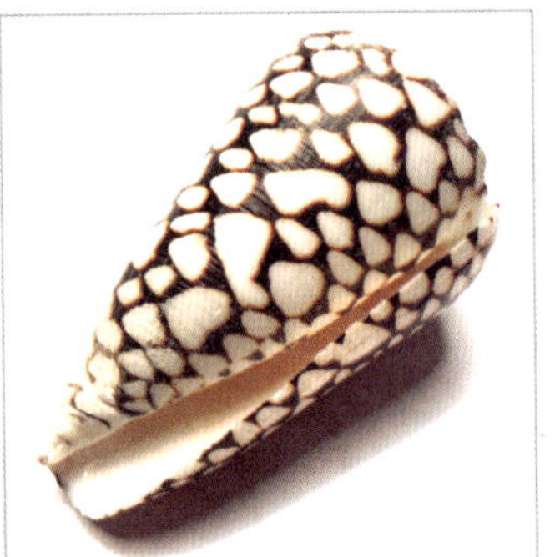

Snail shell

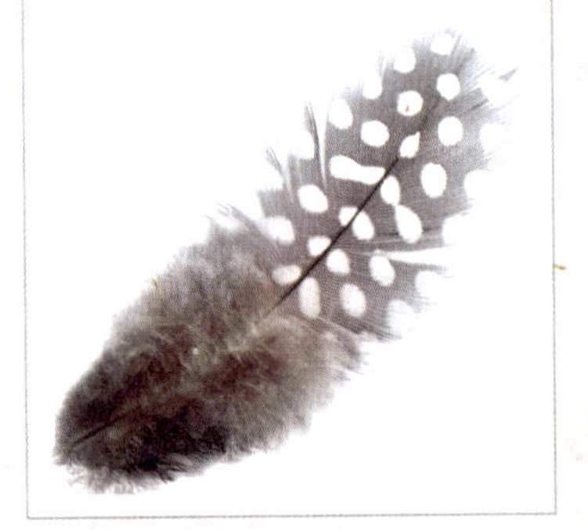

Guinea fowl feather

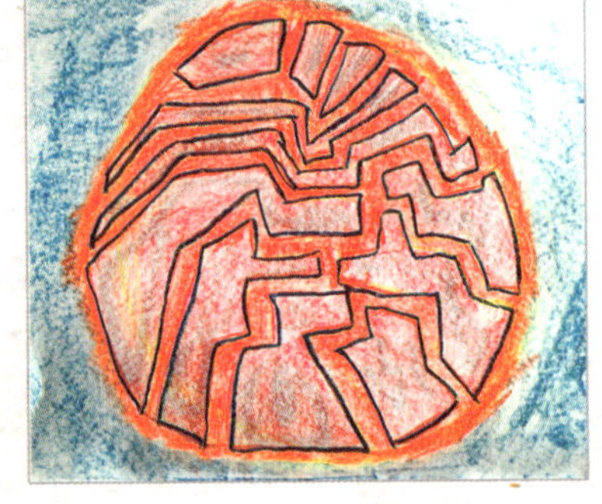

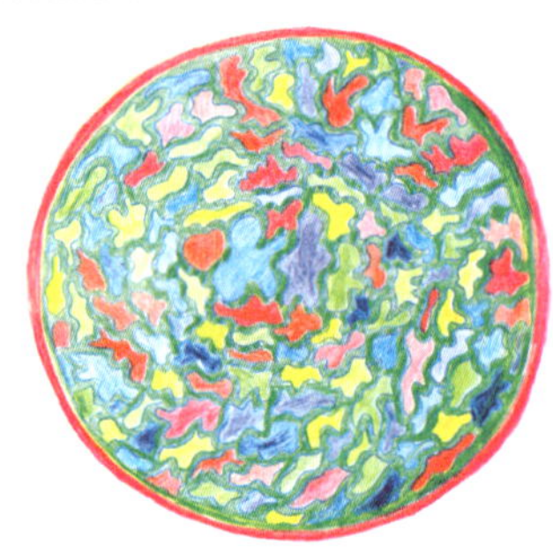

In nature, so-called self-organising patterns or dissipative structures occur under a variety of circumstances. We see evidence of this in the photographs below in ice on water after a frosty night, on the bark of a pine tree, on zebra skin and when snow is driven across the ice.

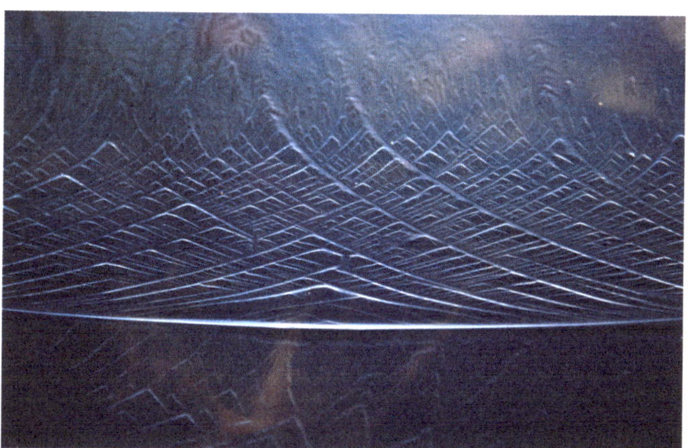
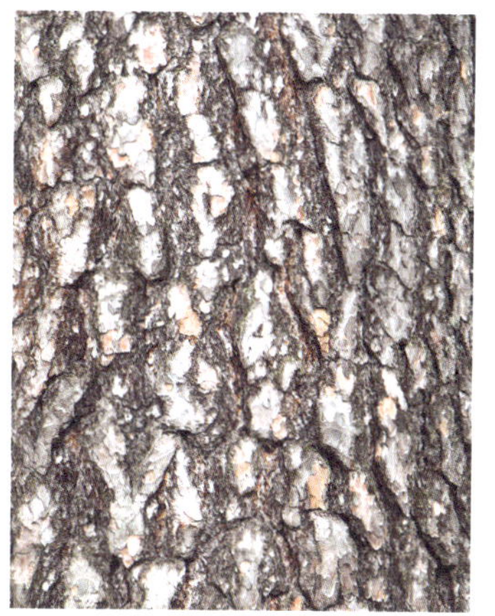
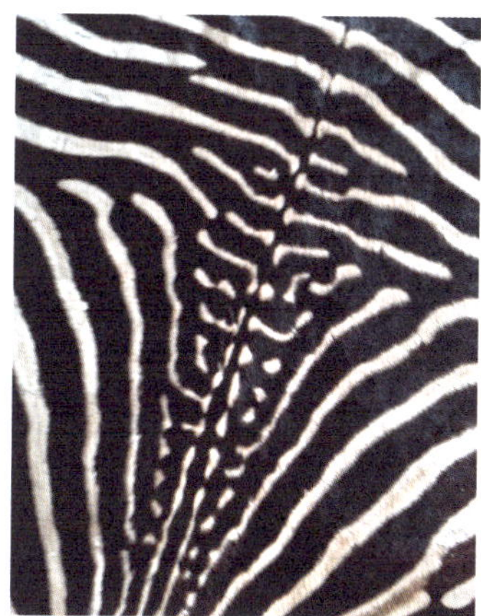

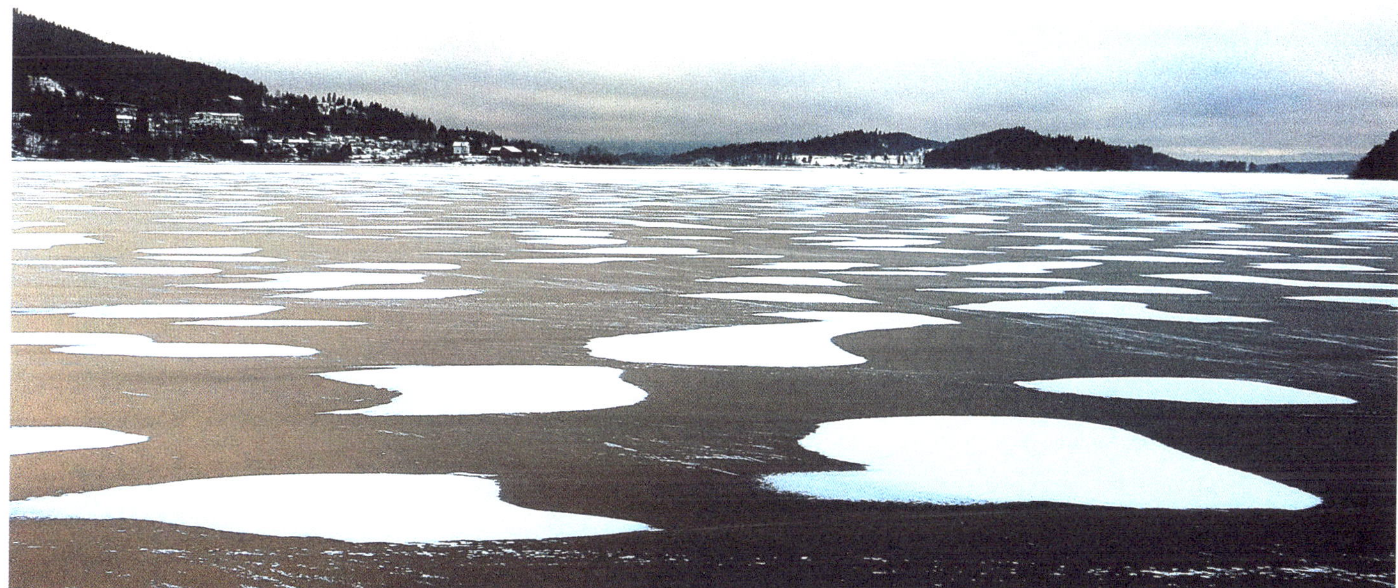

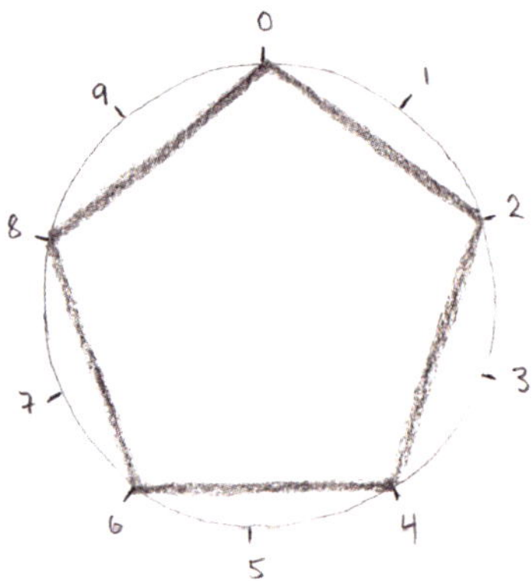

The two and eight times tables

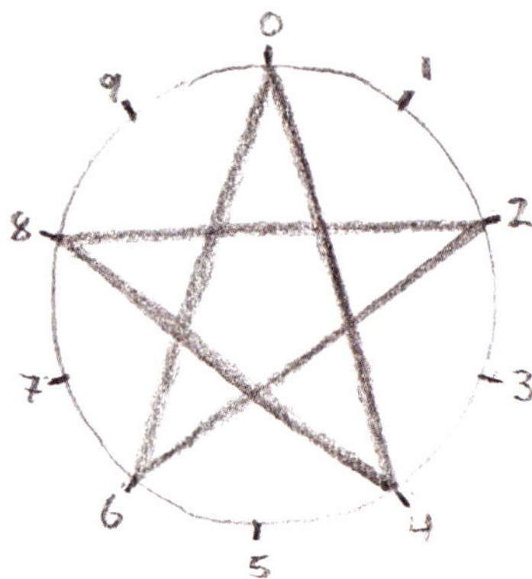

The four and six times tables

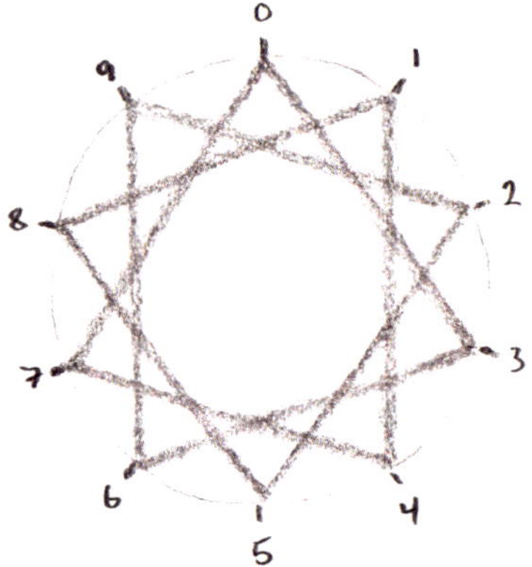

The three and seven times tables

Multiplication tables

Multiplication tables can be explained visually. Mark points numbered 0 to 9 on a circle. To draw the two times table, as shown in the first example, draw a line from zero to two, the first multiple of the times table, then from the two to the four, and so on. Observe the form that emerges. If this is done for all multiplication tables, it becomes clear that each one has a form.

When the number is more than ten, use the final digit (for example, for number 11, it is the final 1 that is relevant).

On the left we see some examples. What would the nine and five times tables look like?

Ask pupils to discover which multiplication tables have the same form. It is interesting and surprising, and easy to get excited about the aesthetics of numbers.

In Class 3 we learned how to display multiplication tables as a row of numbers (see p.84). The next exercise takes this idea further, this time using the decimal scale. Begin with 0 and jump to the next number on the line as far as this is possible. Then jump back to the digit that is now the last digit in the number (as before, when you reach numbers higher than 10, only the final digit is relevant). For example, the 3 times table works like this: 3 − 6 − 9 − 12 − 15 − 18 − 21 − 24 − 27 − 30

Do any of the multiplication tables have the same form? Ask pupils to find out.

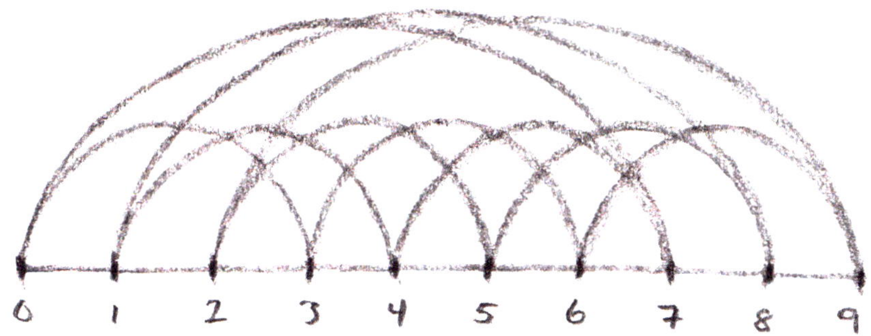

The three and seven times tables

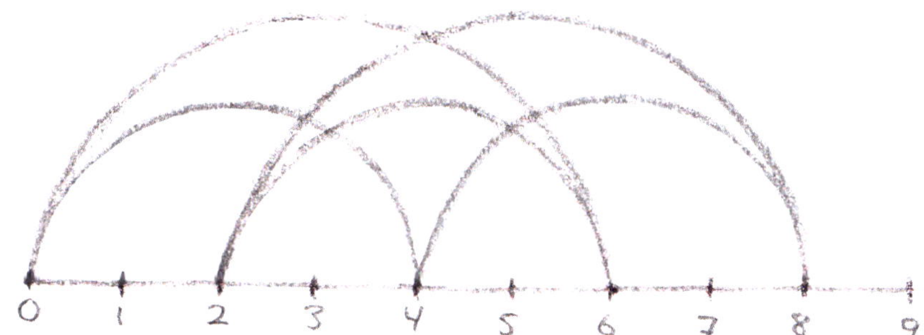

The four and six times tables

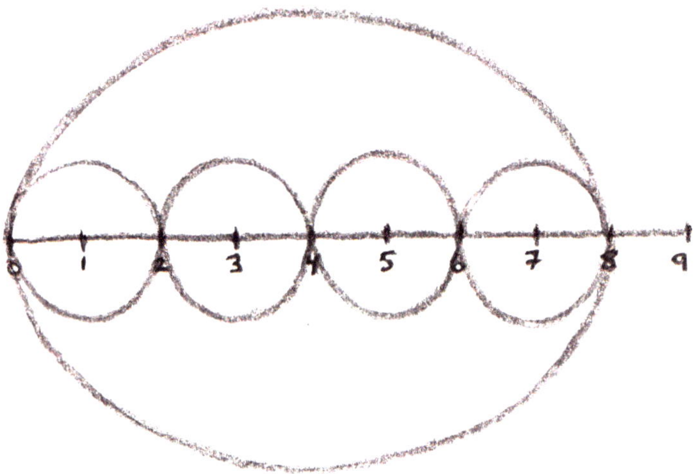

The two and eight times tables

An awareness of space is inherently connected to mathematics, and these exercises will help to strengthen pupils' ability to think mathematically.

A new form occurs when the numbers are drawn using arches alternately over and under a line numbered from 0 to 9. Draw the first arch above the line. Ask your pupils to explore the similarities in the forms that appear.

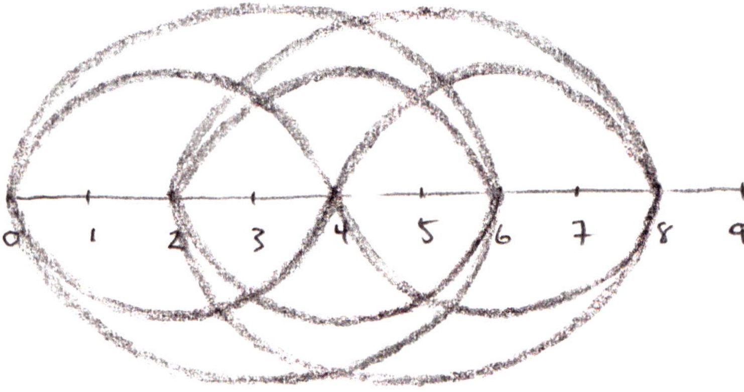

The four and six times tables

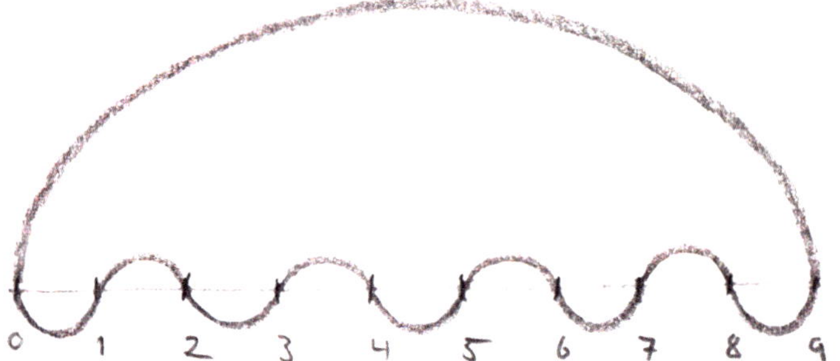

The nine times table

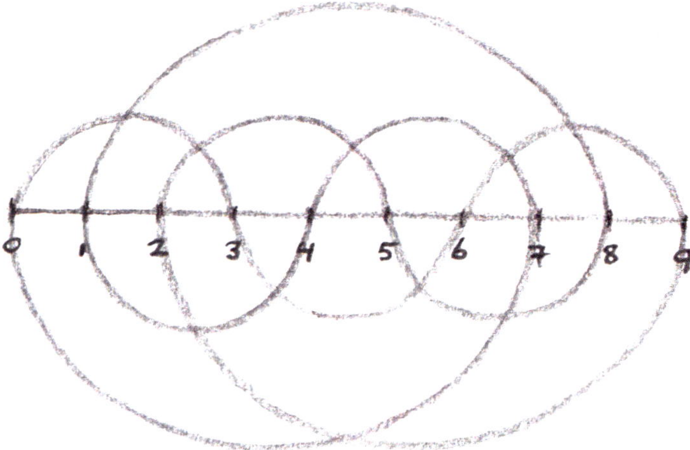

The three times table

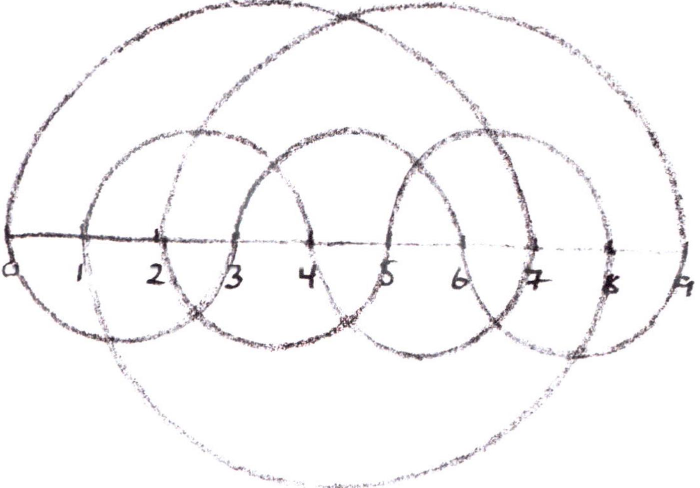

The seven times table

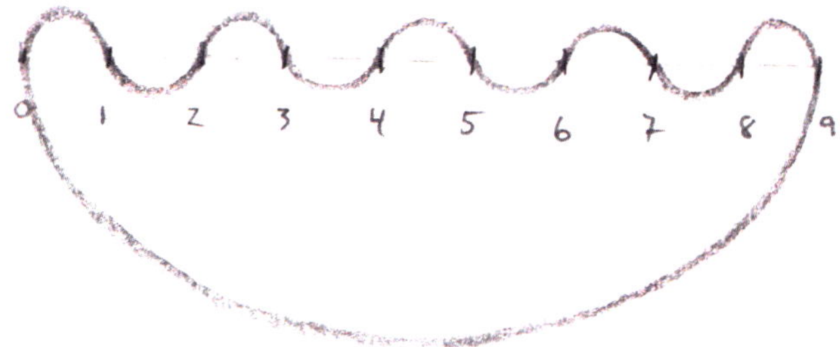

The one times table

Part 5: Class 5 Exercises

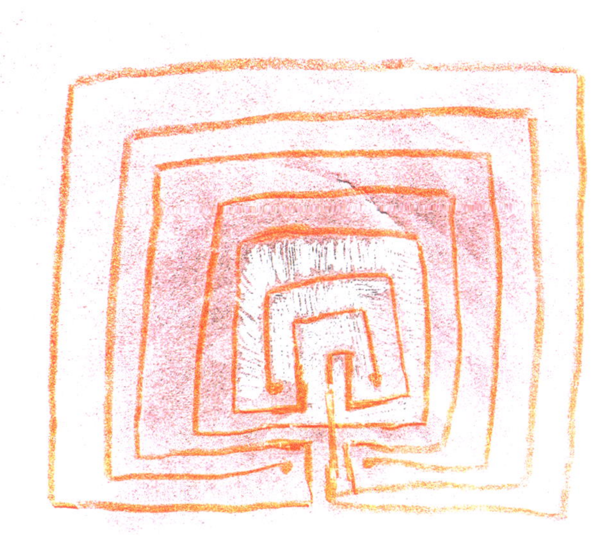

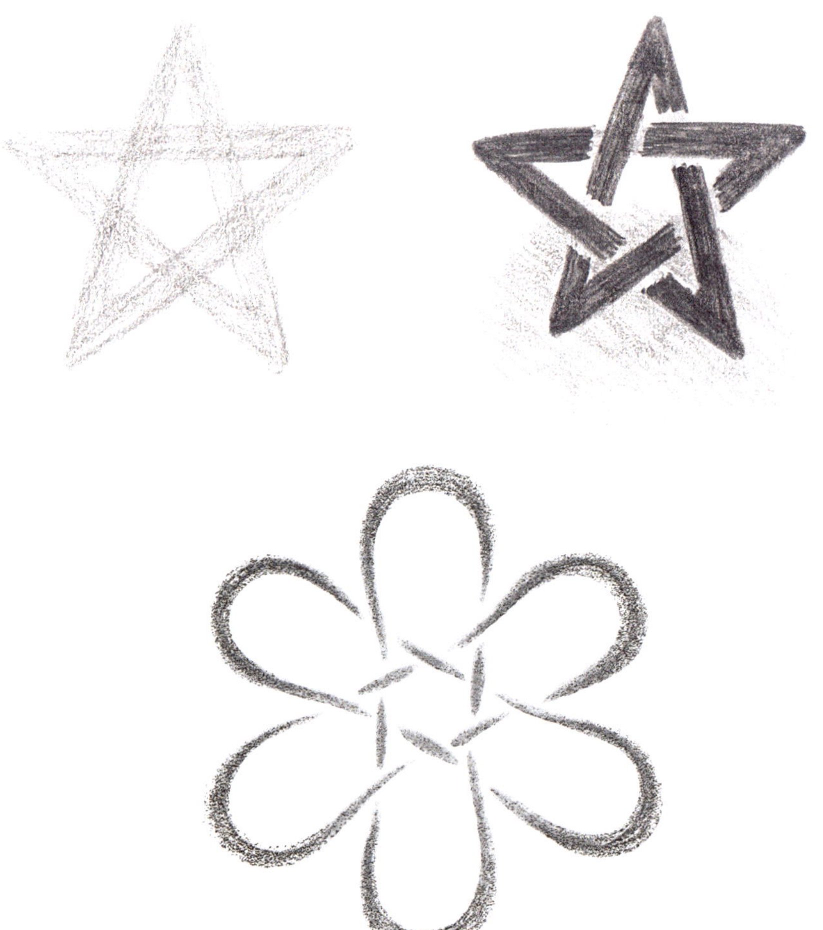

Plaiting

Plaiting requires planning and accuracy. Before drawing, decide on a background colour, which should be paler than the colour used for the figure. Draw the form on the paper lightly in pencil. Next, using the colour you have chosen for the figure, start plaiting: over and under, over and under. Cover the surrounding area with the background colour until the pencilled guidelines disappear.

Will the end result look 'correct' if you plait alternately over and under? If a pupil finds that this doesn't work, ask them to check carefully that they have gone over and under. It should always work.

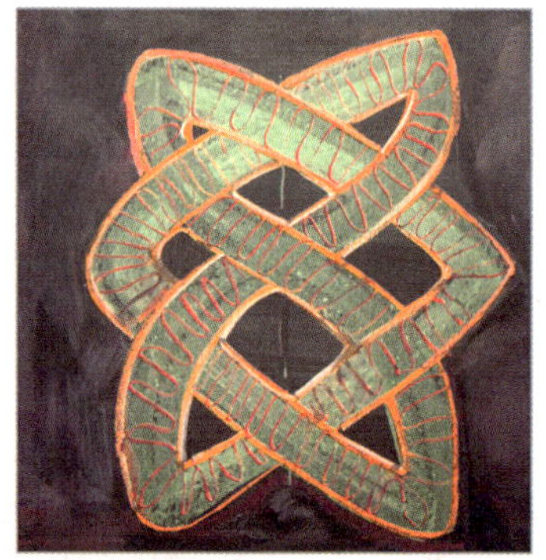

Blackboard drawing

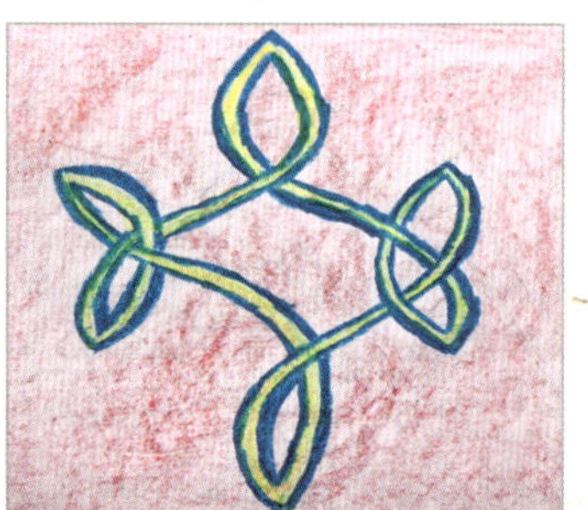

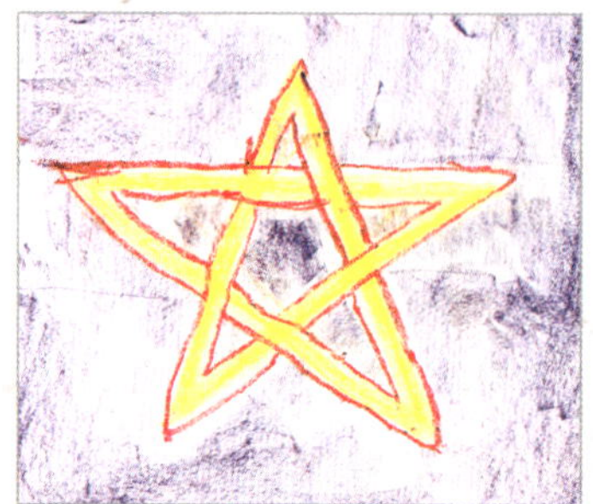

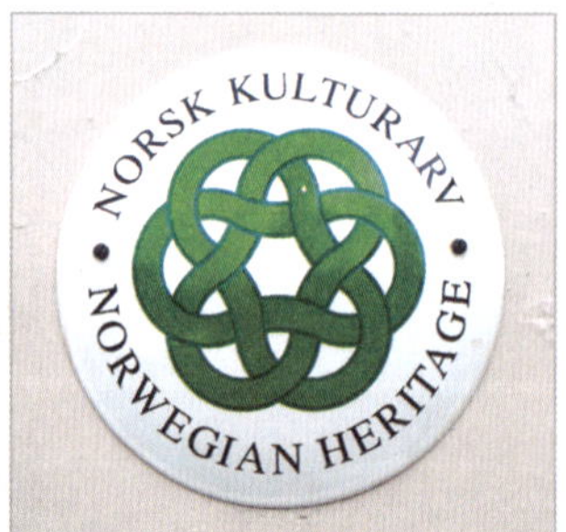

Decorations

Simple or complex plaits can be used for borders and corners. Encourage your pupils to experiment with different designs. Start using a simple form and build upon this by dividing lines and joining them together in new ways.

The three forms at the bottom of the page consist of two simple and identically formed lines (imagine using threads or rope to achieve the same results).

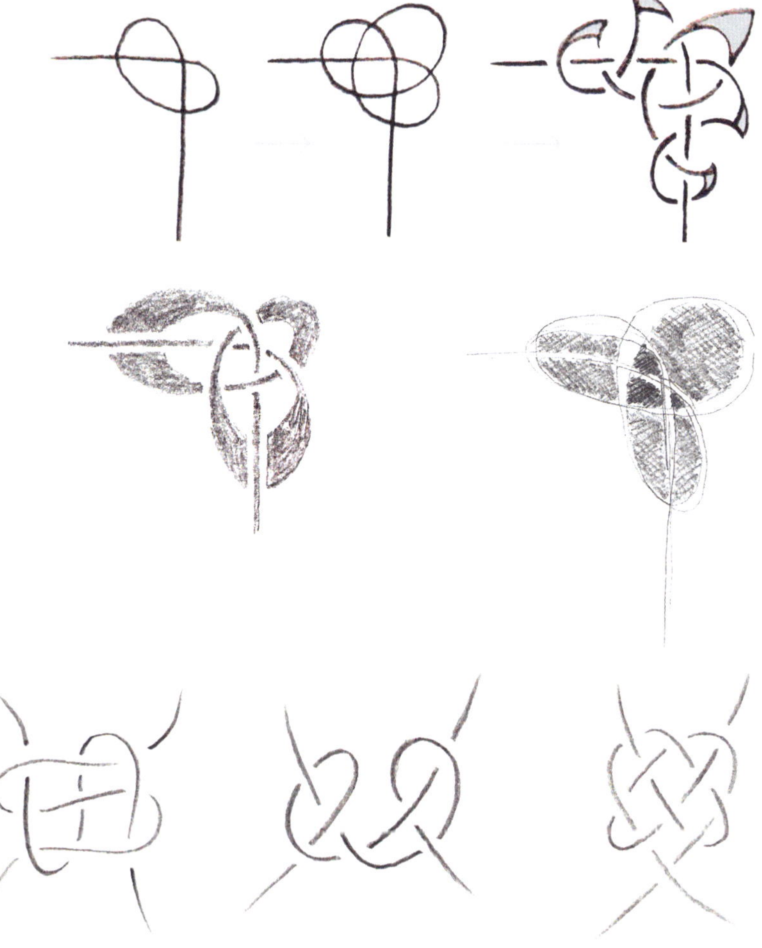

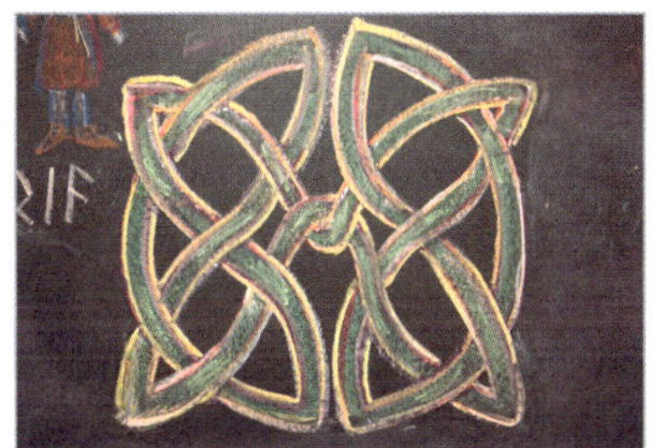

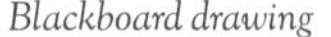

Blackboard drawing

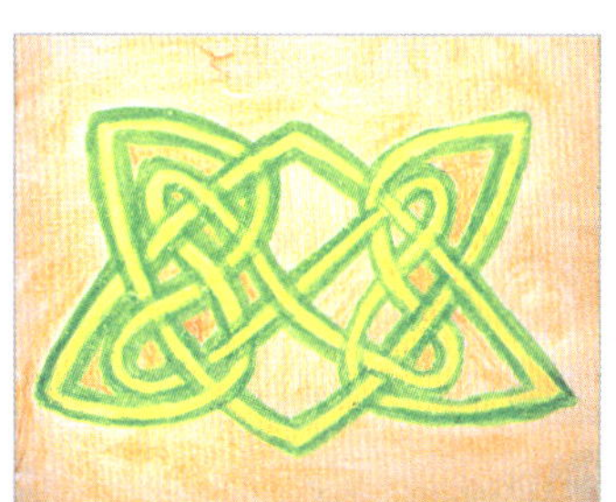

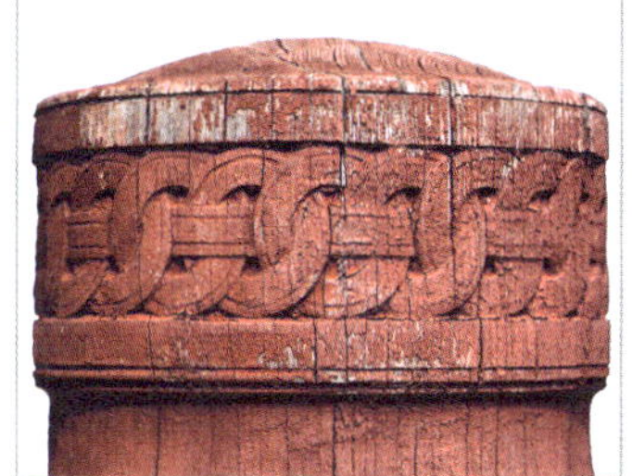

Decorative detail from pillar, Biri, Norway, 1901

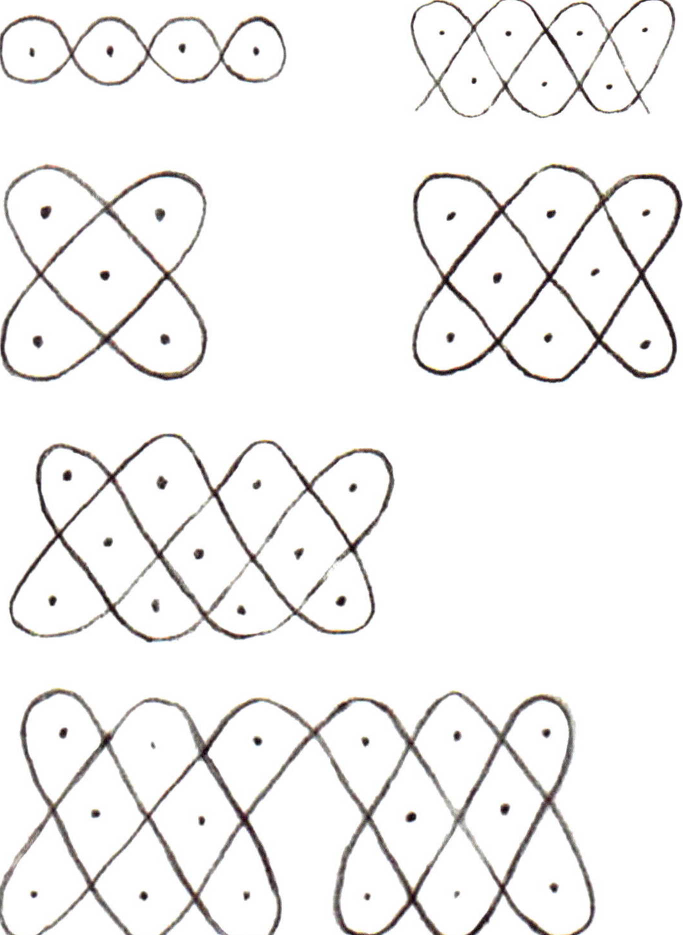

Plaited patterns

Experiment with one, two or three rows of dots. This is a continuation of a technique introduced in Class 4 (see p.94), but now ask your pupils to develop the form to make braided patterns.

When using two rows there will always be loose ends, while three rows result in one or more continuous lines. Allow pupils to discover this themselves if they haven't explored this area before. In this way they can discover additional and more advanced braided patterns.

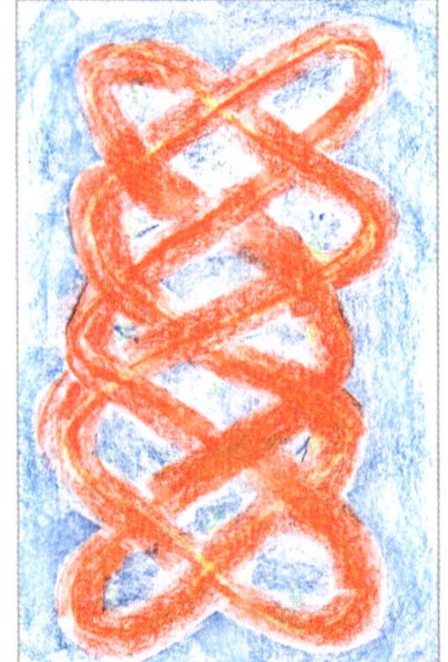

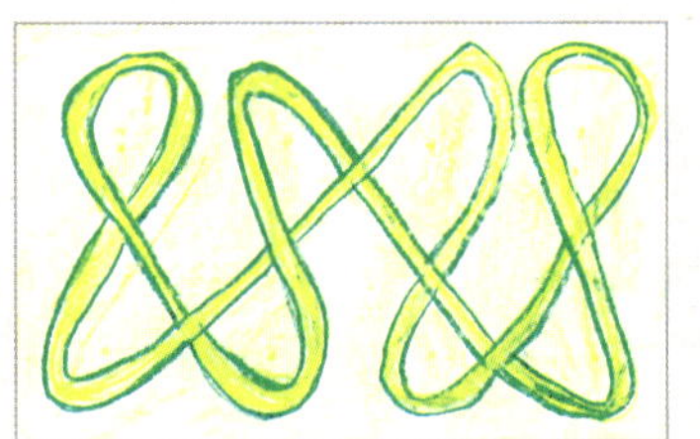

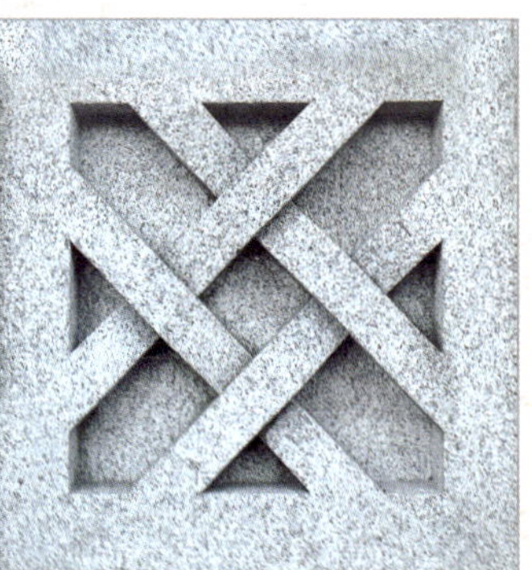

Ornamentation, Vigeland Park, Oslo

Aesthetic problem-solving

This is a demanding exercise, so try it out yourself first and then decide if your pupils are ready to attempt it. Refer back to the Class 4 exercise on p.94 to refresh your memory.

In class, allow pupils to sit together in problem-solving groups so they can deal with obstacles that arise. Ask pupils to draw this wavy line in a circle, then superimpose the same type of wavy line on top. The next step is to create examples using fewer waves: try eight, then seven, six, five and so on, for as long as this is possible.

Sculpting figures

Pupils can 'sculpt' figures in a pale colour before providing definition with edge lines and plaiting, as shown.

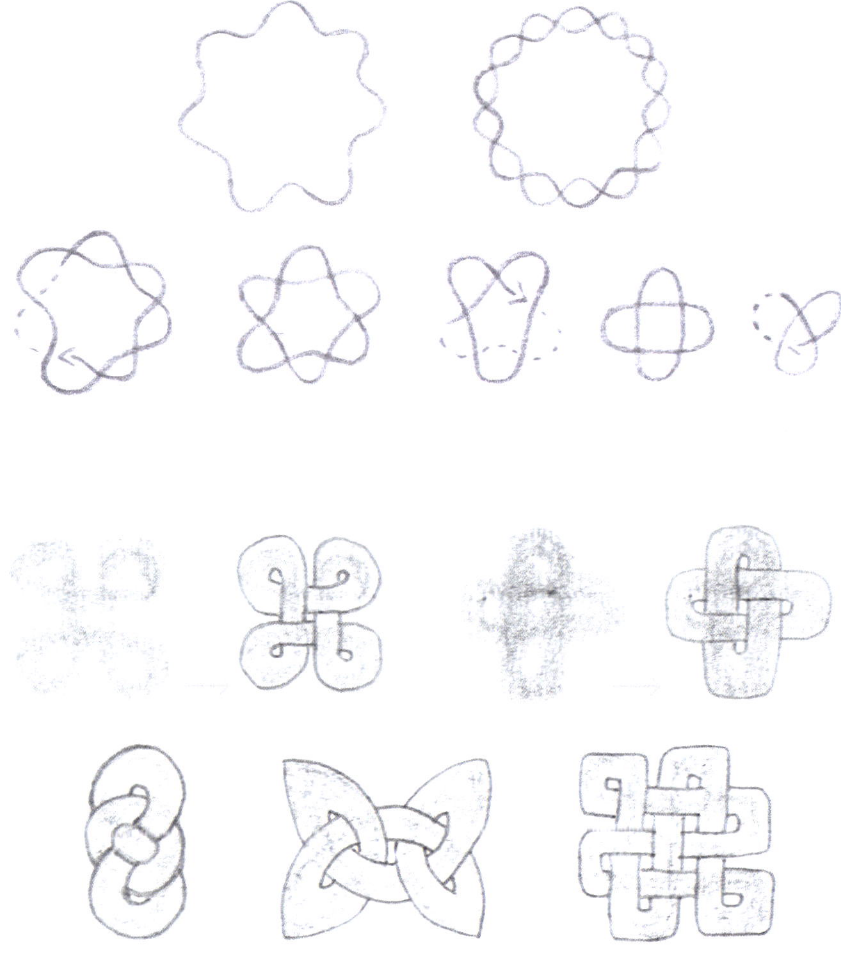

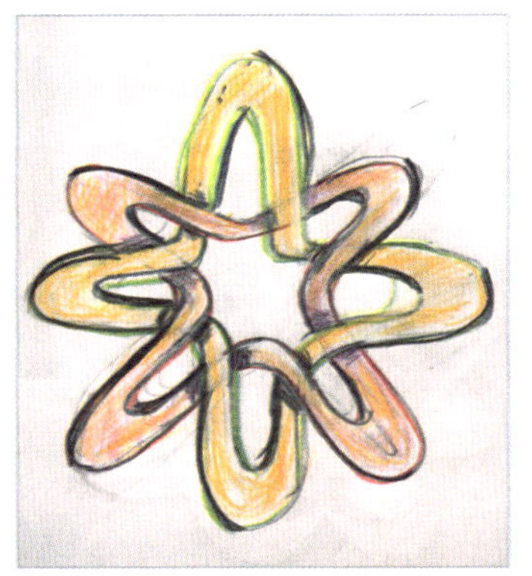

Eight-loop plaiting

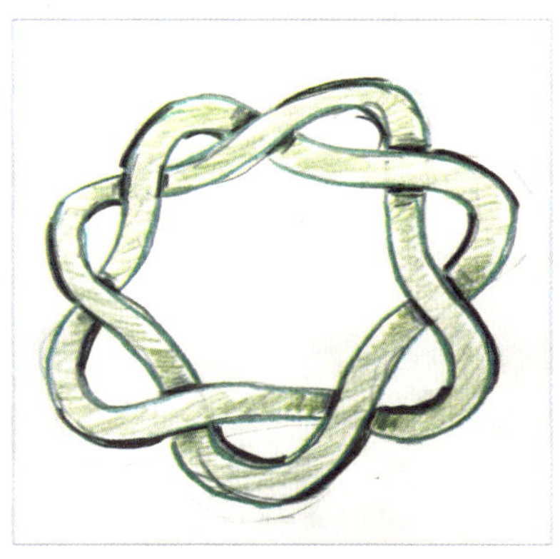

Seven-loop plaiting

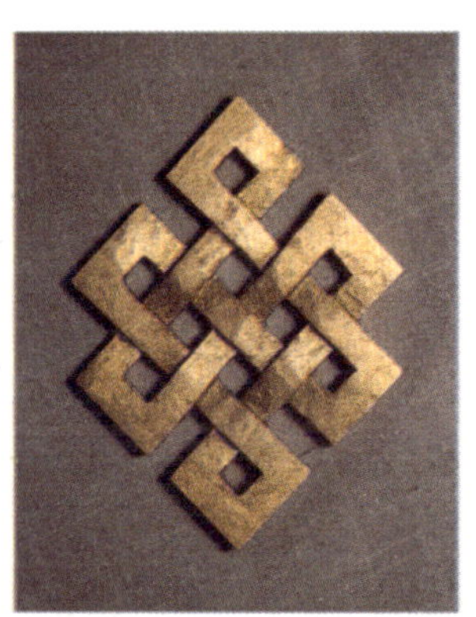

Wooden carved jewellery

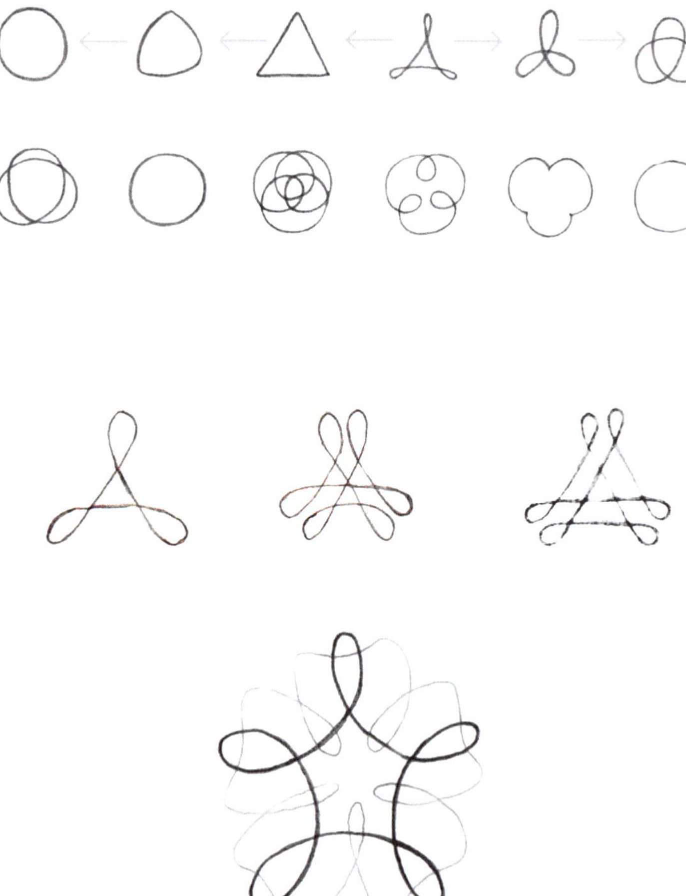

Metamorphoses

Start with the fourth figure in the top row and transform it in both directions, as shown. Allow your pupils to try themselves and see how far they get. They may have done a similar exercise in Class 4 (see pp.90–91), but now they will be able to take it further. Let them work together once the task is complete to discuss results and the process.

Additional exercise

Drawing these three forms will give pupils who need an extra challenge something to work on.

Juxtaposition

To achieve the figure on the bottom left, start with the form drawn with a thick line, as it is simpler, and draw the form with the thinner line around it.

Are there other ways to weave forms into one another? Look at the examples on the facing page.

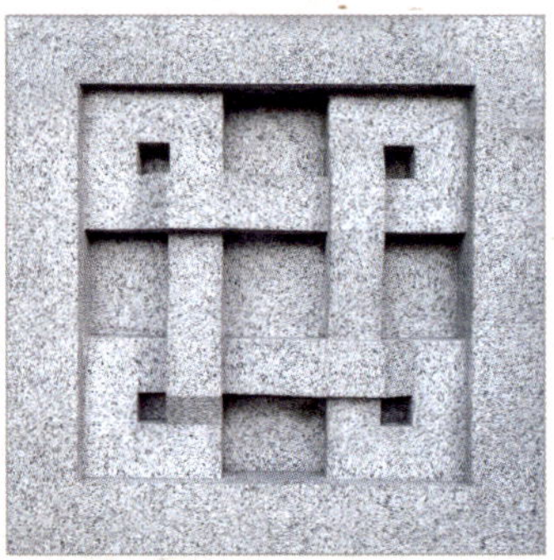

Ornamentation, Vigelands Park, Oslo

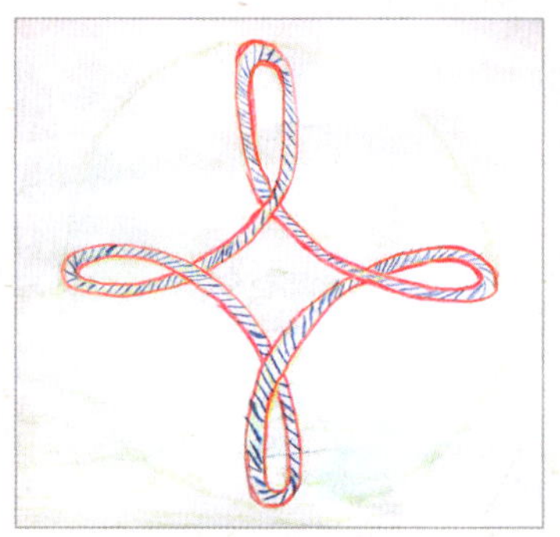

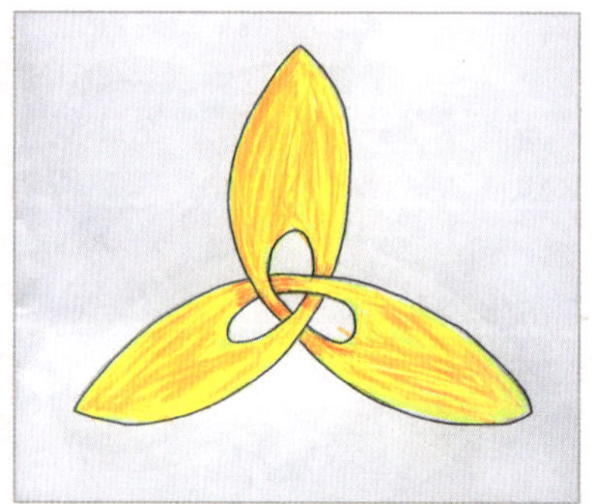

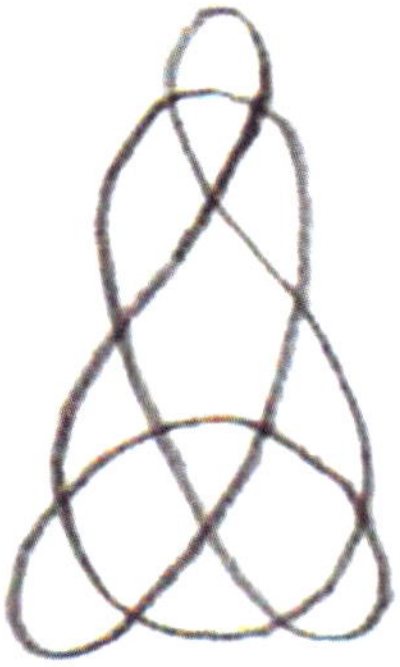

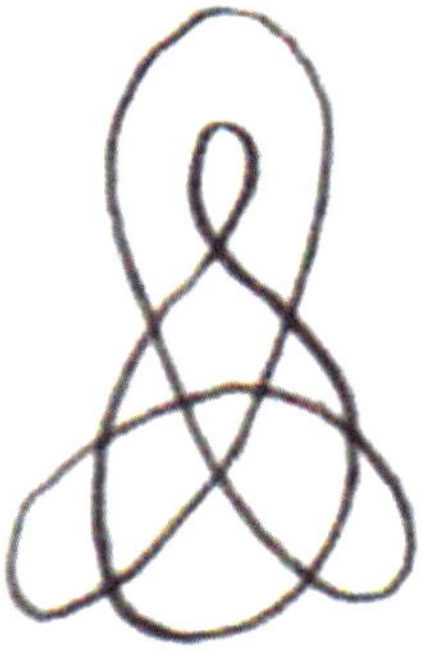

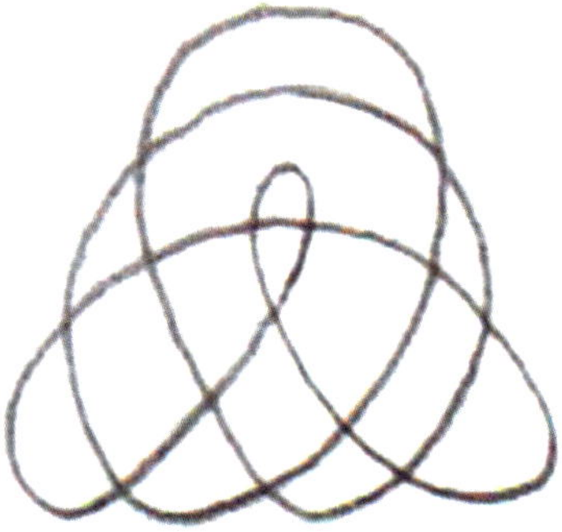

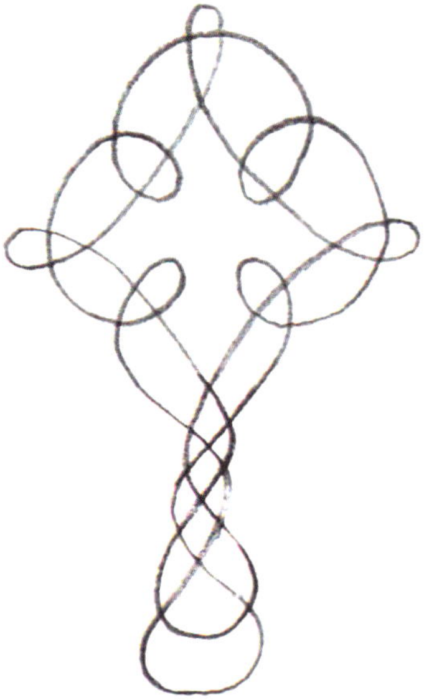

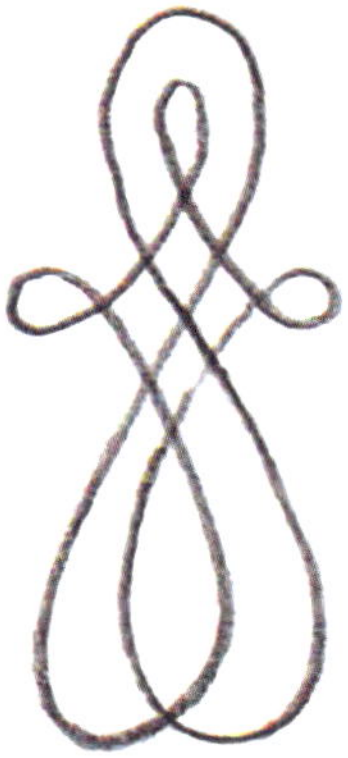

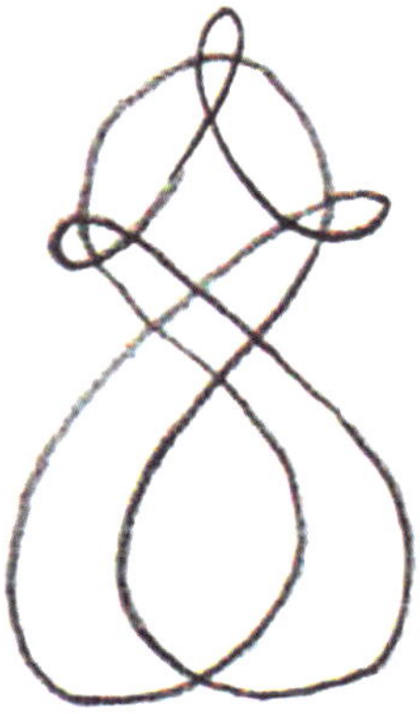

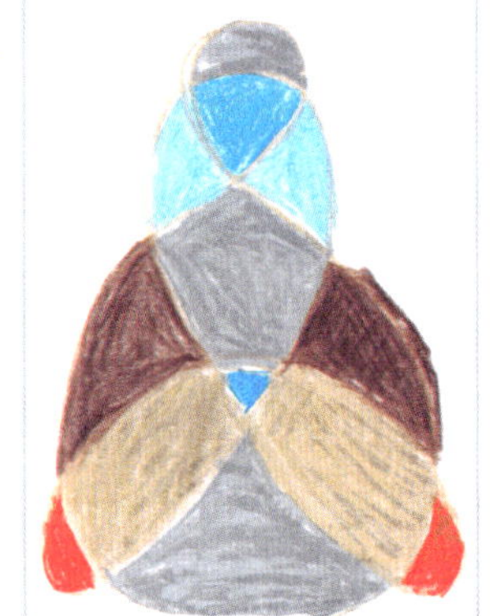

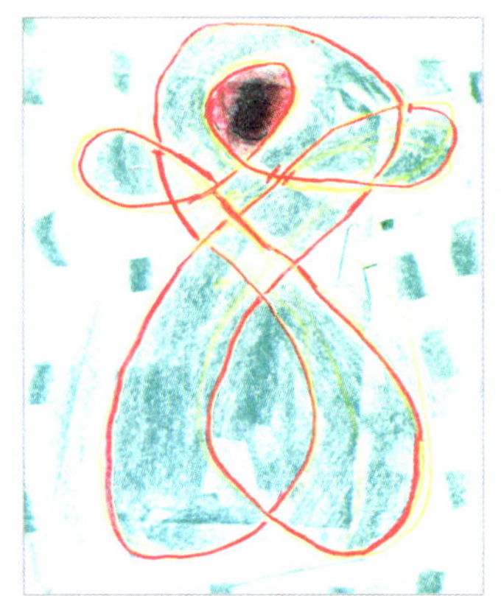

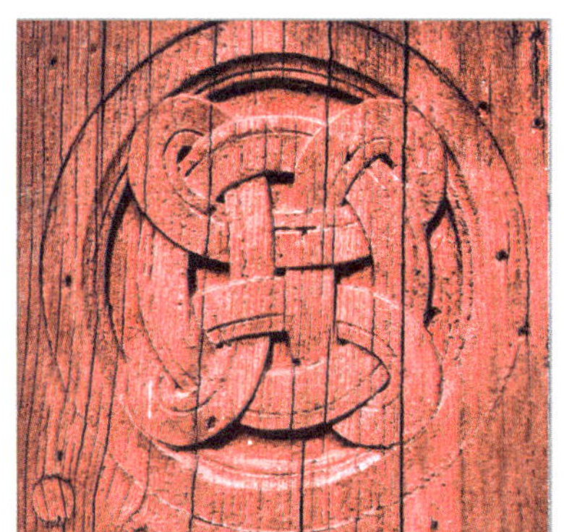

Decorative detail from pillar, Biri, Norway, 1901

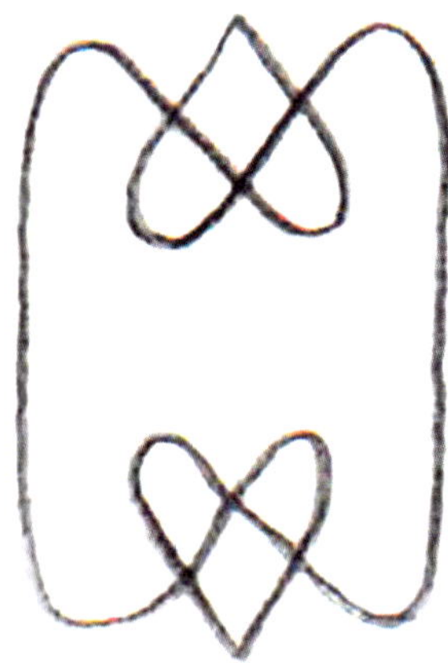

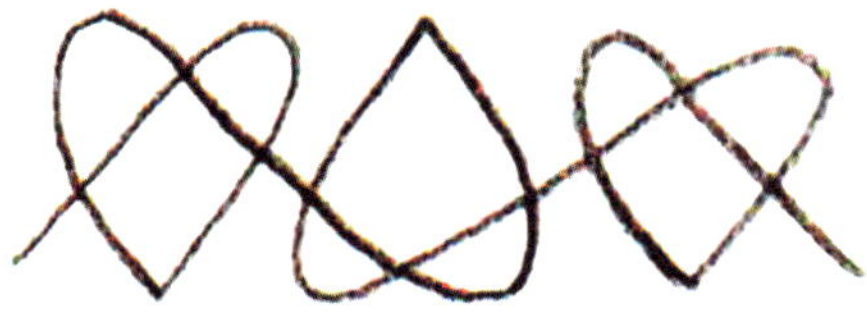

Plaited heart border

The challenge in these forms is to keep the heart shape in mind even when it is upside down. These forms need practice and preparation. Consider whether your pupils are capable of this yet.

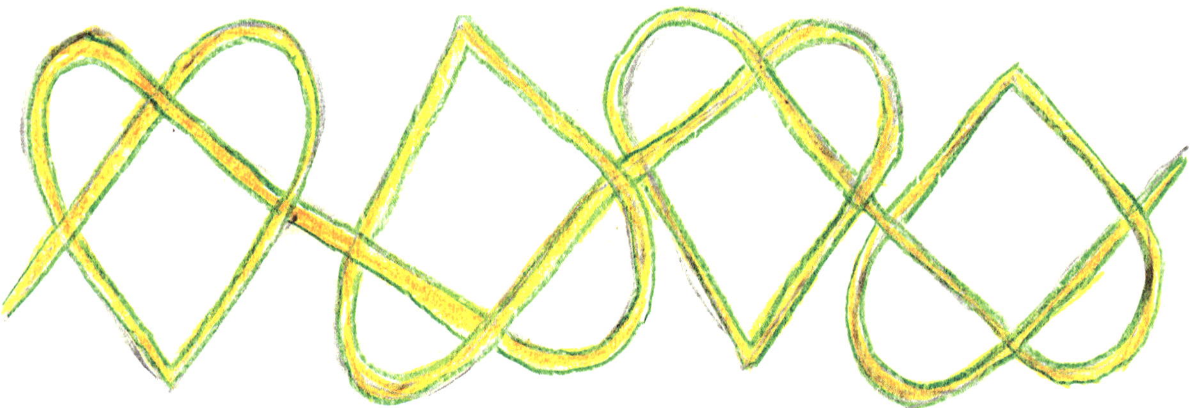

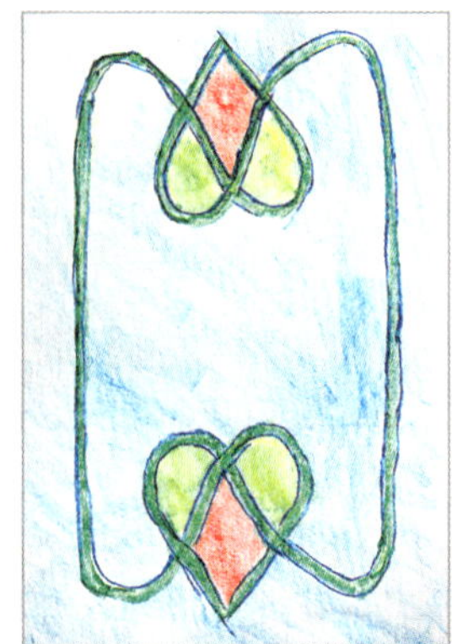

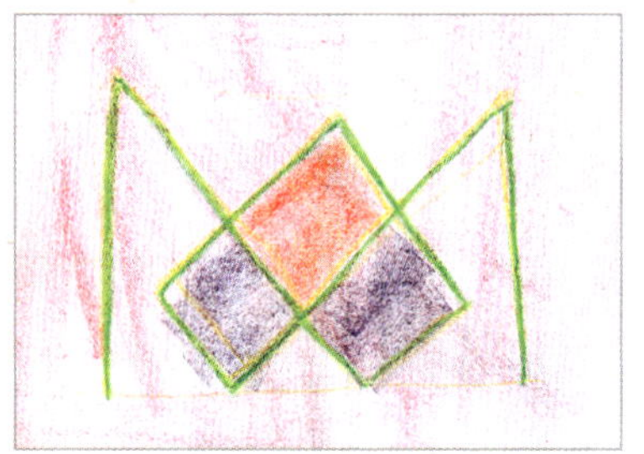

More challenging borders and loops

The border at the top of the page will be familiar from Class 2 (see p.42).

The next step is to bend it downwards and around so that it follows an imaginary circle. Turn it one third of a rotation per loop. You can use the numbering, as shown, to assist the process. The loop at number 4 is supposed to end up above the loop at number 1 in the imaginary circle.

In the figure on the centre right, the border is bent upwards and around to create another form.

The figure at the bottom of the page is also challenging. If you decide to give this to your pupils, ensure they have plenty of time and do preparatory exercises. They may need to use points to assist in its construction.

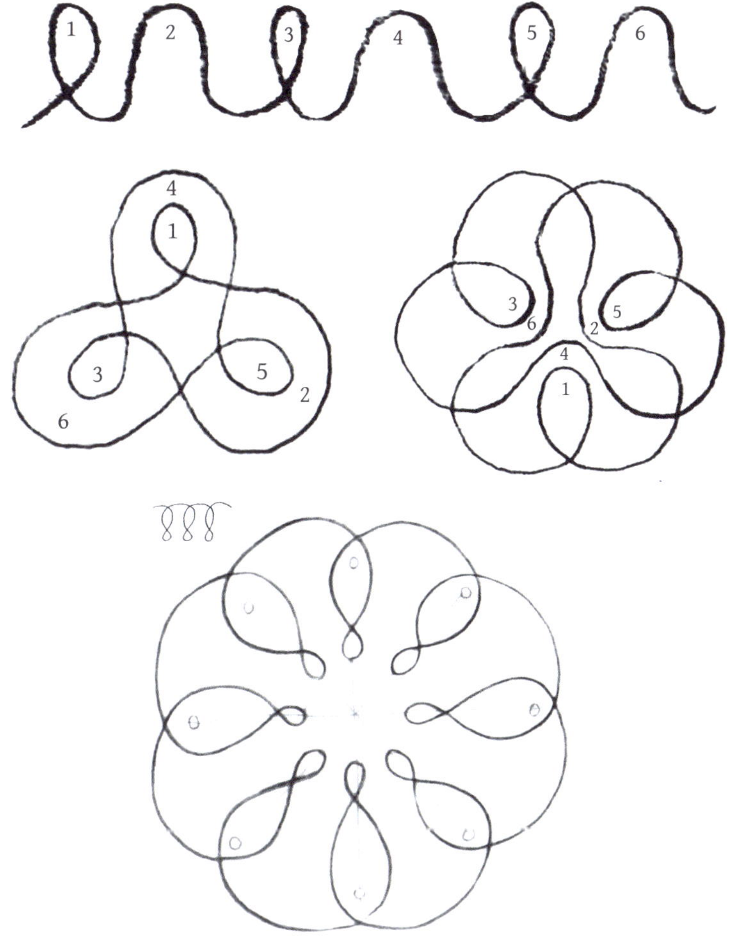

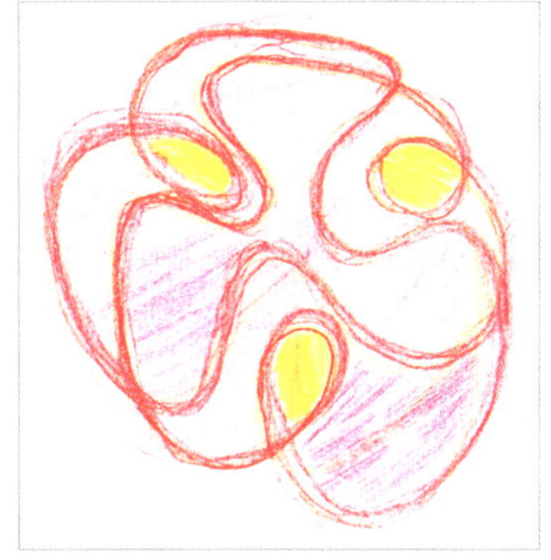

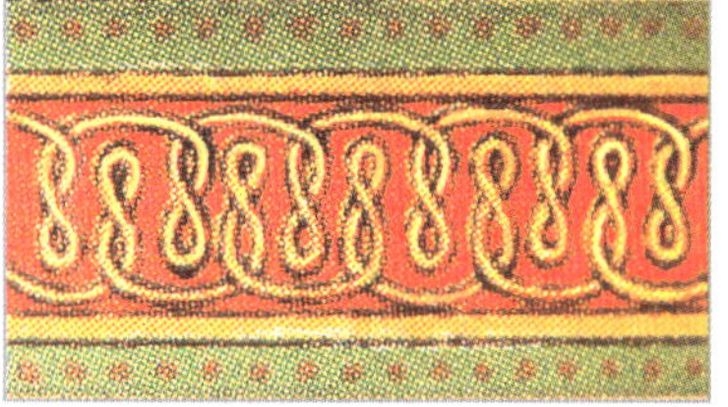

Celtic pattern

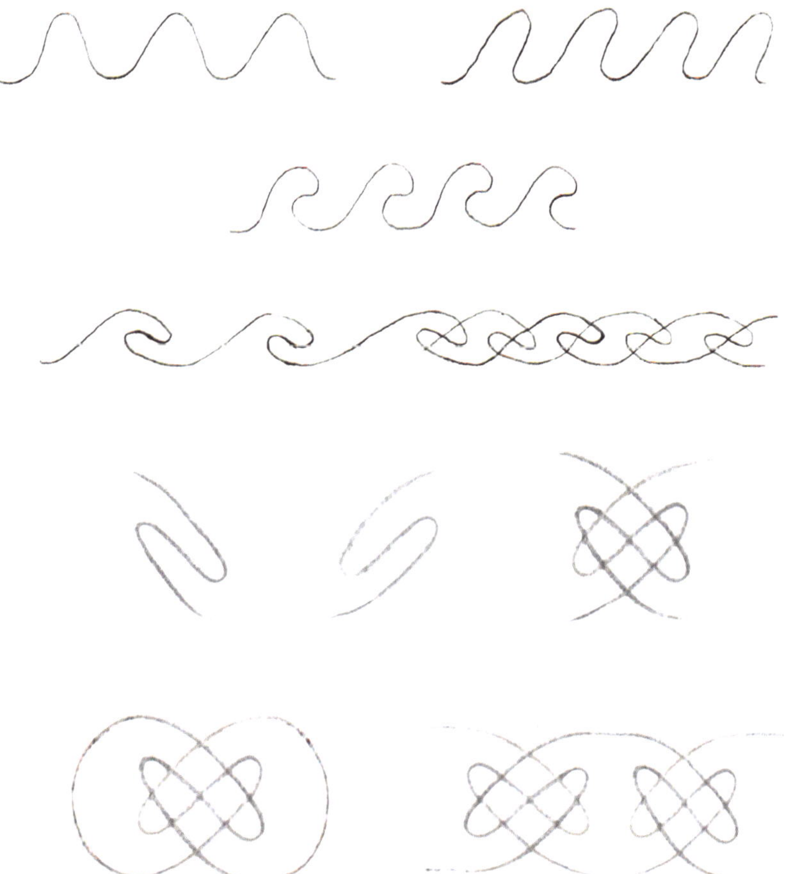

Ornaments

Before this exercise, have your pupils practise making borders in preparation, as shown on the upper three rows on the left.

When you are ready to begin, make two opposing S shapes and plait them together as shown in the fourth row. The challenge is to make the 'waves' long enough and straight enough to be able to plait them.

Tie up the loose ends to complete the ornament. Two can be bound together to create Celtic interlacing (see the bottom row).

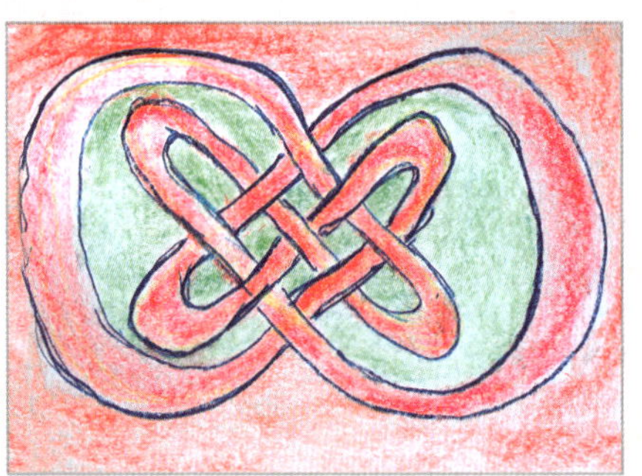

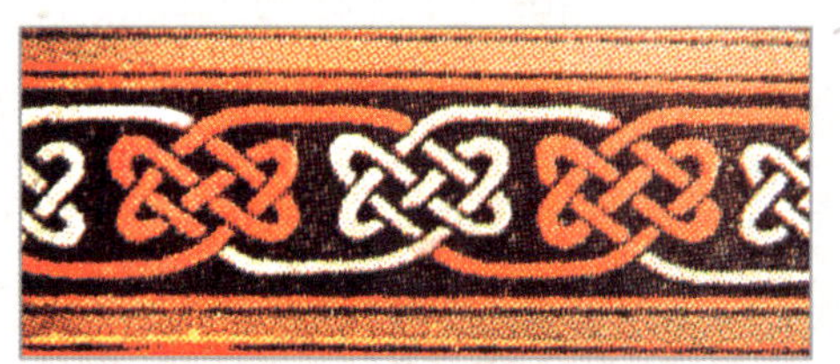

Celtic ornament: interlaced ribbon patterns

Pupils might find it difficult to interweave the borders on the previous page. An alternative approach is to reintroduce this figure from Class 4 (see p.95), then open it up and extend the lines in two larger arcs, as shown.

Ask the class whether they think it is better to colour it in or leave it as it is.

Finally, practise drawing the whole form in one continuous line.

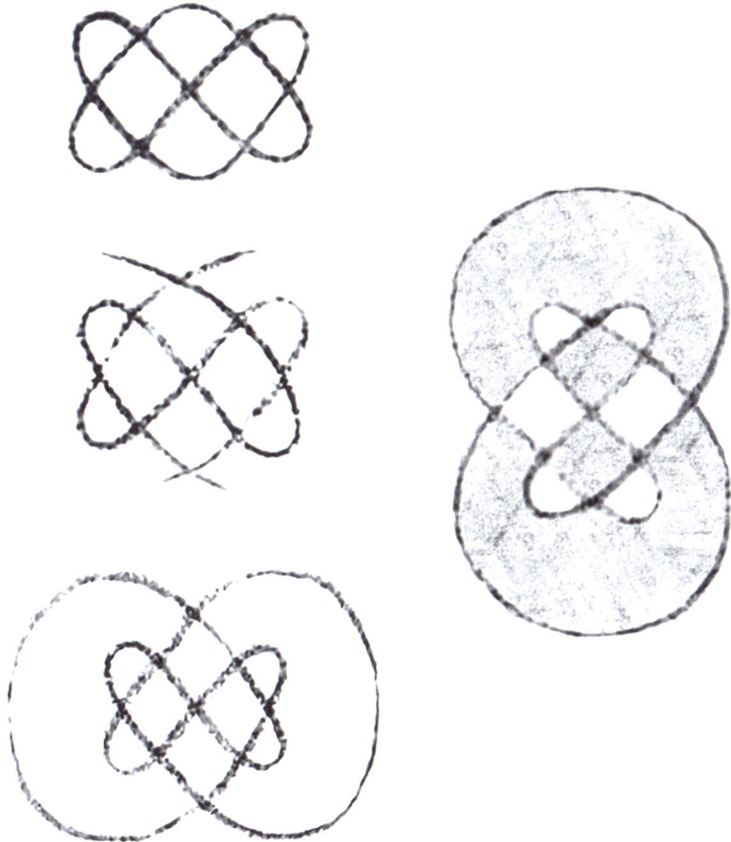

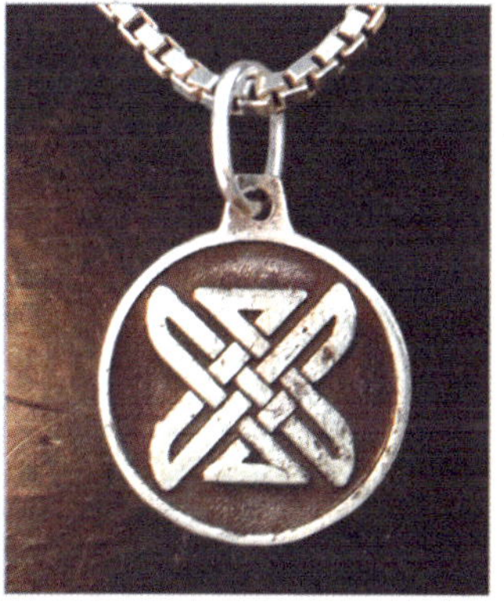

Traditional jewellery motif, Brazil

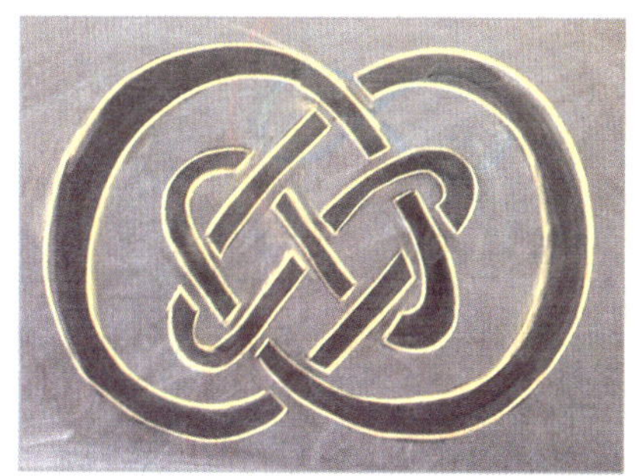

Blackboard drawing in charcoal and yellow chalk

Figures of eight

Take the time to familiarise yourself with the next eight pages before proceeding with these forms.

Start with a figure of eight, or a row of loops. Superimpose another on top, as seen in the central figure.

Explore this form using different lengths and rows that become wider or narrower. It is aesthetically pleasing if one row is thicker than the other, preferably using different colours.

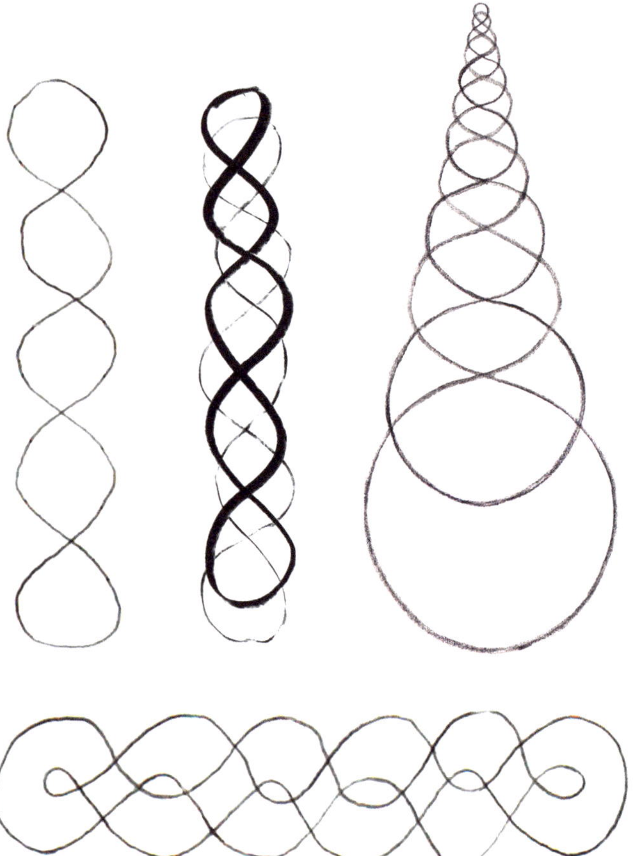

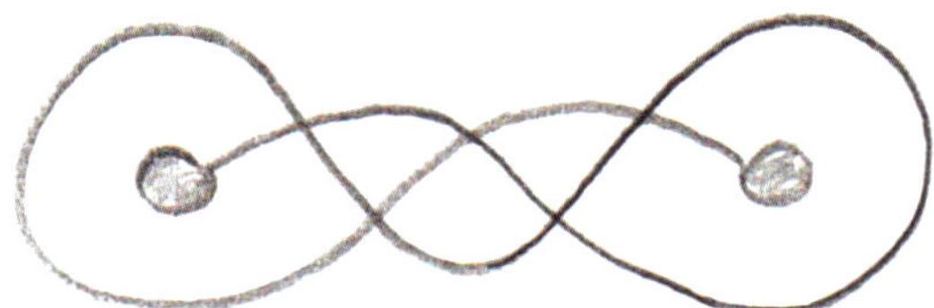

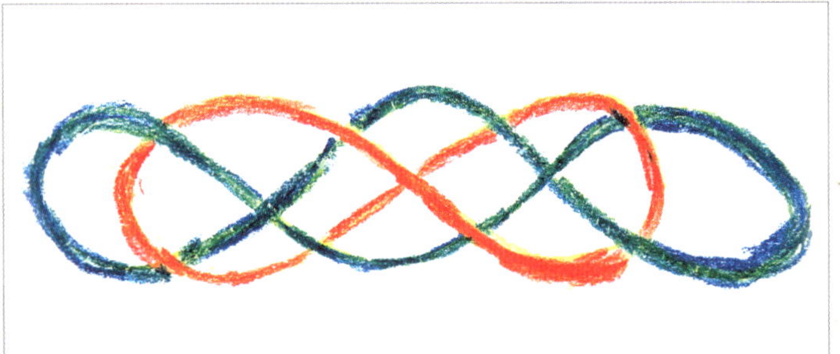

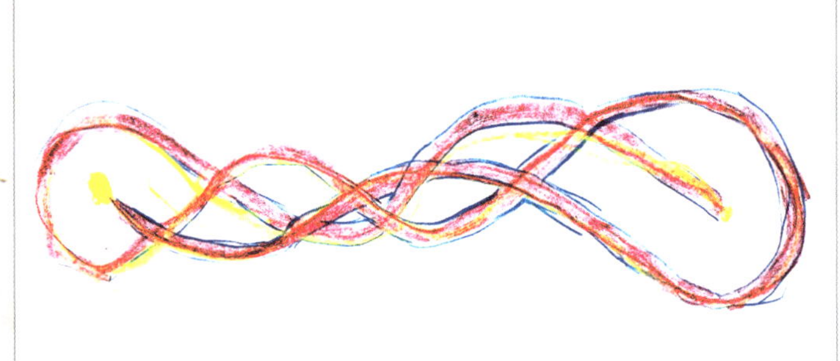

These forms can be constructed with the help of dots, as previously described (see p.124), but here the object of the exercise is to practise using freehand drawing.

Start by using a wavelike movement, taking care that when you work upwards the line weaves towards the first downward line, thus making space for another line to work down. Note that there will always be loose ends when using three 'waves'.

Below, four waves are interlaced in a continuous line completed in the same way. There are no loose ends.

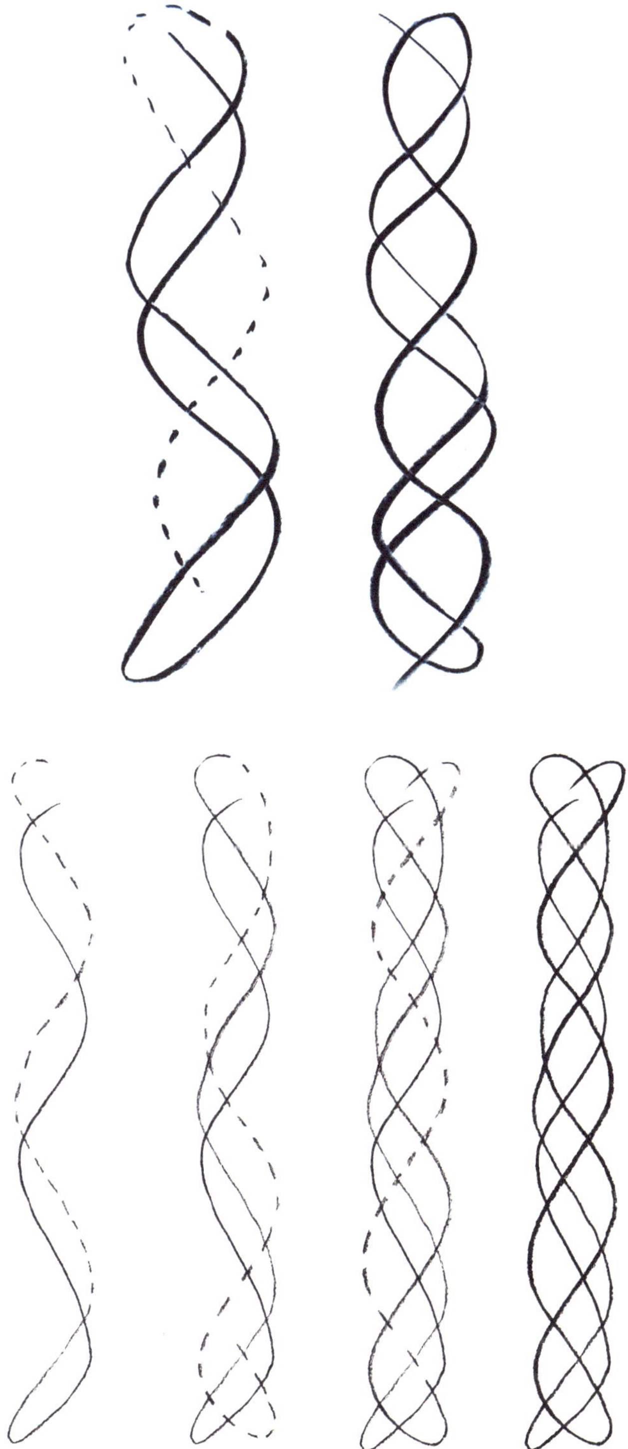

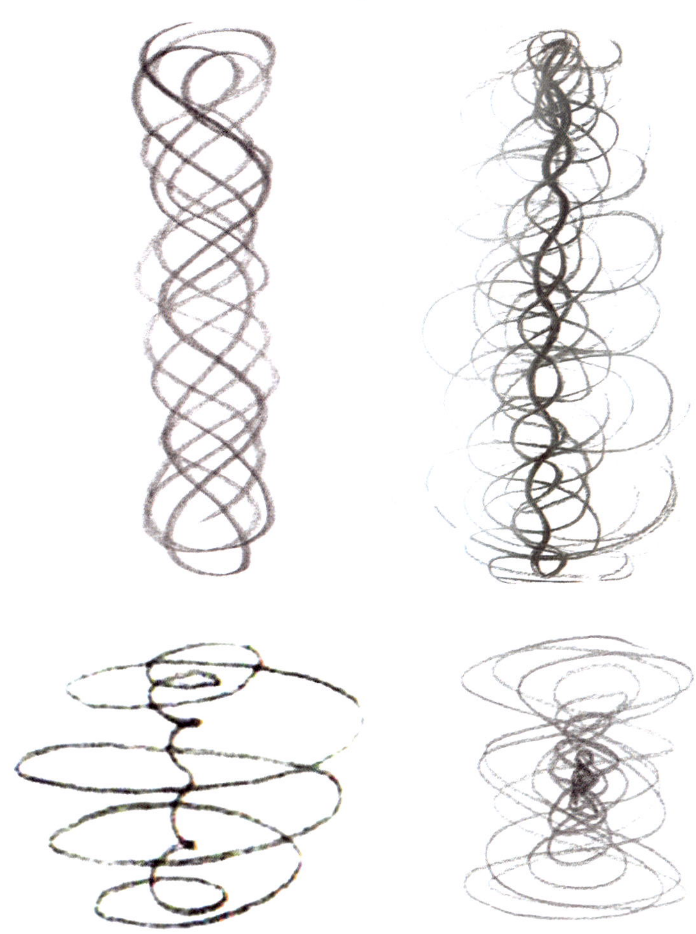

Follow the same principle here, but this time draw freehand and follow rhythms up and down, and left and right. There might be a few waves or many, wide or small, tall or short.

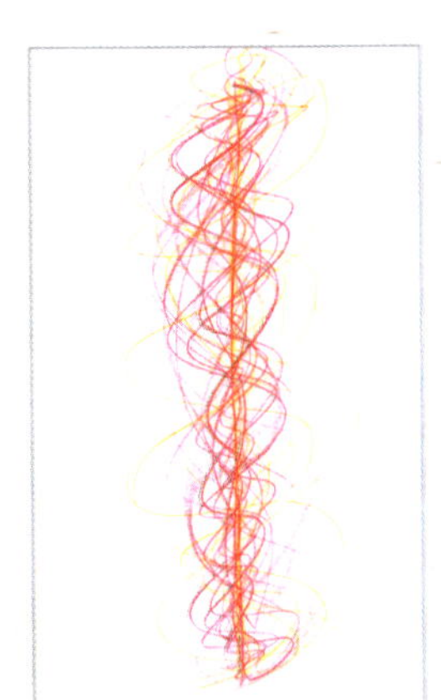

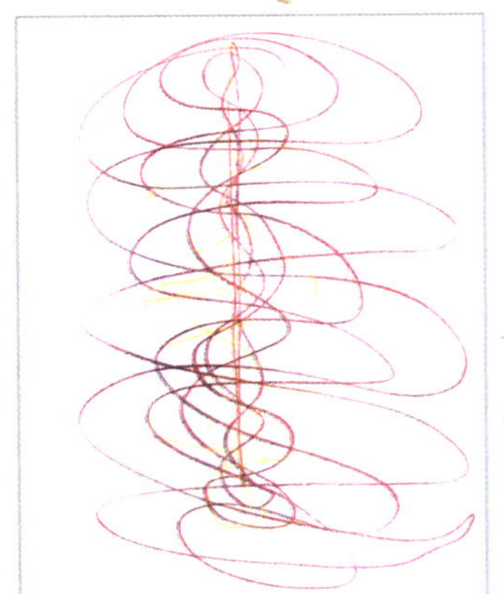

Celtic ornament

This exercise features a border influenced by a Celtic ornament motif, which uses a single curved line as its starting point. Extend spirals from the top and bottom points.

Next, extend lines from the spirals into the curves.

Colour in these spaces using the same colour used for the lines. Finally, give the spirals 'tentacles', as shown.

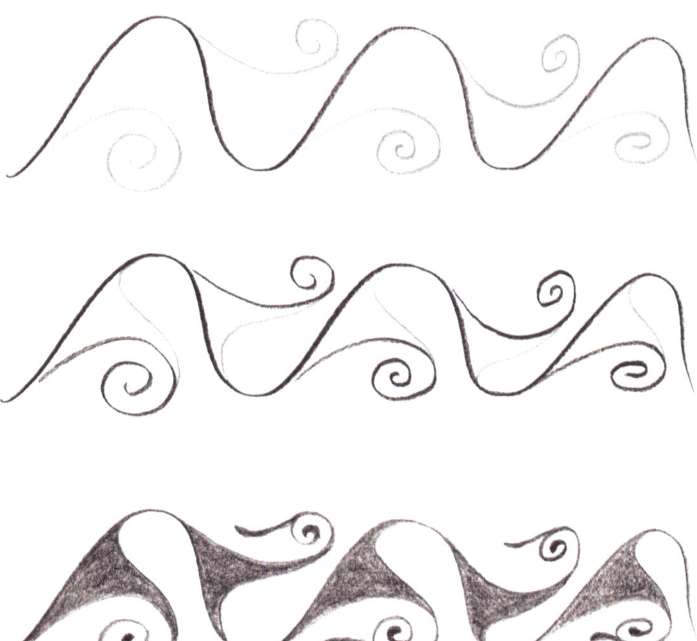

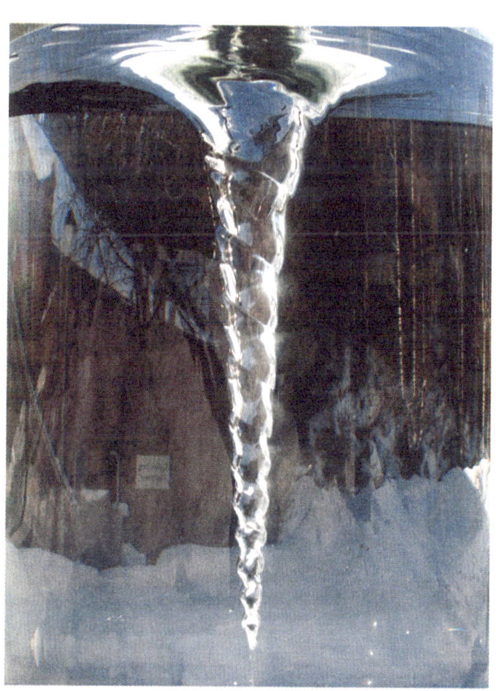

A spiral in liquid from the sculpture Our Energy, Our Matter, Our Space, Our Time, *2006, by Petroc Sesti, Kistefos Sculpture Park, Jevnaker, Norway*

The rhythms of nature

The photographs on these pages show linear movement in nature: the bark on a willow tree, the tracks carved in sand by water, waves streaming through seaweed, light playing in water or spirals in liquid.

Do these natural forms have a relationship to those seen in the photograph of Urnes Stave Church, in Norway (left)? Discuss it with your pupils.

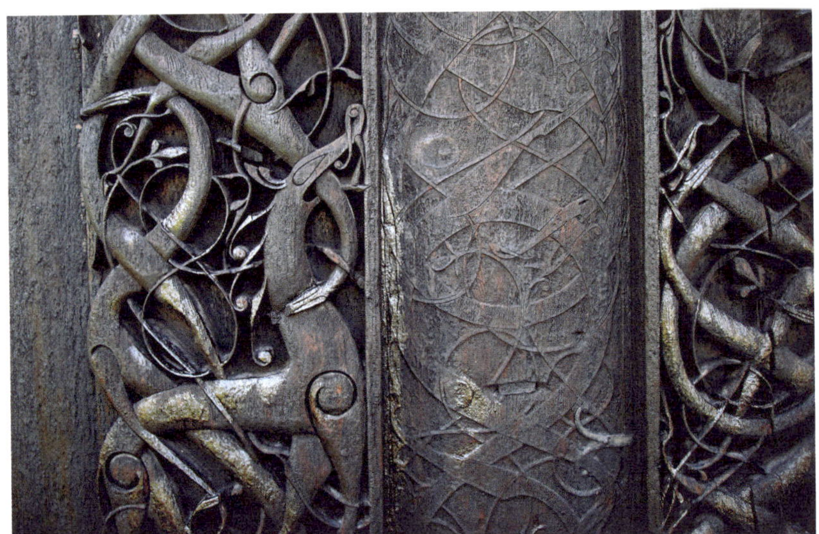

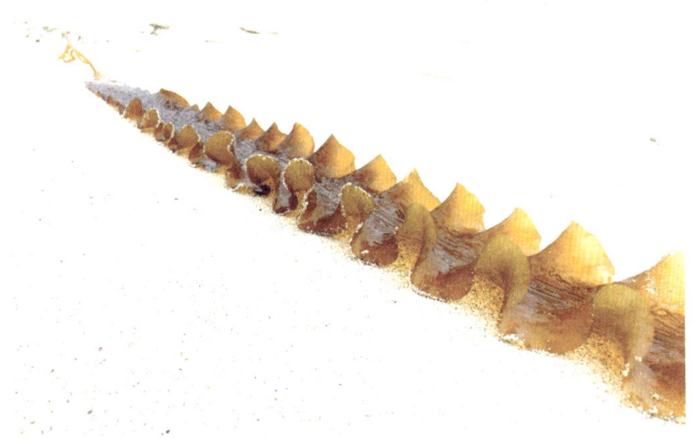

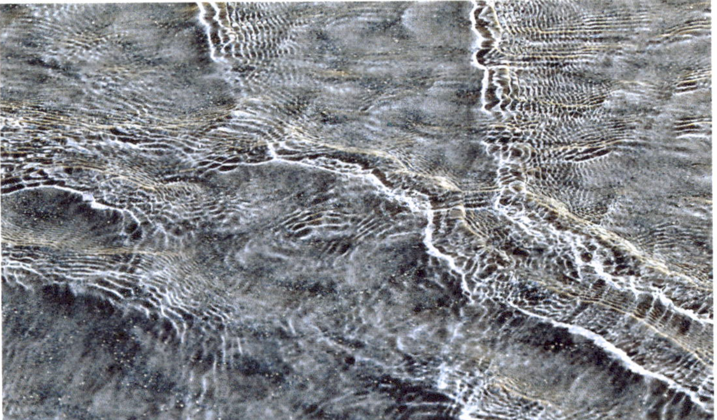

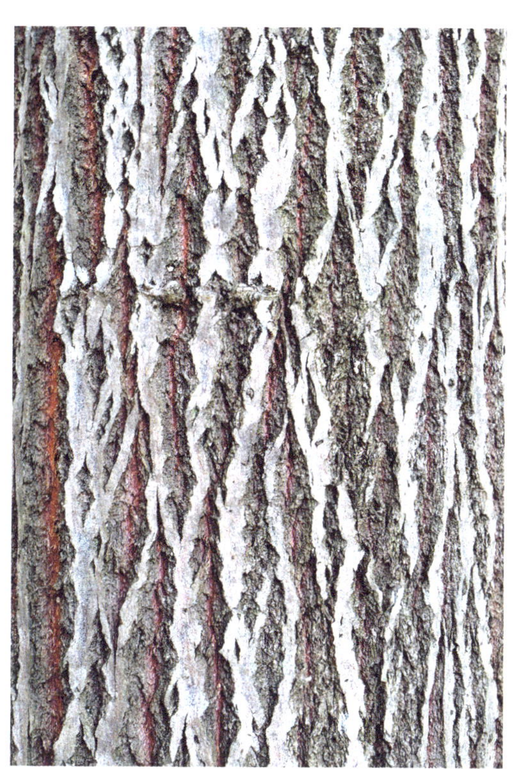

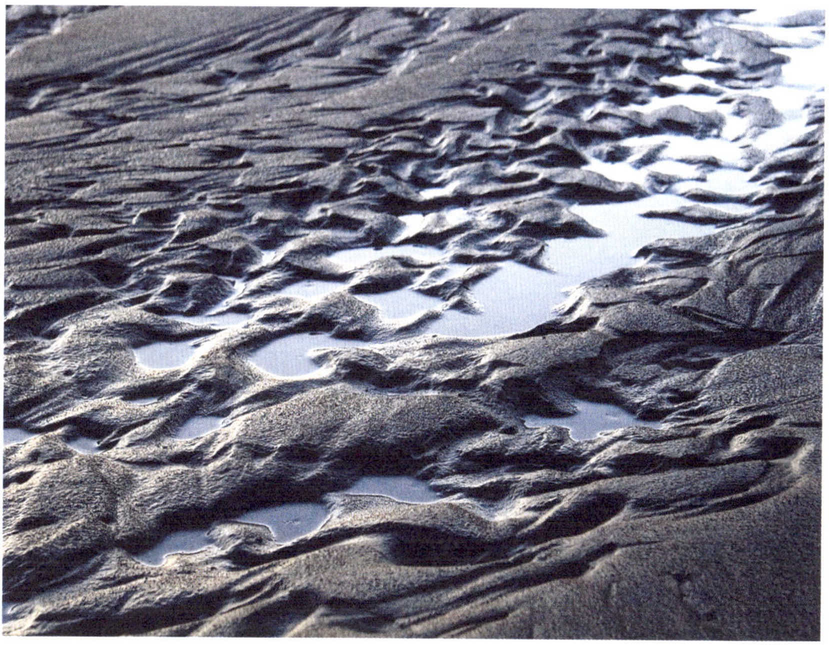

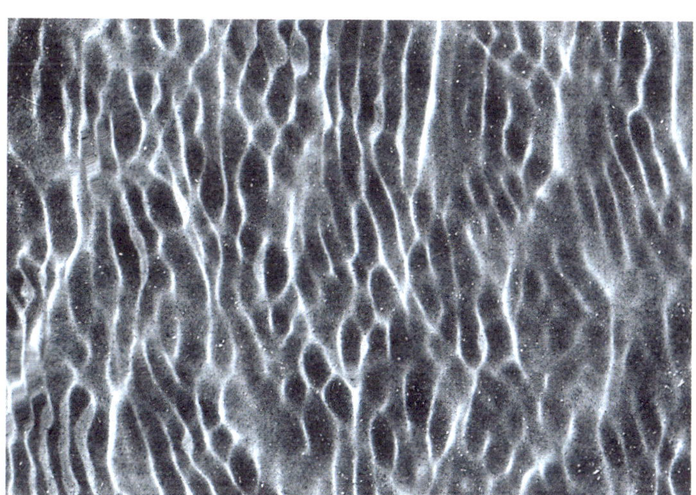

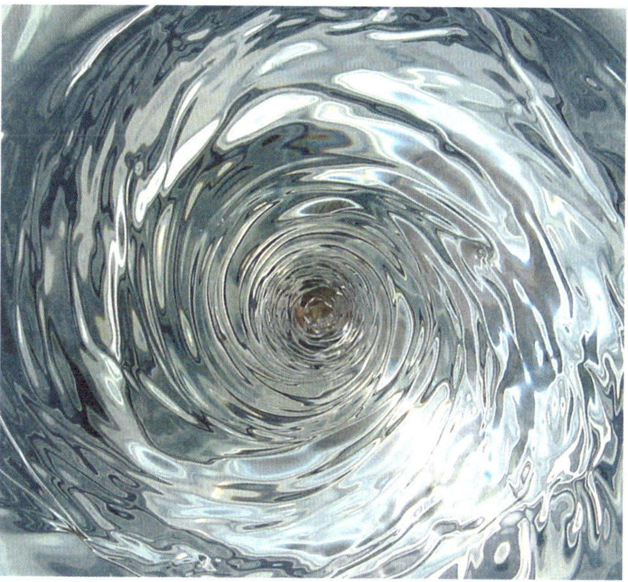

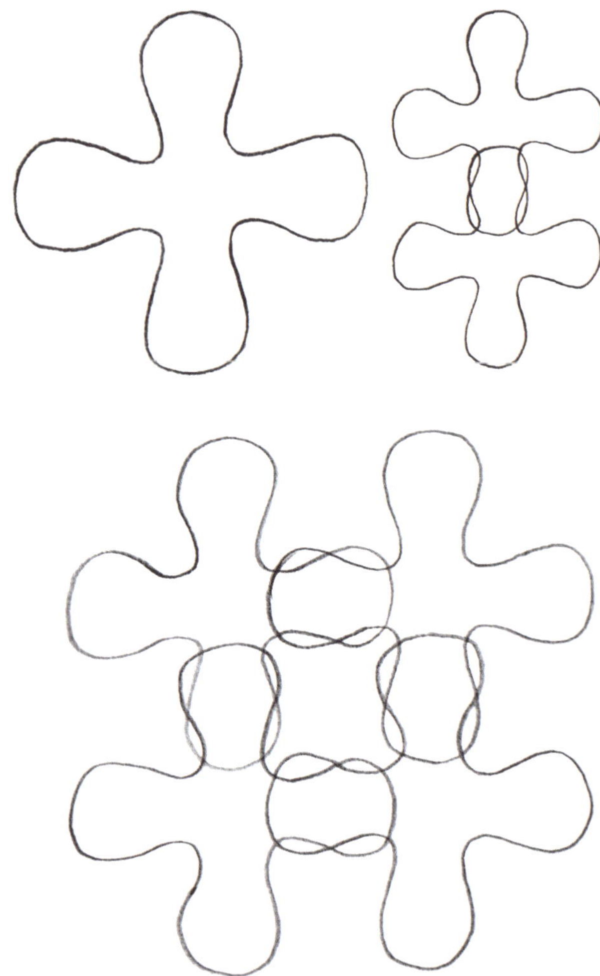

Braided patterns inspired by Byzantium designs

Show your pupils this simple form and draw their attention to how the line needs to swing inwards to knot into another form.

Ask them to make the pattern over an entire sheet of paper. The size can be left up to the pupil. How many forms do they have to use to fill the sheet?

They can also place the figures at an angle and fill in the gaps with flowers, as shown in the illustration of wallpaper below.

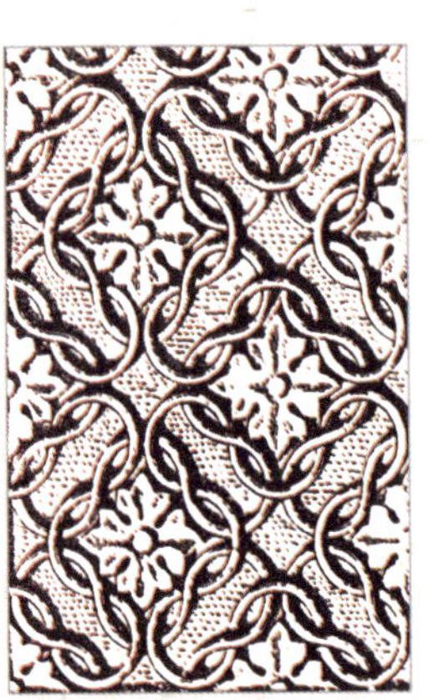

Byzantium 'wallpaper' pattern

Braiding

Your pupils will already have learned how to braid around rows of dots. In this exercise, the challenge is to swivel the borders at a ninety-degree angle and continue the plait.

Pupils can experiment with one, two or three rows of dots. Pupils can put this technique to good use by creating borders on the pages of their workbooks.

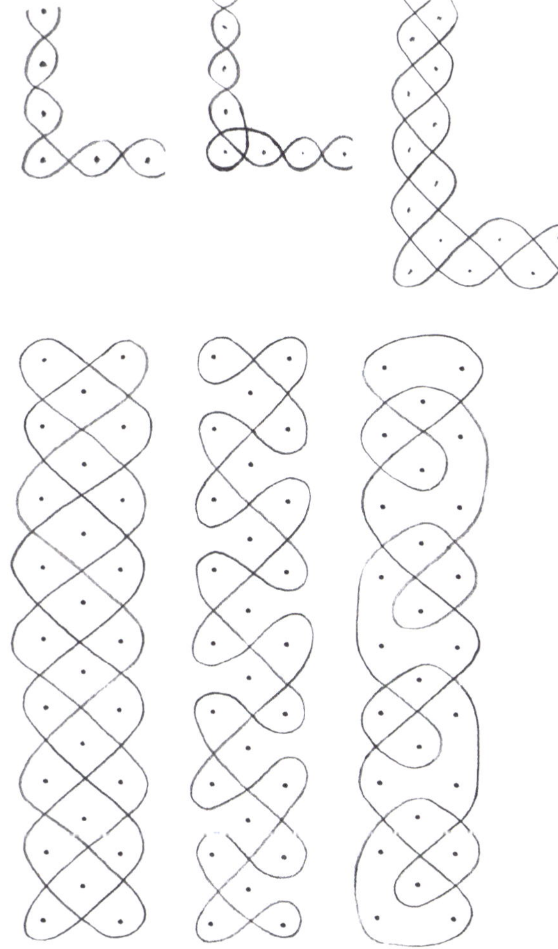

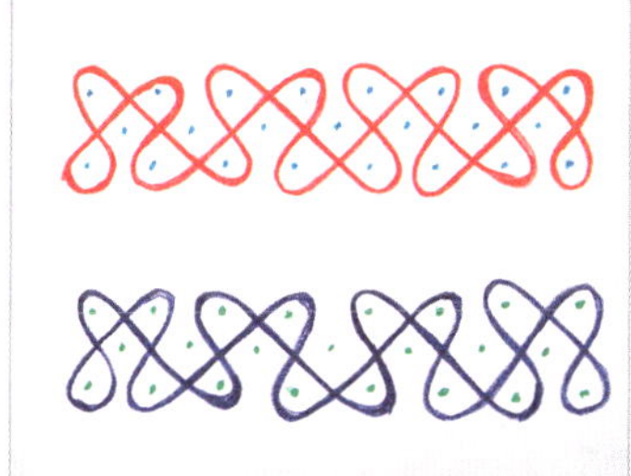

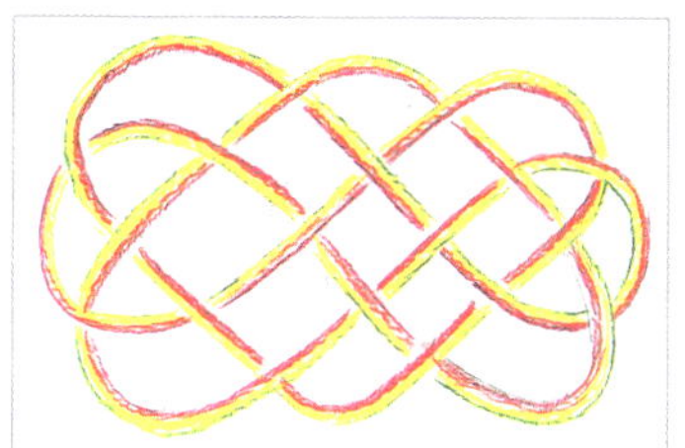

A pattern for rope braiding

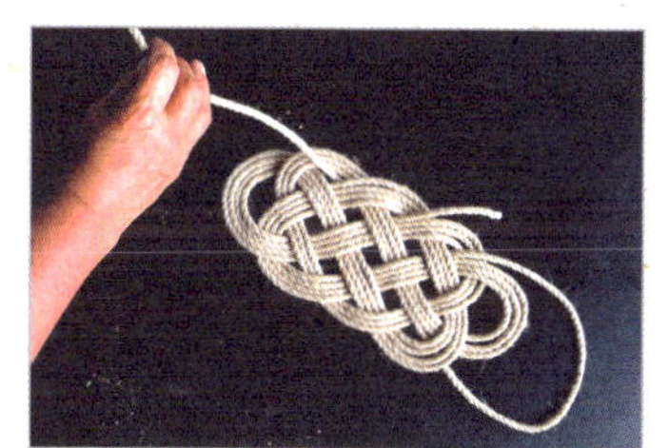

Rope work by pupils

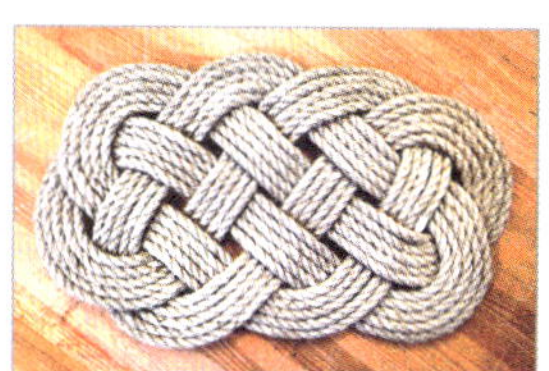

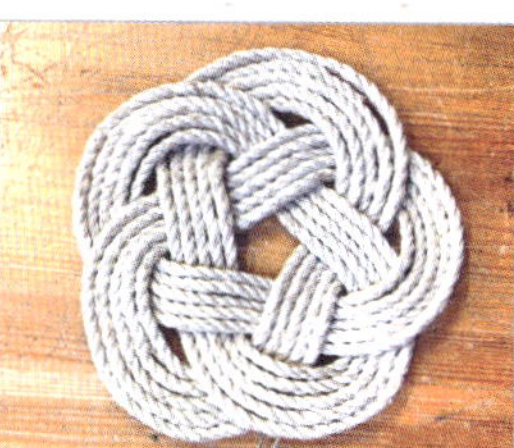

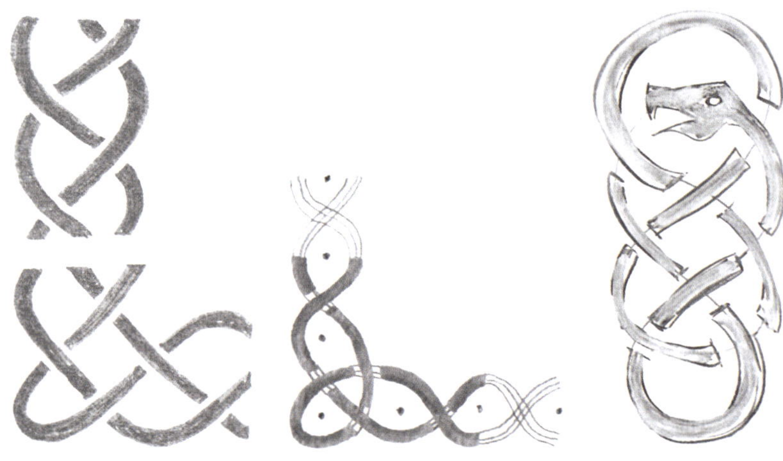

Viking patterns

Your pupils can experiment with simplified Viking patterns, starting with braiding one or two lines, as shown in the first two examples on the upper left.

These figures can be used to make templates to print onto textiles. It is a fun activity for the class to make Viking costumes together. The forms can be as simple or as complex as you like, depending upon pupils' abilities and needs.

The blackboard illustration (lower left) shows templates for a border. Print a series of them and make your border as long as you wish.

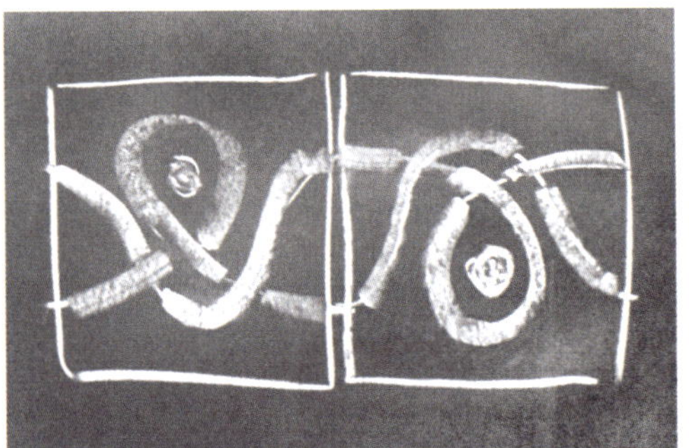

Blackboard example for a template that can be rotated yet still have the parts fit together

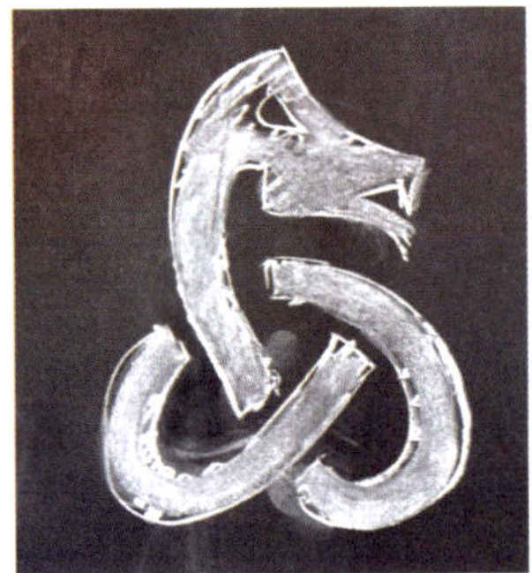

Blackboard example

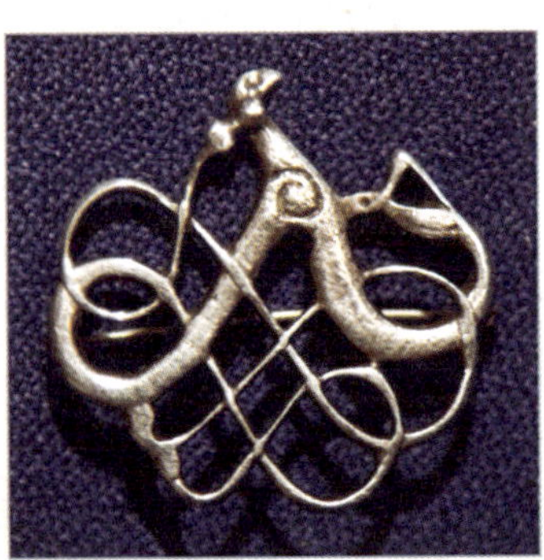

Urnesfibel, brooch from the Viking Age

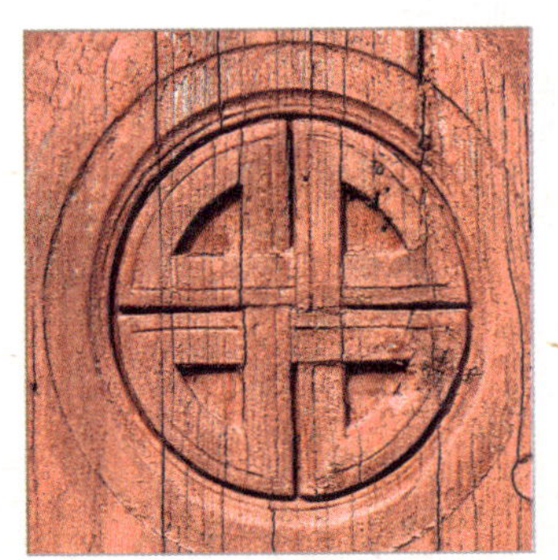

Decorative detail from a pillar, Biri, Norway, 1901

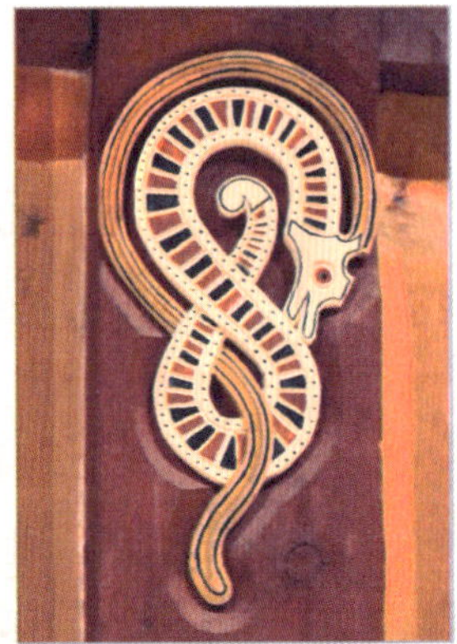

Carved dragon motif

Snake motifs

Brooches from the age of the Vikings often featured snakes. Show your class how to draw a snake motif, but try it out yourself first.

First, draw this simple plait, then go over it with a wax colouring block. Gradually develop the line, as shown, until you have your snake motif.

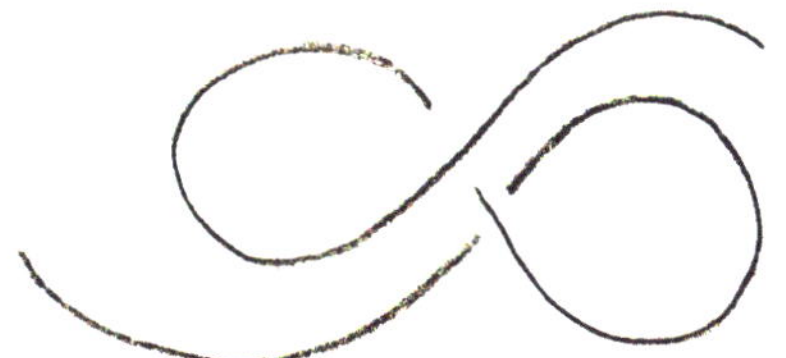
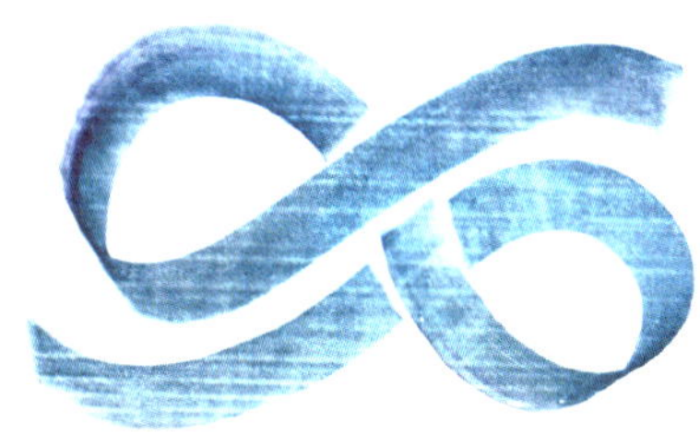

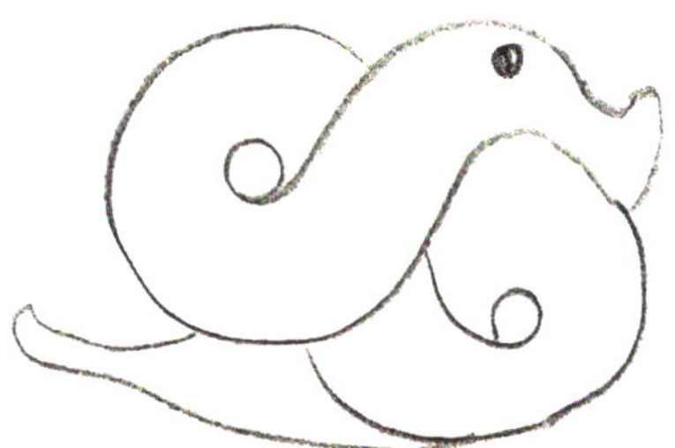
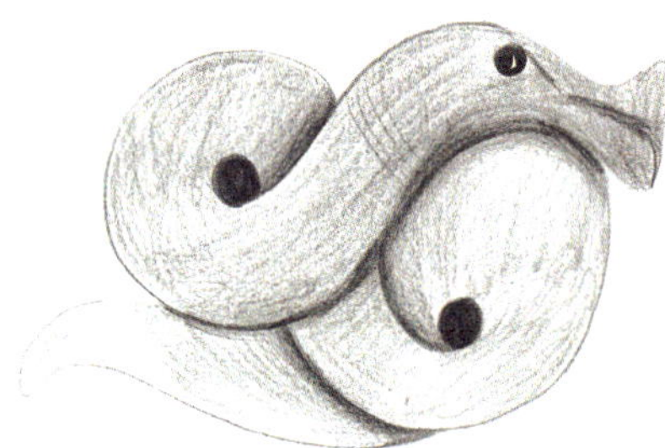

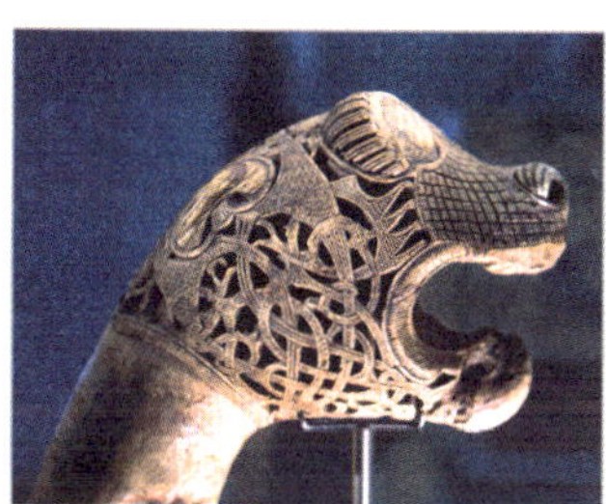

Animal head from the Oseberg ship site, displayed in the Viking Ship Museum, Bygdøy, Oslo

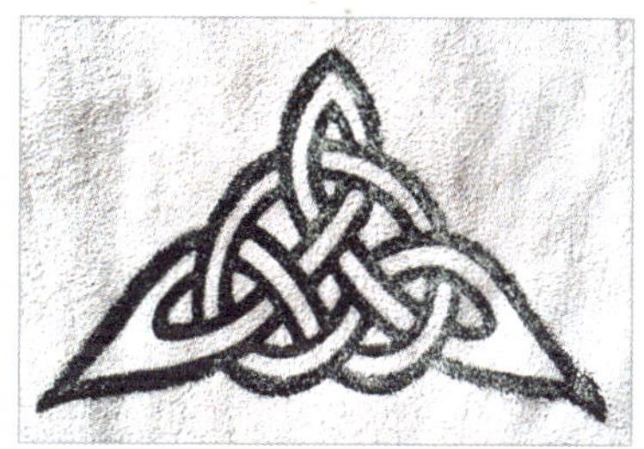

Print on leather

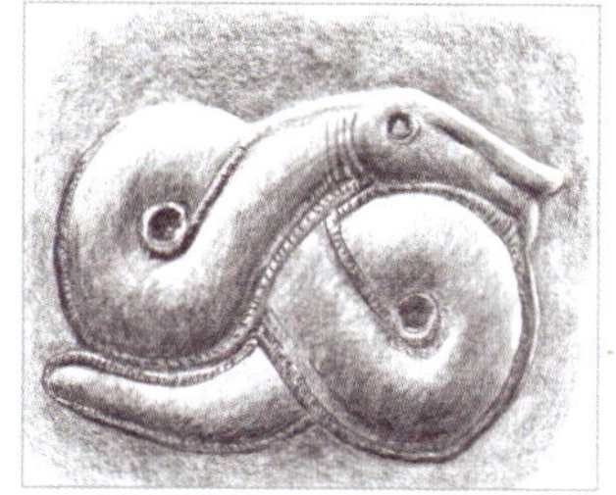

Pencil drawing of brooch from the Viking Age

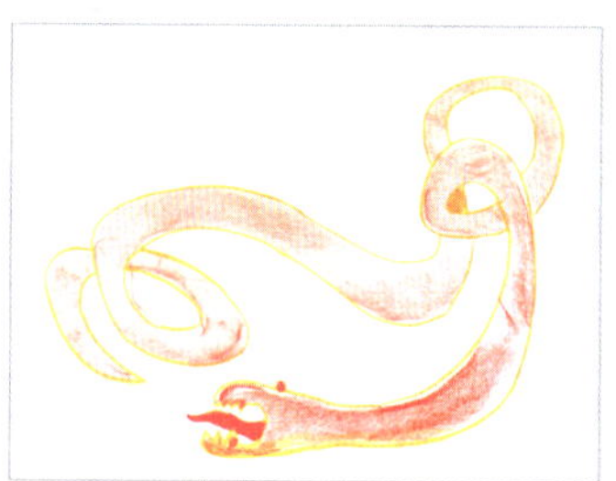

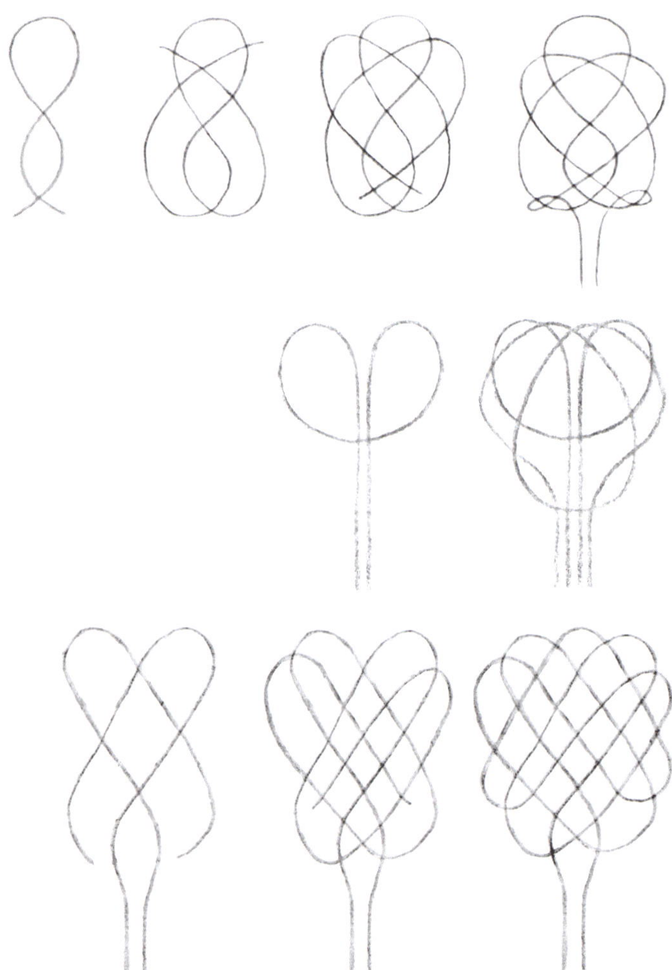

Arabesques

The carpet beaters in the photographs contain Moorish arabesques, originally brought to Europe during the Crusades. They are difficult to draw and are best suited as exercises for those pupils who need greater challenges.

It is easiest if they are built up section by section, as shown in the examples on the left, which demonstrate how to draw each style of arabesque represented in the photographs. With practice, some pupils might manage to draw them in one line.

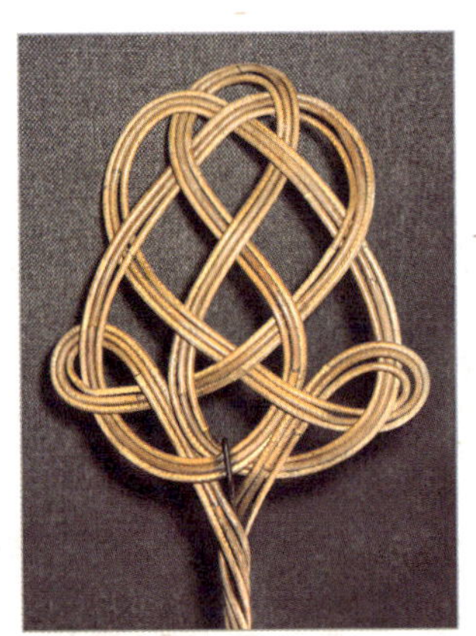

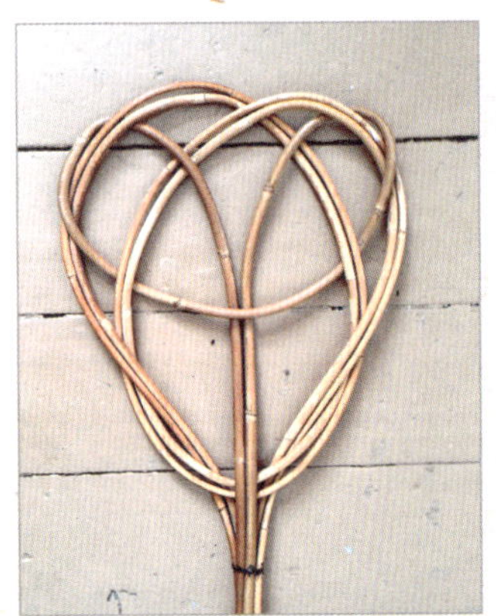

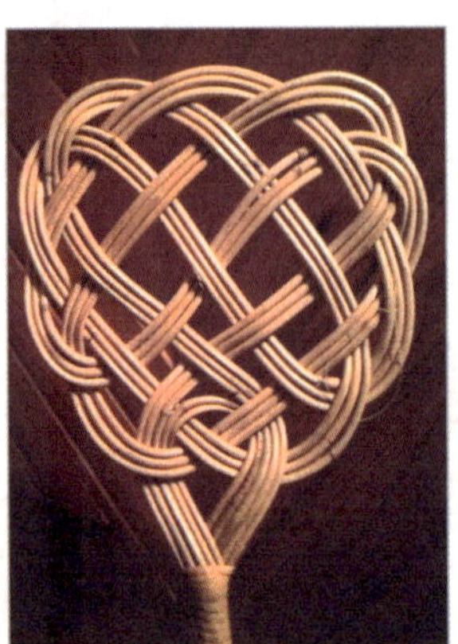

Extra exercises

If your pupils show particular aptitude, consider setting these demanding exercises as aesthetic challenges.

To draw the figures in the top three rows, master the borders first, as shown, using dots for guidance.

To develop this technique, place the dots in a ring of three, four, five or six and make the line go around and through them.

The large figure lower down can be drawn with one continuous line, but it helps to use two other forms to guide you: a circle and a five-pointed star, as shown. Imagine, too, lines in between the star's five points, which cross its centre before extending outwards.

Now, build up the form by starting with the 'heart' shapes that originate from the points of the stars.

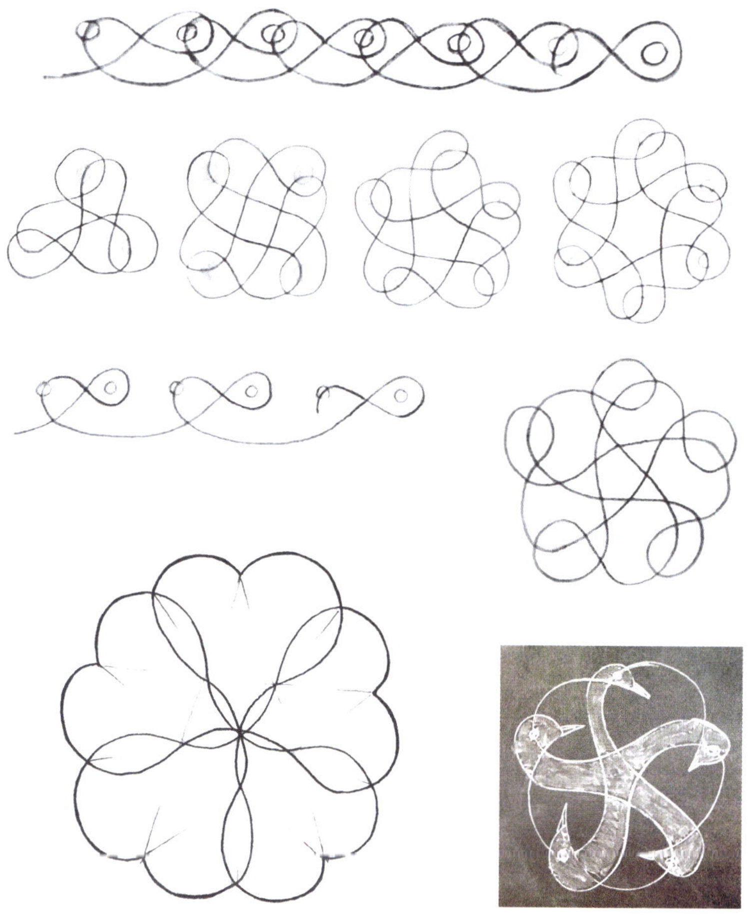

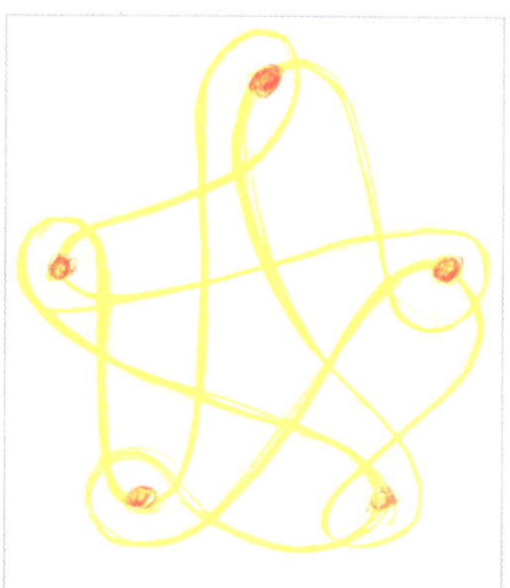

Blackboard drawing

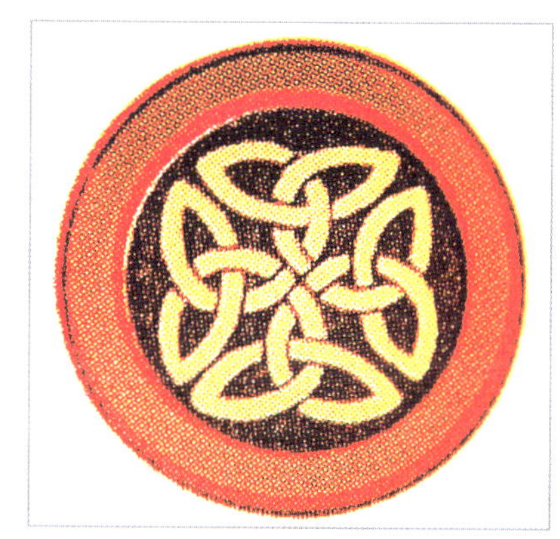

Circular Celtic ornament with four knotted trefoils

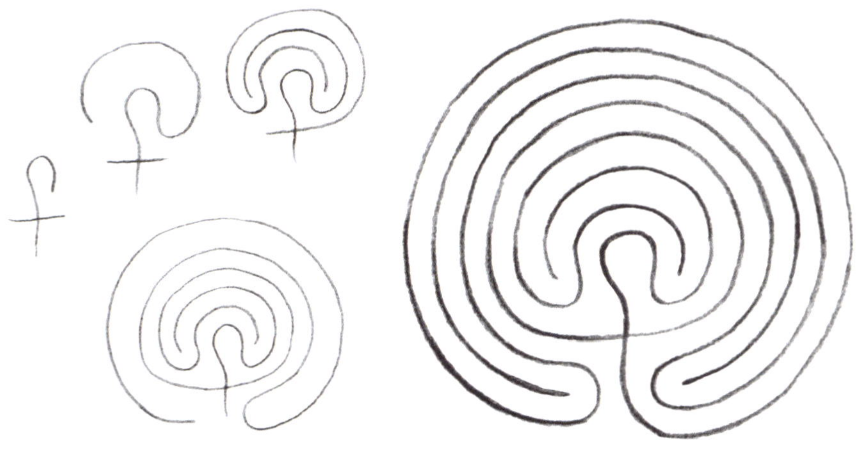

Trojaborg labyrinths

This Trojaborg labyrinth form is at least 3,000 years old and forms one continuous pathway. As a form, the labyrinth provides rich challenges for the drawer. It seems to breathe in and out, to contain living rhythms and symmetries.

Trojaborg are found around the world and are used in different ways by different cultures. Labyrinths can be found as inlaid patterns on church and cathedral floors in several European cities. In certain places, this style of labyrinth is known as the 'Road to Jerusalem'.

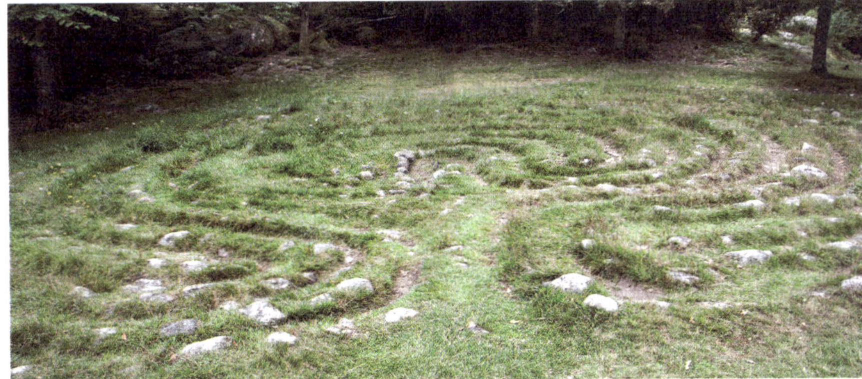

Labyrinth at Grebbestad, Bohuslän, Sweden. Date unknown, but possibly from the early Iron Age, according to related finds in the area

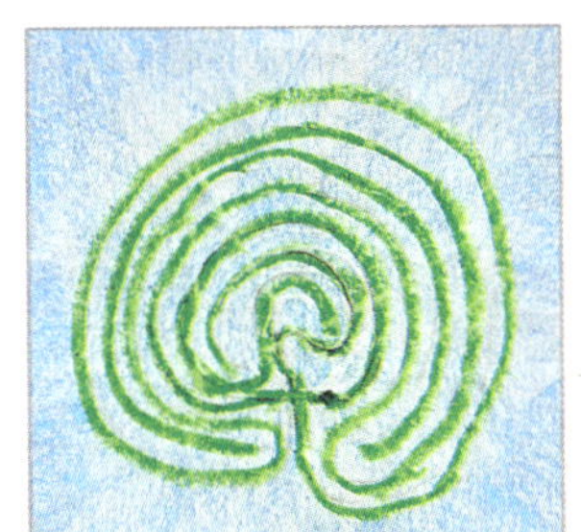

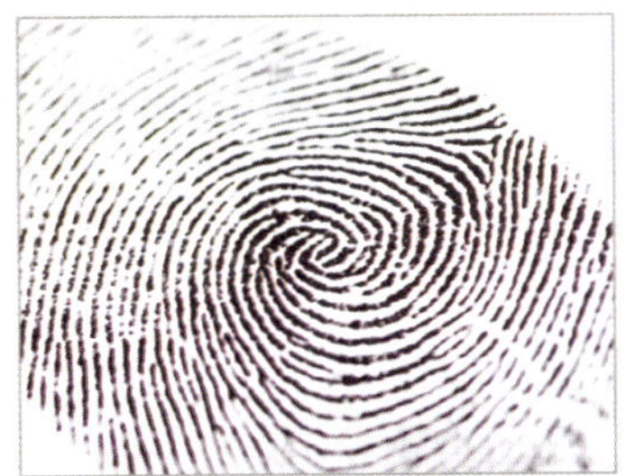

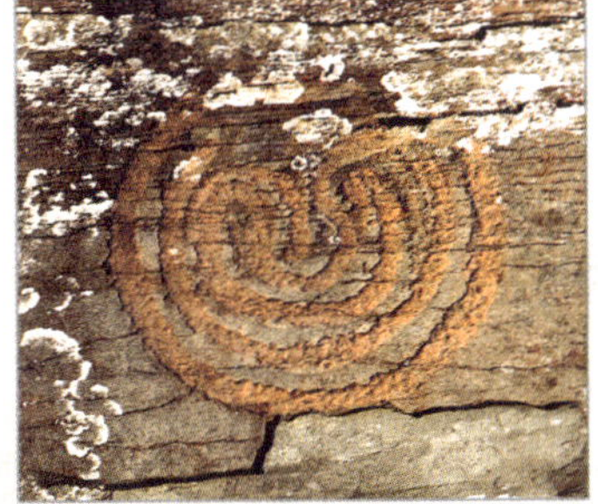

Labyrinth-shaped rock carving on the shores of Tyrifjorden, Buskerud, Norway

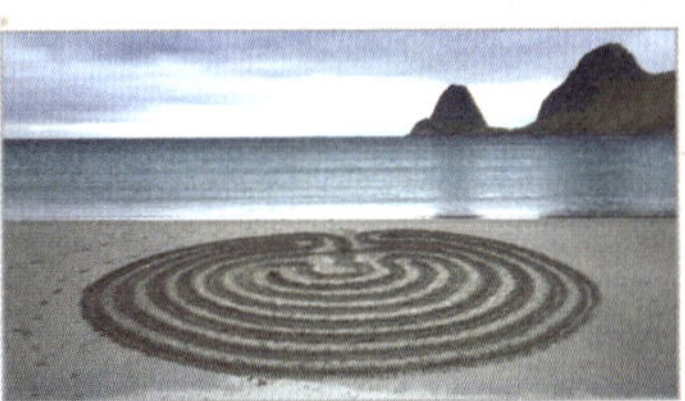

Trojaborg labyrinth drawn on a beach in Vesterålen, Norway, 2015

Your pupils will enjoy drawing Trojaborg labyrinths at full size in sand, or by using chalk in the playground or by placing stones on the ground. It is easy to construct a labyrinth by working from a cross form, as shown in the diagram on the right. However, drawing it freehand, step by step, as shown on the facing page, will enable you to fully relate to the qualities inherent in the labyrinth's form.

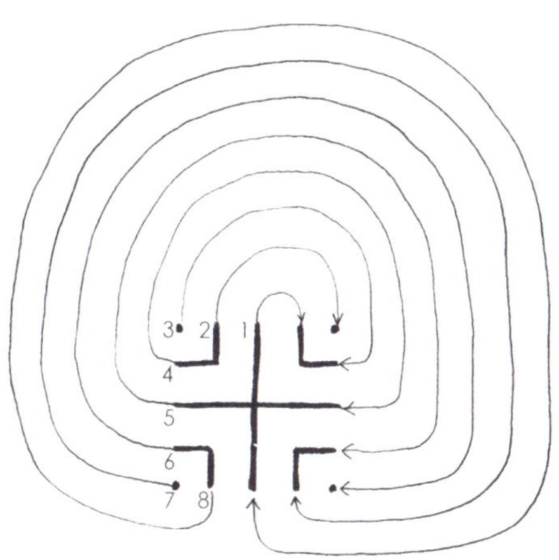

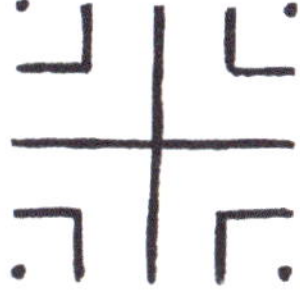

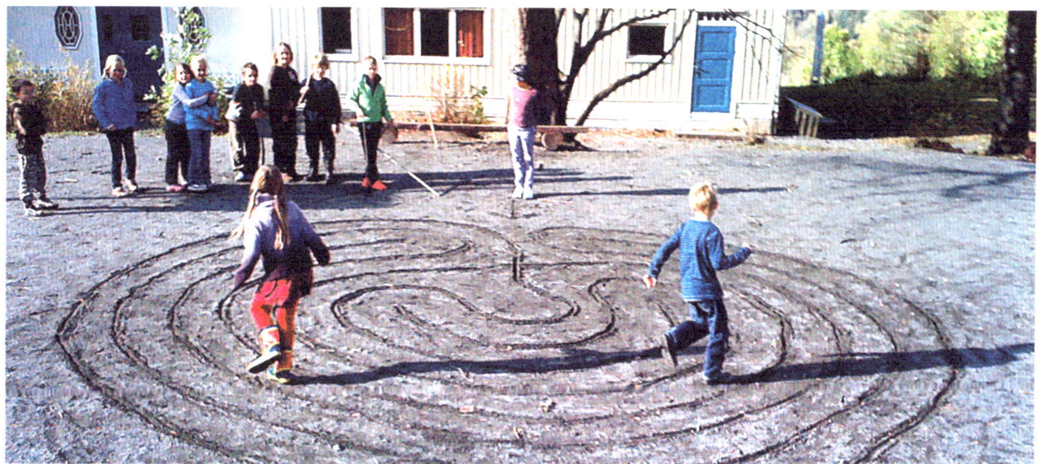

A Trojaborg-shaped labyrinth in a school playground

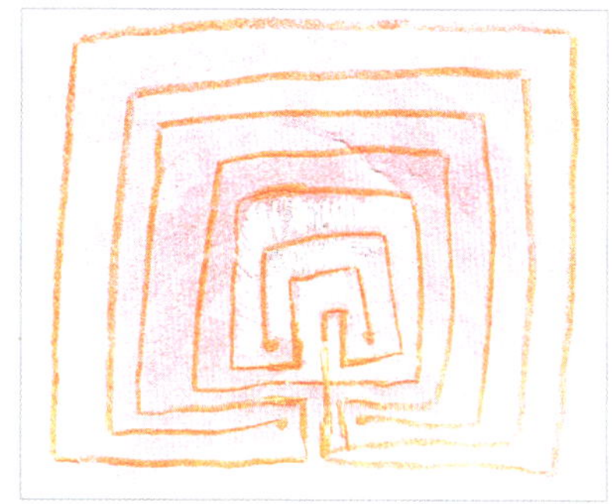

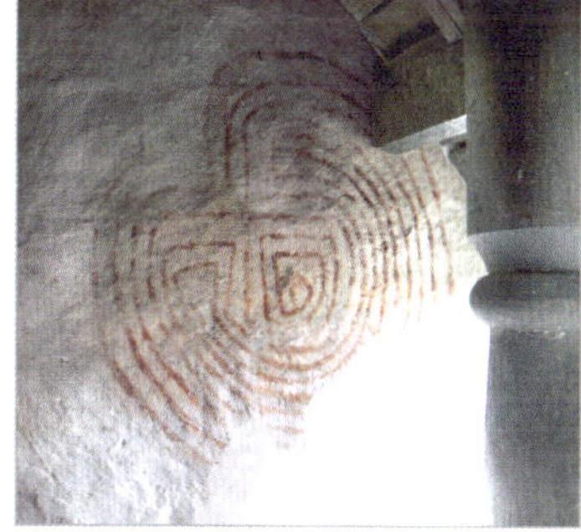

A labyrinth depicted on the wall of a medieval church entrance in Seljord, Norway

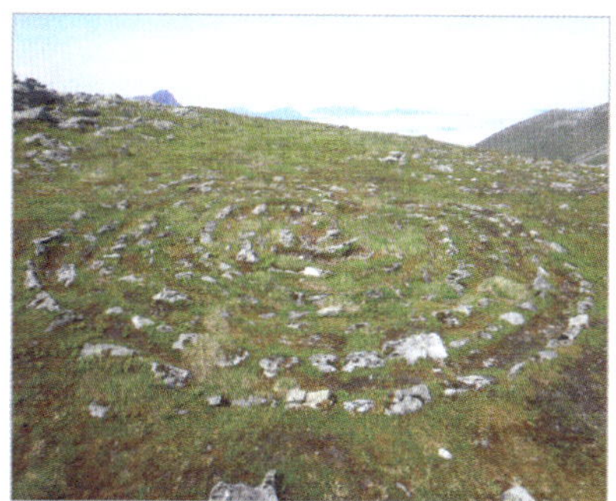

The Julian Castle Trojaborg, Ørsta, Norway, dates from the Bronze Age

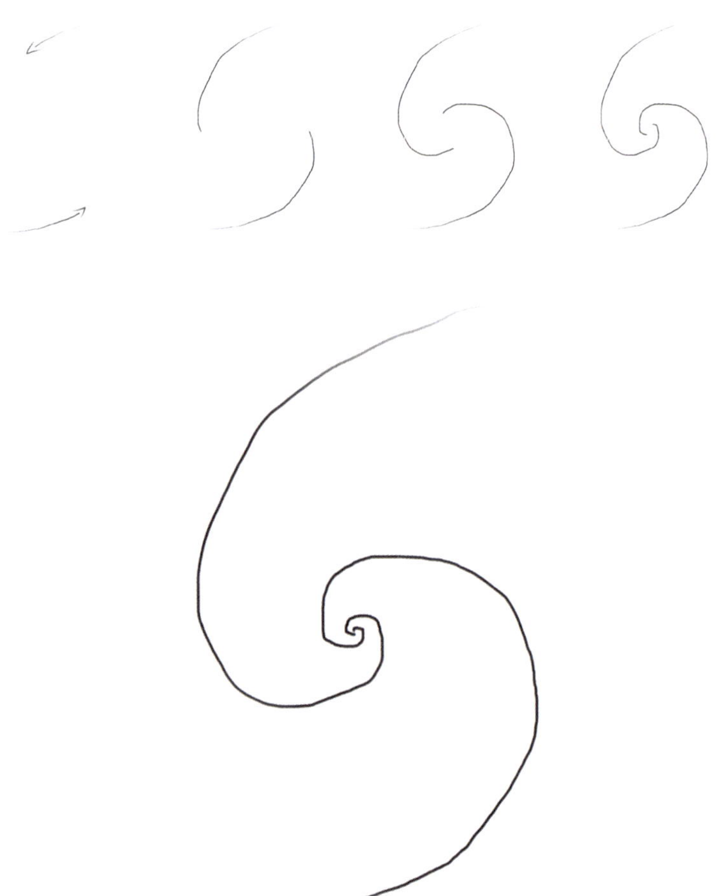

Spirals

A logarithmic spiral is one in which the size of the spiral increases but its shape stays the same with each curve. Drawing them freehand is difficult, but possible. This challenge is also a good example of aesthetic problem-solving, so it is worth spending time on practising this form.

Before the exercise begins, I suggest you do not mention the word 'spiral', so that pupils can discover the form for themselves as it emerges.

Instruct your pupils to start with two lines, one at the top and one at the bottom of the page. Extend each line gradually so that they approach one another but do not meet. In other words, they will turn towards one another, but the end of each line will not 'point' at the other one. Ask your pupils this question: if the lines do not point at one another, does that mean they will not meet?

Your pupils might find the exercise confusing to start with, but it is important that they discover the principle in the spiral that gradually appears. To ensure that they get the idea, repeat the exercise, both on paper and the blackboard.

The sheet of paper will eventually be divided into two surfaces, and when the work is coloured in it will underline the strong dynamism of the spiral.

Logarithmic spirals are often found in natural phenomena, such as in nautilus shells, pinecones or liquid (see photographs).

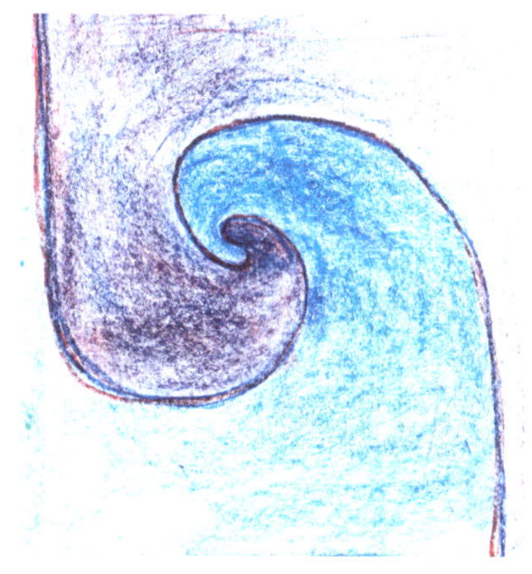

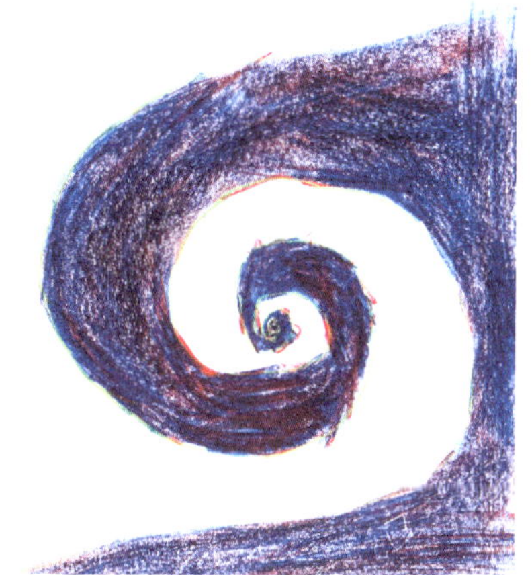

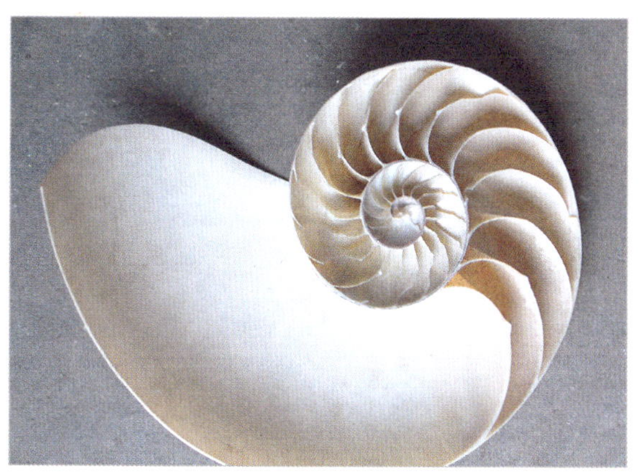

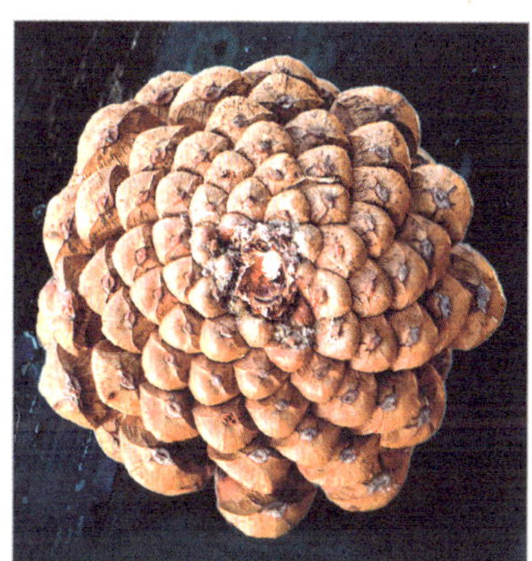

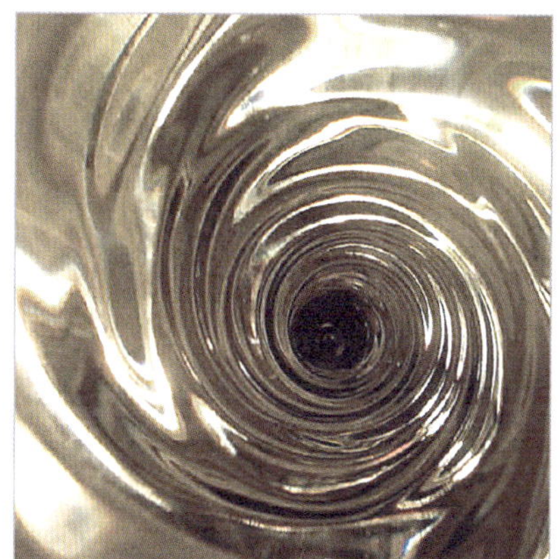

Spirals in plants

In a lot of plants, the so-called Fibonacci spiral is visible. At this level of schooling it is too early to teach your pupils about Fibonacci's number sequences or constructions, but you can prepare them for more advanced mathematics in the future by using freehand drawing to explore the beautiful ratios between leaves.

Choose a colour that matches your background to draw the lines. Mark the middle of a page with a dot, then place three dots equidistant from the central point and equidistant from one another, as shown on the top left. Draw three lines in a spiral shape from the central point outwards, passing through each marked point. Try letting the spirals unfold more and more.

Next, mark five points in the same way (one of these will be in the same place as one of the previous three, as

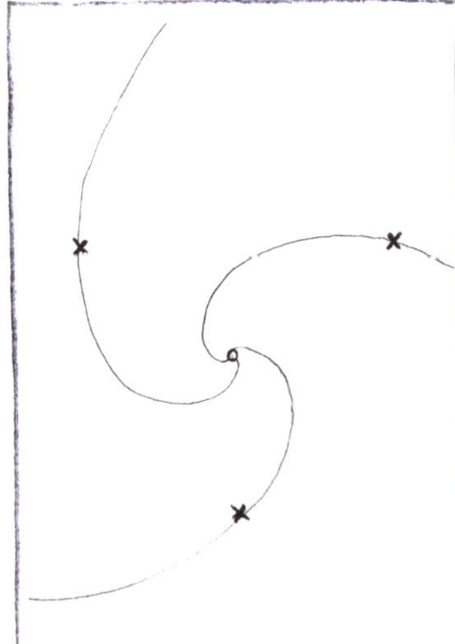

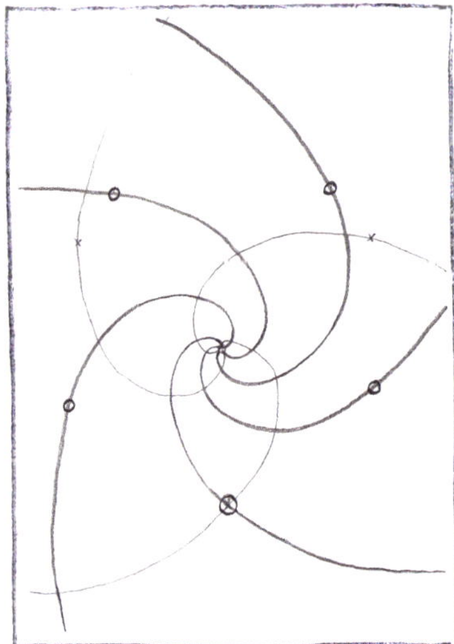

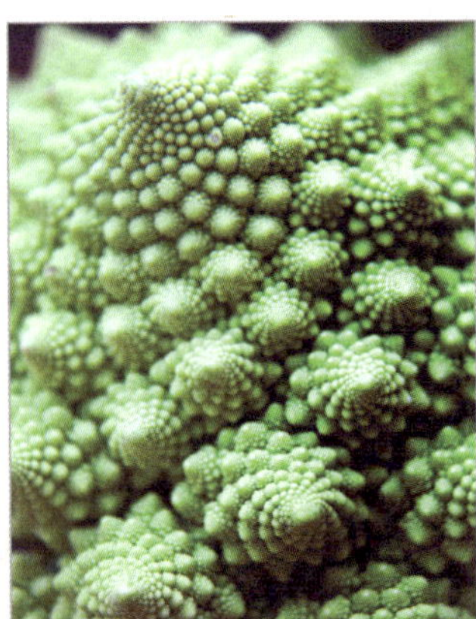

Romanesco broccoli

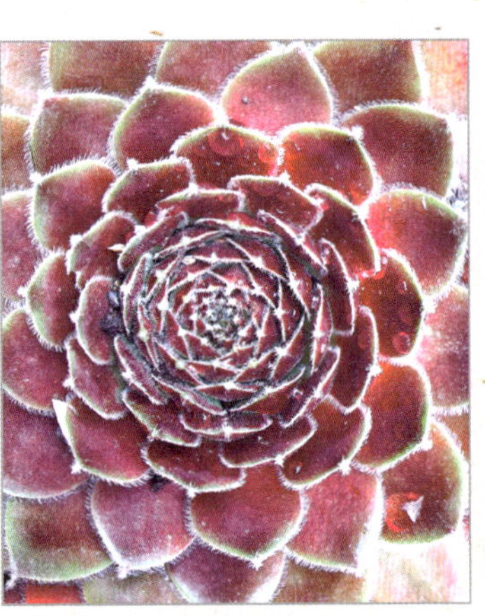

Sempervivum

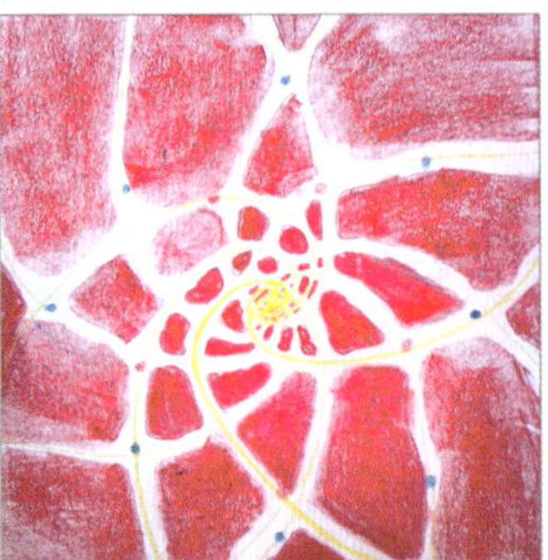

shown on the top right on the facing page – see the small x within the circle). Let the spiral develop from the centre and out through these points, but in the opposite direction.

Now, use a stronger colour to define individual areas in the gaps and colour these. Finally, fill in any spaces with the weaker background colour, so that all guidelines disappear.

Flower forms

To make a flower, draw a small circle about the size of a cherry, then draw a border of loops that constantly touch the circle. The loops can be the same size or different. Colour them in if you like.

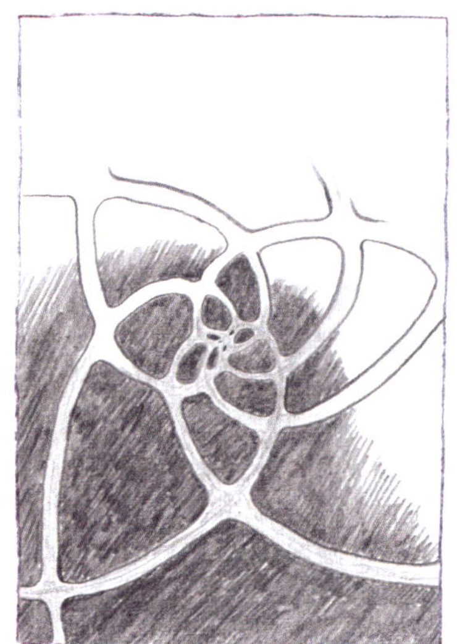

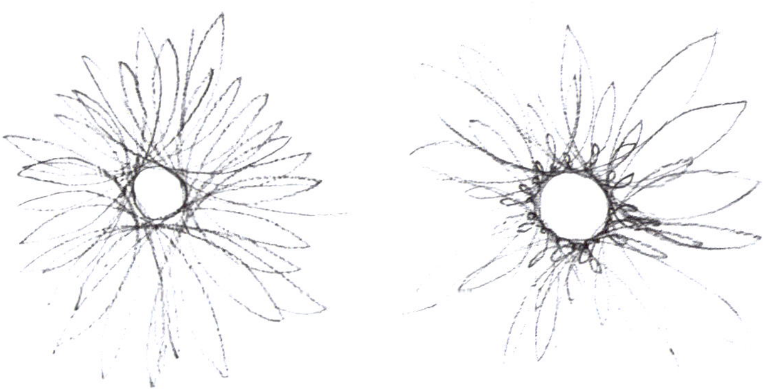

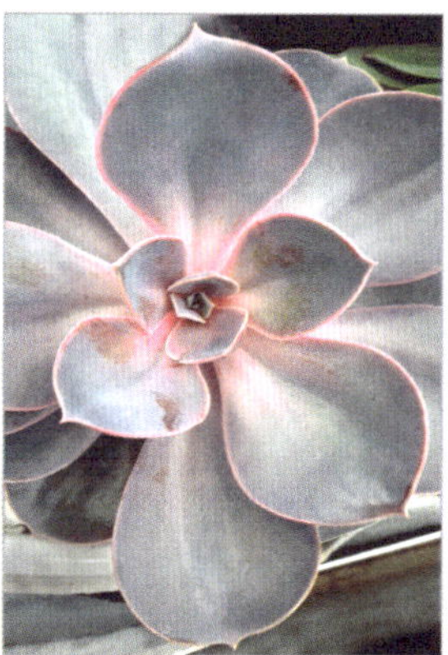

Echeveria

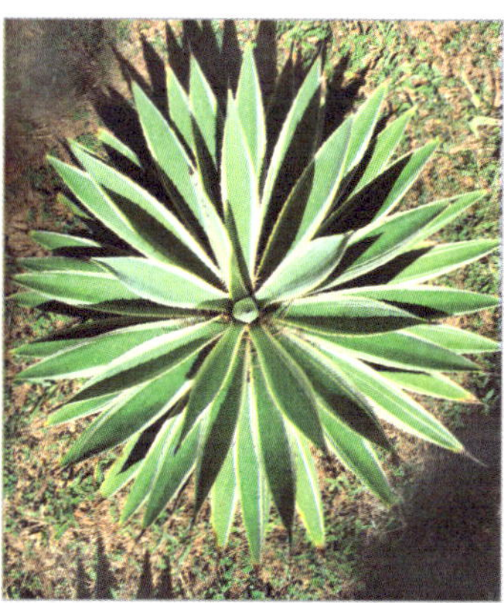

Sisal plant

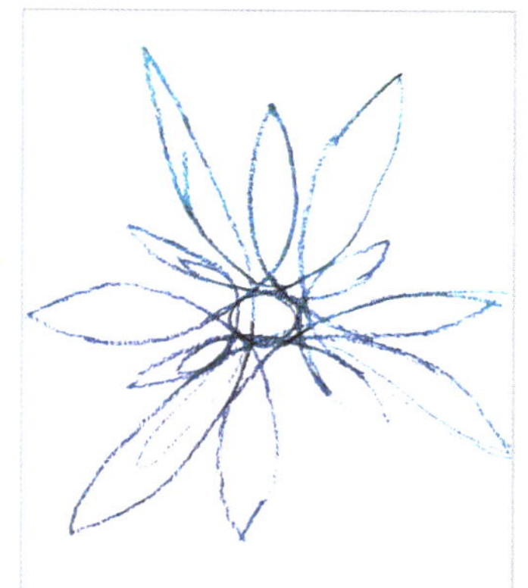

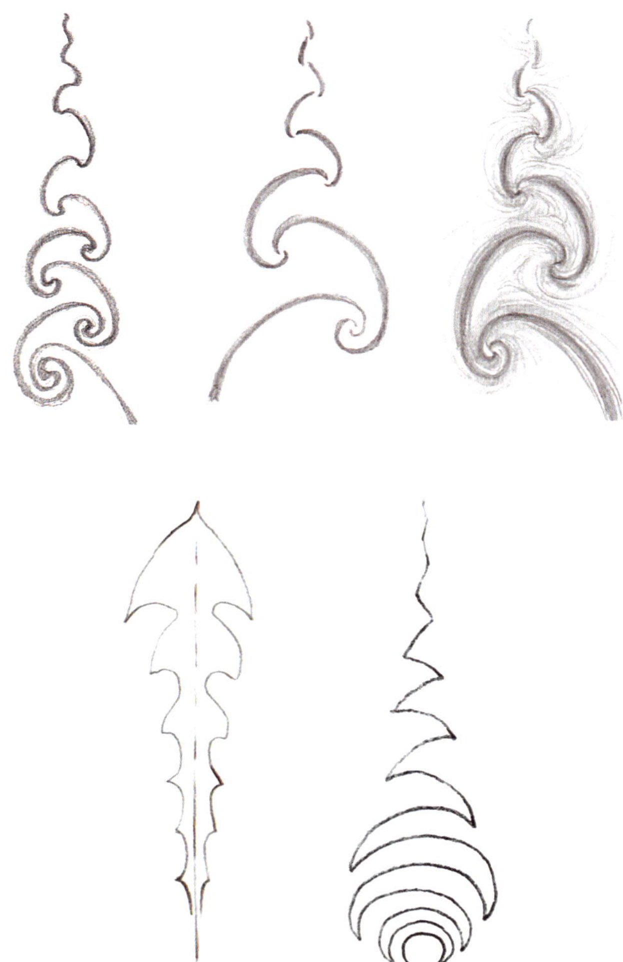

Movement in water and air

Water and air streaming past an object will rhythmically beat from side to side and produce a meandering pattern known as a Kármán vortex street, as shown in these three examples.

Metamorphoses

The two leaf-like forms below include all four types of exercise in this book: line drawing, the basic shapes, mirroring and development of forms (see pp.19–20).

The first resembles a dandelion leaf and can be drawn using mirroring, beginning with the central line. Note the transformation and development of the form on the way up, not least the elegant way in which it finishes.

The other shape transforms from the round to the linear. Start with the small almost-circle at the bottom and allow the movement to progress upwards.

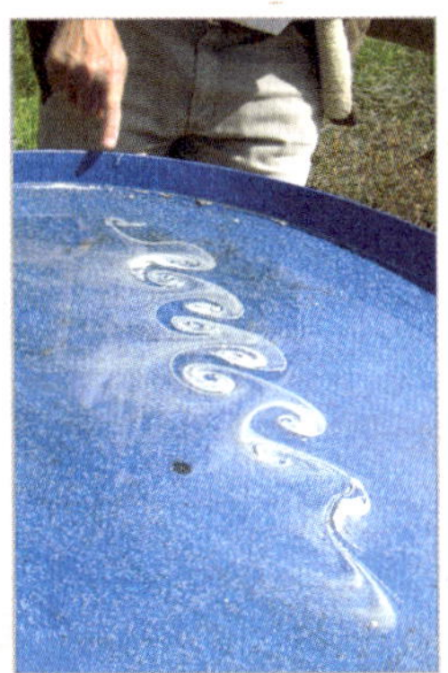

Movement in water. A finger is slowly pulled through water with a powdered surface

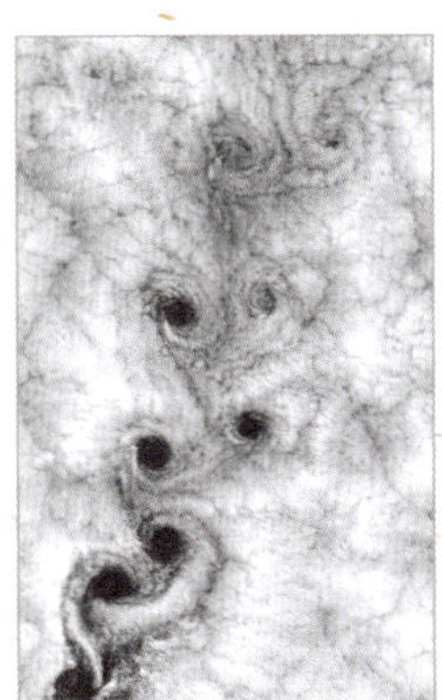

Clouds over the Pacific Ocean. The same meandering movements occur in both water and air

Leaf patterns

Build up a leaf pattern following the steps shown here. Try your own variations.

Seed patterns

Draw a circle the size of an orange and draw semi-circles, or 'seeds', along the inside of its circumference. Continue with a new row of seeds on the inside of the first row so that the start and finish point of the semi-circle is at the top of a semi-circle on the first row. Try to be as accurate as you can so that you can fully enjoy the pattern that arises as you work inwards.

If your circle is not perfect, don't worry; this just makes the exercise more interesting – indeed, it is preferable! This is part of nature's rich mode of expression: the perfect principle of form meeting accidental circumstance.

Add the flower petals at the end. You can colour these, but not the seeds.

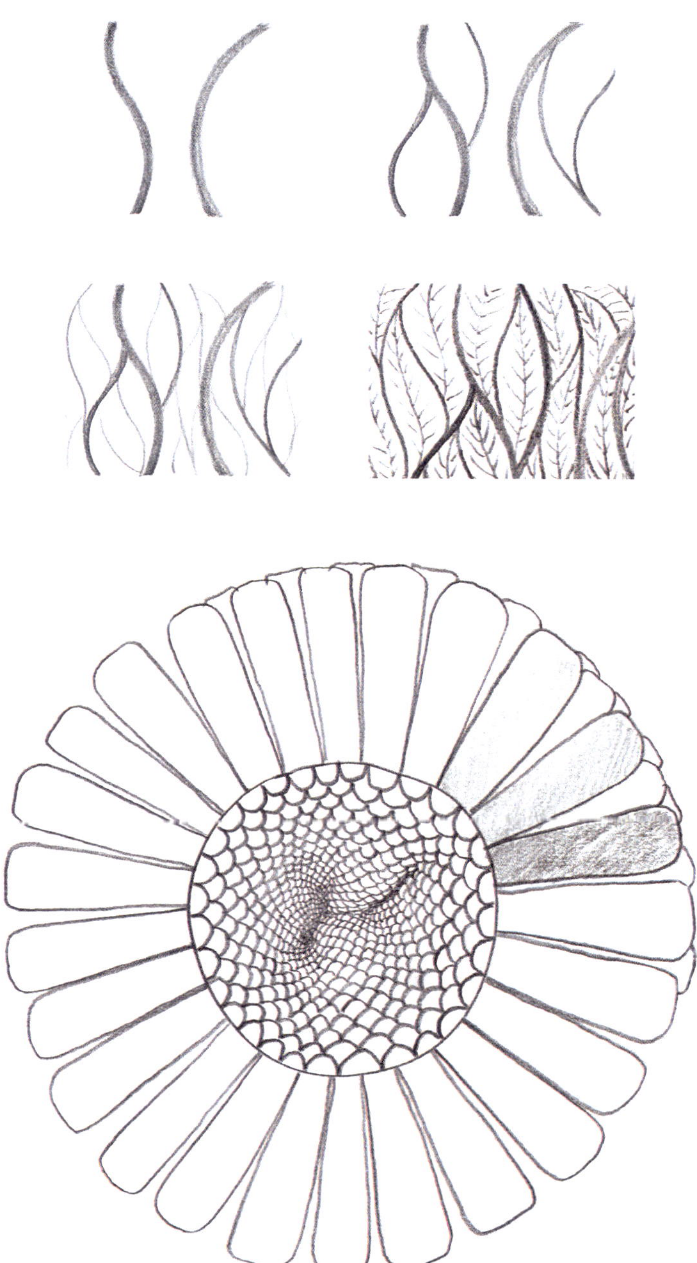

The Sierpinski triangle

A Sierpinski triangle is an equilateral triangle that can be subdivided into more equilateral triangles.

First, draw a large triangle on a sheet of paper using a light colour.

Draw a new triangle inside of the first triangle, as shown in the first drawing, and colour this in. Draw triangles in the same way in all of the new triangular spaces that emerge, and continue for as long as you like.

You can fill in all of the triangles you create with a stronger colour.

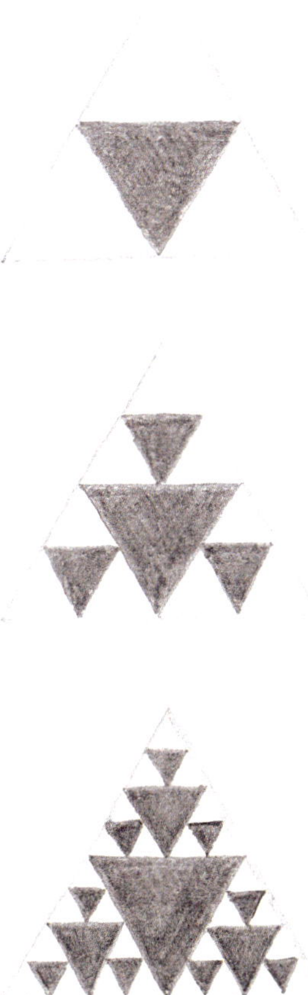

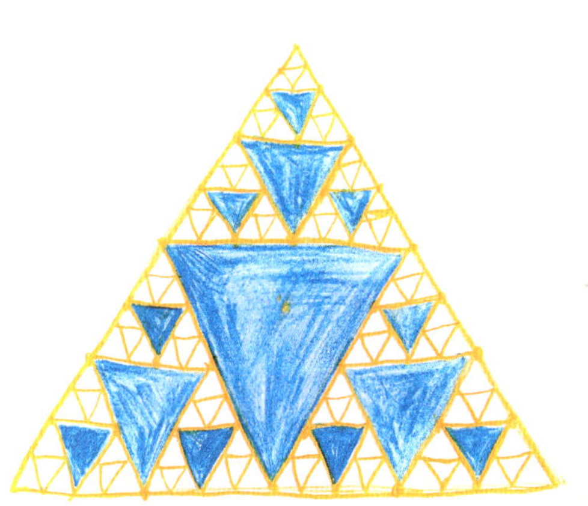

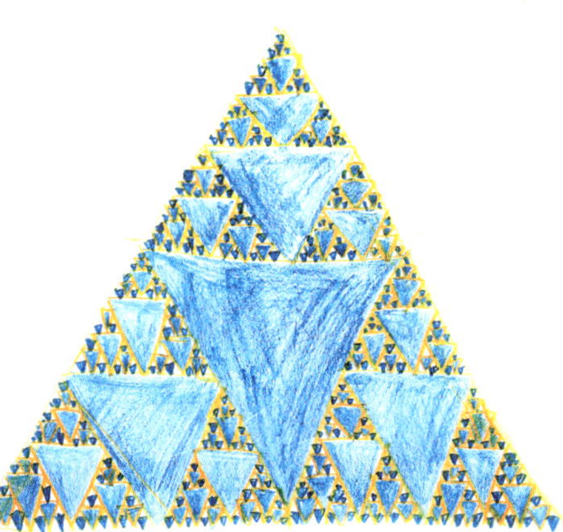

The Koch snowflake

Like the Fibonacci spiral, the Koch snowflake is a feature of mathematics too advanced for this age group, but it is instructive to draw it.

Start by drawing a large triangle in the colour you will use to fill in the finished form. Mark two points on each side of the triangle to divide them into three equal lengths.

Now, draw new triangles from the centre of these parts, as shown (top centre). Continue this with all the lines or sides that appear.

When you decide you have gone far enough, draw an outline around the entire form with a sharp and strong-coloured crayon.

Finally, colour in the form with the original colour so that all the guidelines disappear.

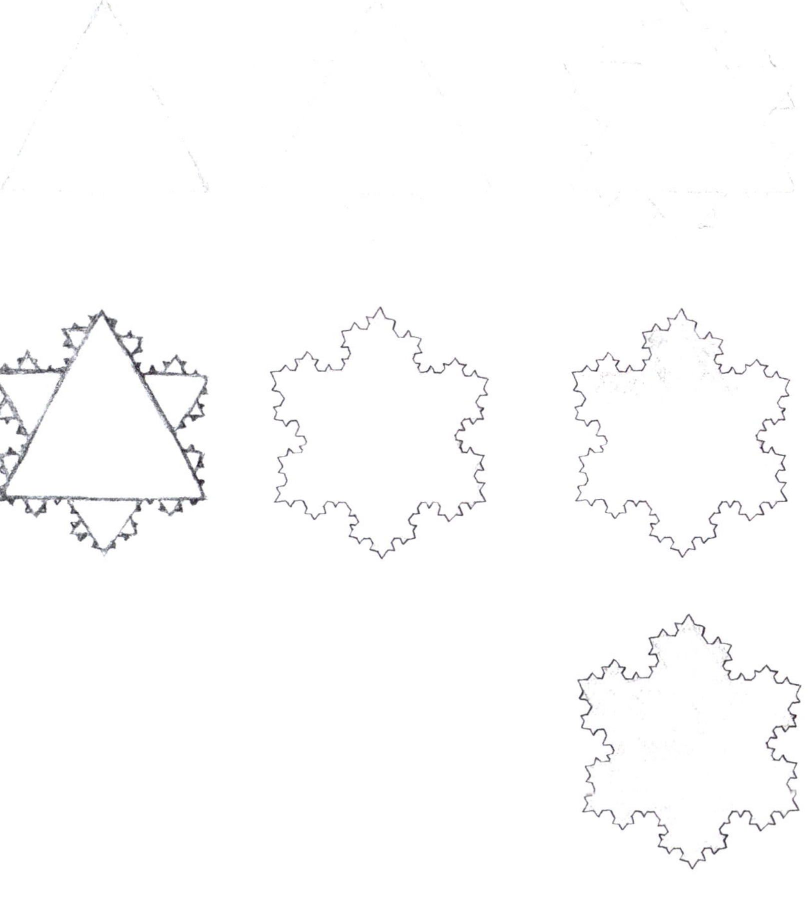

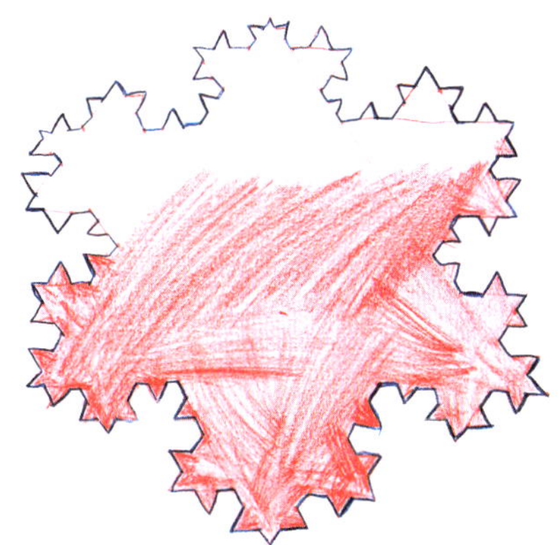

Unfinished work by pupil

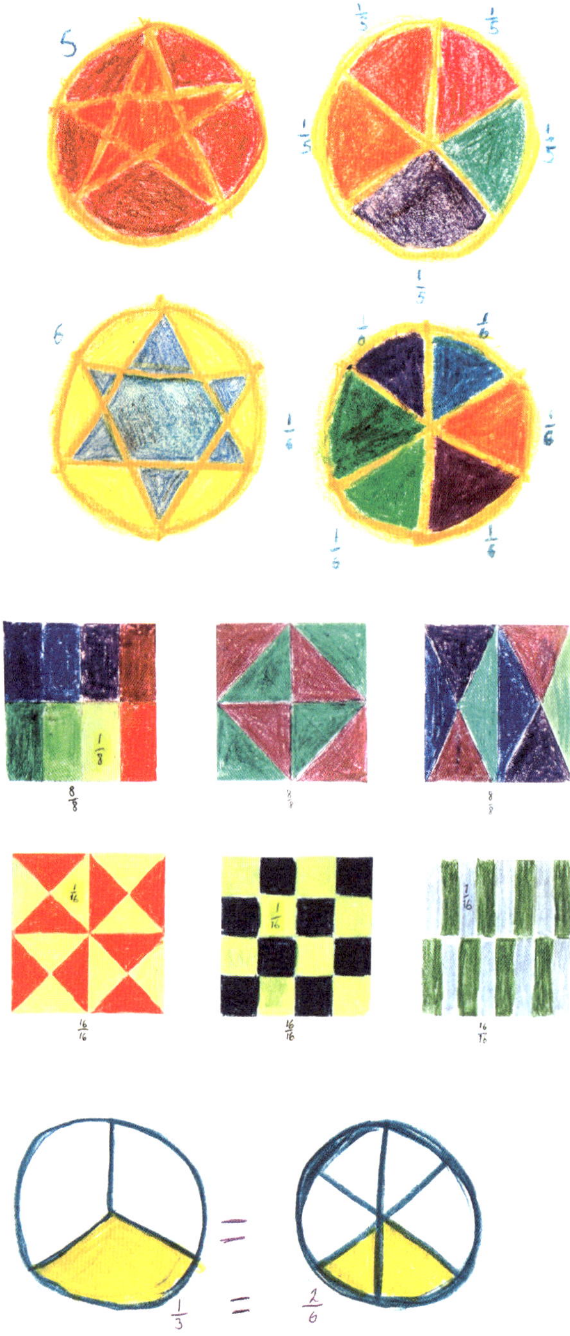

Fractions

Visuals can help your pupils to understand fractions when they have difficulties. For example, the circles illustrated here can be used to introduce dividing a whole into pieces.

You can also fold paper squares in class to divide them into two, four, eight or sixteen equal pieces. The challenge is to do so in as many ways as possible and to work out the different solutions for making each part equal in size. Colour in the sections clearly.

The drawings at the bottom of the page also use circles, this time to demonstrate the equal amounts of 1/3 and 2/6 and of 2/3 and 4/6. All these examples are work by pupils.

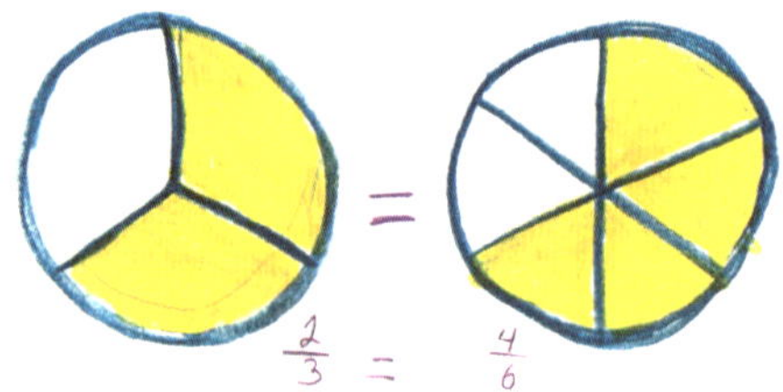

The following exercise demonstrates how values sink towards zero when the numerator stays the same and the denominator increases.

Glue a strip of paper onto a sheet or into a book. The next strip should be folded in two and only the upper part glued in beside the first one. The next strip should be folded in three and so on. A curve will appear that gradually becomes less steep. This is a good way of introducing pupils to logarithms, something they will fully understand at a much later date.

Representing fractions in a circle or as pillars is an exercise in understanding graphical representation. It is necessary to understand fractions in order to be able to understand bar graphs. One version of this can appear as such (taken from a pupil's work):

The left-hand side of the workbook pictured shows ratios 1/1, 1/2, 1/3, 1/4, 1/5, 1/6, 1/7, 1/8. The values reduce and thus will flatten out.

The right-hand side shows the ratios 1/8, 2/8, 3/8, 4/8, 5/8, 6/8, 7/8, 8/8. The values increase evenly in a regular growth pattern.

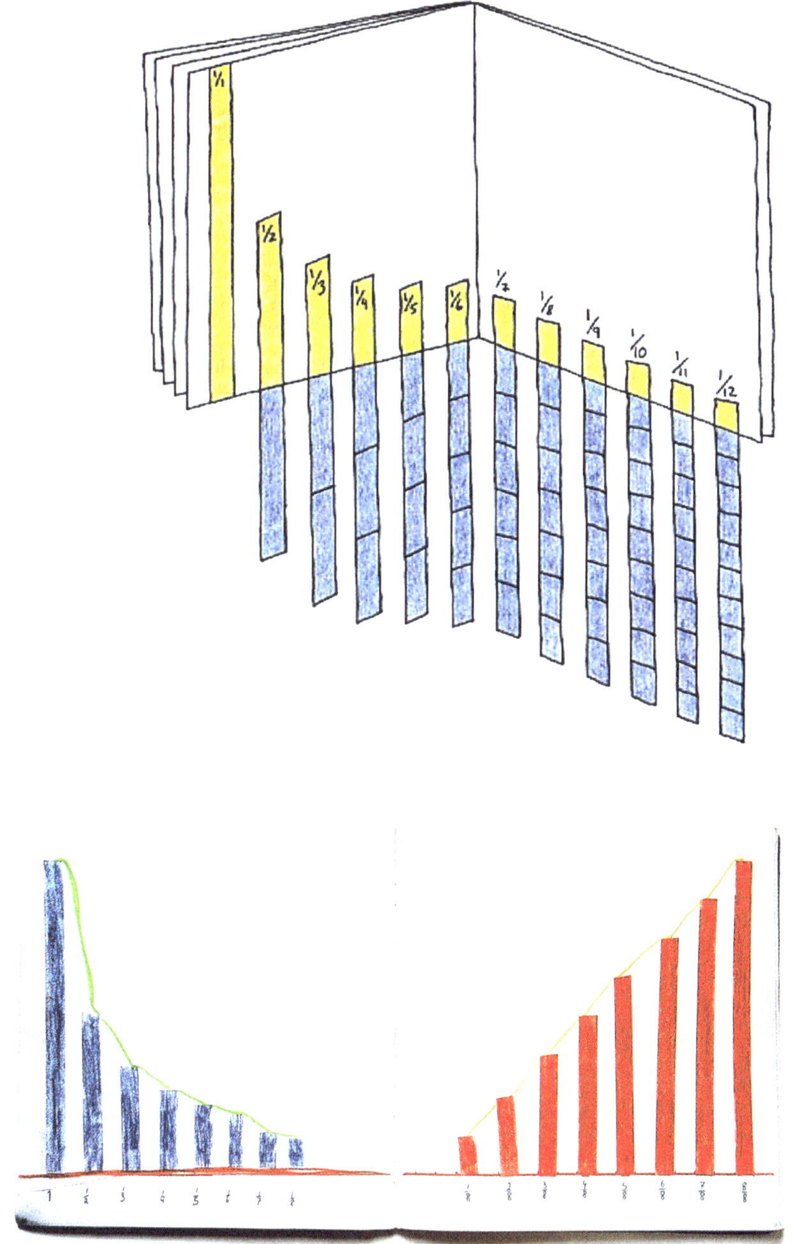

Fractions can also be presented in rows, and this piece of work is called a fraction table. By using a ruler placed on the figure, it is possible to see how 1/2 equals 2/4, 3/6, 4/8 and so on. Pupils can go on a journey of discovery, trying to find similar yet different sizes.

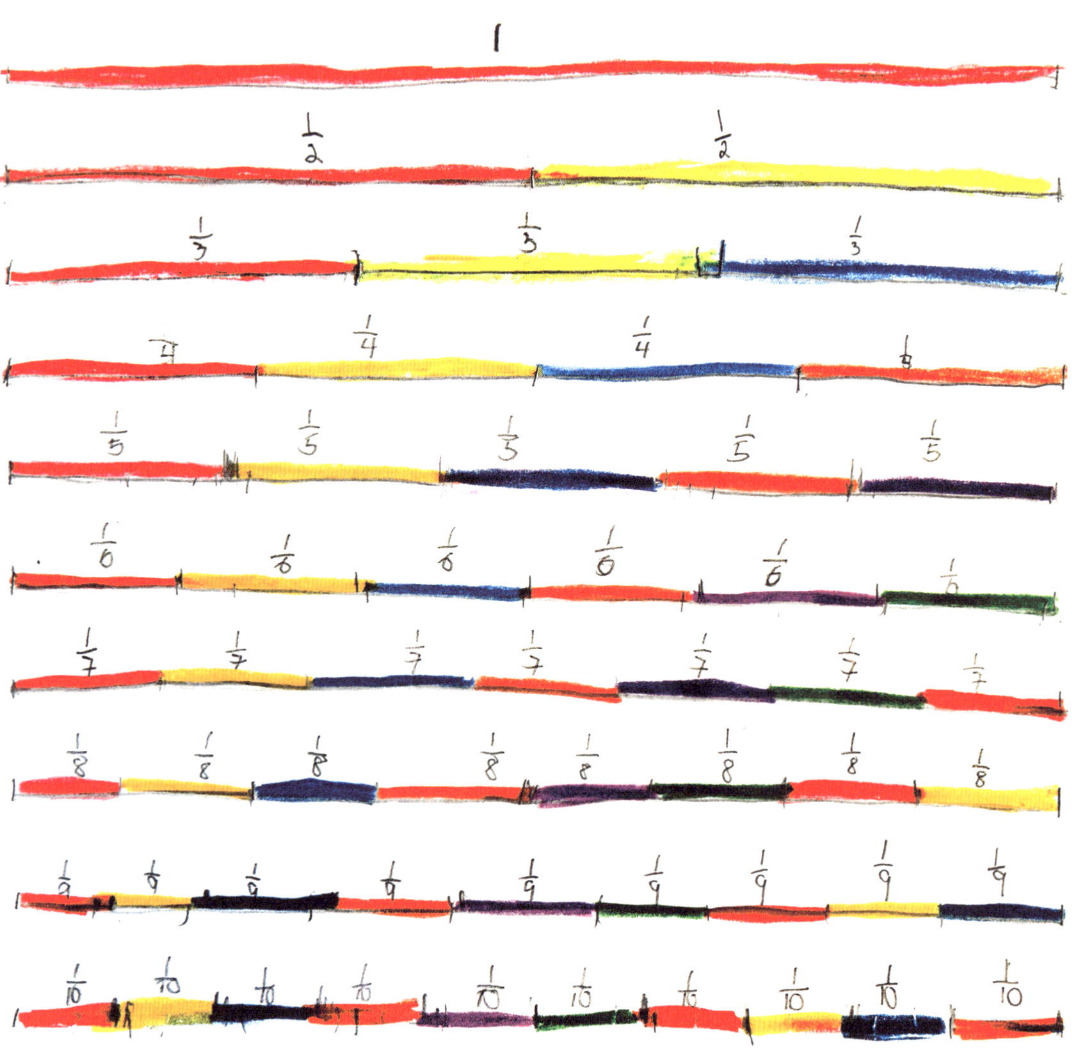

In this exercise, fractions are represented as pieces of pie. Here, the pupil has folded the paper and discovered how this circular, round surface can be folded in half again and again. It helps to visualise how a whole can be divided or put together from many different fractions.

When a part is halved over and over again, it becomes constantly less, yet it never reaches zero. Or does it? Discuss this in class with your pupils.

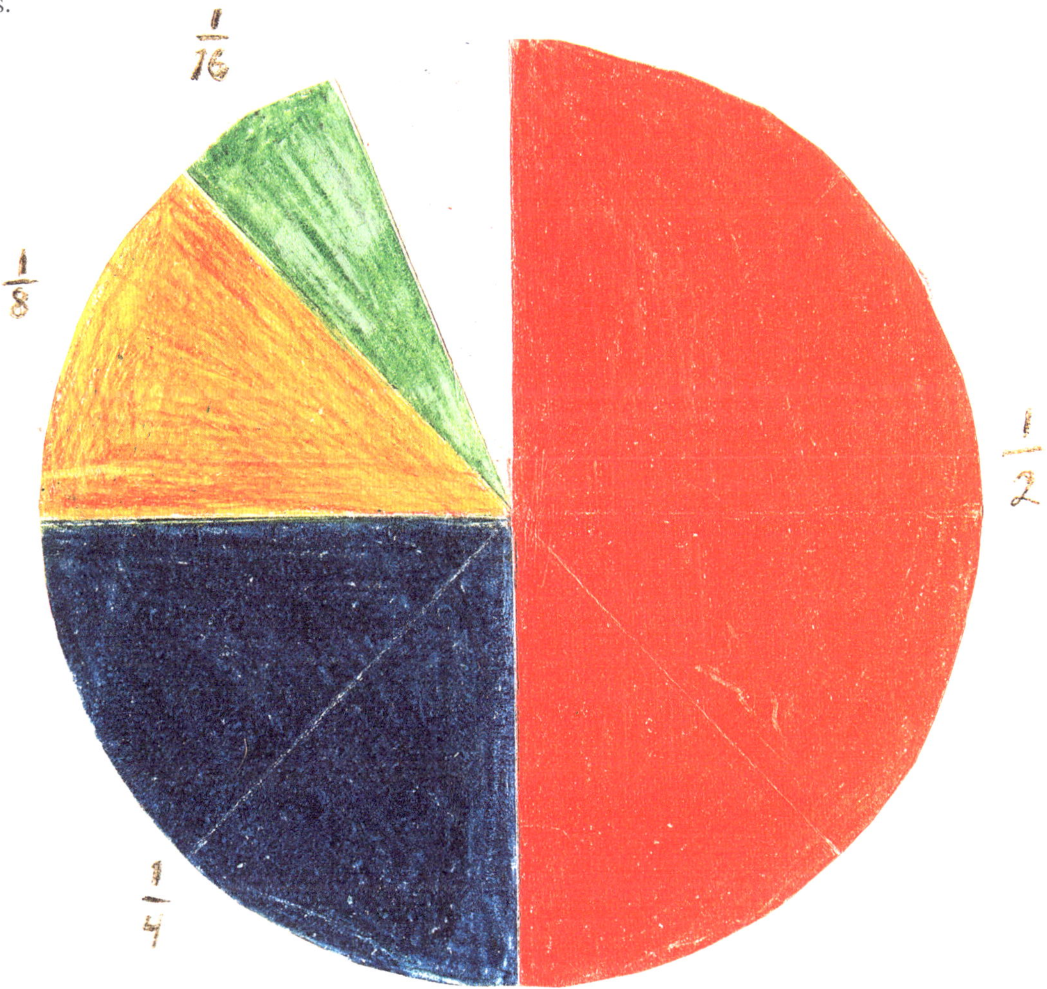

Part 6: Botany Lesson Exercises

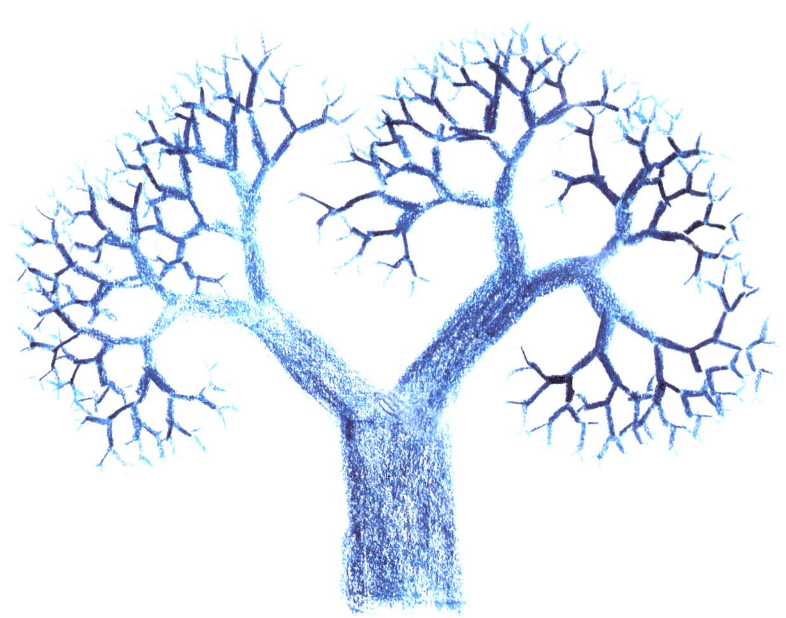

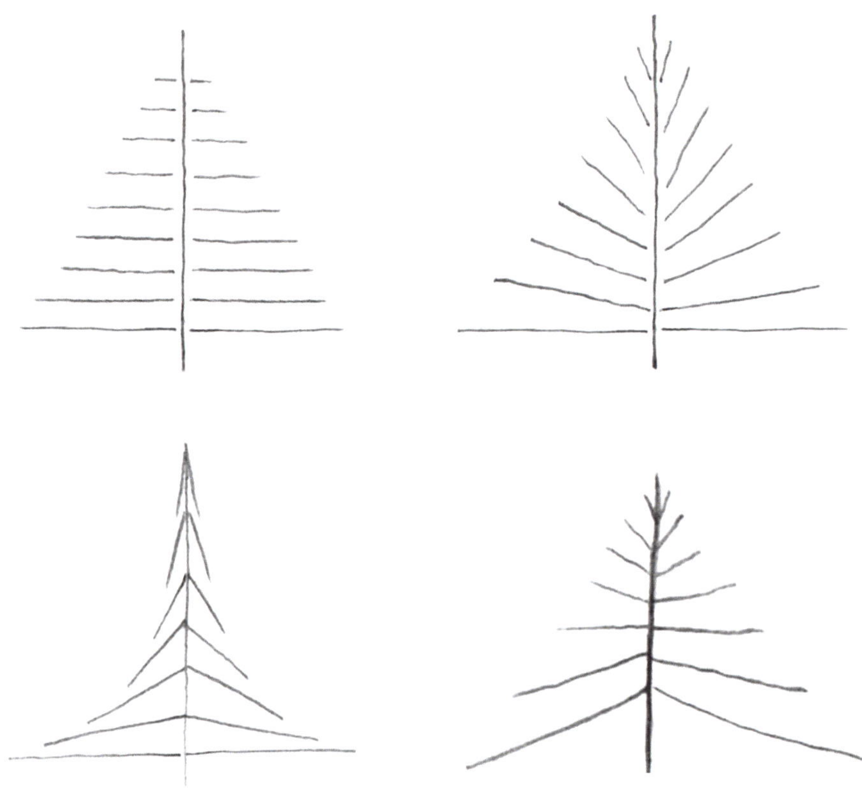

Metamorphosis and plant motifs

Divergence is a large and exciting aspect of form drawing. It is easy to see the principle of how branches divide on trees or annual plants (that is, those that grow from seed to plant and then die within a single season).

Birch, pine and spruce do not form their crowns, or tops, in the same way as other trees; they maintain their shape at the crown. From a form perspective, their growth and development occur at the base of the tree; therefore these exercises should be drawn from the bottom up. You can guide your pupils through a few steps, then leave them to continue drawing to see if they can complete a whole form. Through practice and development, they can gain a sense of both structure and the total form.

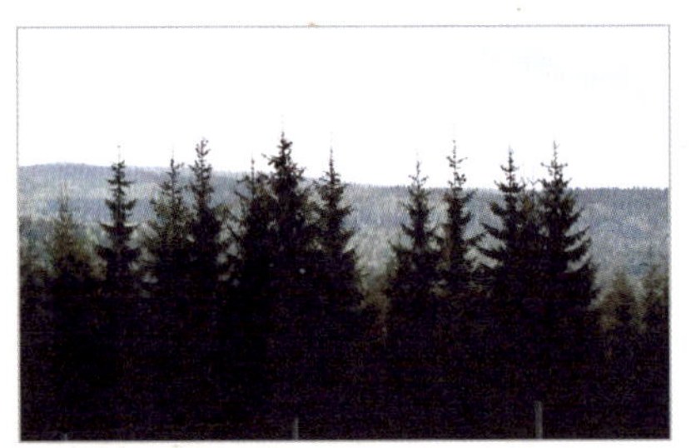

Norwegian spruce forest

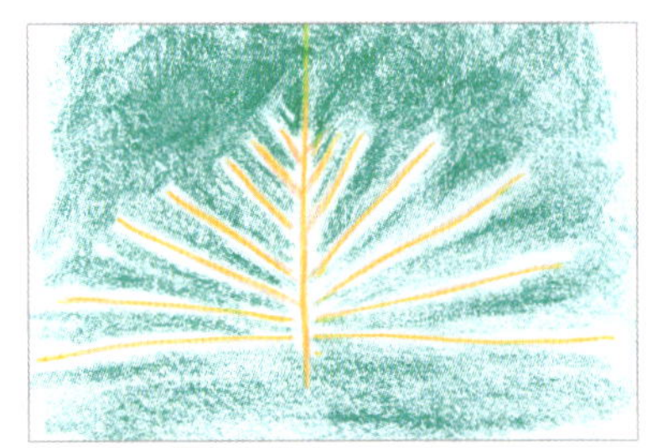

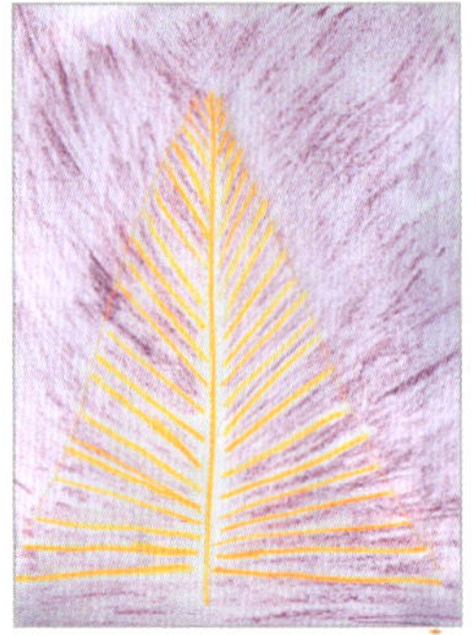

Looking at an elm tree branch (see the photograph below), we can see that the new twigs grow alternately on each side and the stem follows the direction of each new sprouting twig.

The principle of how a branch grows after each division can be represented as shown. You can draw a faint oval or egg shape as a framework for the branches to be drawn within.

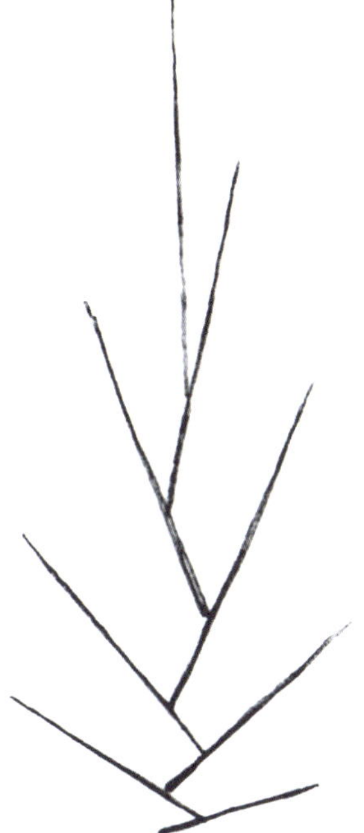

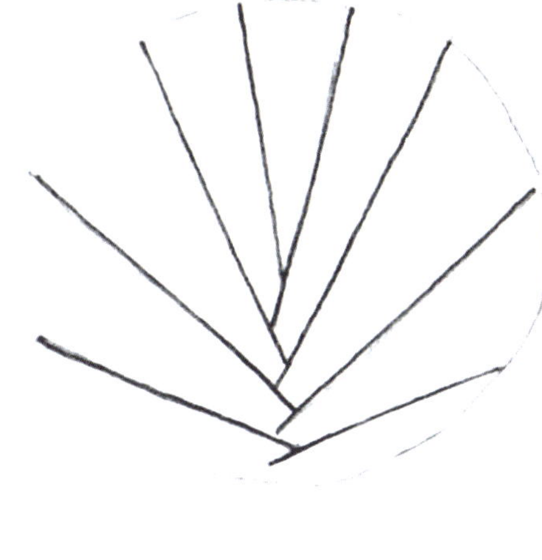

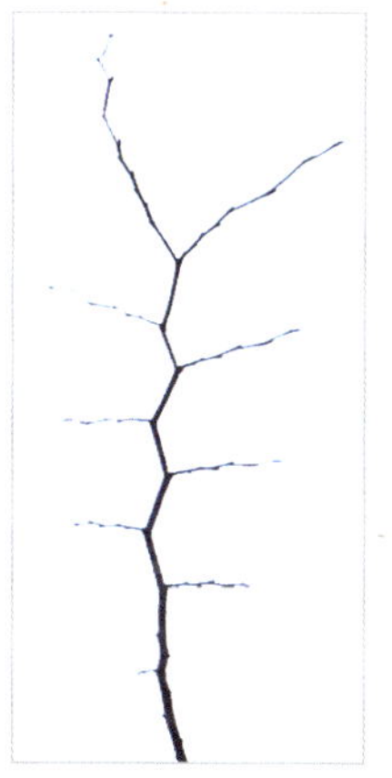

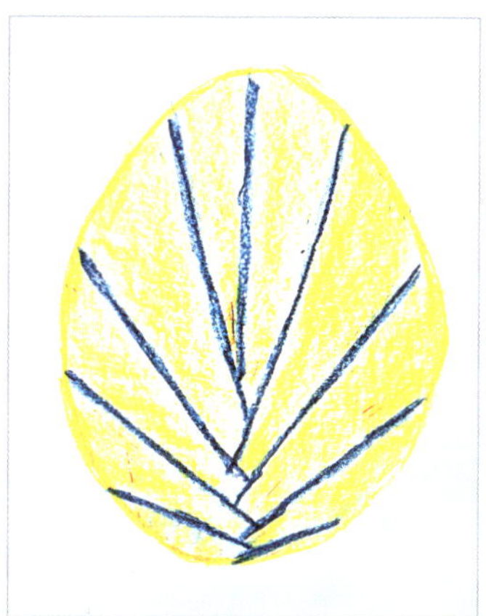

A branch from an elm tree

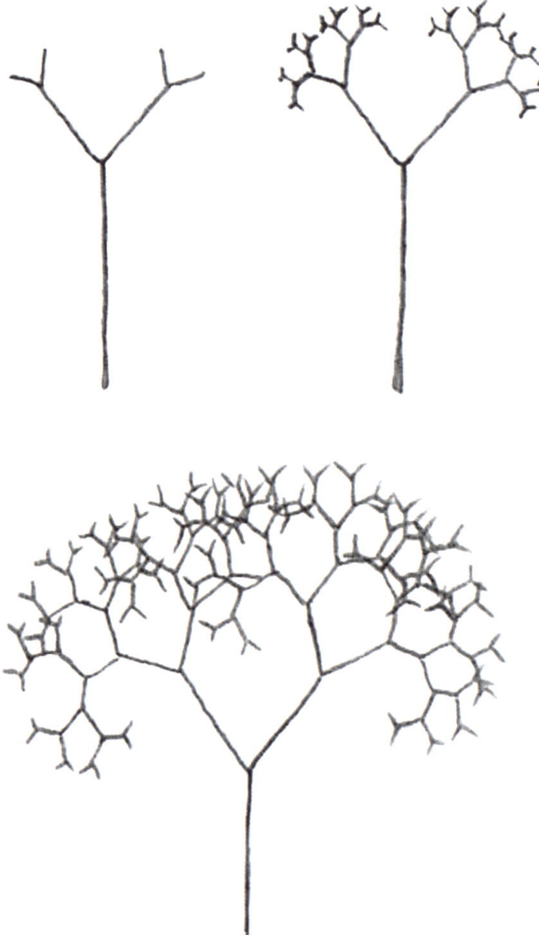

A general rule for the division of branches, particularly among annuals, is that they continually divide into two or three.

There are two main places to introduce variation: the angle where the new branch divides from the stem and the ratio between the lengths of the old and new branches. In the example on the left, the ratio is half the length of the previous branch. The angle remains the same. Let the pupils experiment with different solutions (and see p.167 for more).

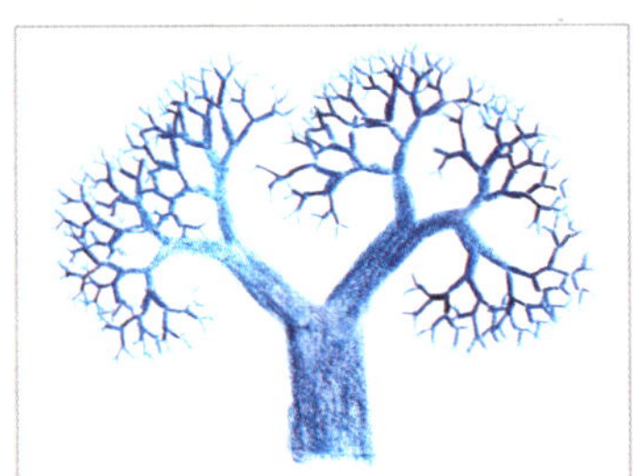

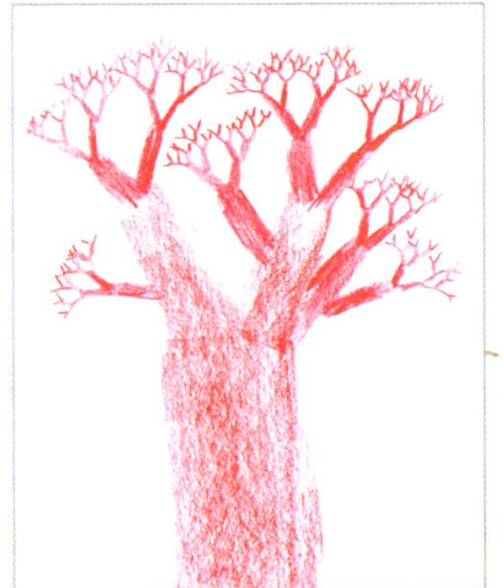

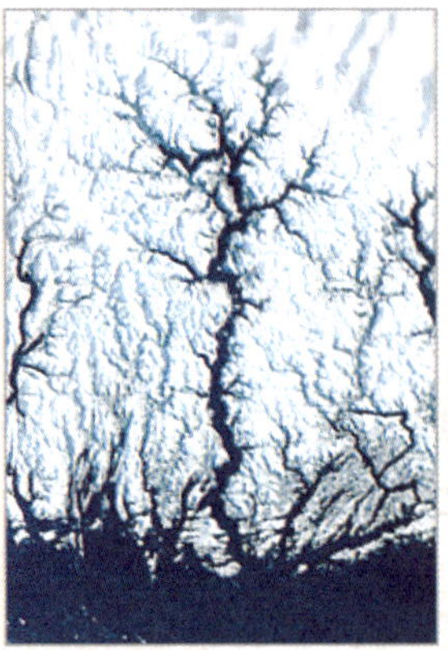

Sogne Fjord, Norway

In this exercise, other rules apply. The first line represents the full height of the form. Now, find the middle of the 'trunk' and extend two branches from here so that there are three equally long branches stemming from this point, then repeat with each new branch that you draw.

Let pupils try with other ratios too (and see related exercises in fractal structures on p.172).

In the photographs below are two ash trees, one two years old, the other almost ten. Notice how the initially strict branch formation of two parallel twigs at the same angle is replaced by another principle for crown formation. (The dimensions of the photograph have been adjusted to allow for comparison.)

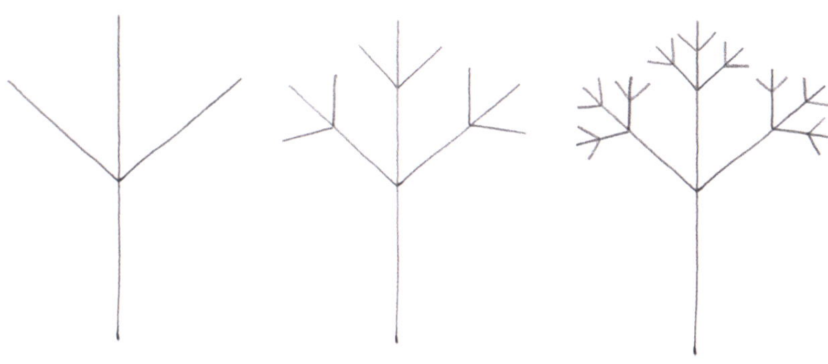

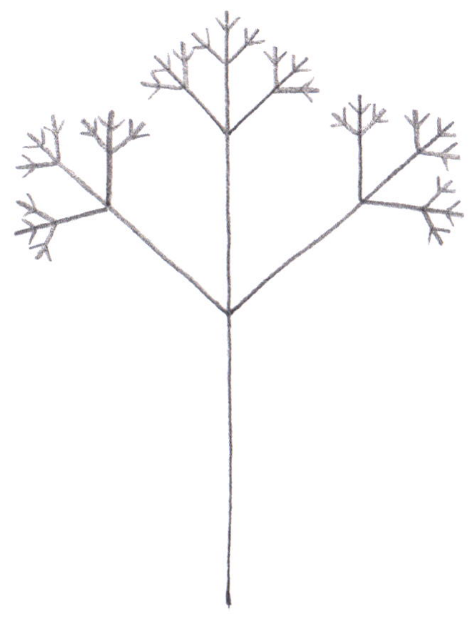

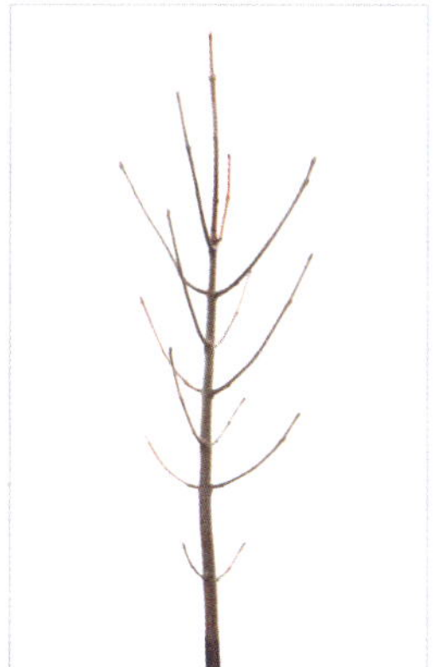

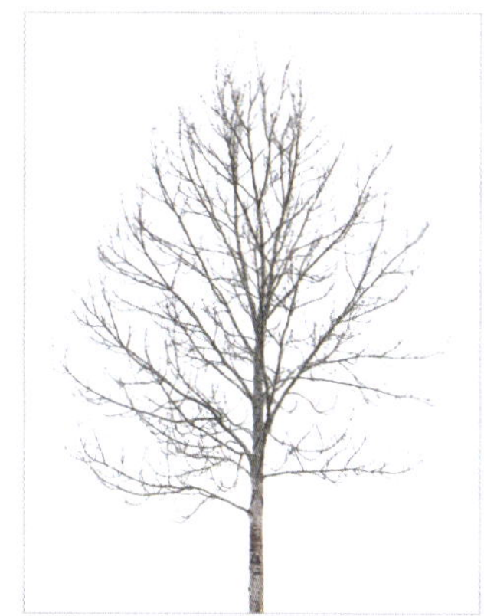

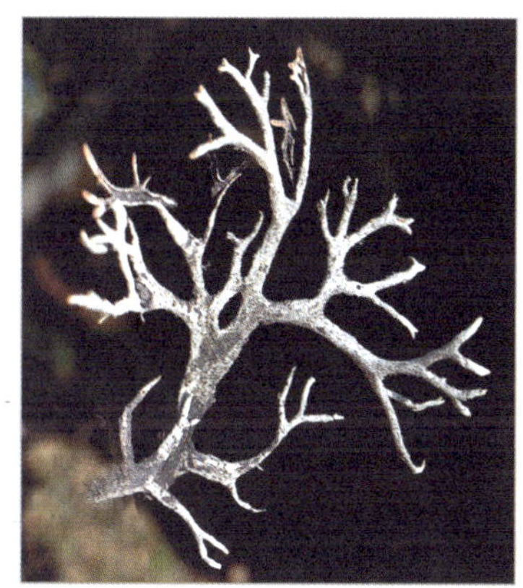

Branching in lichen

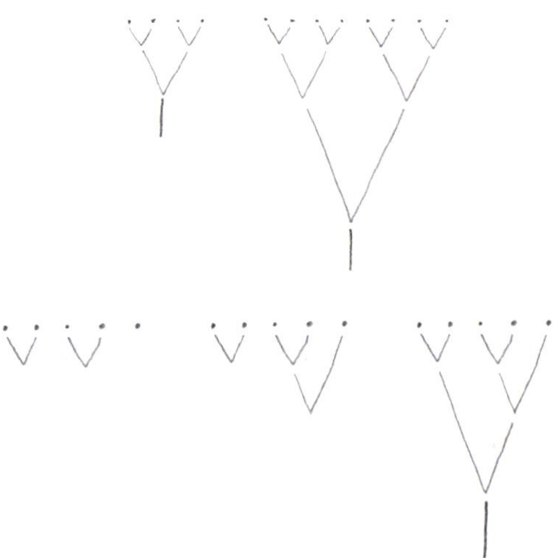

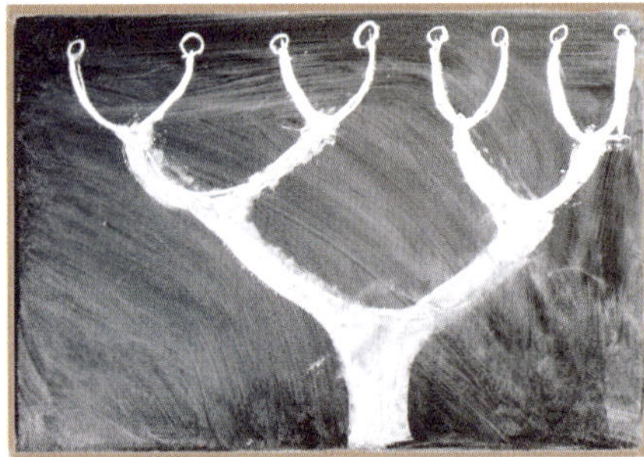

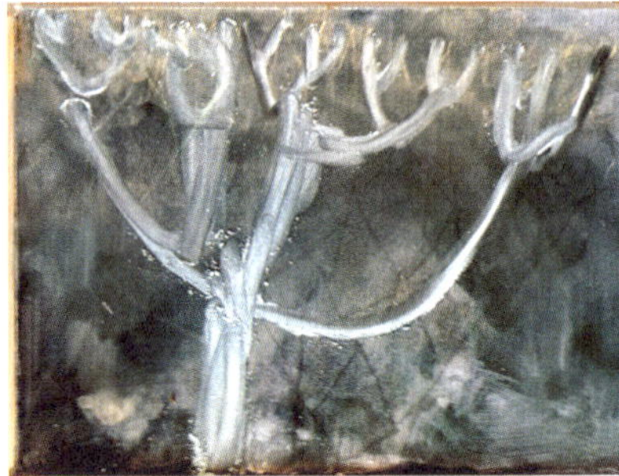

Work by pupils on blackboard

It seems as if plants have a plan for how tall they will be, and for why and how they will stop growing. Some, for example, have planned to form a screen. In a form-drawing exercise it is possible to begin where growth stops, rather than where it starts.

Place dots along a line or a curve, then join them together two by two, as shown in the first two illustrations. Take care not to have more than one join at each point.

If the number of dots or flowers is not even, there will be one left when they are joined two by two. Connect this final flower as shown in the last illustration on the top left. In other words, first connect the flowers from left to right, two by two, then connect them from right to left, before once more working from left to right.

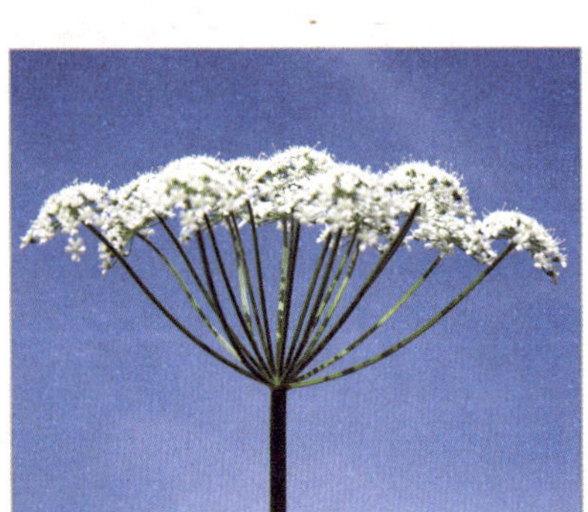

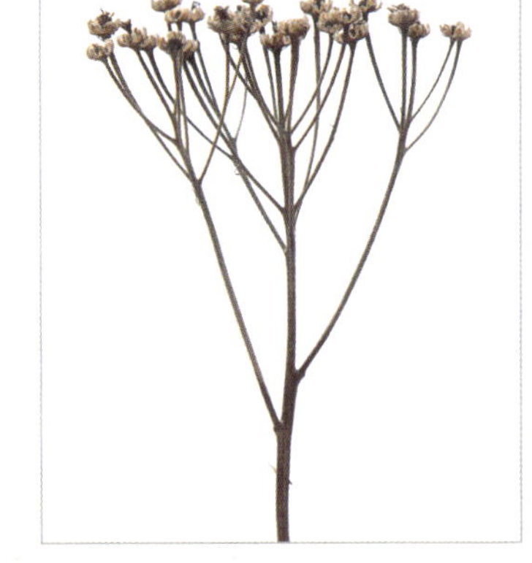

Umbellifer

A decorative alternative is to arrange the points (which can represent flowers, for example, or apples) in a circle or semi-circle. In the example shown in the bottom right photograph, the faint circle that acts as a guideline is drawn in yellow. This disappears later when the colour yellow surrounds the tree.

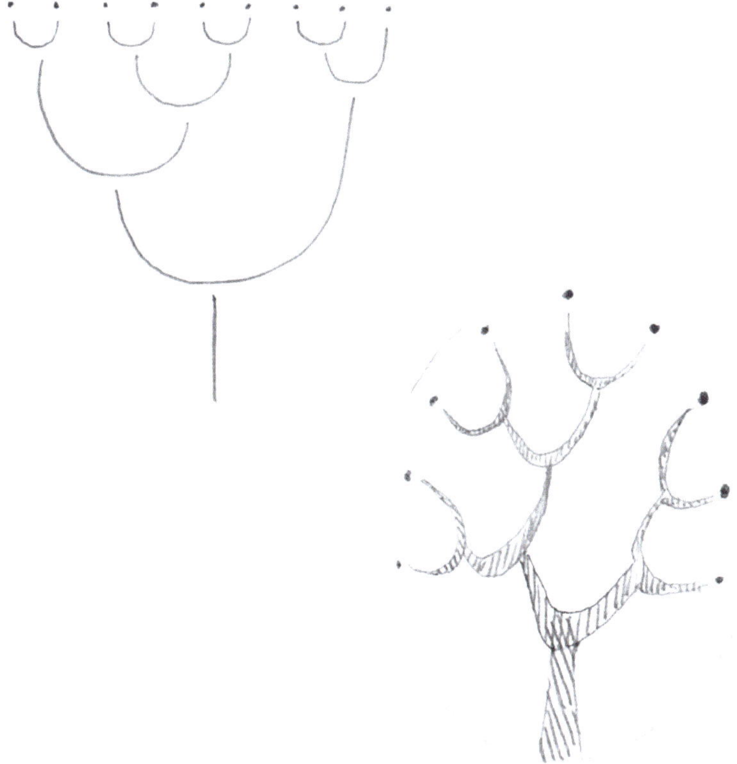

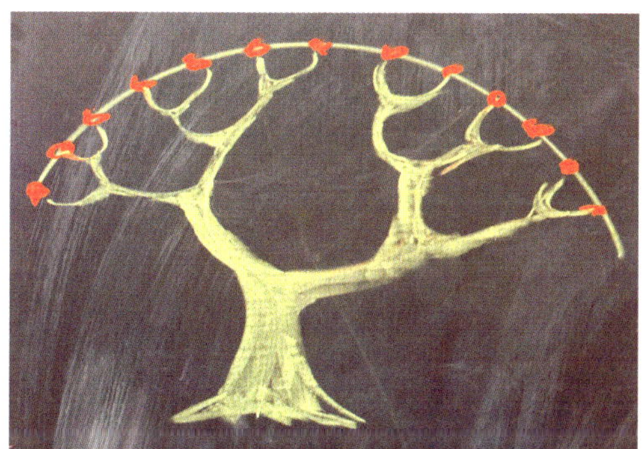

Drawing on blackboard

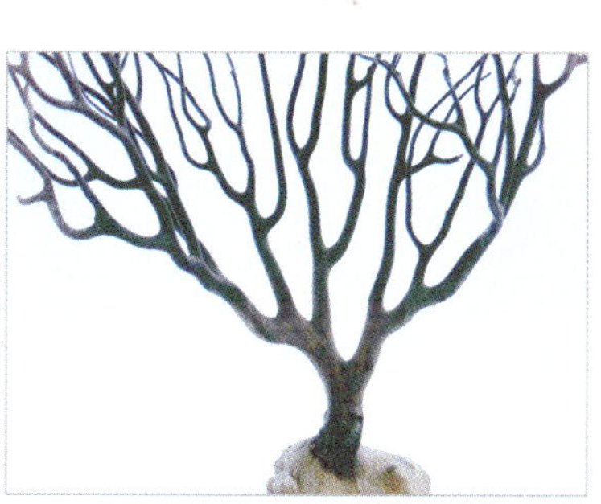

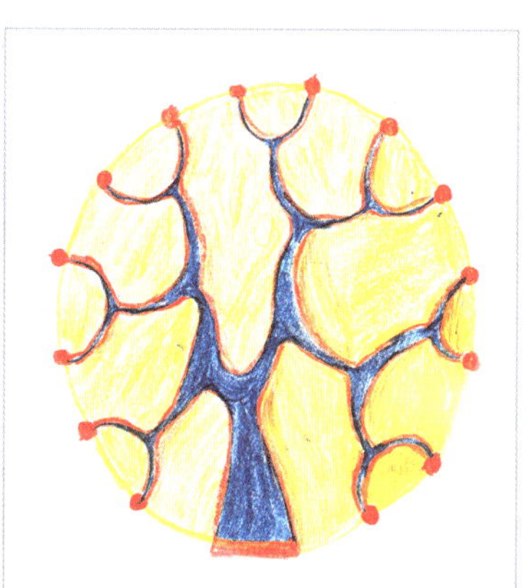

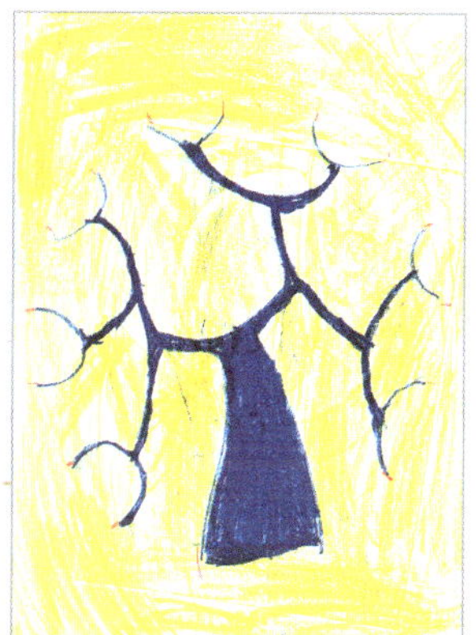

Seaweed

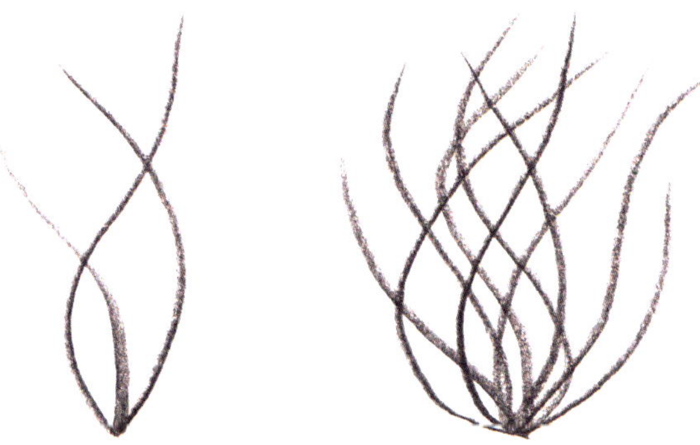

Division of branches can also be drawn as a juxtaposition, as can be seen in bushes. Branches can also divide arbitrarily, rather than following a regular pattern. This is an example of an inherent principle of form that has transgressed, resulting in something more chaotic in nature. This will provide new problems for your pupils to solve, as they will have to consider their drawings from an aesthetic perspective.

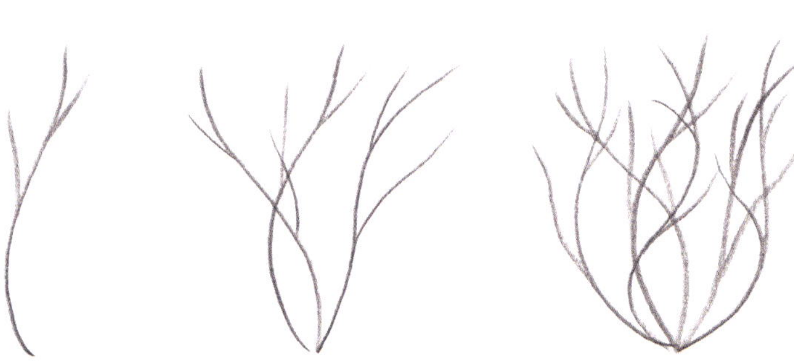

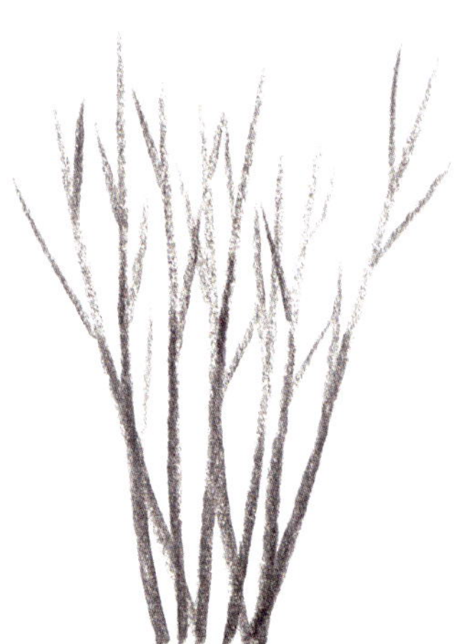

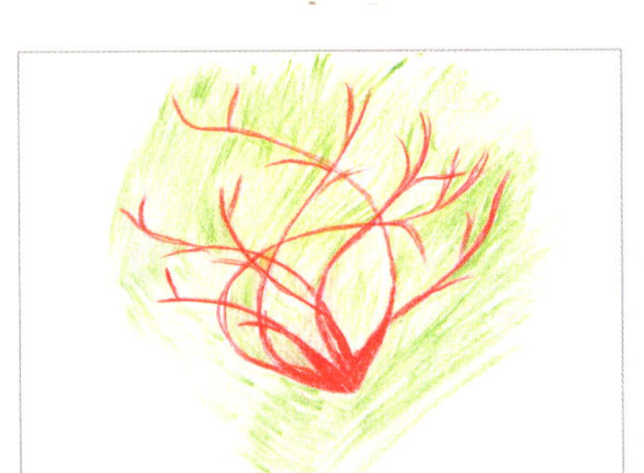

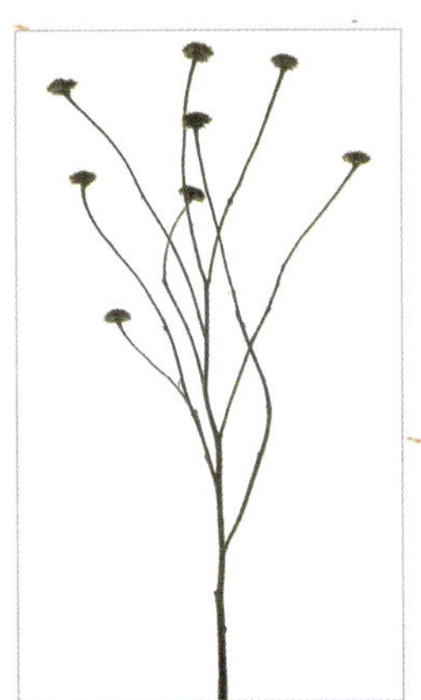

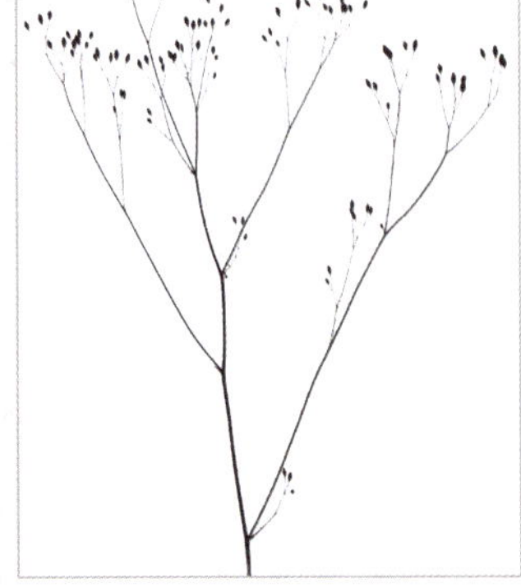

Annual plants

On the right is an example where the angle of division is relatively acute and branches gradually lengthen as they split.

Start drawing this form with a thick, square-shaped trunk from which branches grow, as shown. (Note that this is a continuation of the exercise on p.162.)

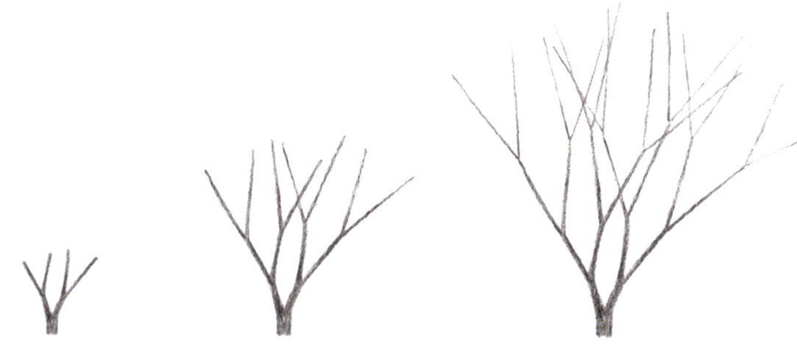

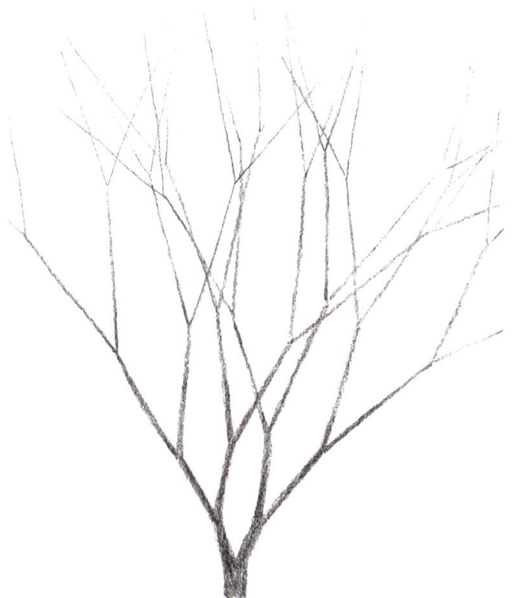

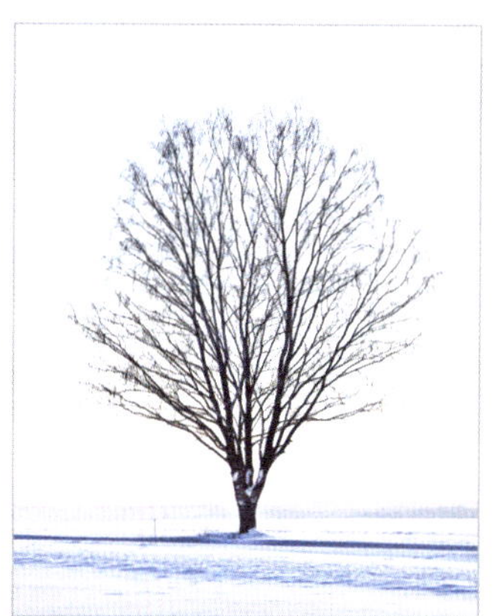

Old birch tree

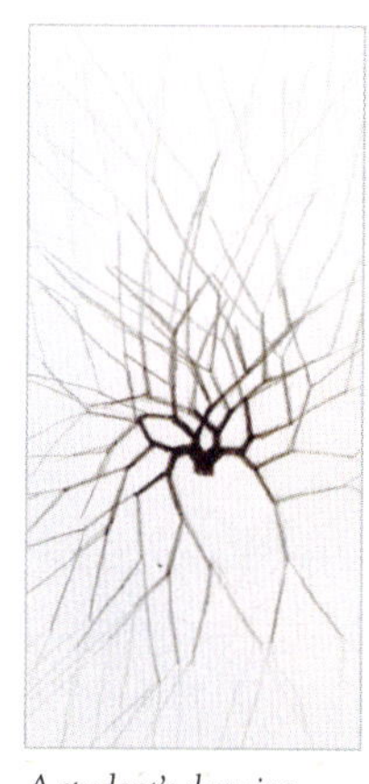

A student's drawing, playing with lines

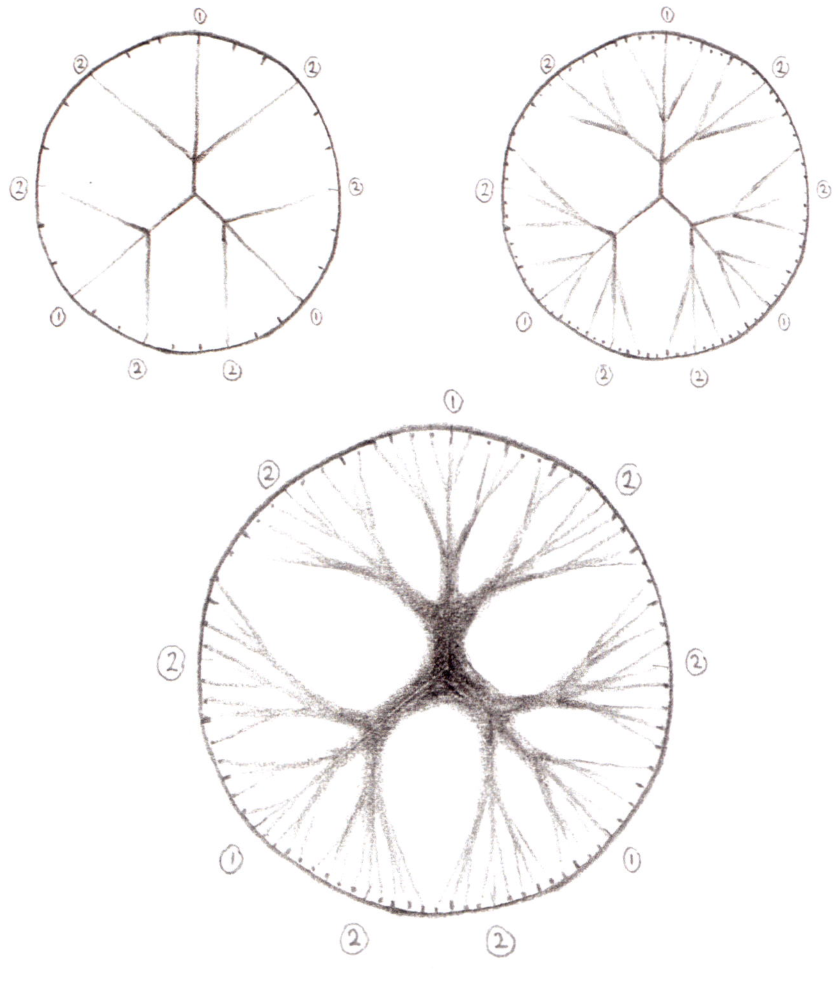

Branching can also be observed in other phenomena, for example cracks in concrete. In this exercise, divide a circle into three (see the points marked 1 in the example shown) and connect the points to the middle. Split the spaces in between into three, using two points (see the points marked 2). Connect these points using branches, as shown in the drawing. Continue to divide the spaces in this way once or twice more, and make the 'trunk' thicker towards the middle. Finally, erase the circle and the points, or colour over them.

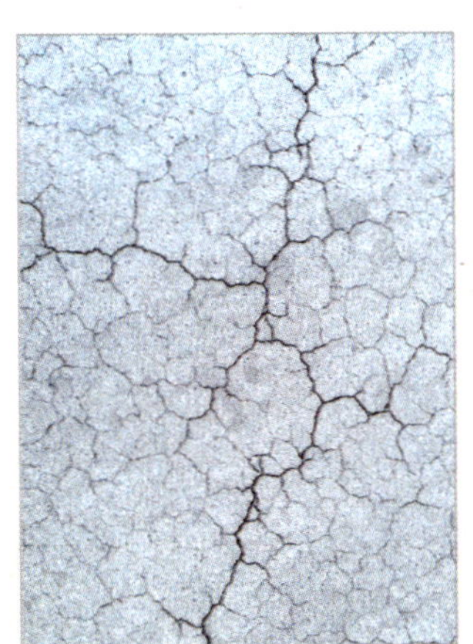

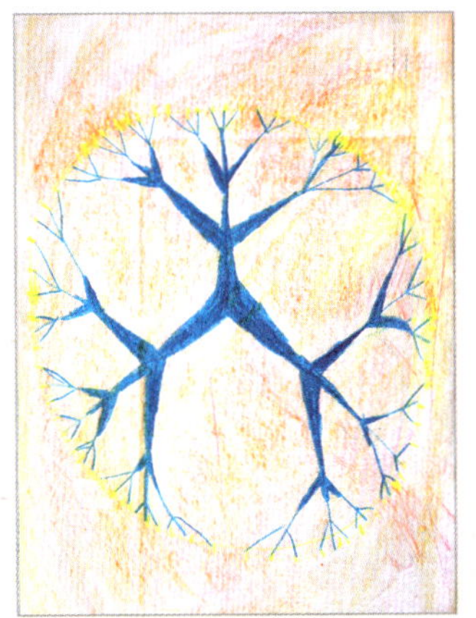

Cracks in concrete

This exercise can be developed into many different forms: let your pupils experiment. Bear in mind that the 'centre' does not need to be placed in the middle, as seen in the figure on the bottom left.

The figure on the bottom right has five main branches, and one smaller branch has been added to fill a gap. In this example, the branches are also curved and the points transformed into 'fruit'.

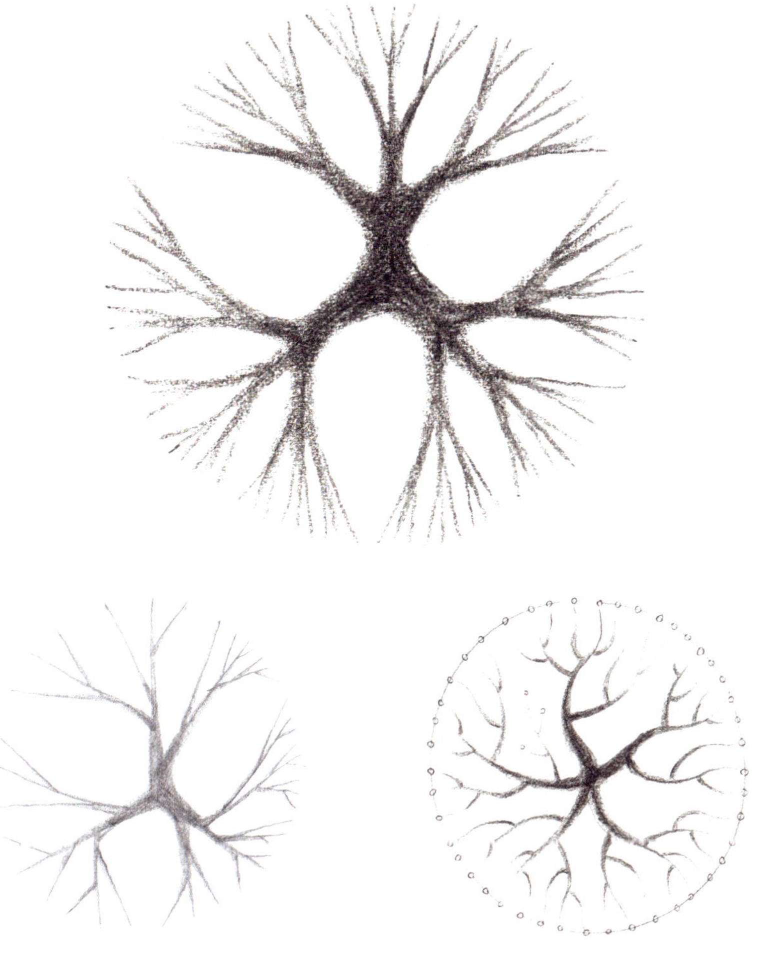

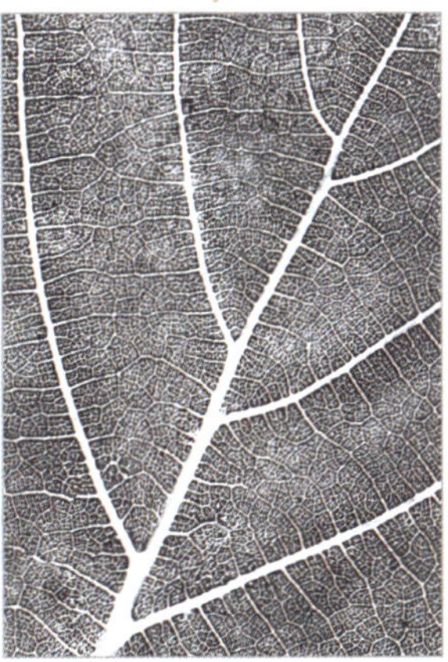

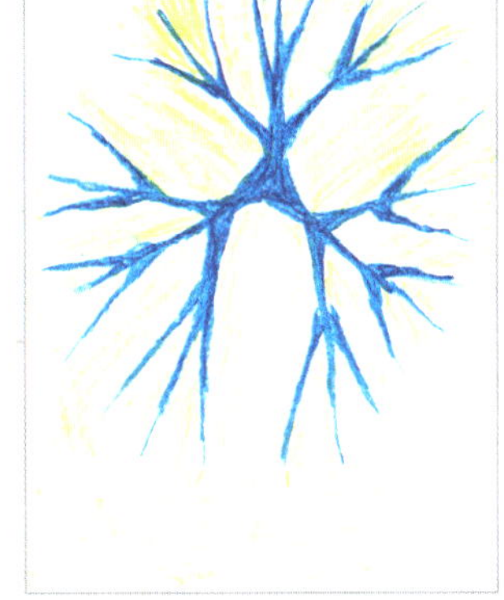

Veins of a leaf

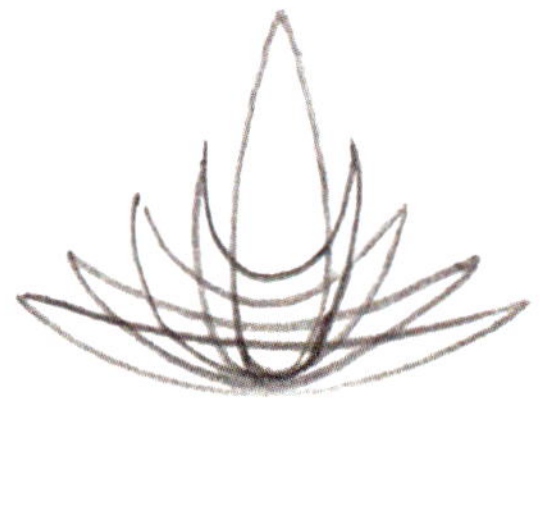

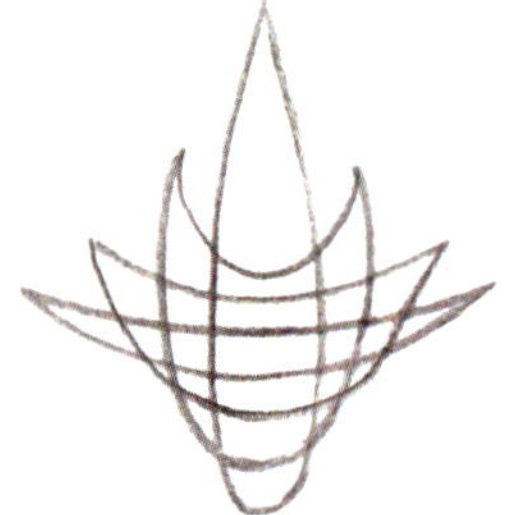

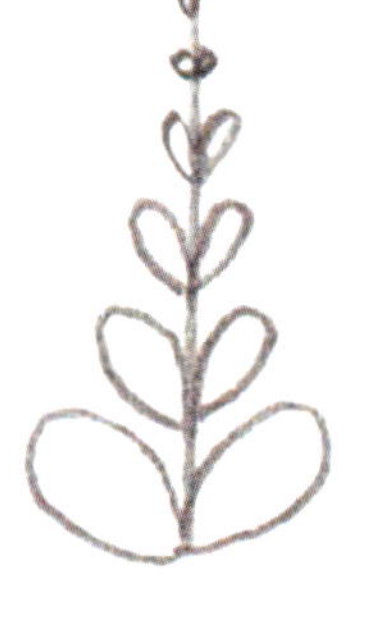

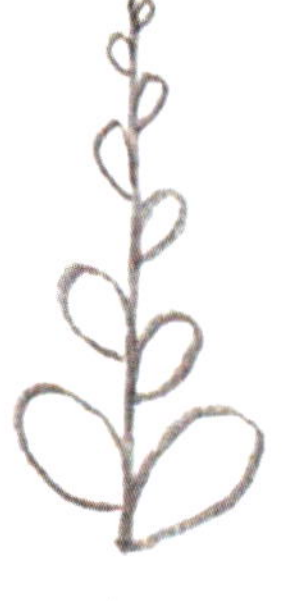

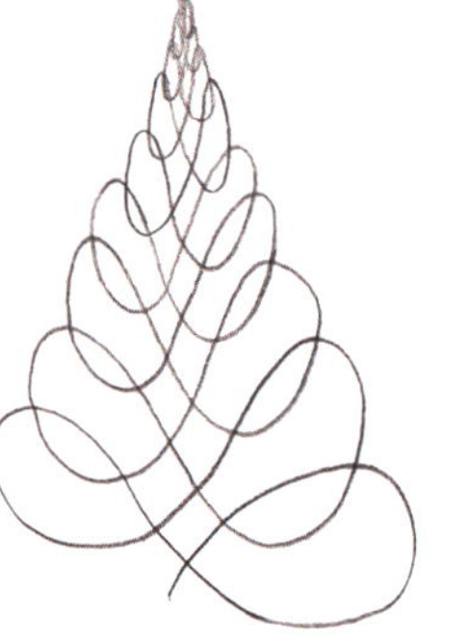

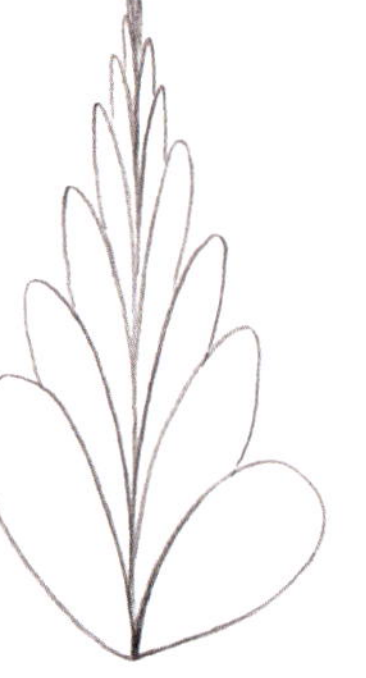

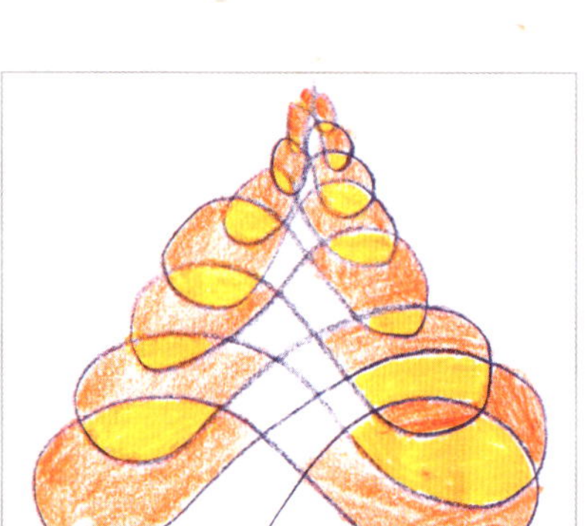

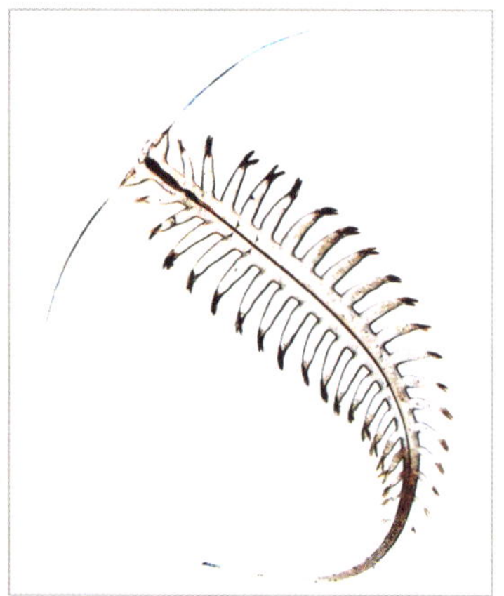

Metamorphoses

Transformation is the inspiration for the following exercises, rather than specific plants. Explore the different principles of growth with your pupils. For the exercises here and on the facing page, always start at the base of each form.

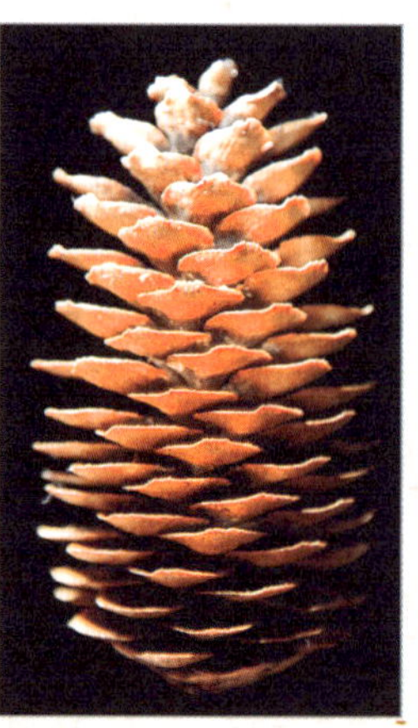

Polychaeta, or bristle worm

Spruce cone

Here we can see how the form of the leaf as a whole is inherent in every single part, and how the individual elements of a leaf can gradually be separated from the main form.

The bottom right photograph shows how nature can 'make mistakes'. The final leaf formation cannot decide if it is going to turn into a leaf on each side, or if it should round off with the middle leaf. In cases like this it is possible to see the plan lying behind the form.

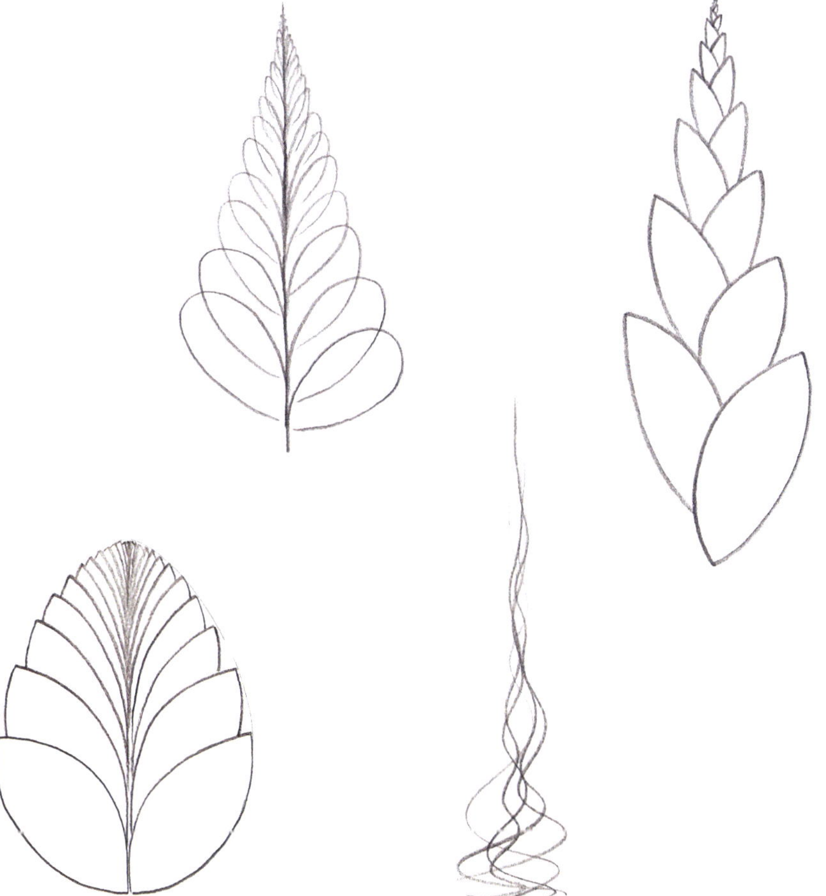

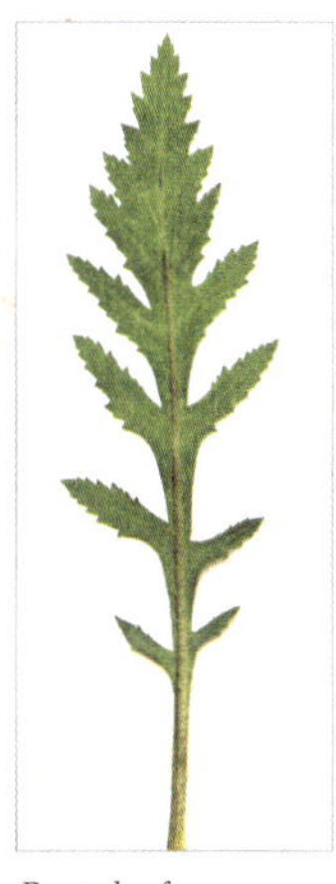

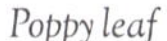

Poppy leaf

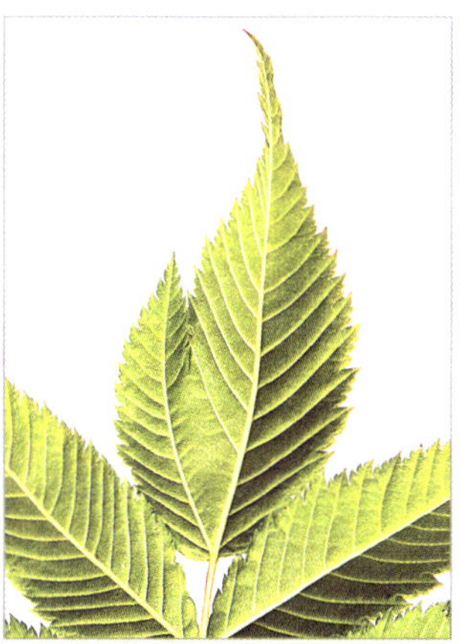

Leaf that 'hasn't made up its mind'

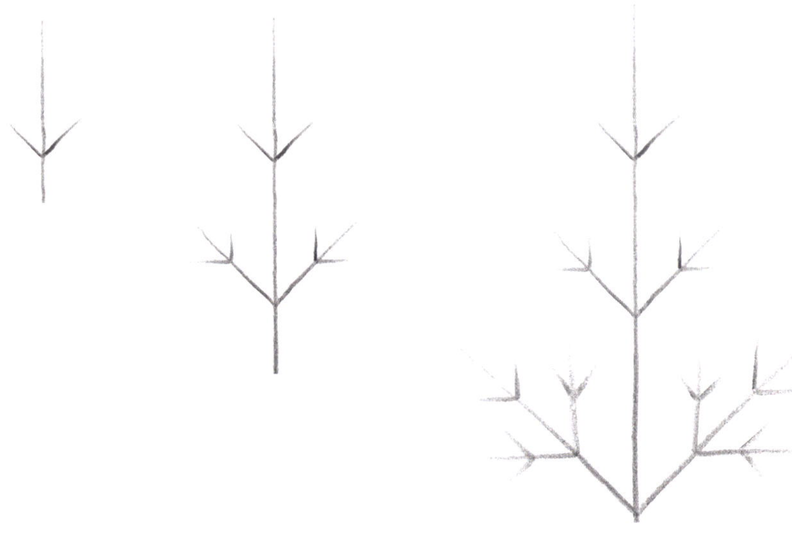

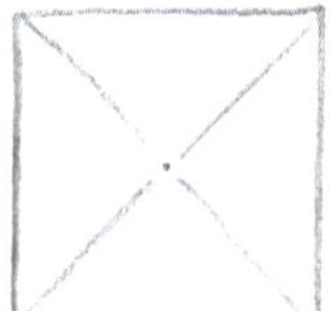 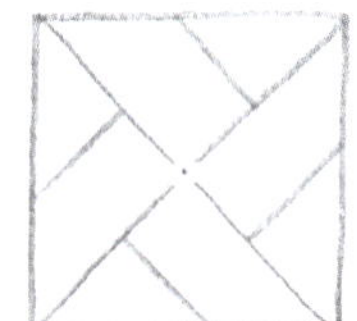 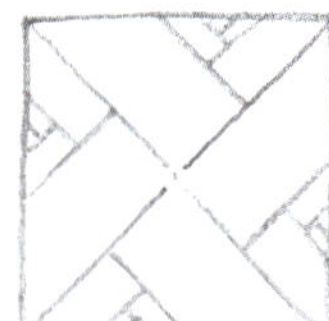 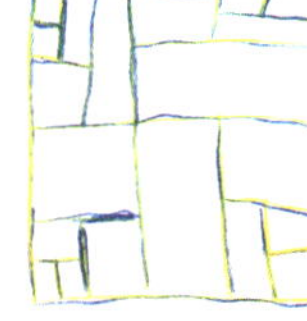

Fractals

Fractals are curves or figures in which the parts resemble the whole. In other words, details are repeated and in turn the whole figure resembles the detail. As an example, look at a fern and explain how each leaf resembles the smaller leaves, which in their turn resemble even smaller leaves. Draw your pupils' attention to how beautifully and freely these leaves form in relation to what is in principle a rigid structure.

To construct a fractal, first show your pupils how to draw the upper section before drawing identical parts underneath on each side. Ask them what should come next, then instruct them to carry on constructing the figure until it becomes impractical to continue.

The squares to the left act as a simple plan for teaching fractal structures.

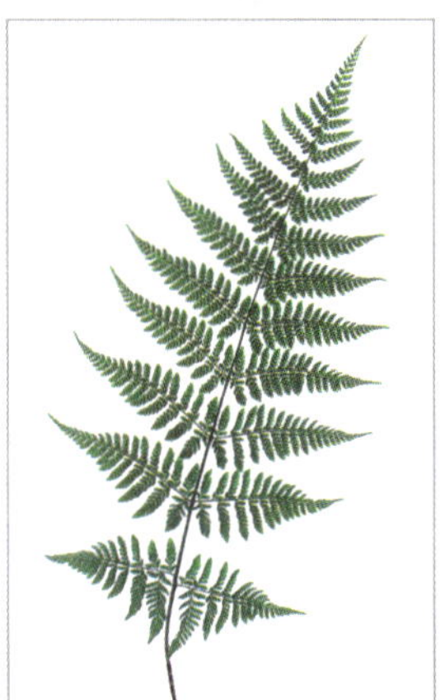 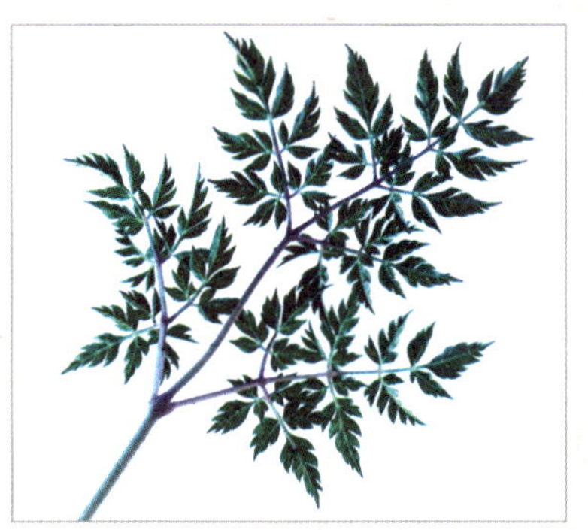 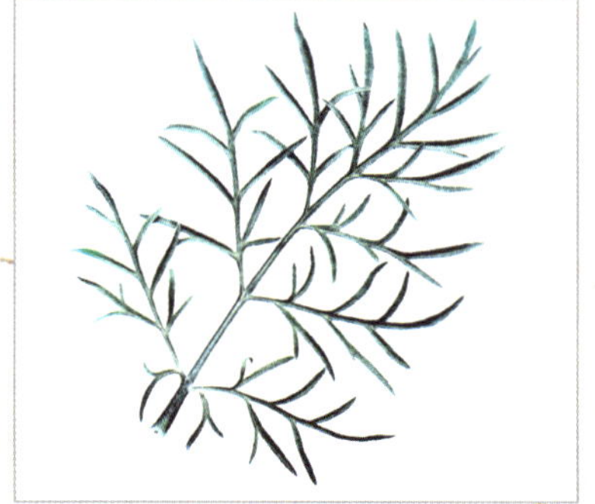

Different leaves formed following fractal theory

Snail shell form

A snail shell form can be drawn with the technique shown. First, draw a vertical line, preferably along the entire length of the paper. Next, from the base draw an arc that reaches halfway up the first line. Continue the line across the first line in another arc, to reach halfway along what remains of the line above. Continue in this manner as far as possible. This is an interesting exercise in itself.

To continue the form, start a new arc one third of the way up the first vertical line and close this one third into the next section, as shown.

Start the final sequence of arcs halfway along the 1/3 arc created in the previous step, as shown, and continue to work upwards.

Note that all of these are guidelines. Complete the form using thick lines, or a colour, as demonstrated in the large figure.

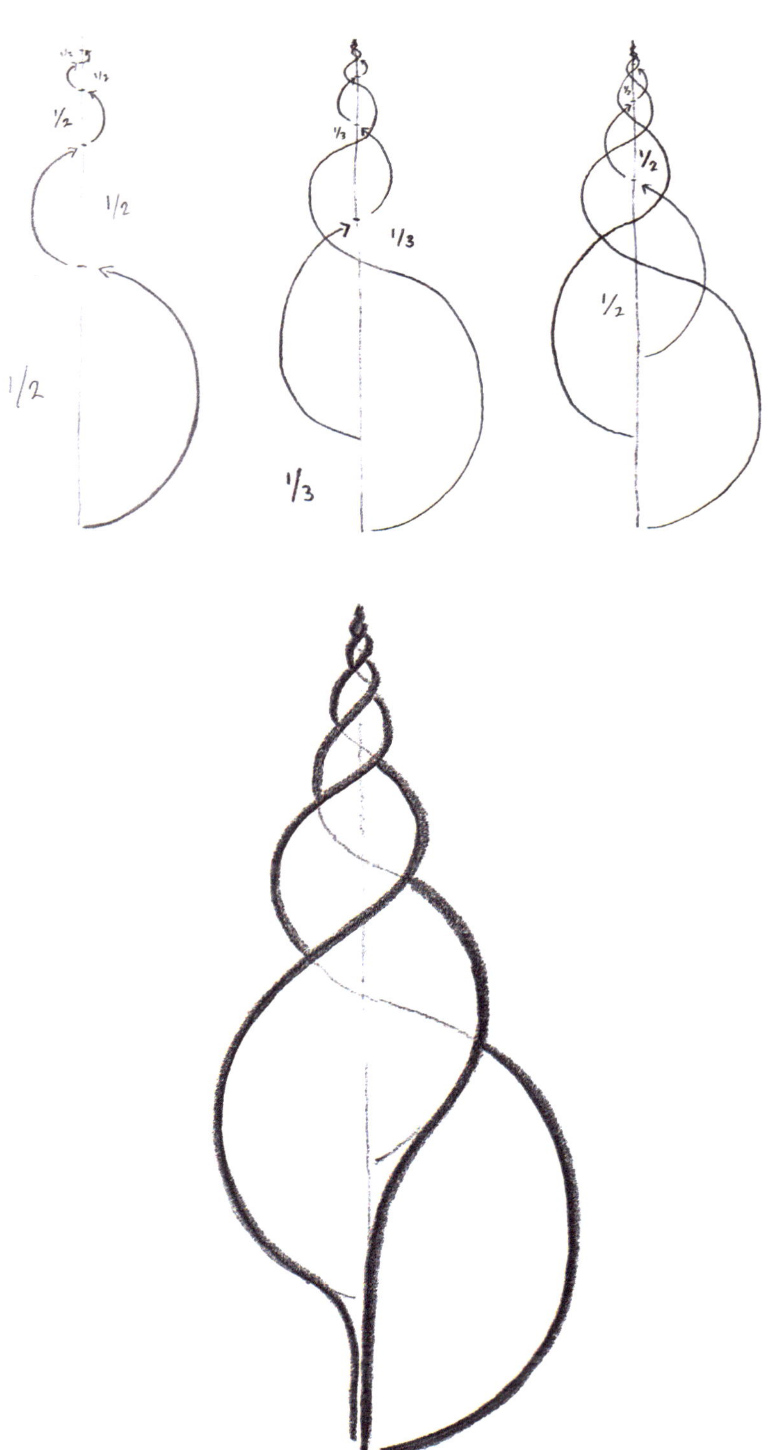

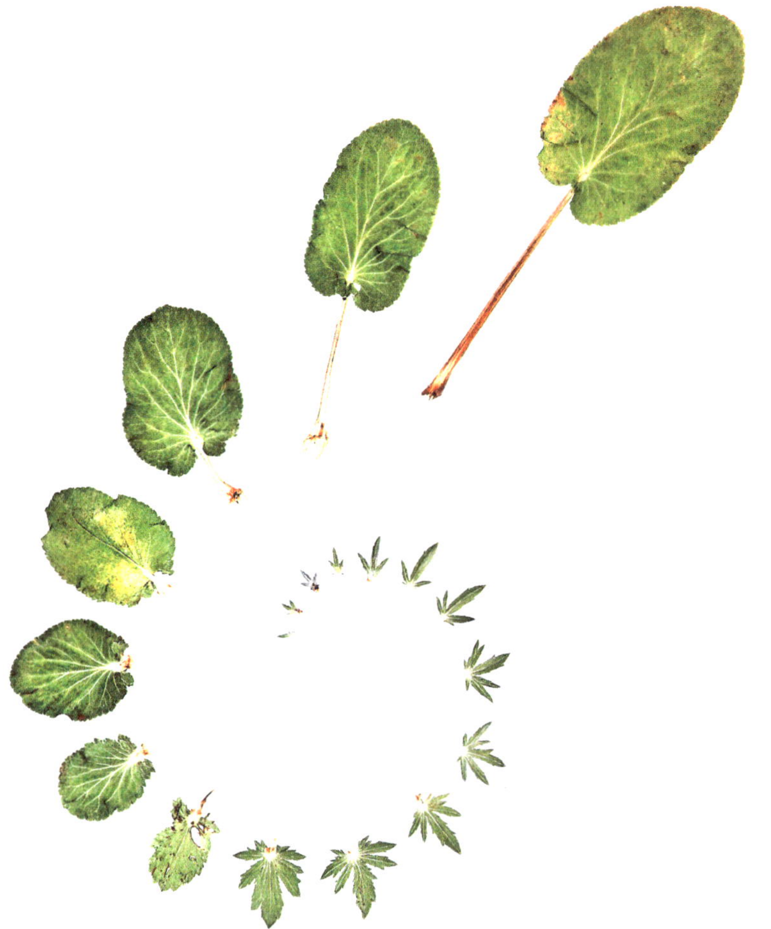

Metamorphosis in leaf forms

Leaf sequences in annual plants can undergo a surprisingly large degree of metamorphosis as new leaves appear further up the stem. In just one plant it is possible to find leaves that change from completely round forms to linear and cross-like formations.

Here, the leaves of this blue eryngo Bethlehem are displayed in a developing spiral to demonstrate how the different forms relate to one another, and how they transform yet still belong together. There is plenty of inspiration here for form drawing; indeed, form drawing provides a useful tool for exploring such diversity.

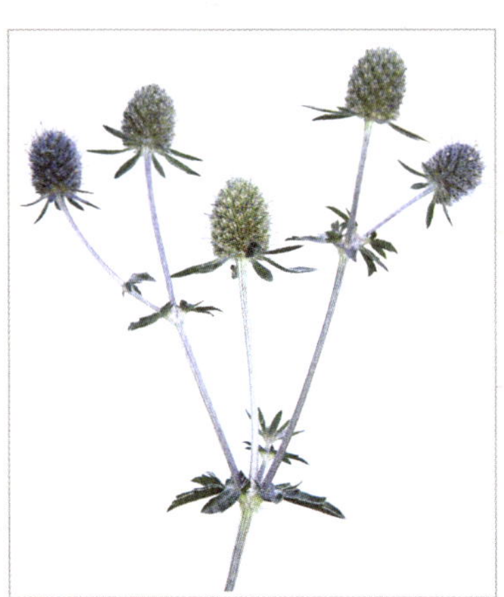

Some of the leaves on the facing page are displayed side by side at the bottom of this page. Their size has been adjusted to allow us to easily see the forms' metamorphosis. On the right are examples of how you and your pupils can explore this type of metamorphosis playfully.

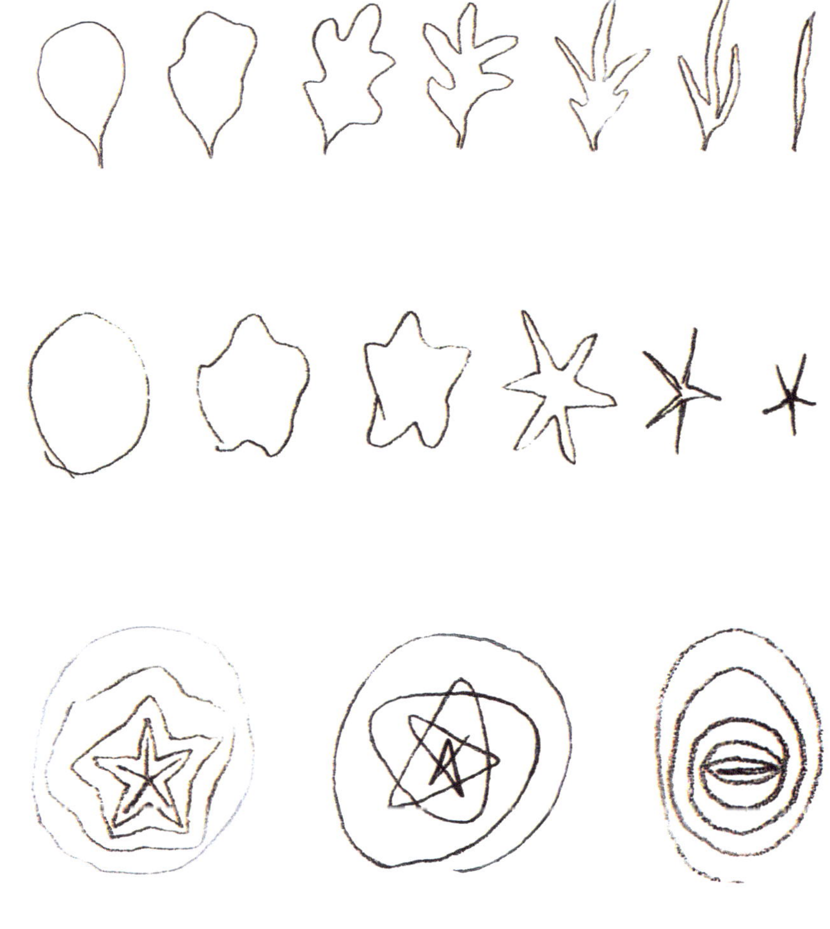

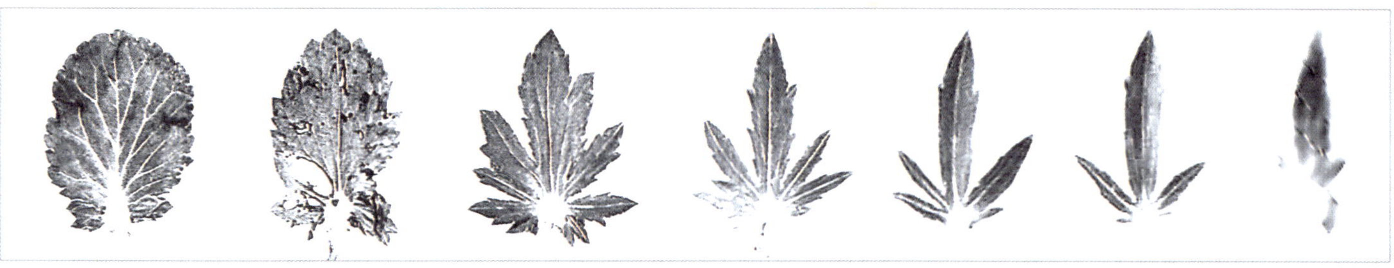

Pythagorus' Tree

This is a fractal structure built on a square, invented by the Dutch mathematics teacher Albert E. Bosman in 1942. Study it with your pupils and work out how to construct it together.

To build on this work, construct a Pythagorus' Tree again using differing pairing squares. For example, the first square might be 5 x 5, the next two 4 x 4 and 3 x 3. This results in the branches being asymmetrical in relation to one another, making the form more dynamic.

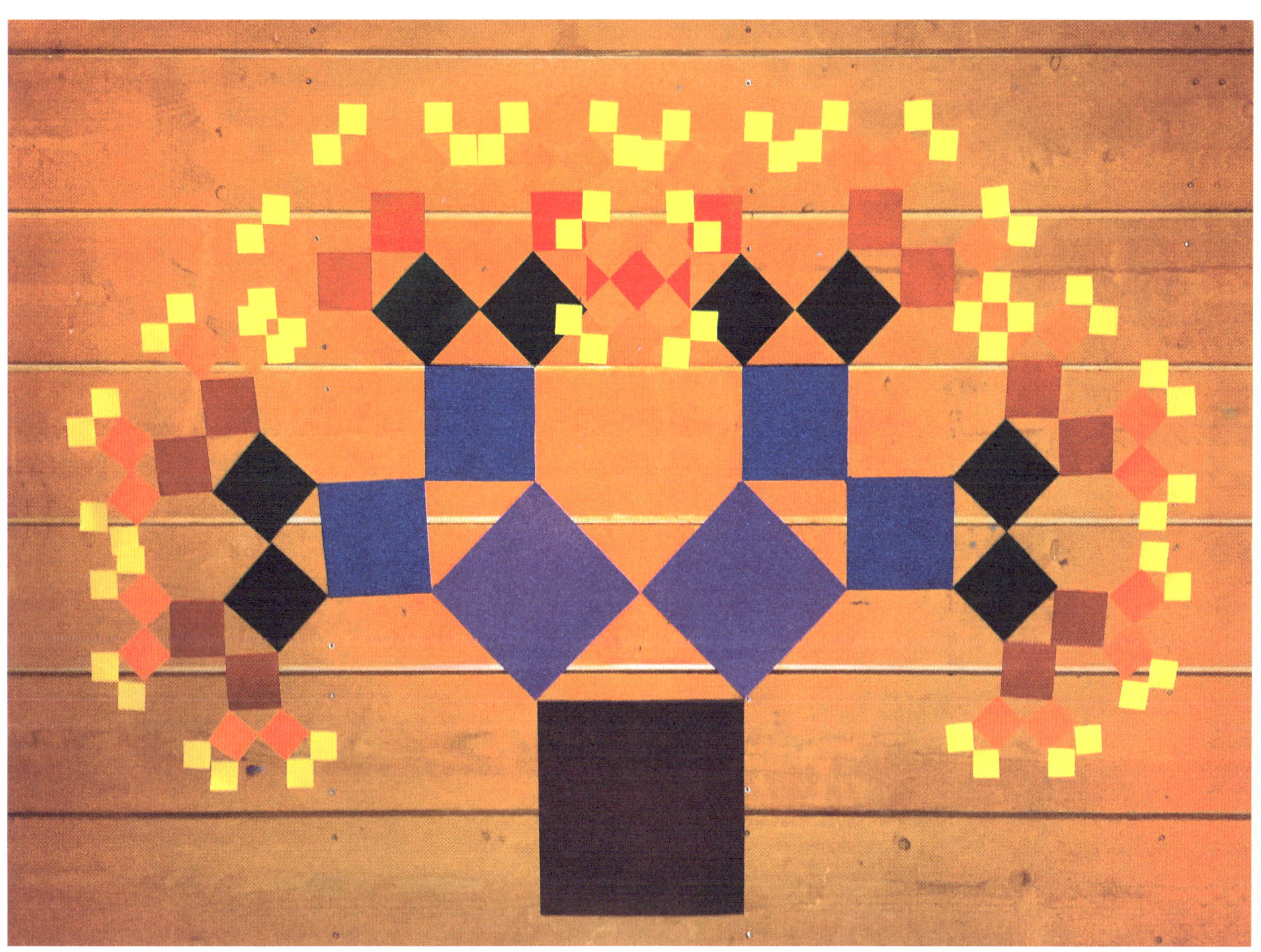

Part 7: Cultural History Lesson Exercises

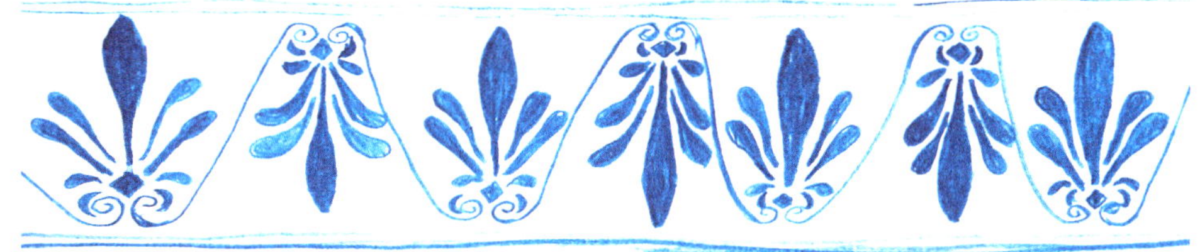

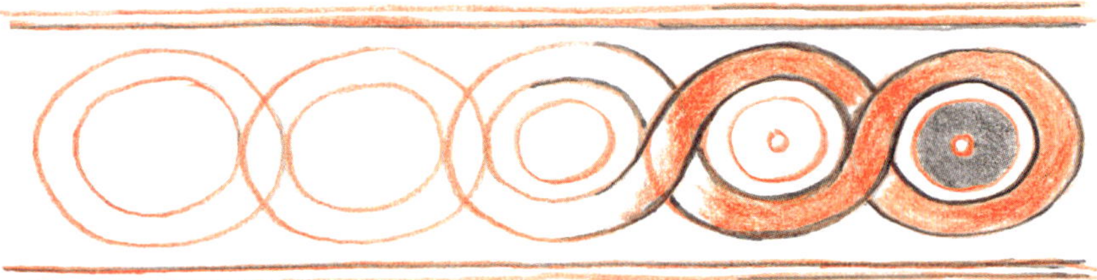

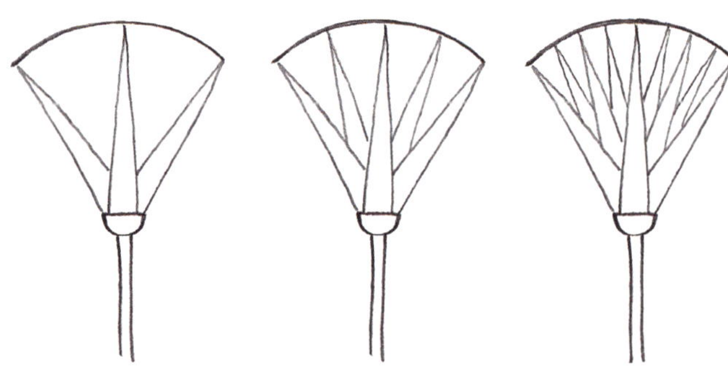

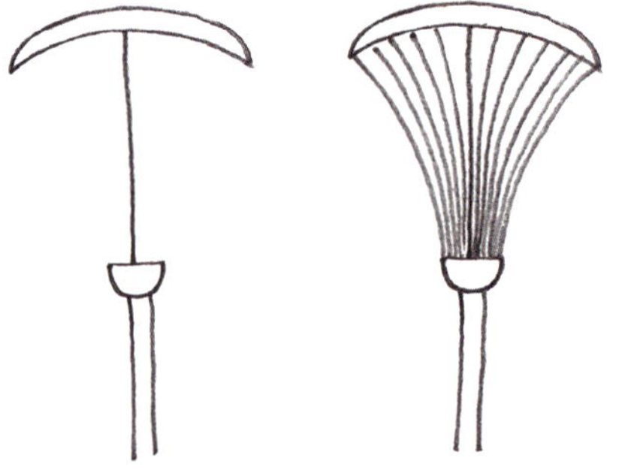

Persian ornamentation

First, draw two parallel lines, leaving a large gap between them. Inside these two lines, but without touching their edges, draw a large circle and then place a small one inside of this. Draw another large circle so that its circumference touches the small circle's, as shown, placing another small circle inside of the new large circle, and repeat until the border is as long as intended.

Use colour to accentuate the plaited pattern that emerges, as shown. If you like, draw extra, smaller rings inside.

Egyptian ornamentation

To draw the lotus flower, start with three leaves, as shown, then place another leaf in each space. Repeat until you have nine leaves.

To draw the papyrus flower, start by drawing the central line, then build up outwards until the flower is complete.

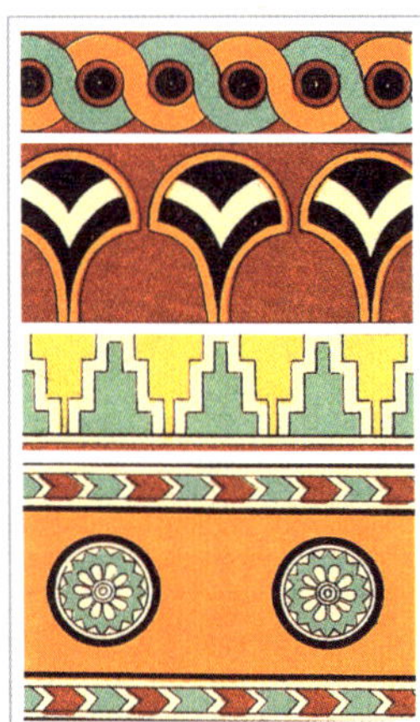

Painted ornaments from Nimrod

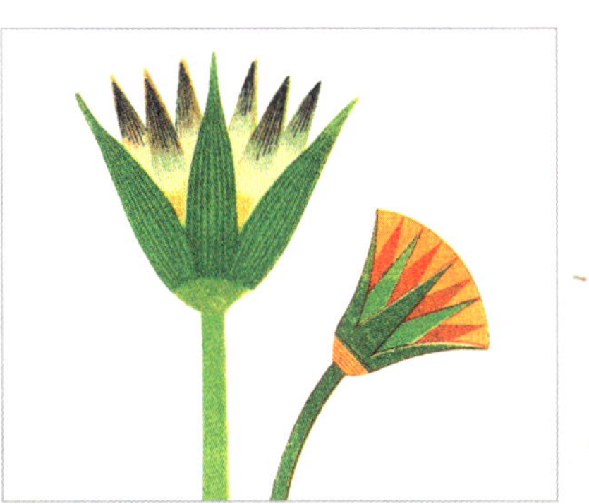

Lotus flower

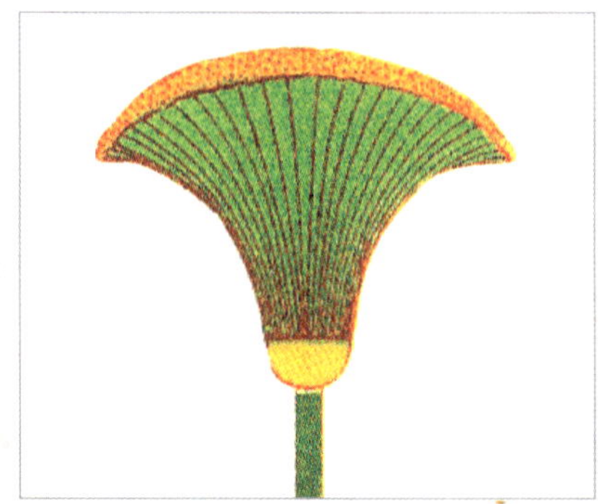

Papyrus flower

Similar to the exercise on Persian ornamentation on the facing page, draw two parallel lines. Next, fill the space with as many large and small circles as will fit, though in this case they should be spaced out and their circumferences should not overlap. Now, develop the form further by drawing stalks and buds. Next, draw a line beneath the top line that will allow you space to draw flowers. First, draw one leaf on each flower, then the two outer leaves, then the petals in the middle, and finally the ones in between those. Repeat the process in the circles: these should look like the flowers seen from above.

In the lower exercise, begin by making a pattern of dots with a ruler. Next, add arcs, as shown, until the whole sheet is covered. In the narrowest part of the forms that emerge, add the three 'fields', as shown. Finish by adding the curved lines to make a papyrus pattern.

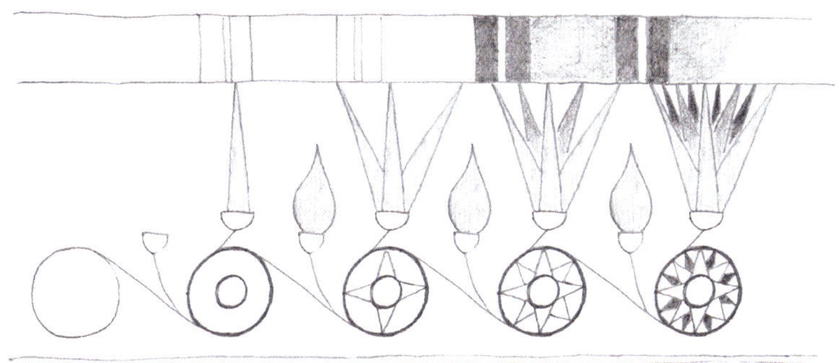

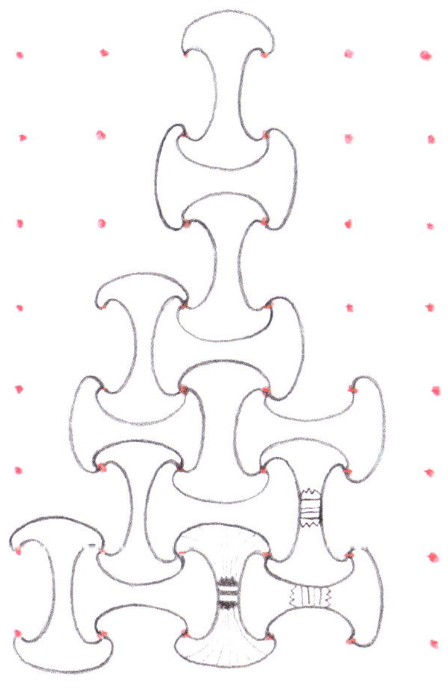

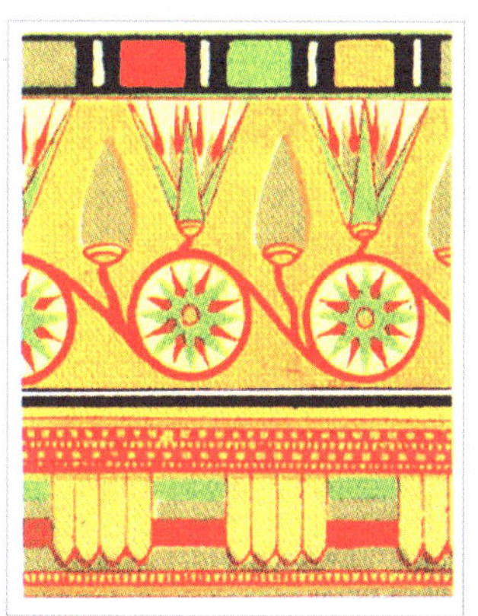

From the wall of a grave in Gourna, Egypt

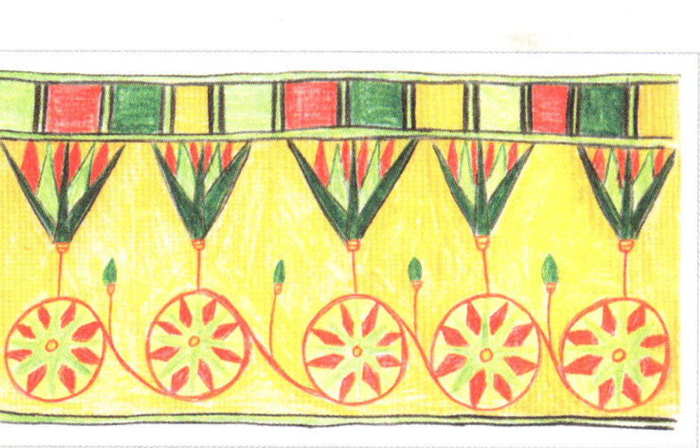

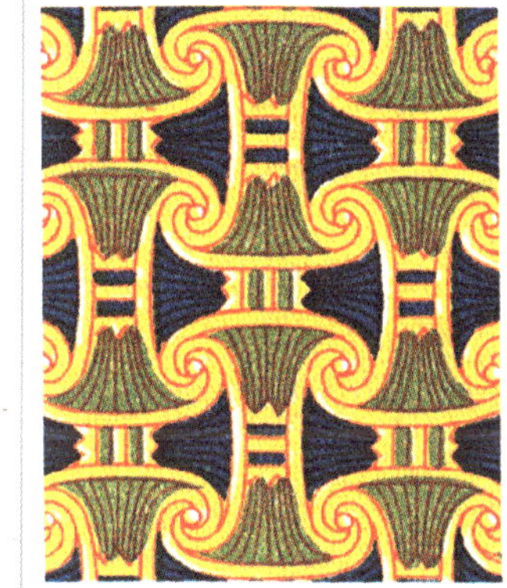

From the roof of a tomb

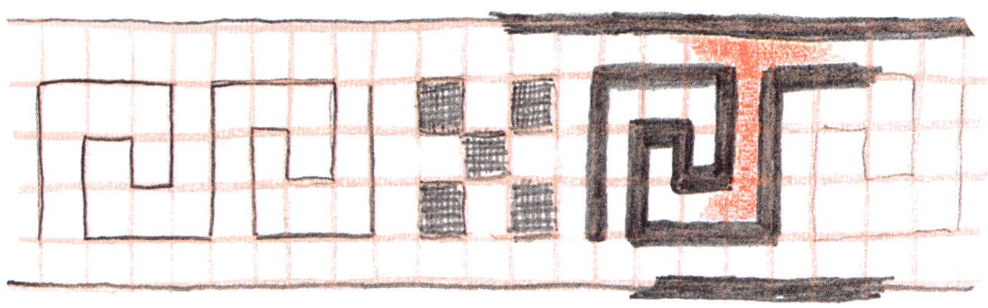

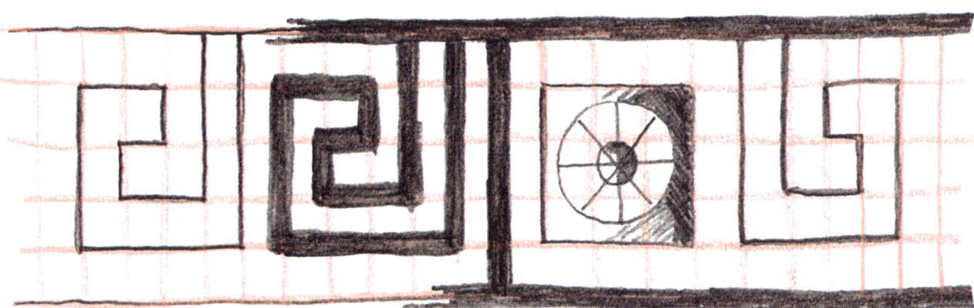

Greek ornamentation

Use orange or brown to draw six horizontal lines, as shown on the top left, and partition them with vertical lines to make a grid. Your pupils will use this as a guideline.

Use brown or black to draw the pattern on the grid, as shown. When the pattern, or meander, is in place, the lines can be thickened.

Finally, the spaces can be coloured with the background colour so that the guidelines disappear.

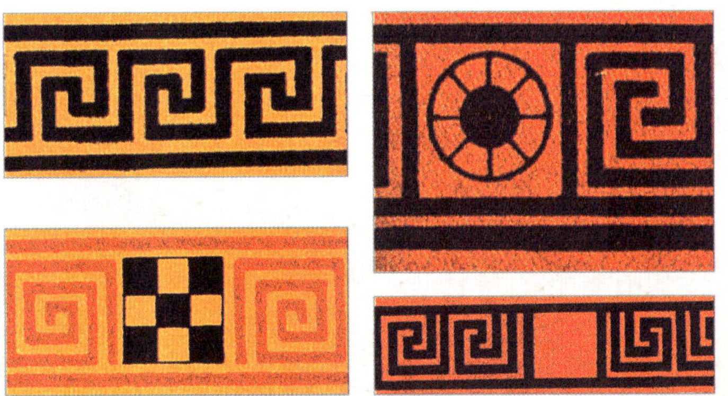

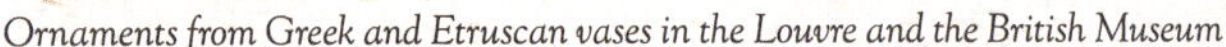

Ornaments from Greek and Etruscan vases in the Louvre and the British Museum

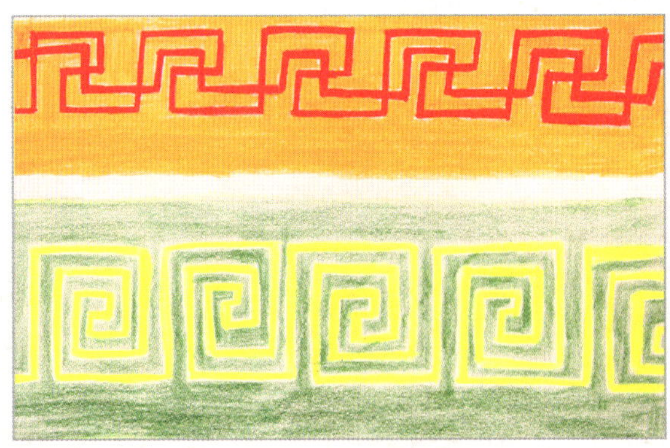

Draw two parallel sets of lines, as shown.

Next, in the space between the lines, draw the long curved lines with a spiral at each end.

In between the two spirals draw in the square or diamond shape, followed by the central leaf and two smaller leaves on either side – note that these should follow the curve of the small spirals.

Now draw in the rest of the leaves and colour the figure.

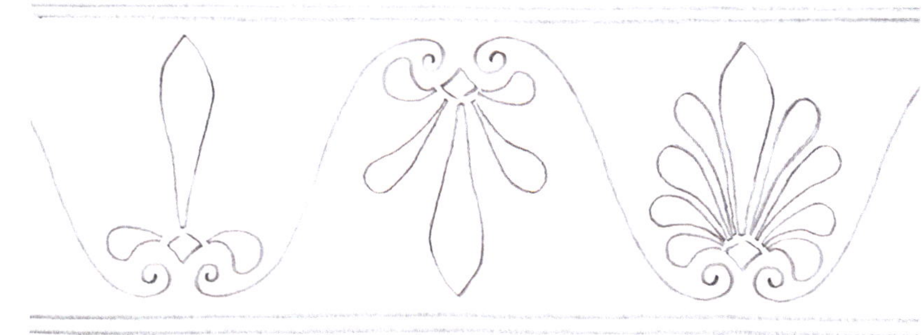

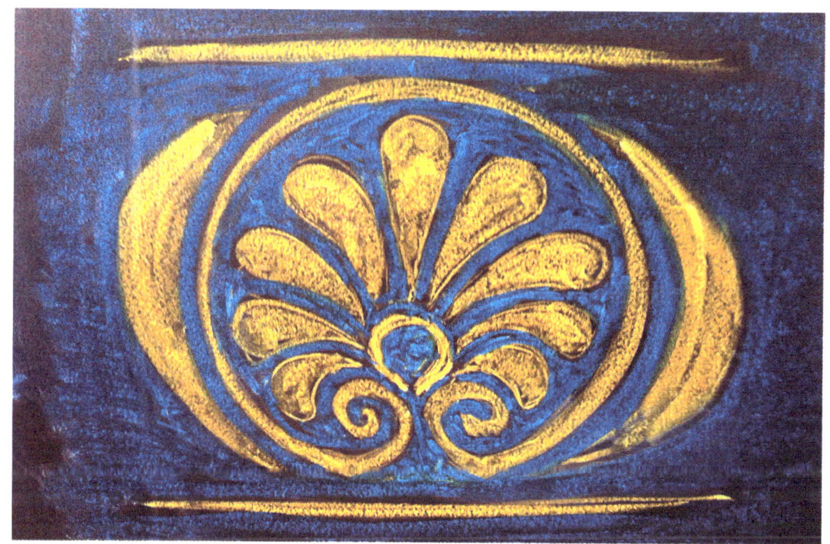

Ornaments from Greek and Etruscan vases in the Louvre and the British Museum

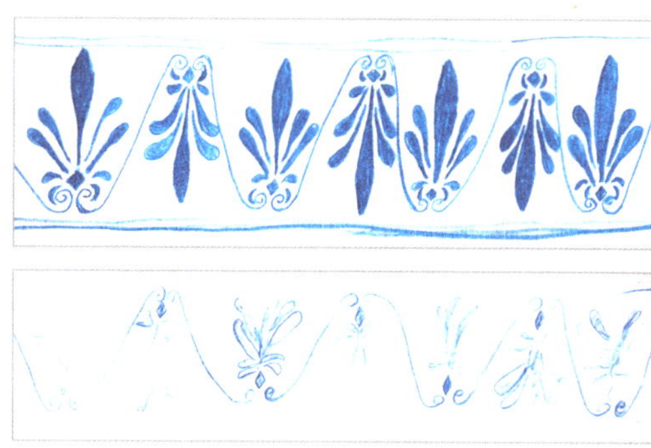

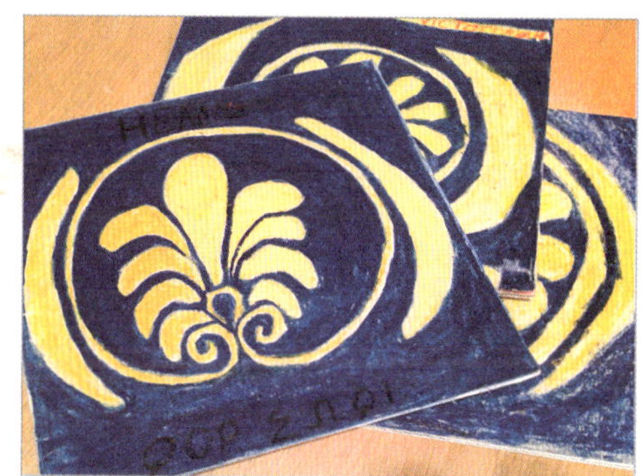

Drawings on covers of pupils' workbooks

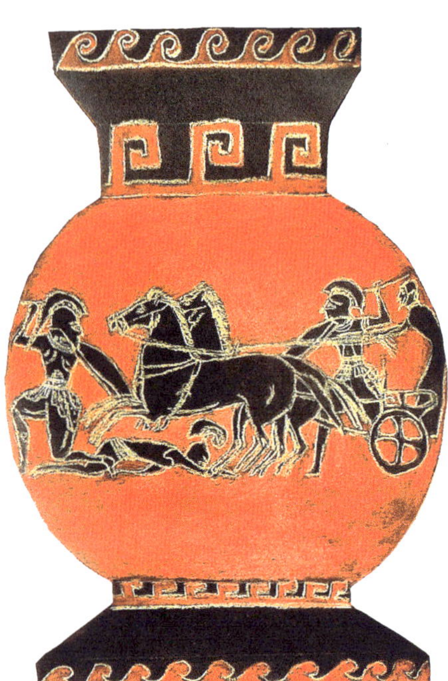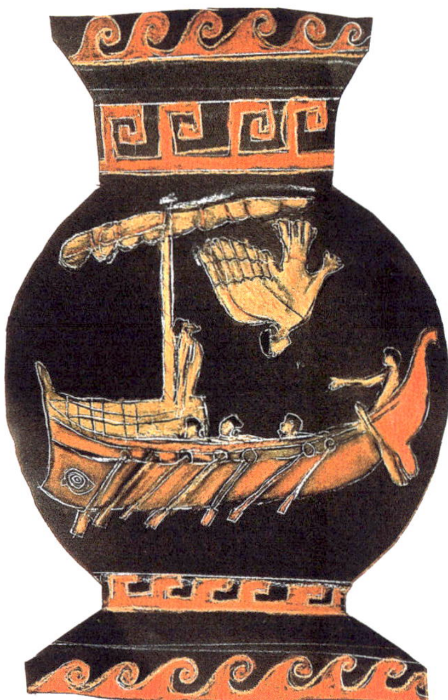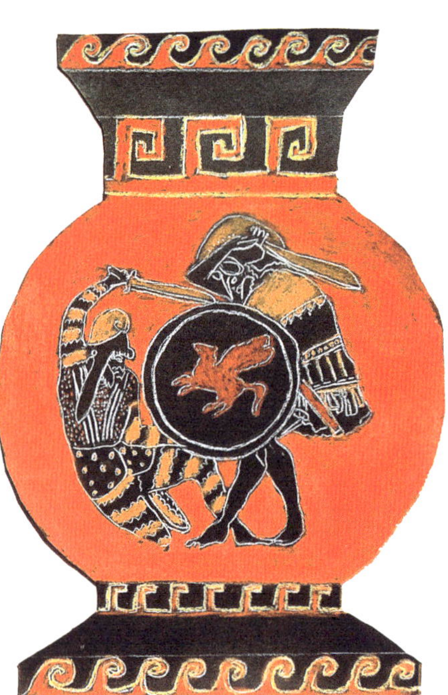

Examples of classwork completed on black cardboard using coloured chalk

These examples can all be drawn freehand, though you should challenge your pupils to find out how to construct the figures themselves.

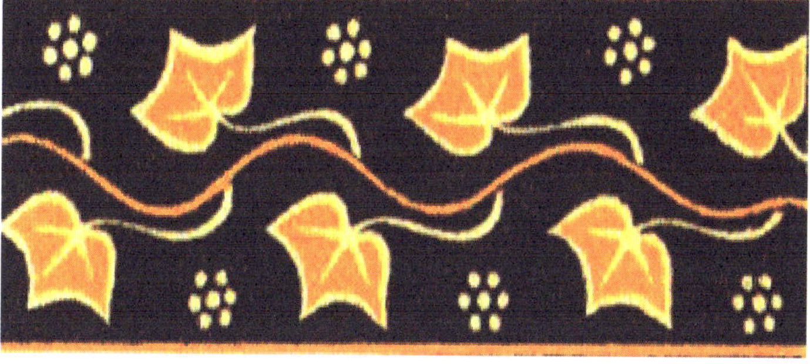

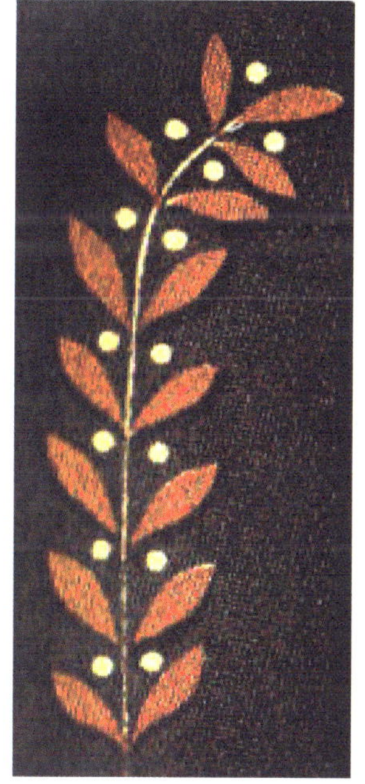

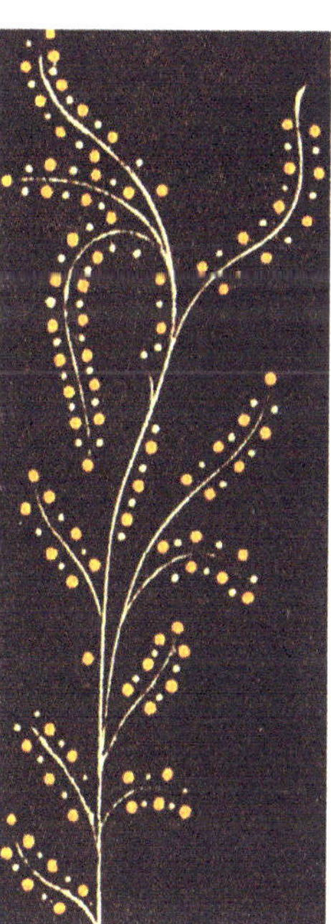

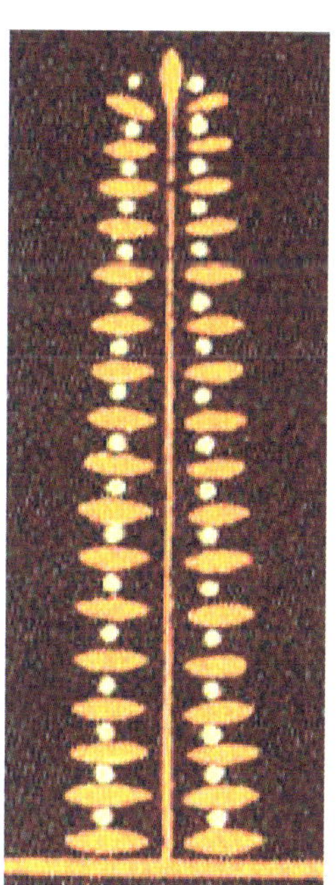

Islamic patterns

Lay eight sheets of rectangular paper in the pattern shown in the photograph.

Next, take a fresh sheet of paper and choose a background colour that you can make 'disappear' later, or a pencil that you can erase at the end of the process.

Now, draw what you see freehand on a smaller scale (see 1).

Mark the centre of the short sides that turn outwards so that you can draw squares (see 2).

Look at what you have drawn so far and find the figure outlined in red (see 3); on your own drawing, mark it using a different colour to your background colour.

Do the same for the figures outlined in red on the next example (see 4).

Finally, plait the whole form together as shown, alternately weaving over and under. Use a strong colour and make the lines suitably thick.

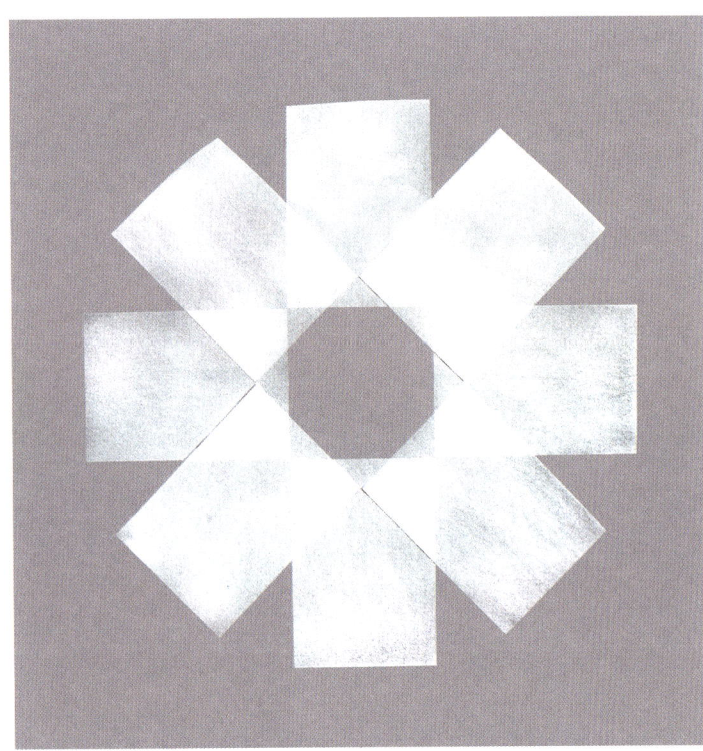

1

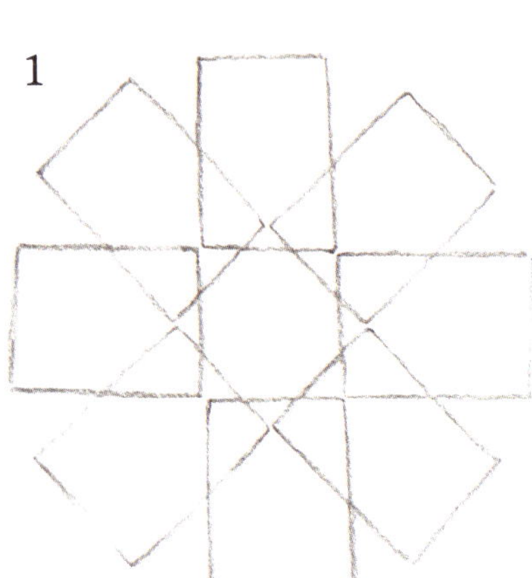

2

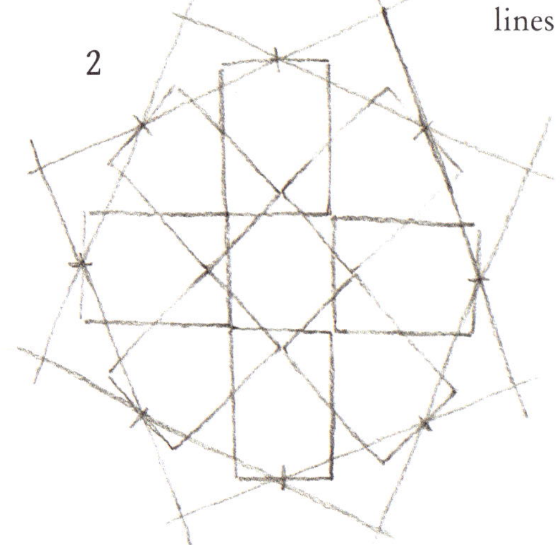

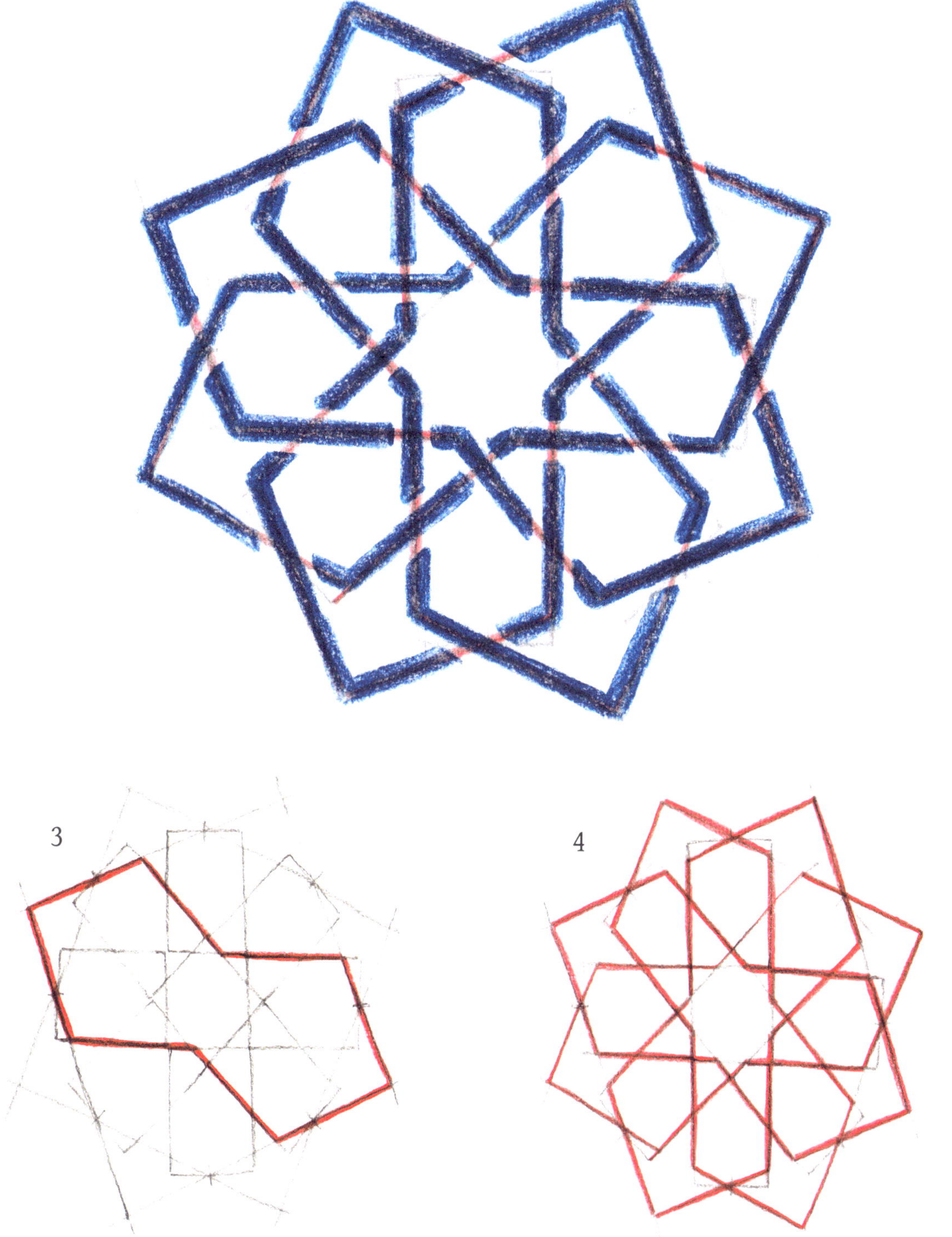

3

4

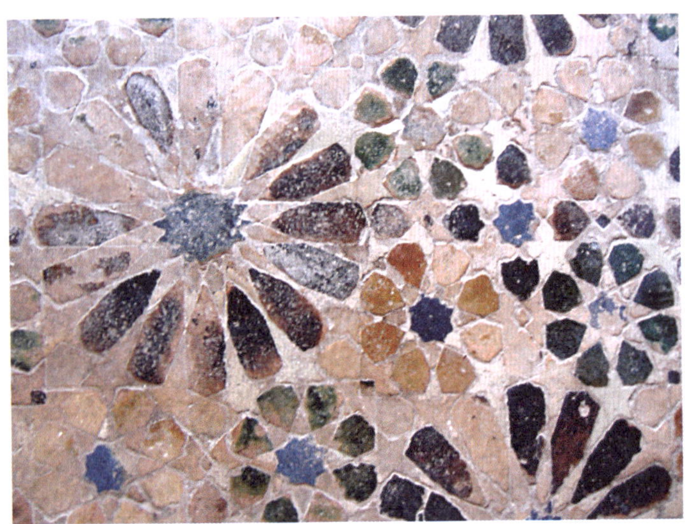

Floor tile detail, Alhambra Palace, Granada, Spain

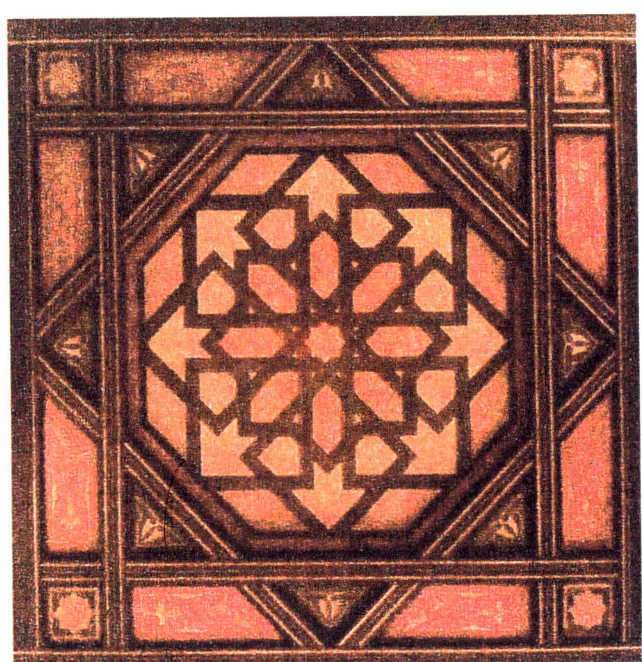

Ceiling detail, house in Granada

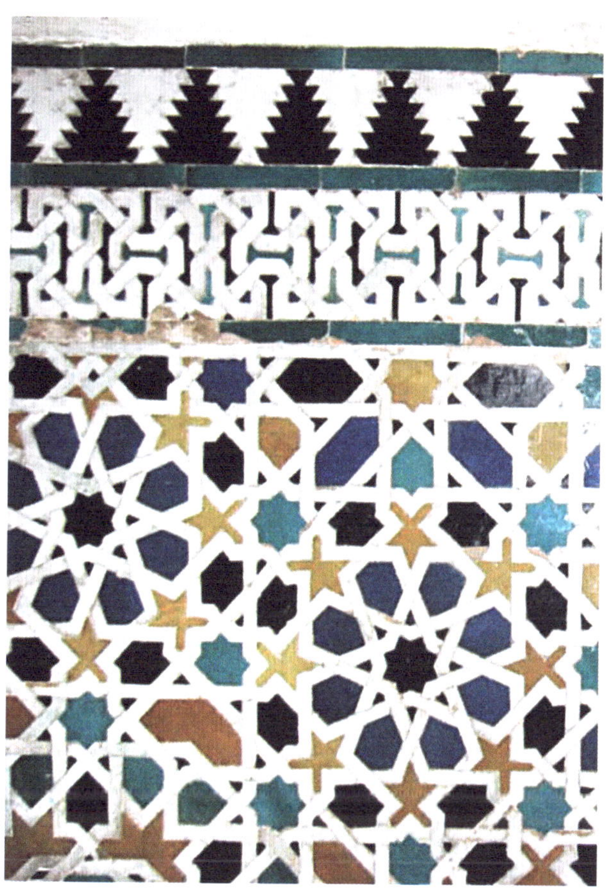

Wall tile detail, Alhambra Palace, Granada

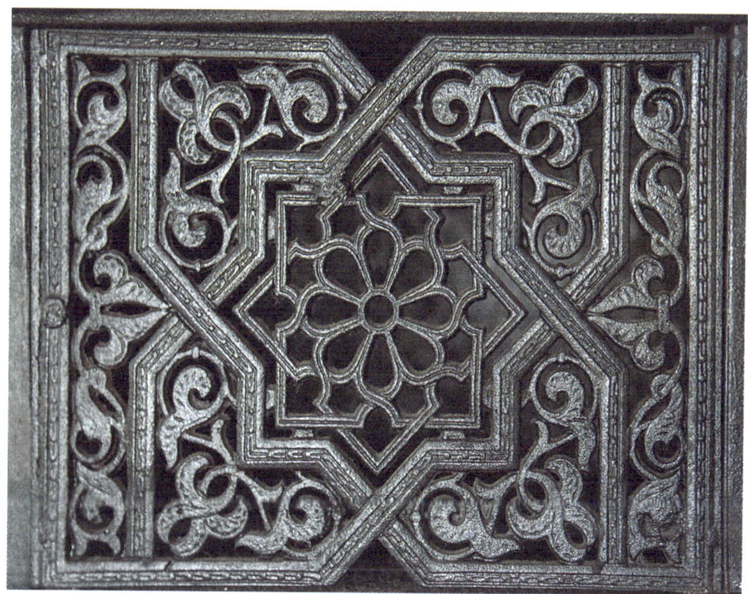

Detail from 19th-century oven, Drammen Iron Works, Norway

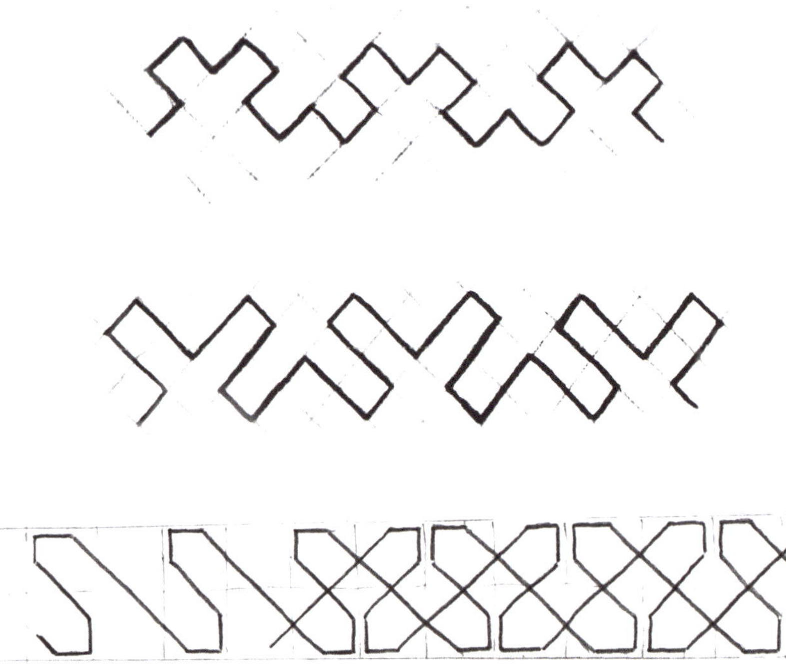

Borders

The aim of these exercises is to show that the borders are identical when mirrored both horizontally and vertically. At first your pupils might find guidelines helpful, as shown, but encourage them to try drawing the forms freehand once they have had some practice.

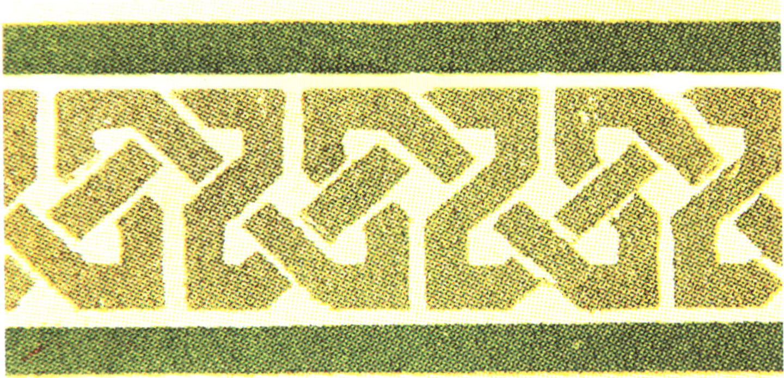

Moorish border, mosaic from Alhambra Palace, Granada, Spain

Begin this exercise by drawing two sets of parallel lines, as shown, to make the border. Within them, draw three wavy lines on top of one another. You can either do this freehand or use points as guidelines to indicate where the lines should go.

Colour in either the form that arises or the gaps between them. In this exercise the guidelines can remain in place if they don't automatically disappear as a result of the colouring process.

Drawing from an engraving on a 16th-century Ottoman brass candlestick

Part 8: Further Thinking

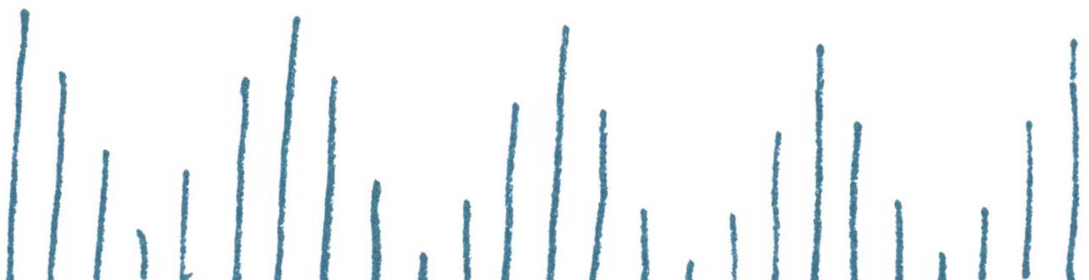

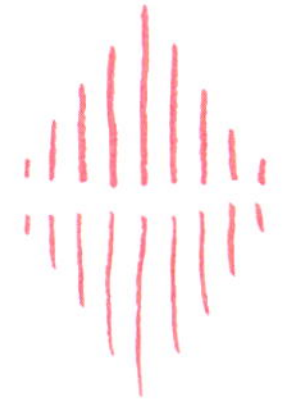 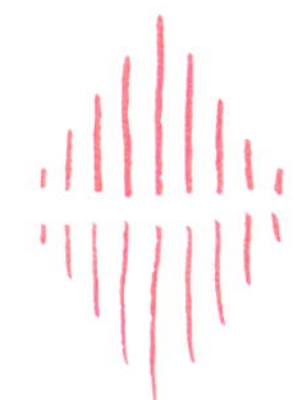

Living Lines: the Dynamics of Form

Form drawing involves close contact not just with what is created, but with the creative process too.

Looking out, now, over the ocean, the birds, the vegetation, I see that absolutely everything in nature arises from the power of free play sloshing against the power of limits. The limits may be intricate, subtle and long-lived like the genetic structure of the orange tree before me. But the patterns of the ocean, the pattern of the orange tree, of the seagulls, arises organically; it is a self-organising pattern. This self-organising activity arises, slowly changes, suddenly shifts, learns from mistakes, interacts with the ways of its fellows and its environment. These creative processes inherent in nature are called by some people evolution, by others creation, the unending flow through time and space of this pattern on patterns is what the Chinese call the Tao. (Nachmanovitch, s.33).

Everything in existence, things that are made and things that grow, is intertwined. They are in formation and decay. Some expand in a moment, some over millions of years. Everything is in motion.

Movement is the cause of a great variety of forms. Air is responsible for ephemeral patterns that can be observed among the movement of the clouds. Water streams in spirals or in wavelike forms. Stones have their own patterns created by incredibly slow formation processes. Everything that grows has its own inherent form.

Although the processes might be different, all these create patterns of movement on their way to creating a more or less permanent form.

Movement and the senses

I know that I can observe these movements visually, yet I am also deeply bound to these movements through my sensory body.

The German doctor and author Hans Jürgen Scheurle claims that we are able to sense things only as a result of movement. While moving, we experience events and actions as transformations. We observe and experience space and time as we happen to pass through it with all of our senses.

Children experience the world by moving with it. For very young children, stimulation of the muscular sense (the kinaesthetic sense), the sense of balance (the vestibular system) and the sense of touch are particularly important. To enable children to sense in this way, they need to move in tune with their surroundings. For example, children learn how gravity works by running around.

If you try to gauge the weight of something in your hand, you have to actively move it in your hand. If you touch an object to see how it feels, you will put your hand on it. Sensory experiences are activated the moment the hand comes into contact with the surface of the object. Yet once the hand has been placed and is stationary, the sensory experience fades. It is the motion of stroking or the varied pressure placed on the object that is essential to sensory experience.

Sensorimotor skills, as they are commonly called, suggest that the words 'sensory' and 'movement' belong together. We experience the world through movement. The neuroscientist Jean Ayres calls this interaction with our physical surroundings *sensory integration* and claims that this provides the basis for later cognitive functions (Ayres 1995). The first seven years of a child's life are spent simultaneously experiencing the world and their own body within it. By the time a child is of school age, they use the skills they have acquired in their first seven years to master the most complex coordination processes, and reading, writing and mathematics. As Ayres writes, 'Visual perception which is necessary for reading, is the end product based on a lot of building blocks that have been laid in the course of the baby's and toddler's sensorimotor activities. The same applies to all academic ability, behaviour and emotional development; everything rests on a sensorimotor foundation' (ibid, p.24) and 'You can think of sensations as "food for the brain"' (ibid, p.13).

Movement and experience

Everything we put into motion relates to its surroundings. If you throw a ball upwards, its speed will elegantly decrease before accelerating towards the ground. When the ball lands it will bounce up. This sensory information is accessible to the person throwing the ball, not only through what they see but because of their own relationship with movement and the knowledge their body holds. In other words, we have knowledge based on movements we have experienced in relation to our surroundings: for example, gravity, mass, acceleration and so on. The movements we execute become an important part of our realm of experience and a major component in our ability to assess our surroundings.

Movement also has its own set of aesthetics, and our bodily experiences and connection with the physical world provide an essential platform for mastering them.

When you are on skis and about to turn on an untouched mountainside covered in loose snow, you will have an inner picture of the path you wish to take or your course of action before you head downwards. You have an awareness of everything unpredictable that can happen upon meeting this type of terrain based on previous experience. The moment you throw yourself into it – or act – it is this inner picture that continues to be your guiding light. The actual action, however, is utterly dependent on your meeting with the terrain. In this meeting between the skier's intentions, experience and technique on the one hand, and the terrain's feedback on the other, intuitive action occurs.

In this case the skis form two parallel tracks that look like they are one track. An experienced skier will surrender themselves to the progress of their skis and simultaneously control the choice of path and display courage when crossing the line of a possible fall. It is very seldom that a skier does not turn to view their own tracks at the end of their trip. (From a conversation with ski instructor and teacher Bård Øvsthus, 2014)

Drawing movement

I have conducted experiments in different groups by asking them to drop a normal sheet of A4 paper on the floor (see photo on p.101), which will fall in a zigzag pattern. When I then ask participants to draw what they have seen,

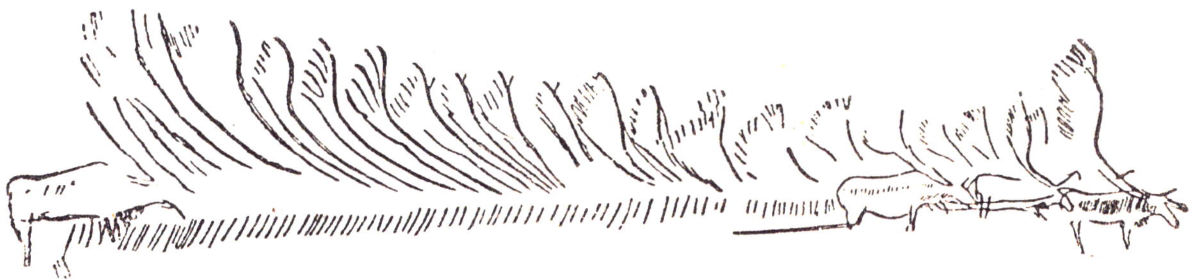

Ice Age art: Nomadic reindeer flock carved on a splinter of bone

the majority draw a simple and systematic zigzag movement. Hardly anyone tries to draw the actual sheet of paper, or the accurate track left by its movement.

It is natural for us to think abstractly or simplify movement forms in this manner. Drawing them involves a deeper understanding of what causes the movement, for example drag, flexibility, weight, gravity, friction and viscosity. As such, our ability to recognise movement and tendencies of form can be expressed and explored through form drawing.

Comprehend the form, grasp the matter

Everything consists of form and matter. Form is an expression of an object's quality or nature: 'When we recognise what something is, it is the form of the object we grasp' (Stigen 1983, p.114). Form therefore becomes an aspect of thought. In order to recognise an object, thought needs to grasp 'either the objects themselves or their form. The former is naturally impossible. It is not the stone that is present within the soul, but its form' (ibid, p.114). The form is abstracted from the material object and becomes universal in human consciousness. Aristotle refers to this as a 'perception', an 'abstraction' or a 'universal term' (ibid, p.114).

Such universal forms are not always easily seen, as they may interweave with one another or be exposed to chance events so that they no longer appear as pure forms. Sudden movements or changes can also make it difficult to isolate them.

Therefore, we must work methodically to explore different forms. This can be done in three stages:

1. Observation

Forms need to be studied. They have to be collected and categorised, even perhaps isolated or separated from other forms. You can find common characteristics such as angles, rhythms and unique shapes, such as circles and squares.

2. Abstraction

Try to remove yourself from your sense impressions and contemplate what you have observed. What often seems to be complicated in nature can often be simplified into a pure form. It is the *idea* of the form that needs to be discovered.

3. Picturing

Finally, what you have discovered needs to be tested out in a drawing. Try out different ways with a pencil and experiment with the essence of the form's idea. This is an important stage, because your hand is actively exploring and a reconnection is made with the phenomenon.

We can draw the form no matter how fluid it is – if only we have observed it as movement or rhythm. Our brains according to teacher, researcher and author Eric Jensen are designed to discover patterns, contrasts and movement. The main process in visual art is the hunt for 'lasting, necessary and essential qualities from our visual experiences' (Jensen, p.56). This leads us to not only revealing patterns but provides us with general knowledge about the world we live in. In this way art, according to Jensen, acts as an extension of our visual brain.

'I don't actually differentiate between art and science apart from as methods. Art is the representation, science the explanation, – of the same reality.' (Read in Jensen, p.62)

To sense the world using the aesthetic dimension can provide a new and extended understanding of it. 'In a life denuded of aesthetic experiences we miss, not only the most characteristic, but also the most valuable, in our world' (Dewey 1984). As an art-based method, form drawing can provide, via play and research, one of many different access points to our surroundings (and different subjects). Pupils can be taught to learn to see, experience and understand the world as it expresses itself via movement and form. They will develop an aesthetic intelligence.

When Malevich painted his *Black Circle, Black Square* and *Black Cross* he stated 'Only with the disappearance of a habit of mind which sees in the painting reproductions of little pieces of nature, madonnas and shameless Venuses, shall we witness the pictoral work. I transformed myself in the zero of form' (Tin, p.226). 'The painter's task is not to paint flowers in the field. Rather to teach ourselves to see the forces, the invisible order in the visible world.' (ibid, p.229)

It is a great joy to grasp a universal idea of form. It is only then that this can be further developed. We can create the most fantastic work, not bound and perfect as in nature, but freely and exploratively.

Living lines

Up until now I have related drawing to something that is in motion, or to something that is a result of movement. My lines are related to something living. Another source of inspiration for such living lines may be found in geometric figures that are drawn freehand. These simple forms – the square, triangle, star, circle and so on – are good to practise on because they are defined, and therefore 'correct' the drawer, regardless of their skill.

As a result, it is important to have already completed such exercises when attempting forms that don't have inherent regulatory aspects to support them. This aesthetic experience will prove useful later. When pupils are released from such strict definitions they develop from being copyists to being creators. They will experience a learning curve while creating forms using their own judgement and sense of aesthetics. They will create forms that cannot be identified by their resemblance to specific things or identifiable as symbols. They will be defined only by their own inherent structure.

The Norwegian artist Jan Groth, known for his line drawings in different materials, says of his work in 1985:

> The movement of the line and its placement on paper are my signals and seismographic readings. They don't show anything in particular, but are rather organic references, independent of a permanent concept. What is important is rhythm, the dialogue between the stiffness of the line and its displacement on paper. In other words it is about control of the surface. Drawing is discharge, elapse and experience. (Hellandsjø, p.11)

Groth's work includes references to nature, but it is more concerned with the line as an independent organism. The elasticity and life in his work is created in 'the charged balance between sign and surface' (ibid, p.64).

Just as forms in nature have their own inherent dynamic, so does a line on paper have its own aesthetic, its inherent order. If you draw a line on a sheet of paper, you have set a tone. You have provided a rhythm, a pattern of movement, a pace. You have defined the language of the form. The line has its own dynamics not only regarding curves, angles or oscillation, but also in its varying degrees of force and thickness or width. It has a beginning, a zenith and an end. It can be a playful action where the process and end product unite in a rapid flow of decisions. You have freedom to create and to improvise.

Living Thoughts:
Exercising the Imagination

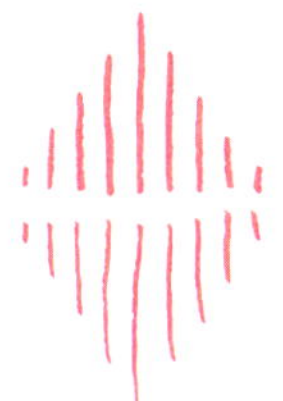
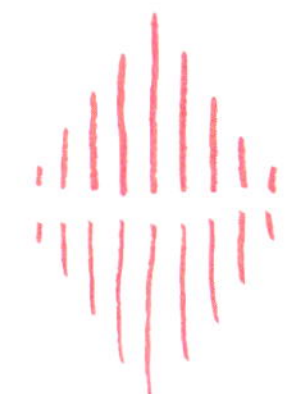

> The Arts nourish our ability to sense and to pay attention, our cognitive and emotional capacities and our motor skills, all of which are the driving forces behind all learning. (Jensen, p.2)

Two sides of me are active when I am form drawing: imagination and action. The imagination is my mental picture of what is to be drawn in the space I have available. This space might be the sheet of paper I am drawing on, which is the framework for the whole. It is within this whole that I am imagining. The action is the act of drawing: I will draw what I have imagined in the time it needs.

Space and time are mutually interdependent, and during form drawing are connected to being present. If I draw too quickly or too slowly, this sense of presence fades.

The imagination is connected to sight as a controller, and the action is dependent upon the hand as a tool. The eye looks back upon what has been done, and the hand pushes the process forward. They are in continual dialogue. As Wilson writes:

> The brain keeps giving the hand new things to do and new ways of doing what it already knows how to do. In turn, the hand affords the brain new ways of approaching old tasks and the possibility of undertaking and mastering new tasks. That means the brain, for its part, can acquire new ways of representing and defining the world. (Wilson, p.146)

What happens within us when we draw?

The interaction between imagination on the one hand and the action of drawing on the other is fundamental to my enquiries into how form drawing is related to thought. It has formed the basis of my methods and the foundation for my ideas. To explain what I mean, take the circle as an example.

The circle is the mother of all forms. It is

the most important form both in form drawing and in geometry. It is easy to admire its pure and perfect form as an expression of both wholeness and context, and it is easy to philosophise about its numeric ratios and formulas. Precisely because it is so simple, it can act as an example of how our thoughts and our hands are engaged in a dynamic process when we draw.

Try to find peace and quiet to carry out this exercise. Draw a circle on a blank sheet of paper and focus fully on this simple action, paying attention to what happens to you while you are drawing. What is it that helps you to make the circle round? What decisions do you have to make during the process? How, even at the start of the process, do you decide upon the correct curvature, which leads to the starting point meeting the end point precisely? What is it that enables you to succeed at such a demanding task?

Before you drew the circle, you had ideas about its placement, its size, the direction you would work in and its curvature. During the exercise, your hand's movements needed to be constantly adjusted in relation to your inner picture of the circle. In addition, the line had to be adjusted in relation to what it actually looked like on the paper. Your imagination represented the ideal, and during the process this ideal met with reality. When you drew the circle, it was your imagination that was in control of the entire form, while at the same time being in constant motion while the line was being formed moment by moment. Your imagination had to be constantly engaged, yet constantly adjusting as your hand drew the line. In other words, there was a constant interchange between the tip of the pencil and its broader surroundings. At the same time, your attention was focused on the start of the curve, where it had to end, and on the demanding and complex process involved in the task of producing the circle.

Your ability to complete the circle's form became clearer during the form-drawing activity and was indeed partially dependent upon the process. The hand's movement depends on your own inner co-movement. In other words, your thinking guides you and solves problems while it is in development.

Using exercises for other forms will help you understand the complex mental processes that are active when completing a simple drawing. In this way, you can become aware of what is active in a child when drawing.

Living thoughts

During the writing of my Masters thesis, 'Form Drawing as Pre-terminological Thinking', I describe a systematic review of equivalent experiences using a numerous variety of figures. To my surprise I discovered that most people don't think about the central point when they imagine a circle. In similar group experiments I have gained insight into hundreds of people and their drawing processes. Almost none have said that they use the concept of the centre of the circle to be able to draw it. Their point of departure is the total form, and when they draw a circle freehand, they pay attention to the space outside of and within the arc of the circle. The imagined circle is a picture that is not necessarily sharply defined, yet totally present and clear: a living concept.

The musician and author Stephen Nachmanovitch mentions Hakuin, a great Japanese painter and Zen Buddhist reformer who is, among other things, renowned for his simple paintings of only a circle. These are completed with a single brushstroke, and this is evident in the curve's distinctiveness, anomalies, blemishes, and variations in weight and texture. In Nachmanovitch's eyes, these express something deeper than an era of style, technical ability or the personality's superficiality.

Those Zen artists with their simple O´s had the knack of concentrating the whole of Self into the simplest acts. The spontaneous, simple O is the vehicle of Self, the vehicle of evolution, the vehicle of passion. It is the big simple breath of God, uncomplicated by was and shall, why and because. (Nachmanovitch, p.30).

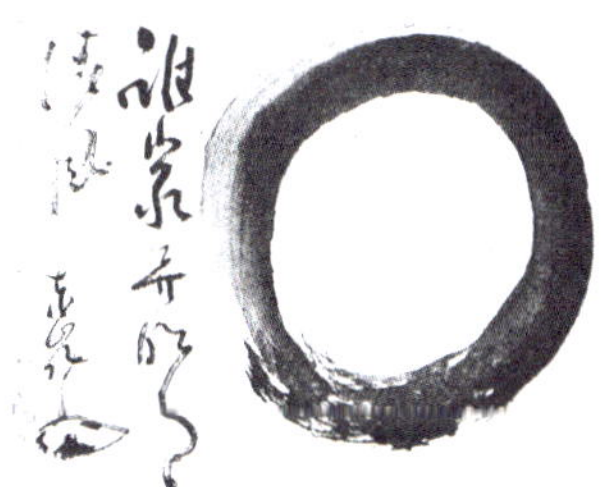

Rudolf Steiner on Form Drawing

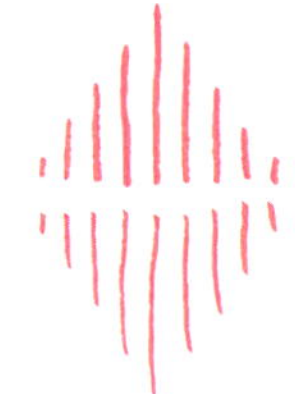

At the start of the twentieth century there was an experimental attitude to modern artistic expression. The composer Arnold Schoenberg abolished the law of gravity in music; he inspired the artist Wassily Kandinsky to free form from figure and colour from form; the architect Ludwig Mies van der Rohe designed the Barcelona Pavillion, in which materials, surfaces and space were liberated from ornament and decoration.

The first Steiner School was founded in this era, in Stuttgart in 1919. From the beginning, drawing exercises were introduced that were separate from the figurative. Colour exercises were freed from form and movement, and instantly related to music and language (eurythmy). Artistic elements were meant to be direct sources of inspiration for the creative individual.

Rudolf Steiner spoke about form drawing on various occasions, and it is my understanding that Steiner intended his thoughts to be further developed by subject teachers.

In the text below, I have gathered some of Rudolf Steiner's thoughts on form drawing.

In 1919 Rudolf Steiner held his first course for teachers. Regarding drawing and form, this quote underlines the reason that pupils should not copy, but rather achieve an inner connection with the form itself.

Next we must develop a fully conscious, ongoing desire to effect harmony of the will, feeling, and thinking, which do, in fact, work together when we teach in this way. It is a matter of continually guiding the will in the proper direction by avoiding false methods. We must stimulate the appropriate expression of a stronger will through the use of artistic methods. From the very beginning, this aim is served by painting and musical instruction. You will notice that, early in the second period of life, children are more receptive to authority in teaching through art. Consequently, we can accomplish the most in this sense during this period of children's lives using artistic methods. They will very effortlessly find their way into what we wish to communicate to them and take the greatest delight in rendering it by drawing or even painting. We should make sure, however, that they avoid merely imitative work.

We must also remember to 'transport' children back to earlier eras, but we should not act as though we still remain in those ages. People were different then. You will transport the children back to those earlier cultural ages that had a different disposition of soul and spirit. This is why, when drawing, we do not aim to make children copy anything. We teach them archetypal forms in drawing by showing them how to make one angle like this or another like that. We try to reveal the circle and the spiral to them. We begin with the form as such; what it imitates is unimportant. We simply try to awaken their interest in the form itself.

You may recall a lecture in which I tried to awaken a feeling for the process of the acanthus leaf's development. There I explained that it is completely erroneous to believe that the acanthus leaf was copied as it appears in legend. It simply arose from an inner formative impulse and was not felt until later; this resembles nature. Thus, it was not a matter of imitating nature. We must take this into consideration in relation to drawing and painting. This will finally put an end to the atrocious error that deadens human minds. Wherever people encounter something artificial, they might say it looks natural or unnatural. It is completely irrelevant to decide whether something is copied properly or not. Resemblance to the external should appear only as a secondary consideration. What should live in people is their intimacy with the forms themselves. Even when drawing a nose, we must relate inwardly to the shape of the nose, so that only later does the resemblance to the shape of a nose become obvious. In children between the ages of seven and fourteen, we can never awaken a sense of the inner laws of phenomena by imitating what is external. We must realise that what we are able to develop in children between the ages of seven and fourteen cannot be developed later. The forces active during that period fade. Later on, all that can arise is a substitution, unless the person is completely transformed through initiation, either naturally or unnaturally.

We both draw and model with our hands, and yet these two activities are completely different. This is expressed with particular clarity when we introduce children to art. When we guide children into the realm of something that can be modelled, we must, as much as possible, see that they follow the forms with their hands. By feeling their way, they make their own forms; by moving their hands and drawing, children are led to follow the forms with their eyes and also with the will emerging through their eyes. It does not violate their naivety to teach children to follow the forms of the body with the hollow of the hand or to make them aware of their eyes – for example, by allowing children to follow a complete circle with their eyes and saying, 'You are making a circle with your eyes.' This does not wound a child's innocence but rather engages the interest of the whole human being. Consequently, we must become aware that we are lifting the lower part of the human being into the higher part, or sensory being. (Rudolf Steiner, *Practical Advice to Teachers*, lecture of Aug 21, 1919 (pp. 9–11, 13), Anthroposophic Press, USA 2000)

When referring to the first day of school Steiner believed that children should be made aware of the different elements connected to learning, among other things that they have two hands, hands that they are meant to work with.

Having spoken with the children about their hands and about working with them, we then proceed to let them do something skilful with their hands. This might even take place in the very first lesson. You might say to them: 'Watch me draw this... Now take your hand and draw it, too.' Then we let the children draw what we have drawn, as slowly as possible.

Actually it will be a slow process if we call the children up one by one to the blackboard, letting them make their mark on the board and then return to their seats. The most important point is that they should digest the lesson properly. Then you might say to the children: 'Now I am going to draw this... And you can use your hands to draw it too.' Each child then draws this as well. When they have all finished, you say: 'This one is a straight line, and this one is a curved line; with your hands you have just made a straight and a curved line.' You can help the clumsier children, but you should see to it that each child does it as perfectly as possible from the start.

Right from the start we let the children do something, and we must make sure that in subsequent lessons this is repeated a number of times. In the following lesson, for example, we let the children make a straight line and then a curved line. Let us consider a subtle distinction. You need at first attach no great value to letting the children make a straight and a curved line from memory; once again you first make the straight line on the board and let the children copy it, and the same with the curved line. Then you ask individual children: 'What is that?' – 'A straight line.' 'What is that?' – 'A curved line.' You use the principle of repetition by letting the children copy the drawing and then, without repeating it yourself first, letting them name it themselves. It is most important to use this subtle nuance. You must make great efforts to cultivate the habit of doing the right things in front of the children; the educational maxims you believe in must become second nature to you. (Rudolf Steiner, *Practical Advice to Teachers*, lecture of Aug 25, 1919 (pp.51f), Anthroposophic Press, USA 2000)

He then proceeds to point out how learning to write has its origins in drawing.

Let us now turn to the next step. We shall assume that you have continued for a while in the exercises with crayons and paints. If what is learned is to be built on good foundations, it is essential that learning to write be preceded by concentration on drawing, so that writing can, to some extent, be derived from drawing. It is also essential that reading print be derived from reading handwriting. We will try to find the transition from drawing to writing, from writing to reading handwriting, and from reading handwriting to reading print. Let us assume that you have reached the stage where the children are finding their feet in drawing and have mastered to some extent how to make the curved and straight forms that will be needed in writing. We now seek the transition to what we have described as the basis for writing and reading lessons. Today I will start with a few examples of how you might proceed. (Rudolf Steiner, Practical Advice to Teachers, lecture of Aug 26, 1919 (pp.62f), Anthroposophic Press, USA 2000)

Steiner claims that the three-dimensional is difficult for pupils to grasp in younger classes:

You are assuming that the solid is the actual thing and the line abstract; but this is not so. A triangle is in itself something very concrete; it exists in space. Children see things mainly in surfaces. It is an act of violence to force a child into the third dimension, the idea of depth. If children are to apply their imagination to a solid, then they must first have the necessary elements within to build up this imaginative picture.

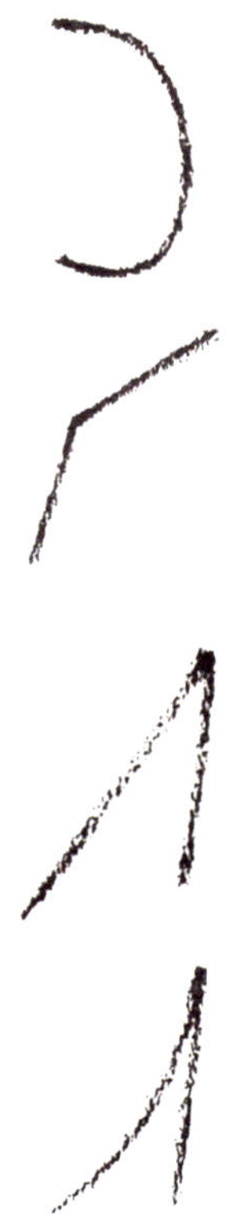

For example, children must really have a clear picture of a line and a triangle before a tetrahedron can be understood. It is better for them to first have a real mental picture of a triangle; the triangle is an *actuality*, not merely an abstraction taken from the solid.

I would recommend that you teach geometry, not as solid geometry first, but as plane geometry, giving figures with plane surfaces between them; this is preferable, because children like to use

their powers of understanding for such things; beginning with plane geometry will support them. You can add further to the effect by connecting it with drawing lessons. Children can draw a triangle relatively early, and you should not wait too long before having them copy what they see. (Rudolf Steiner, *Discussions with Teachers*, discussion of Aug 25, 1919 (p.51), Anthroposophic Press, USA 1997)

Here Steiner emphasises the child's own sense of form without first attempting to portray anything.

As we have already seen, in the drawing lessons in the first few classes, we first teach the children to have a specific feeling for rounded or angular forms, and so on.

From these forms, we develop what we need for teaching writing. In these very elementary stages of teaching drawing, we avoid imitating anything. As much as possible, you should initially avoid allowing the children to copy a chair or a flower or anything else. As much as possible, you should have them produce linear forms – forms that are round, pointed, semi-circular, elliptical, straight, and so on. Awaken in the children a feeling for the difference between the curve of a circle and the curve of an ellipse. In short, awaken their feeling for form before their urge to imitate wakes up! Wait until later before allowing them to apply what they have practised in drawing forms to imitating actual objects. First have them draw angles so that they understand what an angle is through its shape. Then you show them a chair and say, 'Look, here's an angle, and here's another angle,' and so on. Do not let the children imitate anything until you have cultivated their feeling for independent forms which can be imitated later. Stick to this principle even when you move on to a more independent and creative treatment of drawing and painting. (Rudolf Steiner, *Discussions with Teachers*, second lecture, Sep 6, 1919 (p.199), Anthroposophic Press, USA 1997)

This quote addresses the importance of awakening the senses to the reality of life through beauty:

What children need is a sense of reality. Again I will choose a very simple example to show you what I mean. One could draw a pattern such as this (see figure to the right). Teachers must be able to evoke a feeling in children that such a pattern is intolerable because it does not represent reality, and a little practice with students who react in healthy ways will soon enable you to do

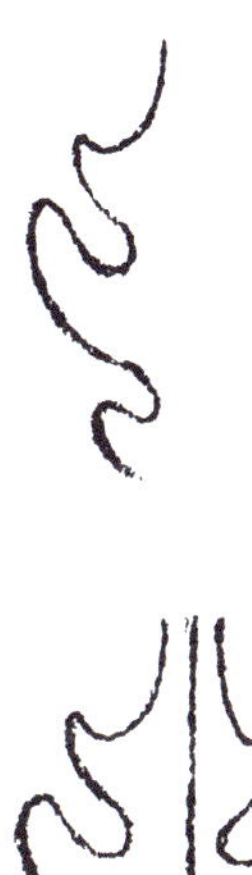

so. Teachers should intensify this healthy feeling – not through suggestions, but by drawing it out of the students – to the extent that, if they see such a pattern, it will be as though they were seeing a person with only half a face or one arm or foot. Such a thing goes against the grain, because it does not represent reality. This is the kind of reaction teachers should induce in students, for it is all part of an aesthetic sensibility. In other words, teachers should allow the students to feel that they cannot rest until they have completed a pattern by drawing the missing, complementary part. In this way one cultivates in children an immediate, living sense of beauty. In German, the word *schön* ('beautiful') is related to the word *Schein* ('shine' or 'glory'). Such an approach stimulates the child's astral body to become flexible and to function well as a living member of the human being.

It is important for teachers to cultivate an aesthetic sense also in themselves. Teachers quickly see how this enlivens the children. Thus, they also nurture an artistic approach to the other activities, as I have already stated in these lectures. I pointed out that everything teachers bring to children when they enter class one should be permeated by an artistic element. And when talking to children about their surroundings, teachers should do so with real artistry, since otherwise they might easily slip into anthropomorphism, restricting everything to narrow human interests. For instance, when using fairy tales or legends to clothe their lessons, teachers may be misled into telling a class that certain kinds of trees spring from the ground just so people can make corks from the bark and seal their bottles. A pictorial approach must never be presented in such terms. The pictures used at this particular age must be created from a sense of beauty. And beauty demands truth and clarity, which speaks directly to human feeling. Beauty in nature does not need anthropomorphism.

If we encourage prepubescent students toward an appreciation of beauty in everything they encounter, after puberty they will take human qualities with them into the practical life, harmonising their views of the world with the practical tasks that await them. (Rudolf Steiner, *Soul Economy*, lecture of Jan 5, 1922 (pp. 241–43) Anthroposophic Press, USA 2003)

Here Steiner emphasises how form drawing is life giving and uplifting for the pupil:

In geometry, therefore, we must not begin with abstract, intellectual constructs, which are usually considered the right foundation. We begin instead with inner perception by stimulating, for example, a strong sense of symmetry in children.

We can begin to do this with even the youngest children. For example, one draws some figure on the blackboard, adds a straight line, and indicates the beginning of symmetry. Then we try to help the children realise that the figure is incomplete and, using every means possible, get them to complete it themselves. Thus, we awaken an inner, active urge to complete what is unfinished. This helps them activate the correct image of a reality. Teachers, of course, must have creative talent, which is always good. Above all, they must have

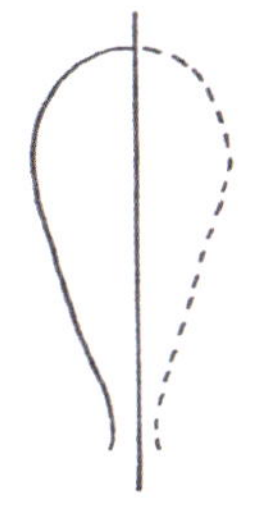

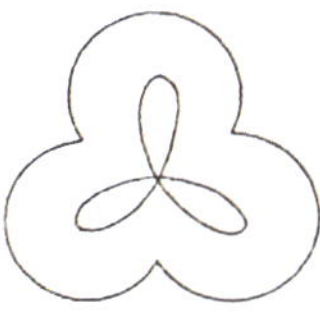

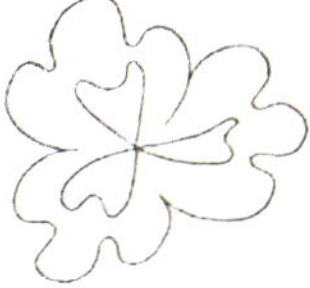

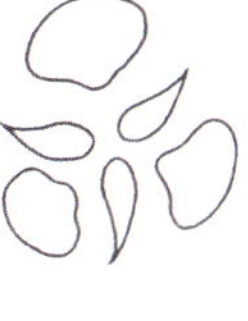

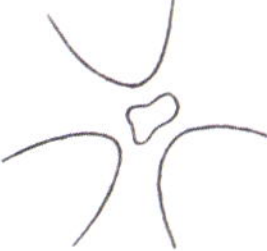

flexible, creative thinking. After assigning these exercises for a while, the teacher moves on to others. For example, we may draw a figure like this on the blackboard, and try to awaken an inner, spatial impression of it in the children. We then vary the outer line and they gradually learn to draw an inner form corresponding to the outer.

In one, the curves are simple and straightforward. In the other, they curve out at various points. We should explain to the children that, for the sake of inner symmetry, in the inner figure, they should curve inward exactly where the lines curve outward in the outer figure. In the first diagram, a simple line corresponds to another simple line, whereas in the second, an inward curve corresponds to an outward curve.

Or, we may draw something like this, followed by corresponding outer forms, so that we make a harmonious whole. We now try to move from this to another exercise, in which we do not let the outer figures come together but make them run away from each other into the 'undefined.' The children get the impression that this point wants to move off, and perhaps one has to chase after it with these lines but cannot catch it; it got away. Then they realise that the corresponding figure must be arranged so that, because *this* ran away, *that* must be especially bent inward. (I can only suggest these principles.) Briefly, by working like this, we give children an idea of 'asymmetrical symmetry,' thus preparing the ether body during waking life so that it continues to vibrate during sleep. And, in those vibrations, it perfects what has been absorbed during the day. Then the children awake in an ether body – as well as a physical body – inwardly and naturally stimulated to activity. They will be filled with life and vitality. This cannot be achieved, of course, unless the teacher has some knowledge of the ether body's activity; if such knowledge is not present, any effort in this way will be mechanical and superficial.

True teachers are concerned not only with the waking life, but also with events during sleep. In this sense, it is important to understand certain things that occasionally happen to all of us. For example, we think over some problem in the evening and fail to find a solution. In the morning, however, the problem is resolved. Why? Because the ether body of formative forces continued its activity independently during the night.

In many respects, waking life is not a process that perfects, but one that disturbs. We need to leave our physical and ether bodies alone for a while so that we do not make them stupid through the activities of the astral body and the self. Many things in life substantiate this fact; using the example just mentioned, when you wake up in the morning, you might feel slightly restless, but you suddenly discover that the solution came to you unconsciously during the night. These things are mere stories; they happen just as conclusively as any experiment. What occurred in this particular case? The work of the ether body continued through the night, and you were asleep the whole time. This is not normal or something to strive for. But we should strive to help that etheric activity continue during sleep, and we do this when we begin by communicating a concrete representation of space, instead of beginning geometry with triangles and the like, in which the intellect is already in evidence. In arithmetic, too, we must proceed in this way. (Rudolf Steiner: A Modern Art of Education, lecture of Aug 14, 1923 (pp.141–44), Anthroposophic Press, USA 2004)

On the development of thinking in a figurative context:

We will now consider another branch of this pictorial method of education. We must remember that with the very little child the intellect that in the adult has its

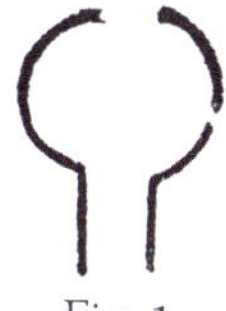

Fig. 1

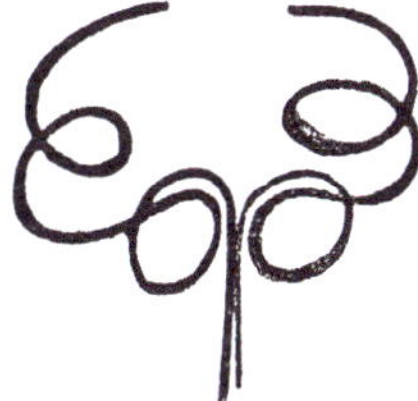

Fig. 2

Fig. 3

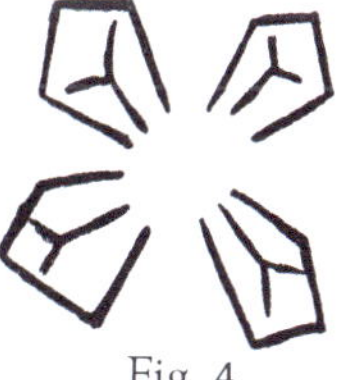

Fig. 4

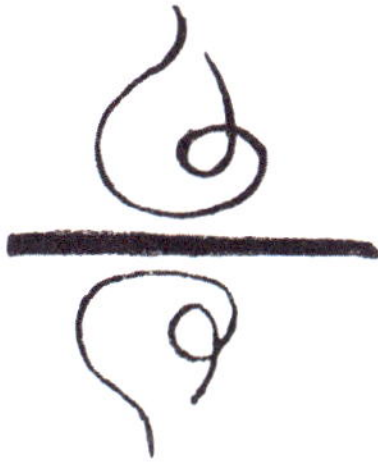

Fig. 5

own independent life must not yet really be cultivated, but all thinking should be developed in a pictorial and imaginative way.

Now even with children of about eight years of age you can quite easily do exercises of the following kind. It does not matter if they are clumsy at first. For instance you draw this figure [see Fig. 1]. You must try in all kinds of ways to get the children to feel that this is not complete, that something is lacking. How you do this will of course depend on the individuality of each child. You could for instance say: 'Look, this goes down to here (left half) but this only comes down to here (right half, incomplete). But this doesn't look nice, coming right down to here and the other side only so far.' Thus you will gradually get the child to complete this figure; the child will get the feeling that the figure is unfinished, and must be completed; finally, the child will add this line to the figure. I will draw it in red; the child could of course do it equally well in white, but I am simply indicating in another colour what has to be added. At first the attempts will be extremely clumsy, but gradually through balancing out the forms the child will develop observation that is permeated with thought, and thinking that is permeated with imaginative observation. All of the child's thinking will become imagery.

And when you have succeeded in getting a few children in the class to complete things in this simple way, you can then go further with them. You can draw some such figure as the following [see Fig. 2], and after making the children feel that this complicated figure is unfinished you can induce them to put in what will make it complete [right-hand part of Fig. 2]. In this way you can arouse a feeling for form that will help the children to experience symmetry and harmony.

This could be continued still further. You could, for instance, awaken in the children a feeling for the inner laws governing this figure [see Fig. 3]. They would see that in one place the lines come together, and in another they separate. This closing together and separating again is something that you can easily bring to their experience.

Then you pass over to the next figure [see Fig. 4]. You make the curved lines straight, with angles, and they then have to make the inner line correspond. It will be a difficult task with children of eight, but, especially at this age, it is a wonderful achievement if you can get them to do this with all sorts of figures, even if you have shown it to them beforehand. You should get the children to work out the inner lines for themselves; they must bear the same character as the ones in the previous figure but consist only of straight lines and angles.

This is the way to inculcate in the children a real feeling for form, harmony, symmetry, correspondence of lines, and so on. And from this you can pass over to a conception of how an object is reflected; if this, let us say, is the surface of the water [see Fig. 5] and here is some object, you must arouse in the children's minds a picture of how it will be in the reflection. In this manner you can lead the children to perceive other examples of harmony to be found in the world. (Rudolf Steiner, *The Kingdom of Childhood*, lecture of Aug 15, 1924, (pp.66–68), Anthroposophic Press, USA 1995)

Bibliography

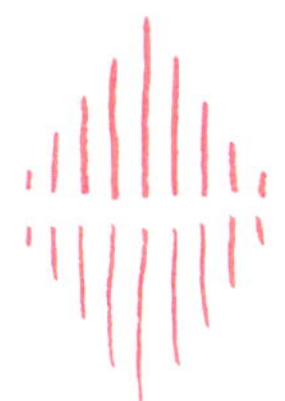

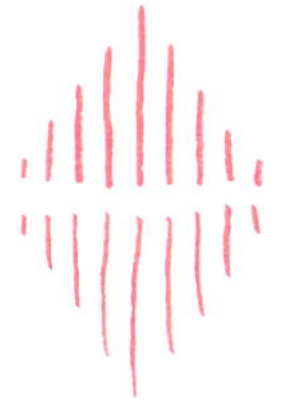

Ayres, A. Jean (1995) *Sensory Integration and the Child*, Western Psychological Services, Los Angeles

Boydston, Jo Ann (ed.) (1984) *John Dewey: The Later Works, 1925–53, Volume 2: 1925–1927*, Southern Illinois University Press, Carbondale

Hellandsjø, Karin (2000) *Signs: Jan Groth's Art*, Museum for Contemporary Art, Oslo

Jensen, Eric (2001) *Arts with the Brain in Mind*, Association for Supervision and Curriculum Development, Alexandria, VA

Jones, Owen (2001) *The Grammar of Ornament: A Visual Reference of Form and Colour in Architecture and the Decorative Arts*, Ivy Press, Lewes

Nachmanovitch, Stephen (1990) *Free Play: Improvisation in Life and Art* Tarcher/Penguin, New York

Scheurle, Hans Jürgen (1984) *The Total Internal Organization: Overcoming the Subject-Object Split in the Theory of the Senses*, New York, NY

Steiner, Rudolf (1995) *The Kingdom of Childhood*, lecture of Aug 15, 1924, Anthroposophic Press, Great Barrington, MA

— (1997) *Discussions with Teachers*, second lecture, Sep 6, 1919, Anthroposophic Press, Great Barrington, MA

— (2000) *Practical Advice to Teachers*, lecture of Aug 21, 1919, Anthroposophic Press, Great Barrington, MA

— (2003) *Soul Economy*, lecture of Jan 5, 1922, Anthroposophic Press, Great Barrington, MA

— (2004) *A Modern Art of Education*, lecture of Aug 14, 1923, Anthroposophic Press, Great Barrington, MA

Stigen, Anfinn (1983) *Tenkningens historie Vol. 1 (The History of Thought)*, Gyldendal, Oslo

Tin, Mikkel B. (2007) *De første formene: Folkekunstens abstrakte formspråk (The First Forms: The Abstract Language of Form in Folk Art)*, Novus, Oslo

Wilson, Frank R. (1998) *The Hand: How Its Use Shapes the Brain, Language and Human Culture*, Vintage Books, New York

Acknowledgements

I would like to thank a number of people who have helped me with pictures, their own form drawing curricula, good advice and proofreading. I would like to give special thanks to Axel Hugo, not only because he supervised my Master's dissertation in form drawing, but also because he taught me to explore form.

Thank you for the kind permission given to use illustrations from the Ivy Press's edition of *The Grammar of Ornament* from 2001. The first edition from 1856 represents cultural expressions from the entire world, collected and reproduced by Owen Jones. It is a rich and reliable source, providing much inspiration. Owen Jones's pictures are used several times throughout the book.

Thank you also to the Ariadne fund for vital financial start-up support.

Picture Credits

Andersen, Jan Arve: p.71 Newtongrange passage tomb; pp.136–37 photos of light in water

Bäuerle, Erich: p.150 movement in water photo

Borgnes, Kirsten M.: p.139 lesson plan, ropework photos

Broby-Johansen, R., *Everyday Art, World Art* (Oslo: Cappelen, 1947): p.138 Byzantium 'wallpaper' pattern; p.197 Ice Age art

Cahalan, Bob, NASA GSFC: p.150 Kármán vortex street caused by wind flowing around the Juan Fernández Islands off the Chilean coast

ESA: p.162 Sogne Fjord, Norway. Satellite picture ESA ENVI – SAT 9. Feb 2010

Fornæss, Marianne: pp.176–77 lesson plan

Frøystadvåg, Stine: pp.86–87 photographs; pp.122–23 blackboard drawings

Jones, Owen, *The Grammar of Ornament* (Lewes: Ivy Press, 2001): p.93 Celtic borders; p.129 Celtic pattern; p.130 Celtic ornament; p.143 circular Celtic ornament; pp.180–85 painted ornaments, wall of a grave, roof of a tomb, ornaments from Greek and Etruscan vases; p.190 Moorish border

Kaumer, Annichen: p.112 lesson plan

Kroken, Ingunn: pp.96–97 photographs

Kutzli, Rudolf, *Creative Form Drawing* (Gloucestershire: Hawthorne Press, 2006): p.139 Celtic forms inspired by examples from Kutzli

Museum of Contemporary Art, Oslo: p.113 cushions

Schimmele, Michael, VESGO: p.101 Piccaninny Creek photo

Sesti. Petroc: p.135 from the sculpture *Our Energy, Our Matter, Our Space, Our Time*, 2006, in Kistefos Sculpture Park, Jevnaker, Norway, reproduced with the artist's permission; p.136 spirals in liquid; p.147 liquid logarithmic spiral

Viking Ship Museum, Oslo: p.90 Oseberg Burial Mound; p.141 animal head from the Oseberg ship site

Wikipeda: https://no.wikipedia.org/wiki/Den_julianske_borg: p. 145 Julian Castle photo

Resources

Suppliers

The following websites provide resources for crafting and more.

Australia

Morning Star
www.morningstarcrafts.com.au

North America

The Waldorf Early Childhood Association of North America maintains an online list of suppliers at www.waldorfearlychildhood.org

UK

Myriad Natural Toys
www.myriadonline.co.uk

Waldorf Schools

There are currently over 1,000 Waldorf schools and many more kindergartens in over 60 countries around the world. The following organisations can provide up-to-date information.

Australia

Association of Rudolf Steiner Schools in Australia www.steinereducation.edu.au

New Zealand

Federation of Rudolf Steiner Schools www.rudolfsteinerfederation.org.nz

North America

Association of Waldorf Schools of North America www.whywaldorfworks.org

South Africa

Southern African Federation of Waldorf Schools www.waldorf.org.za

UK

Steiner Waldorf Schools Fellowship
www.steinerwaldorf.org.uk

You might also be interested in:

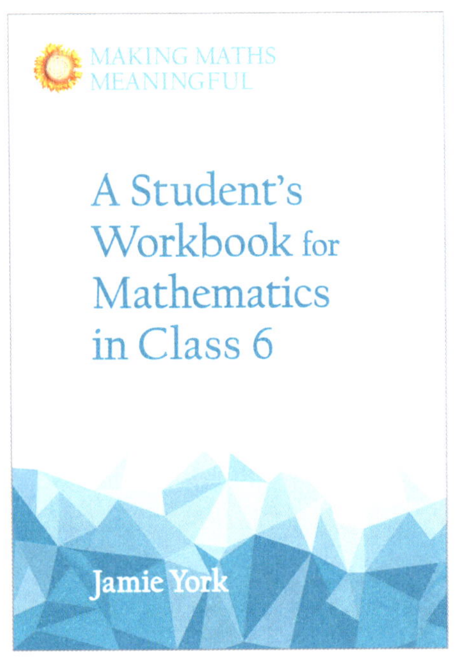

A Student's Workbook for Mathematics in Class 6

Jamie York

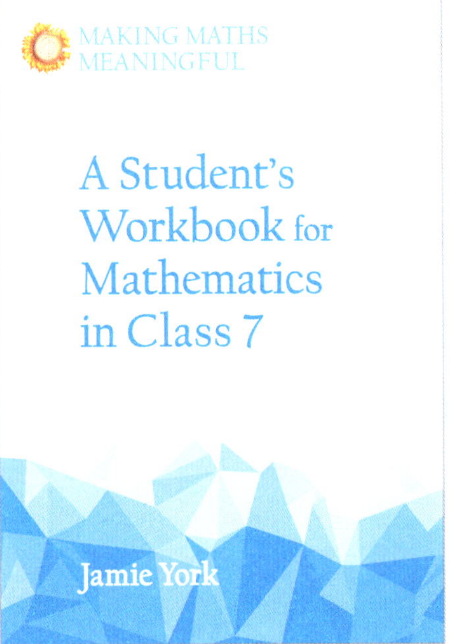

A Student's Workbook for Mathematics in Class 7

Jamie York

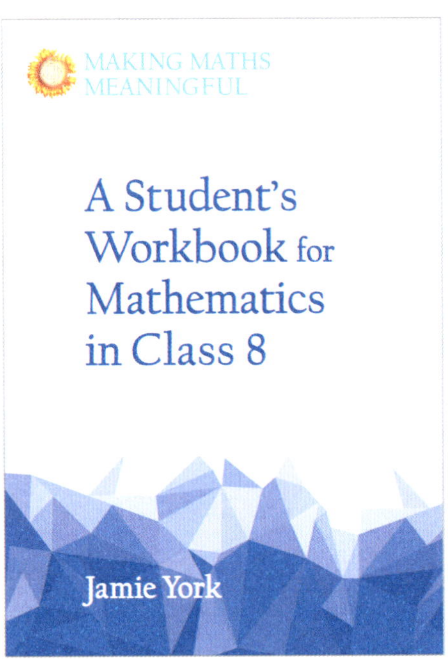

A Student's Workbook for Mathematics in Class 8

Jamie York

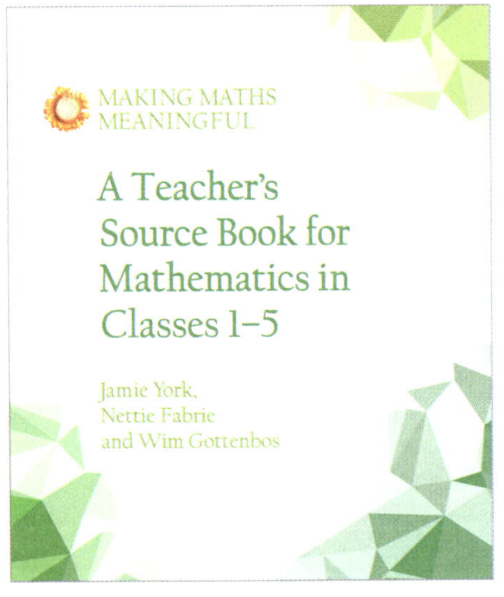

A Teacher's Source Book for Mathematics in Classes 1–5

Jamie York, Nettie Fabrie and Wim Gottenbos

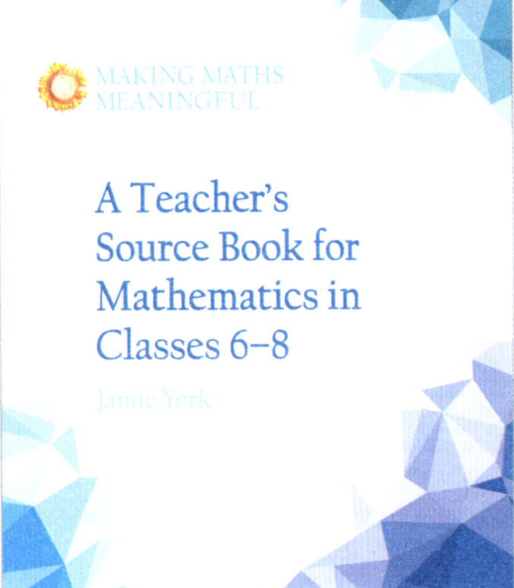

A Teacher's Source Book for Mathematics in Classes 6–8

Jamie York

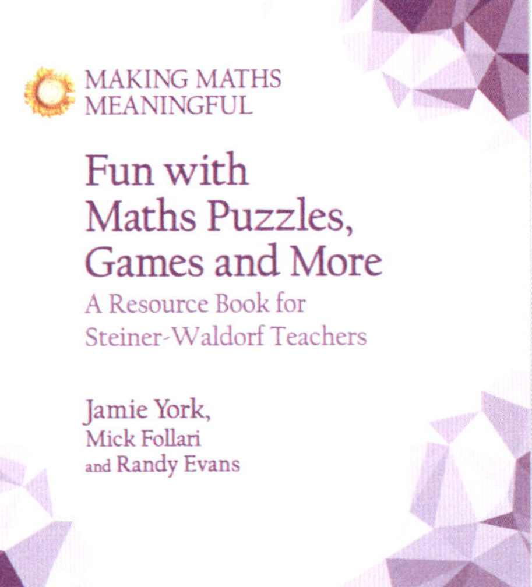

Fun with Maths Puzzles, Games and More

A Resource Book for Steiner-Waldorf Teachers

Jamie York, Mick Follari and Randy Evans

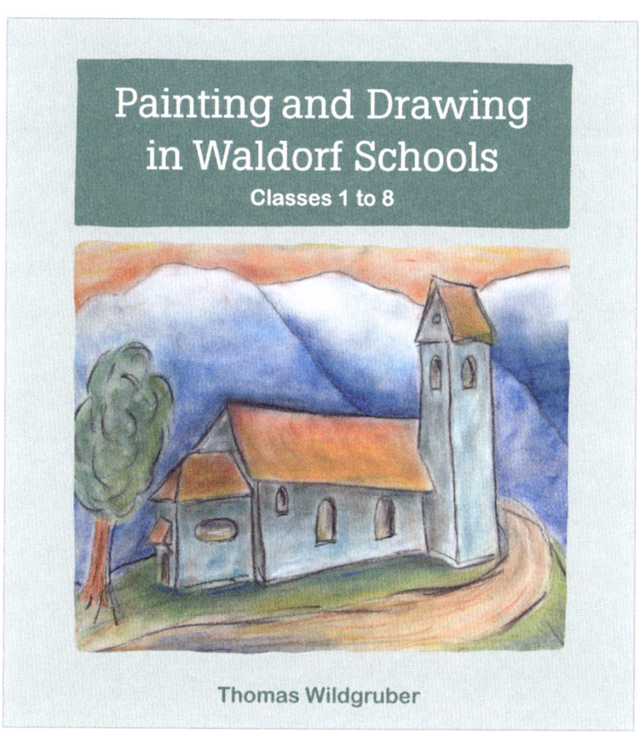

Painting and Drawing
in Waldorf Schools
Classes 1 to 8
Thomas Wildgruber

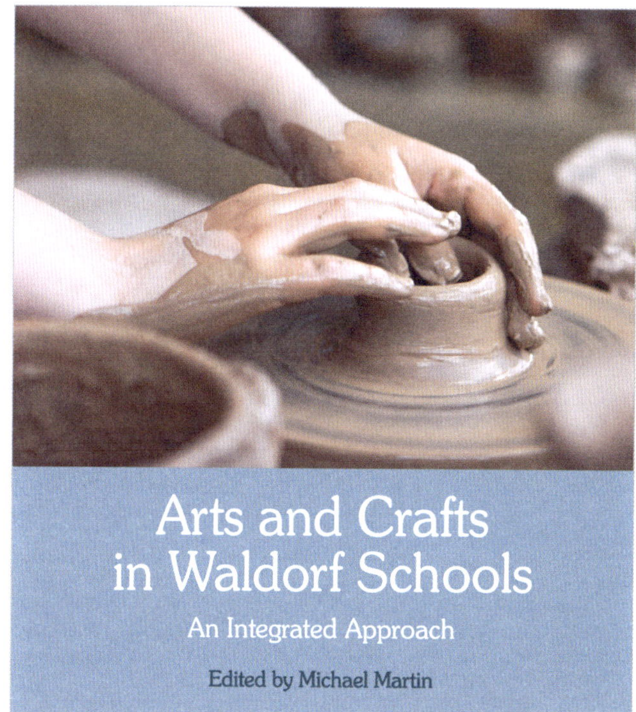

Arts and Crafts
in Waldorf Schools
An Integrated Approach
Edited by Michael Martin

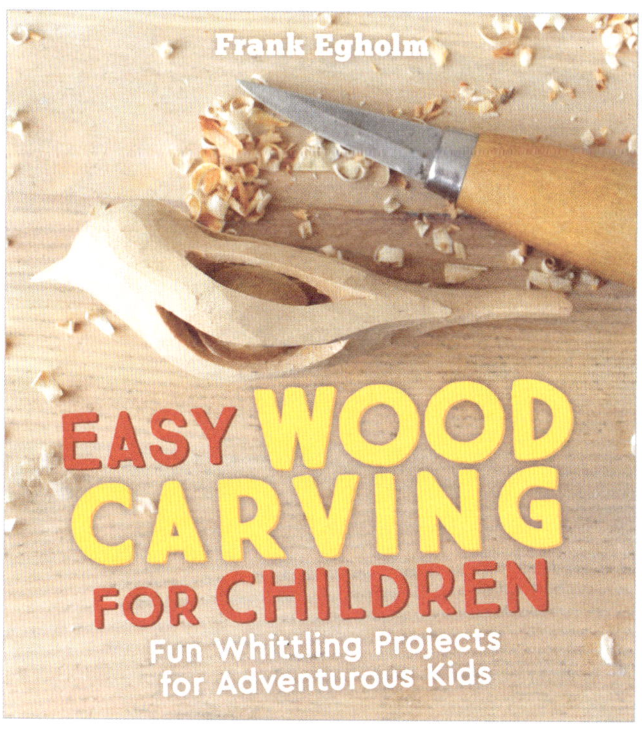

Frank Egholm
EASY WOOD
CARVING
FOR CHILDREN
Fun Whittling Projects
for Adventurous Kids

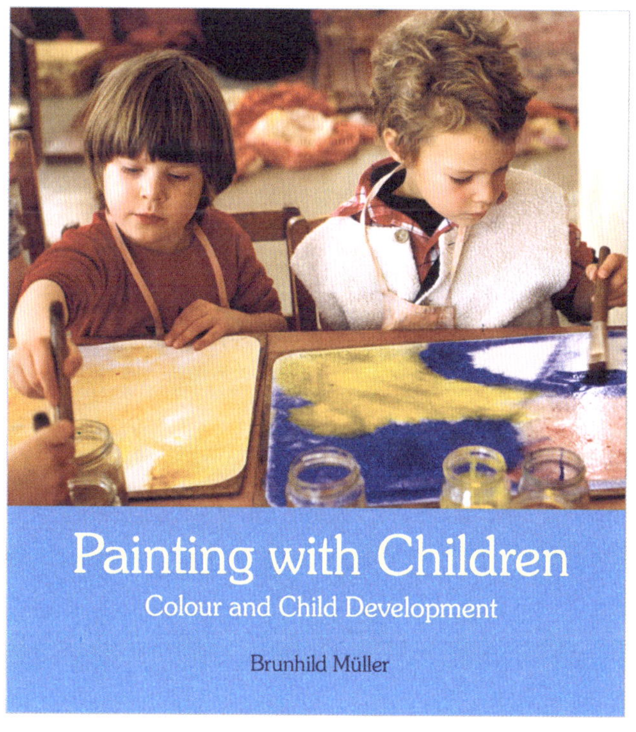

Painting with Children
Colour and Child Development
Brunhild Müller

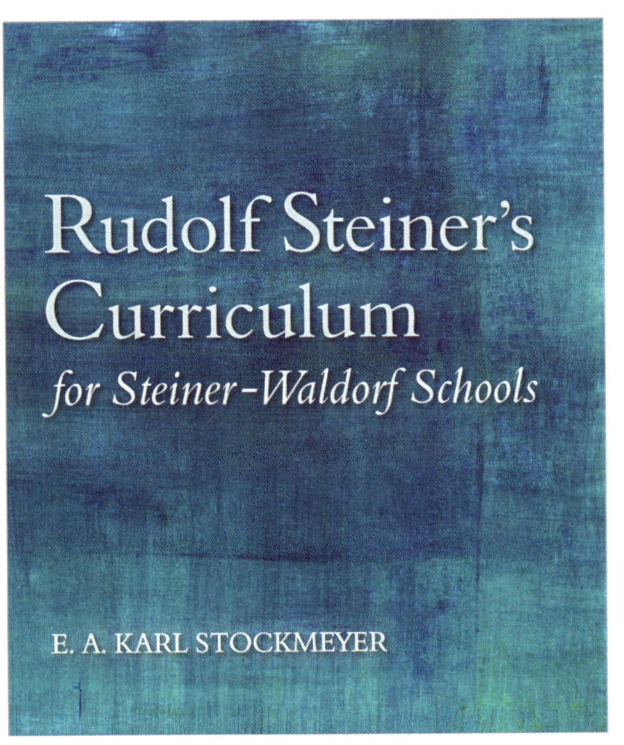

A Handbook *for* Steiner-Waldorf Class Teachers

Written and compiled by
Kevin Avison

The **Tasks** and **Content** of the Steiner-Waldorf Curriculum

Edited by
MARTYN RAWSON,
TOBIAS RICHTER
and KEVIN AVISON

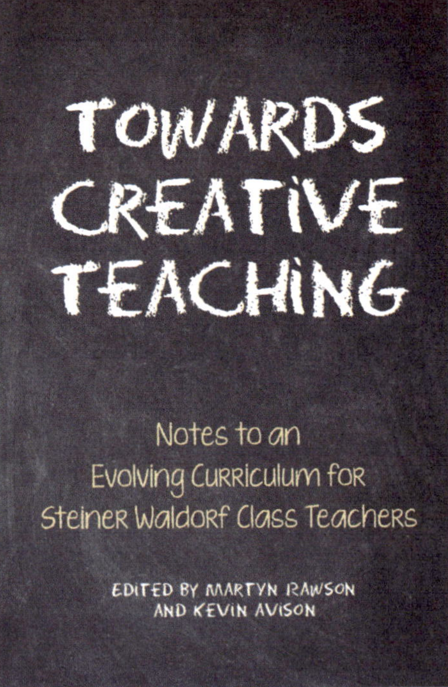

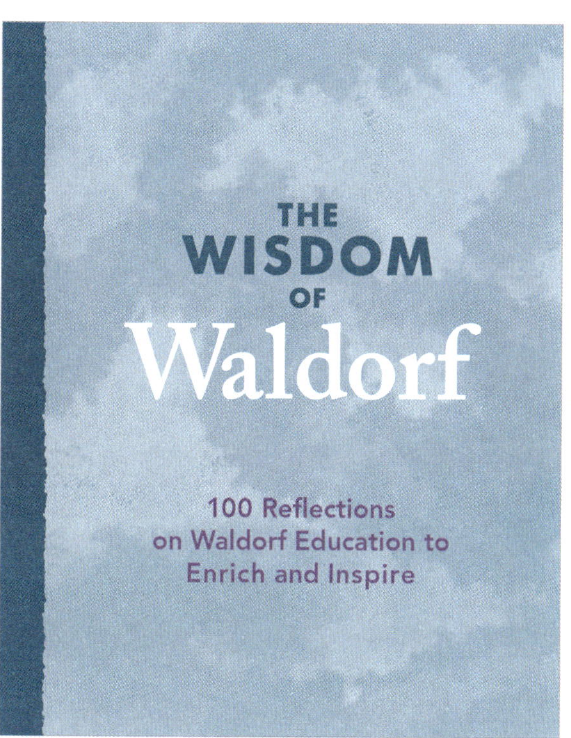
THE
WISDOM
OF
Waldorf
100 Reflections
on Waldorf Education to
Enrich and Inspire

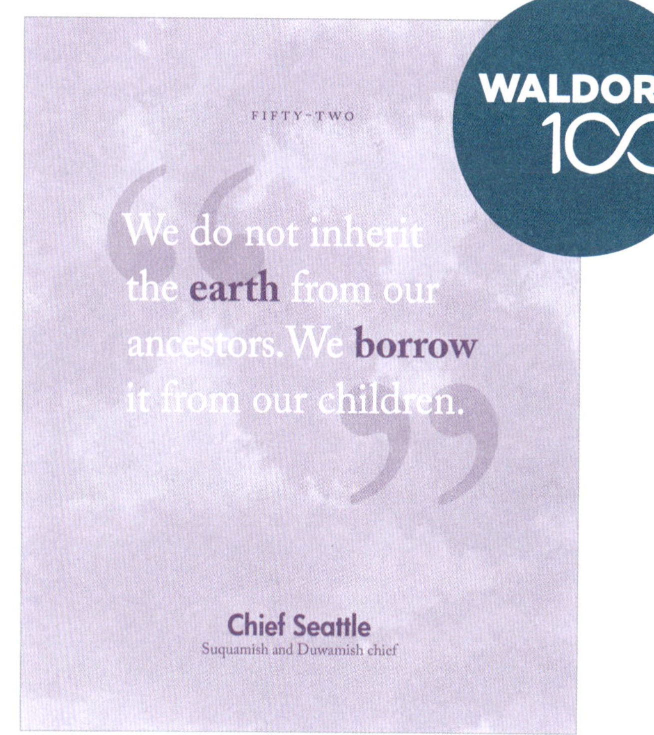
FIFTY-TWO
We do not inherit
the earth from our
ancestors. We borrow
it from our children.
Chief Seattle
Suquamish and Duwamish chief

WALDORF
100

TEN
Every human being is
a teacher, but they are
sleeping and must be
awakened, and art is
the awakener…
Rudolf Steiner

THREE
Little thoughts will
get us nowhere,
so we must pluck up
the courage to think
big thoughts.
Rudolf Steiner

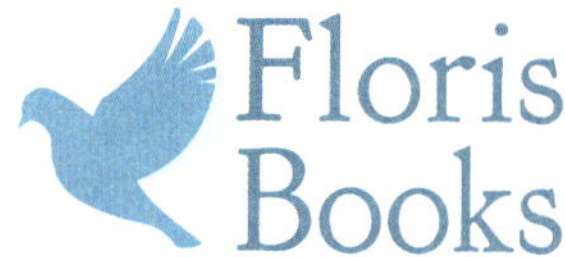

For news on all the latest books, and to get
exclusive discounts, join our mailing list at:

florisbooks.co.uk/mail/

And get a FREE book
with every online order!